# DIVIDED ON D-DAY

EDWARD E. GORDON AND DAVID RAMSAY

# DIVIDED ON D-DAY

## HOW LEADERSHIP FAILURES THREATENED THE NORMANDY INVASION

Prometheus Books
Essex, Connecticut

Prometheus Books

An imprint of Globe Pequot, the trade division of
The Rowman & Littlefield Publishing Group, Inc.
4501 Forbes Blvd., Ste. 200
Lanham, MD 20706
www.rowman.com

Distributed by NATIONAL BOOK NETWORK


Originally published as *Divided on D-Day: How Conflicts and Rivalries Jeopardized the Allied Victory at Normandy* by Prometheus Books



British Library Cataloguing in Publication Information Available

**Library of Congress Cataloging-in-Publication Data**

The Library of Congress has cataloged the hardcover edition of this book as follows:

Names: Gordon, Edward E. (Edward Earl), 1949- author. | Ramsay, David, 1933- author.
Title: D-Day : how conflicts and rivalries jeopardized the Allied victory at Normandy / by Edward E. Gordon and David Ramsay.
Description: Amherst, New York: Prometheus Books, [2017] | Includes bibliographical references and index.
Identifiers: LCCN 2017010411 (print) | LCCN 2017011242 (ebook) | ISBN 9781633883192 (hardcover) | ISBN 9781633883208 (ebook)
Subjects: LCSH: World War, 1939-1945—Campaigns—France—Normandy. | Operation Overlord. | Allied Forces. Supreme Headquarters—History. | Combined operations (Military science)—Case studies. | Great Britain—Military relations—United States. | United States—Military relations—Great Britain. | Normandy (France)—History, Military,—20th century.
Classification: LCC D756.5.N6 G68 2017 (print) | LCC D756.5.N6 (ebook) |DDC 940.54/2142—dc23
LC record available at https://lccn.loc.gov/2017010411

ISBN 9781633889071 (pbk. : alk. paper)

™ The paper used in this publication meets the minimum requirements of American National Standard for Information Sciences—Permanence of Paper for Printed Library Materials, ANSI/NISO Z39.48-1992

*To the OVERLORD commanders who led the path to victory*
*and the soldiers, sailors, and airmen*
*who fought valiantly to achieve this triumph.*

# CONTENTS

# LIST OF CHARTS AND MAPS

(In Insert)

## CHARTS



## MAPS

# LIST OF PHOTOGRAPHS

# BACKGROUND AND ACKNOWLEDGMENTS

Behind every book there is a team of people who are responsible for its ultimate publication. The authors met over ten years ago when Ed Gordon gave a presentation entitled "The Secrets of D-Day" at the Palm Springs Air Museum. Afterward David Ramsay introduced himself as a fellow historian. We then began what turned out to be our decade-long dialogue on the Normandy invasion.

David has a unique link to the events of D-Day. His special interest spans almost an entire lifetime since his father, Admiral Sir Bertram Ramsay, was Allied commander in chief of the seven-thousand-ship D-Day fleet, and principal author of NEPTUNE the naval/amphibious assault plan that was a vital part of the OVERLORD operation.

The authors gathered information from many published and archival sources. Elaine Gordon, who spent a large part of her career as an instruction librarian at DePaul University, had a major role on our team as a researcher and a very insightful editor. We are deeply indebted to her for all the expert suggestions she provided into making *Divided on D-Day* a far better history.

Valerie Collier at Loyola University Chicago spent many hours in preparing our manuscript. Her outstanding work helped us produce a more readable book.

Charlene Meers utilized her great talents in graphic design to help us create original, detailed maps that enable readers to better understand the geography of the OVERLORD campaign. She also assisted us in the selection and formatting of the photographs that appear throughout *Divided on D-Day*.

Denise Goolsby, a reporter at the *Desert Sun* in Palm Springs, California, was very generous in giving us access to her interviews of World

War II veterans. These fascinating accounts of soldiers who participated in the OVERLORD campaign add unique perspectives on these events.

We wish to thank the staff at the Pritzker Military Museum and Library in Chicago. In particular Theresa A. R. Embrey, chief librarian, has been very helpful in showing us pertinent research materials at their library and gathering many other materials for us from across the United States. Also the staff at the University of Ohio Libraries, home of the Cornelius Ryan Collection, has been of assistance to complete our research.

We are also grateful to Steven L. Mitchell, the vice president and editor in chief at Prometheus Books, for all of his many helpful suggestions and advice on improving *Divided on D-Day* and bringing it to a wider audience of readers.

Finally, we wish to heartily thank John Willig of Literary Services Inc. for his outstanding efforts in successfully bringing this book into the marketplace and encouraging us to persevere as authors. His wise counsel has been invaluable.

For all of the content, historical judgments, or unintended factual errors that are found in *Divided on D-Day*, the authors take sole responsibility.

Edward E. Gordon, Chicago, Illinois

David Ramsay, Indian Wells, California

## INTRODUCTION

# REMEMBERING D-DAY IN HISTORY AND MEMORY

> "History will hear me out, particularly as I shall write that history myself."
>
> —Winston Churchill[1]

The Allied D-Day invasion of Normandy on June 6, 1944, and the subsequent campaign rank high in the annals of military history. The final result was the destruction of most of the German army in Western Europe, which played a major role in ending the Second World War in the West. Some of the Allies' finest commanders provided the key leadership.

Even Field Marshal Erwin Rommel, German senior commander in Normandy, was impressed. "Technically and strategically the landing in Normandy was a brilliant achievement of the first magnitude. . . . The functioning of the Allied fighting machine, with all its complexity, surprised even me, and I already had a fairly high opinion of their powers."[2]

In keeping with the seventy-fifth anniversary of D-Day, it is fitting that we commemorate the courageous acts of these countless soldiers, sailors, and airmen who were the most important contributors to the Allied victory. The Americans buried above Omaha Beach at St. Laurent; the British, Canadians, and other Allies at Bayeux; and many military cemeteries across northern France provide mute testimony to the cost of the Allied campaign to free Europe from the yoke of Nazi Gcmany.[3]

Dwight D. Eisenhower expressed this best when he said that "the American soldiers who rest forever near the beach-head they won, and in the land they helped to free, will never be forgotten. Their memory will always help strengthen the bonds of friendship between our countries, historic allies for the cause of human freedom."[4] By 2015 only 5 percent of the sixteen million World War II veterans were still alive. About five hundred were passing away every day.[5]

Many people have commented that the history of war has been written by its winners. The Normandy campaign has been largely represented as a triumphant Allied success story. Martin Blumenson believes that the Anglo-American alliance that directed it "was probably the most successful alliance in history."[6]

The pursuit of a common goal—the defeat of the Axis at times held a difficult partnership together. The "sheer depth, scale and scope of the alliance," says Niall Barr, "between Britain and the United States . . . is hard to comprehend even now."[7] The combined Allied Supreme Headquarter Allied Expeditionary Force (SHAEF) that planned and executed Operation OVERLORD contrasted sharply with the confused German (OKW) armed forces high command. "Alongside the command structure of their enemies, that of the Allied Force was a masterpiece of reason and understanding," asserts historian Max Hastings.[8]

Though it was victorious, the Normandy campaign was far from perfect. The working relationships among the Allied OVERLORD commanders was often marred by disagreements over tactics, strategy, and national agendas exacerbated by rivalries and personality conflicts.[9]

Over the past decades a vast quantity of literature has chronicled the events and the controversies of D-Day. This barrage of sources includes the following:

- Memoirs, autobiographies, biographies of the British, American, Canadian, French, and German commanders.
- National official histories.
- D-Day anniversary books.
- First person accounts by soldiers and officers.
- The published papers of the principal commanders.
- Unpublished archival documents, letters, and reports.

These materials have helped to define the identities of the participant commanders and the aspirations of the Allied nations. However great the triumph, it in itself does not provide conclusive evidence on the quality of the command decisions. This literature also includes myths that have little or no basis in the historic record. Fortunately, the perspective of time has helped us sharpen our historical assessments.

The major focus of *Divided on D-Day* is an analysis of the quality of leadership and the relationships among its principal commanders. Their command decisions proved crucial at key points in the Normandy campaign. Our roster of political leaders and principal commanders include Prime Minister Winston Churchill, President Franklin D. Roosevelt, General Dwight D. Eisenhower, Field Marshal Sir Bernard Montgomery, General George C. Marshall, Field Marshal Sir Alan Brooke, General George S. Patton, General Omar Bradley, General Charles de Gaulle, Air Chief Marshal Sir Trafford Leigh-Mallory, Air Chief Marshal Sir Arthur Tedder, Air Chief Marshal Sir Arthur Harris, Admiral Sir Bertram Ramsay, Admiral Ernest J. King, and many other Allied and German commanders.

*Divided on D-Day* is the first general history of this campaign to be written by an Anglo-American team of historians. Our aim to provide a fresh, balanced critical perspective on controversies that still surround D-Day:

- What caused the Allied failure to implement their beachhead breakout strategy?
- Why was Caen, a top D-Day objective, not captured by the British?
- How could Rommel's Omaha Beach orders have defeated the Allied D-Day invasion?
- Why did Eisenhower refrain from issuing direct orders to his commanders?
- What decisions forced the Americans to fight in the bocage/hedgerow hell?
- Who issued the "phantom order" stopping Patton from closing the Falaise Pocket?
- Why did Eisenhower stop Patton's drive to outflank Germany's West Wall?
- Why did Montgomery delay opening the vital supply facility, the Port of Antwerp, for nearly two months?
- How could have the MARKET GARDEN/Arnhem disaster and the Battle of the Bulge been avoided?

- What decisions could the Allies have made to end the war in 1944 or early 1945?

*Divided on D-Day* provides the behind-the-scenes stories of crucial command decisions, or a lack of them, that led the invasion to first come close to failure, then experience a long period of stalemate on the ground, and eventually win the long, bloody struggle for victory. By raising questions about the Allied commanders' key strategic and tactical decisions, we seek to provide new insights into some of the most vexing controversies that have long surrounded the Normandy invasion.

What lessons can we learn from the OVERLORD campaign? These mighty battles contained both triumphs and personal tragedies. They were fought to sustain great ideals. This is what gives glory to the Allied effort, whatever the rivalries and tangled relations among its commanders.

As we recall OVERLORD's higher purposes, even in the midst of the hard conflicts of a twenty-first century world, the high level of cooperation achieved by the Allies in spite of conflicting goals and objectives may also inspire us to do better. For most of us that is the most important lesson of all.

# CHAPTER 1

# SETTING THE STAGE: STRUGGLE OVER OPENING THE SECOND FRONT

"Well, there it is; it won't work, but you must bloody well make it."

—Sir Alan Brooke, chief of the imperial general staff[1]

## "WE ARE ALL IN THE SAME BOAT"

D-Day's seeds were first planted on Dunkirk's beaches. Almost from the day in 1940 when the British and French forces were evacuated from France, the British began to consider where, when, and how they would return to free northwestern Europe from Nazi occupation. Much of this speculation was premature. Only when the United States dropped its neutrality would the combined manpower and firepower of Britain and America be available to guarantee the success of such a massive amphibious invasion of northwestern Europe. In this chapter, we will detail how difficult it was for the Allies to decide on when and where to launch this invasion.

Soon after Japan's surprise attack on Pearl Harbor on December 7, 1941, Britain's prime minister Winston S. Churchill called Franklin D. Roosevelt. "Mr. President, what's this about Japan?" "It's quite true," Roosevelt replied. "We are all in the same boat now."[2] Churchill immediately proposed traveling to Washington, DC, so that "[w]e could review the whole war plan in the light of reality." On December 14, 1941, he left for America. Churchill spent Christmas with Roosevelt as his guest at the White House.[3]

In their wide-ranging discussions, Roosevelt and Churchill made several unprecedented decisions that had a broad impact on future military operations. First, in order to unify Anglo-American strategy, they agreed that one supreme commander would be appointed in each theater of operations with final authority over all British/American land, sea, and air operations. Secondly, a new Combined Chiefs of Staff based in Washington, DC, would be appointed with representatives from the British and American chiefs of staff to coordinate joint strategic military decisions. They also decided that the Allies should be called the "United Nations" instead of "Associated Powers."[4]

Fig. 1.1. Meeting of Combined Chiefs of Staff, Quebec Conference. August 1943.
Left to right (at Chateau Frontenac): Vice Admiral Lord Louis Mountbatten, Admiral of the Fleet Sir Dudley Pound, General Sir Alan Brooke, Air Chief Marshal Sir Charles Portal, Air Marshal L. S. Breadner, Field Marshal Sir John Dill, Lieutenant General Sir Hastings Ismay, Admiral Ernest J. King, General Henry H. Arnold, Admiral W. D. Leahy, Lieutenant General K. Stuart, Vice Admiral P. W. Nelles, and General George C. Marshall.
(© Imperial War Museums [A 18826])

Achieving this complete unification of military operations proved to be easier said than done. It set the stage for the future Allied invasion of France, an operation filled with controversy that extended to the war's final conclusion.

Germany did not necessarily have to declare war on America after the Pearl Harbor attack. Since Japan was the obvious aggressor, under the terms of the Tripartite Alliance (Germany-Italy-Japan), Germany was not obligated to help the Japanese. However, on December 11, 1941, Hitler elected to make a formal declaration of war against the United States, and America reciprocated on the same day. Hitler seriously underestimated America's industrial might—an error he would live to regret.[5]

## "WHY ARE WE TRYING TO DO THIS?"

Once the industrial might of America was mobilized, there was little doubt that the Axis powers would face inevitable defeat. It became a question of strategy.

In spite of the Pearl Harbor debacle and the growing number of Japanese victories across the Pacific, the US government reaffirmed its prewar policy of defeating Germany first. To the relief of the British, both President Roosevelt and General George C. Marshall, the chief of staff of the US Army, acknowledged that Germany's war-making capacity was far more dangerous. They agreed that Japan's defeat would soon follow the collapse of the Third Reich. The most contentious issue between Britain and America became how to best defeat Germany.

From the first day of the war, America's leaders were determined to speedily confront and defeat the German army by invading northwestern Europe. But because the British had recently been decisively defeated by German forces at Dunkirk and in Norway and Greece, Churchill and the British armed forces chiefs of staff were much more cautious. They also remembered the slaughter of an entire generation in Flanders field battles of the Somme and Passchendaele during World War I. Winston Churchill recounted,

> While I was always willing to join with the United States in a direct assault across the Channel on the German sea-front in France, I was not convinced that this was the only way of winning the war, and I knew that

> it would be a very heavy and hazardous adventure. The fearful price we had to pay in human life and blood for the great offensives of the First World War was graven in my mind.[6]

Britain's war leaders also harbored grave doubts about the battle readiness of US soldiers, believed that American generals lacked combat experience, and were skeptical about America's ability to rapidly increase the production of war materials.[7]

From December 1941 to June 1944 this British foreboding cast a pall over the very idea of mounting a successful cross-channel invasion. "Why are we trying to do this?" Churchill was shouting even as late as February 1944. Almost up to the day of the actual Normandy landings, Churchill continually bombarded the Americans and his own generals with alternatives such as invading Norway, Portugal, or the Balkans. This continued insistence on these diversionary maneuvers weakened his relationships with the American commanders.[8]

The British chief of the imperial general staff, Sir Alan Brooke, voiced similar doubts about a Normandy invasion.[9] From the beginning of the American push to speedily invade northwestern Europe, he instead advocated first invading Italy to weaken German forces in the West. Alan Brooke also insisted that the Allies must win the Battle of the North Atlantic before launching a massive invasion. More time was also needed for a bomber offensive to severely cripple German arms production and win air superiority over Europe.

Overall Brooke did not believe that the Wehrmacht would be sufficiently weakened before 1944. Furthermore he doubted that US war production would be able to turn out the huge quantity of goods required for an invasion and that America could train an adequate number of troops before this date.

Above all Brooke believed that the way to victory was conducting a war of attrition. This strategy had been the linchpin for the Allied victory in World War I. He continued to preach this attritional doctrine throughout World War II, much to the annoyance of Churchill and US war leaders. As we will see the final irony is that during the Normandy campaign, the US commanders applied their adaptation of attritional warfare to end the war in Europe.[10]

On the eve of D-Day Brooke wrote in his diary, "At least it will fall so very short of the expectations of the bulk of the people, namely all those who know nothing of its difficulties. At the worst it may well be the most ghastly disaster of the whole war."[11]

## THE SECOND FRONT DEBATE

The exact timing for an invasion of northwestern Europe became the key decision of the Second World War in Europe. It took a long time in coming.

Even before the United States entered the war, American, British, and Canadian military staffs had met at the ABC Conference in Washington, DC (January–March 1941). They agreed on a "Germany first" strategy to defeat the Axis. After Pearl Harbor a bewildering succession of military meetings and conferences convened to argue over Allied differences in strategy and tactics. The future invasion of northwestern Europe was postponed again and again.

At the Washington, DC, Arcadia Conference, the first war meeting of the Allied political and military leadership (December 1941–January 1942), the United States committed to Operation BOLERO, the buildup of American forces in the United Kingdom prior to the invasion of Europe. Shortly afterward the US Joint Chiefs of Staff (JCS) agreed to combine with the representatives of the British Chiefs of Staff (BCS), creating the Combined Chiefs of Staff (CCS) (February 9, 1942). They would meet over two hundred times, mostly in Washington, DC, during the course of the war.[12]

That March Admiral Ernest J. King, the new chief of US naval operations, met with General George C. Marshall, the chief of staff of the US Army. They agreed on a two-stage plan for an immediate invasion of northwestern Europe. Operation SLEDGEHAMMER, stage one, envisioned a landing in mid-September 1942 on the French Cherbourg Peninsula. The second stage, Operation ROUNDUP, in the spring of 1943 called for either an expansion of the original SLEDGEHAMMER invasion area or another landing in the Normandy region.

The plans for Operations SLEDGEHAMMER and ROUNDUP had originated in the US War Department's War Plans Division. Major Albert Wedemeyer prepared the report entitled the Victory Program and submitted it on July 9, 1941, to fulfill President Roosevelt's request for an operations plan if the United States ever went to war with Nazi Germany.

The strategy behind these plans was eventually developed into Operation OVERLORD for D-Day in 1944. The Victory Program was approved by General Dwight D. Eisenhower before its submission to Roosevelt and Marshall. William Weidner observes, as a result, "It could honestly be said that Eisenhower helped to determine the strategy, while General Montgomery prepared the operational plans."[13]

In April 1942, Churchill met with Marshall in London and agreed to this plan, overriding objections from his own chiefs of staff. Soon afterward, the British designated Admiral Sir Bertram Ramsay as the Allied commander of the Naval Expeditionary Forces (April 23, 1942). Ramsay's appointment was the result of his unrivalled experience in commanding the massive Dunkirk military evacuation of British and French forces across the English Channel in June 1940.[14]

However, it soon became apparent that the manpower and logistical shipping numbers just did not add up. America's mobilization was rapidly expanding its military forces, but there were other demands. At the Arcadia Conference the United States agreed to occupy Iceland and Ireland to free up British troops, and the Pacific war with Japan had urgent manpower requirements.

Marshall's SLEDGEHAMMER/ROUNDUP plan envisioned 800,000 troops being shipped to England by the spring of 1943. However in the fall of 1942, only 105,000 men were available.[15] More time was needed to amass the American forces required for a cross-channel invasion of France.

The sealift capacity in 1942 was also insufficient for such an operation. In the fall of that year, all the landing craft available in the United Kingdom could carry only 20,000 men. At least another year was required for US shipyards to build a sizeable invasion armada.[16]

Churchill and Brooke continually evidenced a lack of enthusiasm for the Normandy operation. Neither opposed it outright but believed it impossible in 1942. Perhaps the summer of 1943 might be possible, if the Allies secured both air and naval superiority, and America produced the promised vast numbers of weapons, ships, supplies, and men required for a successful enterprise. The British preferred to avoid a direct assault on a powerful German Wehrmacht, an army that many historians today consider the overall best professional fighting force in World War II.

Since being pushed off the European continent at Dunkirk, Britain had been fighting a peripheral war. The Royal Navy confined the Germans to the European mainland and kept the Allied supply lines open. British bomber command pursued an all-out strategy of strategic saturation raids to destroy German industry, infrastructure, and morale. The British Special Operations Executive (SOE) supported the underground resistance movements in occupied countries to, in Churchill's words, "set Europe ablaze."[17] Because of its economic and manpower limitations, an indirect war strategy better suited Britain.

Manpower and war production concerns also fueled British reluctance to mount an invasion of France. Its already-battered empire could ill afford the prospect of huge casualties. By the time of the actual invasion, spring 1944, the British army was at the very limit of its final growth—2,750,000 soldiers. In contrast the US Army numbered 5,750,000, and was still not at its potential maximum. Britain's production had fallen from fulfilling over 90 percent of the Commonwealth's war needs in 1940, to only about 61 percent by 1944.[18] American shortages of war materials lessened as the war continued. For the British such shortages were perpetual, to be lived with indefinitely. As a result of all of these issues, difficulties continually arose between the two allies regarding planning, logistics, and tactics.

Churchill and the British general staff saw many hazards in haste and great virtue in delay. After the German invasion of the Soviet Union in 1941, their implicit game plan was to allow the Wehrmacht and Russian armies to bleed each other to death. Their preferred underlying strategy called for the British and other Allied forces to strike when the Nazi regime was on the verge of collapse. With a weakened Germany and Soviet Union, the Allies could invade and establish a "new order" for the European continent. Churchill hoped to thereby prevent the potential Communist Russian dominance of postwar Eastern Europe.

Operation RANKIN was the British chiefs of staff plan to implement this peripheral strategy with attacks in the Mediterranean region, the Balkans, Norway, and elsewhere. These thrusts would help to wear down the Nazi empire in Europe until it collapsed. Perhaps it was all wishful thinking on their part, but as late as November 1943 the British chiefs still considered the possibility of implementing RANKIN as an alternative to a major landing in Normandy. Thus by the time of the Second Washington

Conference in June 1942, Churchill had persuaded Roosevelt to issue a joint veto for a 1942 Allied landing in France.[19]

## THE MEDITERRANEAN STRATEGY

However, pressure for Allied action in Europe was building. In early 1942 the American public was clamoring for some immediate major military operation as revenge for Pearl Harbor. Stalin was also pressing the Allies for a major invasion of Western Europe that would open a second front, thereby siphoning German forces out of the Soviet Union. British and American military commanders needed to agree soon on a significant Allied military operation in the European area.

Alan Brooke offered his own plan, Operation GYMNAST, a joint Anglo-American invasion of French North Africa. With Churchill's approval, the British argued that GYMNAST would encircle Hitler's Europe. It could help prevent a potential German occupation of Spain, Portugal, and Gibraltar. Also this operation would clear Mediterranean shipping lanes to the Suez Canal and the Far East. Field Marshal Erwin Rommel's Afrika Korps was in full retreat after their defeat by the British forces led by Field Marshal Viscount Bernard Montgomery at the Battle of El Alamein (October 23–November 4, 1942). The goal of GYMNAST was an Allied entrapment of Rommel through an East-West pincer envelopment and the destruction of the Afrika Korps. This would ideally position the Allies to invade the so-called "soft underbelly" of Europe, thereby knocking Italy out of the war. However the British reassured the Americans of their full support for ROUNDUP in the spring of 1943.[20]

Marshall and King were angry at being forced by Roosevelt to commit to GYMNAST. This was one of the few times during World War II that Roosevelt intervened in a military decision. Marshall and King perceived it as a "sideshow" operation in the Mediterranean much more in line with British Imperial interests than Allied strategic goals.[21]

But as historian John Keegan points out, from the British perspective, "It was, however, deeply psychological. Not only was the sea a bridge between the homeland and the East, it was also the amphitheater in which for two hundred years they had played grand strategy, longer indeed than they had played it in India with quite as much personal involvement."[22]

Here two fundamentally opposing conceptions of war—the indirect versus direct approach—collided. For the British an invasion of northwestern Europe would come only as a final knockout blow. First the German Wehrmacht had to be worn out by fighting on many fronts. The Americans contended that the Allies should be using the Clausewitzian principle of concentration of their forces at the decisive point. Their dispute was never resolved and repeatedly hampered the successful course of the Normandy campaign.[23]

The Joint Chiefs of Staff reluctantly approved GYMNAST that became the Operation TORCH landings in November 1942. To prevent any backsliding by Marshall and King, Churchill insisted that an American be appointed commander in chief of Operation TORCH.

A Marshall protégé was selected, Lieutenant General Dwight D. Eisenhower, who was then serving in Britain as commander of US Army forces. The remaining principal commanders would all be British. Ramsay, the deputy to Admiral Sir Andrew Cunningham who was the TORCH Naval Commander, was tapped to plan the two landings staged from Britain. Thus Eisenhower and Ramsay worked together, as they would later for the Normandy D-Day invasion.[24]

## "DO THE BRITISH REALLY BELIEVE IN OVERLORD?"

In January 1943 while the fighting still raged across North Africa, the Allied leadership met at Casablanca for their second major conference. They chose this site largely for propaganda purposes, as they hoped to lure Soviet leader Joseph Stalin, the third member of the "Big Three," into a face-to-face meeting. This did not happen. He was too busy fighting the Battle of Stalingrad that would soon end in a great Soviet military victory. In declining Roosevelt's personal invitation, Stalin added a barbed reminder: "Allow me to express my confidence that the promises about the opening of the second front in Europe given by you, Mr. President, and by Mr. Churchill in regard to 1942, and in any case in regard to the spring of 1943, will be fulfilled."[25]

The Combined Chiefs had met fifty-six times since July 1942. At Casablanca it soon became apparent that they were still on two different planets. There Marshall and King sought to force a decision on the cross-channel Operation ROUNDUP later in 1943. They believed that an operation from the United Kingdom was essential to ultimate victory.[26]

Fig. 1.2. Casablanca Conference, North Africa. 1943. Seated: President Franklin D. Roosevelt (left) and Prime Minister Winston S. Churchill (right). Standing from left: Lieutenant General Henry H. Arnold, Admiral Ernest J. King, General George C. Marshall, Admiral of the Fleet Sir Dudley Pound, Field Marshal Sir Alan Brooke, and Air Chief Marshal Sir Charles F. A. Portal. (© Imperial War Museums [A 14122])

Brooke cautioned that any immediate Allied invasion of France would pit twenty-five Allied divisions against forty-six German divisions.[27] This offered the Germans a potential easy victory. Instead as a follow-up to TORCH, he argued that the Allies should mount an invasion of Sicily or Sardinia to knock a weakened Italy out of the war. This would force the Germans to overstretch their forces in order to replace Italian troops in Italy and the occupied Balkan and Greek territories.

The Combined Chiefs of Staff unwillingly came to a final compromise agreement on January 19, 1943. They would invade Sicily (Operation HUSKY), but also continue building manpower in England for a thrust across the English Channel if "the German strength in France decreases."

Brooke finally acknowledged at Casablanca that "we could definitely count on re-entering the continent in 1944 on a large scale." However, he did not say whether this meant Italy or France! The Americans were now adamant about no further delays in invading northwestern Europe.[28]

At the Trident conference in Washington, DC (May 12–27, 1943), British opposition to a cross-channel invasion appeared to soften. A provisional date of May 1, 1944, was set for the cross-channel invasion ROUNDUP, now renamed OVERLORD. This was later confirmed at the Quebec Quadrant Conference (August 17–24, 1943). Much to the British dismay the Americans also added Operation ANVIL. This was a simultaneous landing in southern France to coincide with OVERLORD.[29]

Meanwhile Allied battlefield successes were mounting. On May 12, 1943, all Axis forces surrendered in North Africa.[30] Sicily was then invaded by the Allies on July 10. By August 17 the last German soldier was banished from the island. These positive Allied developments also precipitated an anti-war coup d'état in Italy that overthrew Benito Mussolini on July 25. The Italians then asked for an armistice.[31]

This string of successes and the relentless Allied bombing of factories and rail yards around Paris raised hopes in France that the Allies would soon launch a cross-channel invasion from England. When would the Allies attack? In the fall of 1943, an ironic joke circulated widely across France: "Stalin's army crosses Germany, then France, until it reaches the English Channel. Taking up a loudspeaker, the leader of the USSR bellows across the Channel to the British and Americans: 'You can come over now!'"[32]

The Axis collapse was so rapid that it gave the Allies many military opportunities. For once they jointly agreed on an immediate plan for an assault on mainland Italy. On September 3, the Allies crossed the narrow Straits of Messina (Operation BAYTOWN). US general Mark Clark's Fifth Army then launched an amphibious invasion at Salerno on September 9 (Operation AVALANCHE). Simultaneously, British general Bernard Montgomery's Eighth Army landed at Toronto (Operation SLAP STICK) in the Puglia region.

The Germans rapid response to these assaults moved additional armored and infantry divisions into Italy. They strongly contested the Allied Salerno landing before successfully withdrawing to the heavily fortified Gustav defensive line. This stretched across the mountainous width of the Italian peninsula. Here the Germans would halt the Allied armies until May 1944.[33]

During the autumn and winter of 1943, preparation for OVERLORD advanced. Yet behind the unified Allied front, the British grew increasingly apprehensive. In a cable to Marshall, Churchill stated, "We are carrying out our contract, but I pray God it does not cost us dear."[34]

On November 11, a British Chiefs of Staff memo recorded, "We must not regard Overlord on a fixed date as the pivot of our whole strategy. . . . The German strength in France next Spring may . . . be something that makes Overlord impossible [or] Rankin not only practicable but essential."[35]

The Americans reacted angrily to the British advocacy of RANKIN at this advanced date. A US chiefs of staff memorandum that autumn expressed their deep dismay:

> It is apparent . . . that the British . . . now feel OVERLORD is no longer necessary . . . continued Mediterranean operations coupled with POINT BLANK [major aerial bombing of German strategic war infrastructure] . . . will be sufficient to . . . [assure] her military defeat without undergoing what they consider an almost certain "bloodbath."[36]

Brooke finally had driven the Americans to their breaking point. Marshall was determined to force the British into a final non-revocable commitment to OVERLORD.

This opportunity presented itself at the Tehran Conference in Iran (November 28–December 1, 1943). This was the first joint meeting of the "Big Three"—Joseph Stalin, Winston S. Churchill, and Franklin D. Roosevelt.

Stalin was impatient for major military relief through the long-promised Anglo-American second front in France. Without actually knowing about RANKIN, he began to suspect that a plot existed to weaken Russia's armies by making them face the brunt of the German military machine. Churchill still supported the idea of gradually wearing down the Germans and avoiding potentially high British casualties from such an invasion. Roosevelt backed US military policy that was still committed to a major invasion as soon as possible.

The Tehran Conference gave Stalin's generals a chance to pin the British down on their OVERLORD commitment. With Americans present,

Russian marshal K. E. Voroshilov, a member of the State Defense Committee, pressed Brooke by asking him if the American stance on OVERLORD's importance coincided with British thinking. Brooke equivocated repeating the old arguments about the need to drain off German divisions in France through ancillary military operations.[37]

The Russians pressed on the Normandy operation remorselessly. During another session at which Roosevelt was present, Stalin looked at Churchill across the table and asked, "Do the Prime Minister and the British Staff really believe in Overlord, or are they only saying so to reassure the Soviet Union?" Churchill hedged saying that under agreed conditions they would attack the Germans with "every sinew of our strength."[38] Stalin continued to press harder, demanding an exact invasion date, and the naming of the OVERLORD supreme commander.

At Tehran the Allies finally agreed to an OVERLORD launch date sometime in May 1944, and a supporting operation in the south of France. The naming of the supreme commander was promised in the near future.[39]

Churchill and Brooke had been backed into a corner by the Russians and Americans and finally ran out of maneuvering room. Major General John Kennedy, a British planner, later conceded, "Had we had our way, I think there can be little doubt that the invasion of France would not have been done in 1944."[40]

Even after the Tehran Conference, Churchill tried to get OVERLORD postponed for some more assaults "around the ring." In April 1944, he told an American general that if he were planning OVERLORD, it would not be executed until the Allies had rctaken Norway, invaded the Aegean islands, and secured Turkey's support.[41]

After interminable delays all the Allies had finally accepted the OVERLORD concept. The die was cast! It had been a hard, bruising process.

Now began an even harder phase. Appointing OVERLORD's leadership and successfully planning the largest amphibious invasion ever attempted in the history of warfare.

# CHAPTER 2

# FIRST SHOTS: CONTROVERSIES OVER D-DAY PLANNING

"We had worked like beavers for months."
—General Frederick Morgan,
author of the original invasion plan[1]

## THE COSSACS ARE COMING!

Though the Allies had agreed to an invasion in northwest Europe, this was only the beginning of their prolonged struggle to determine where and when to launch D-Day. At Casablanca the British were successful in securing the postponement of a cross-channel attack and substituting an agreement to mount Operation HUSKY, the invasion of Sicily. To appease the Americans, Winston Churchill suggested appointing a commander for the invasion of northwestern Europe. He proposed that a member of the British Chiefs of Staff be named as a temporary deputy commander.

Marshall liked the idea. While Churchill thought this was a harmless consolation prize, Marshall perceived that appointing a deputy commander or a chief of staff gave the invasion planning a new lease on life. On January 22, 1943, the Combined Chiefs of Staff ordered such an appointment and an independent US-British staff to plan the future amphibious assault.

In March a relatively unknown lieutenant general, Frederick Morgan, was appointed chief of staff to the supreme Allied commander designate (i.e., not yet appointed). As commander of the British I Corps, Morgan had gained significant experience in operational planning. Brigadier General Ray Barker was made his American deputy. Their staff was built from people who already had been planning the buildup of Allied soldiers in England for the cross-channel invasion.[2]

Fig. 2.1. Lieutenant General Sir Frederick E. Morgan. (© Imperial War Museums [EA 33078])

Morgan was given the bulky files already developed by the British since 1942 containing plans for cross-channel operations. He was ordered to plan what came next for 1943 and 1944 and develop an outline for the British Chiefs of Staff.

Morgan found little enthusiasm from the British military establishment. They didn't take his organization seriously. This operation was assigned space in Norfolk House on St. James Square in London. Morgan was very aware that the building was considered a jinx because of its prior history. It was thought to be a symbol of lost causes. Henry VIII and Elizabeth I had beheaded several members of the Norfolk family, its original owners, for high treason because of their refusal to renounce Catholicism.

Initially it was unclear to Morgan how much of his assignment was just a smoke screen for hiding British intransigence. The first part of his orders was to conduct an elaborate disinformation campaign to confuse the Germans on the Allied invasion intentions (Operation COCKADE). This subsequently became Operation FORTITUDE.

Morgan was also charged to prepare for two other contingencies: (1) "a return to the Continent in the event of German disintegration" (Operation RANKIN), and (2) "a full scale assault against the Continent in 1944 as early as possible."[3] No one had told Morgan what had priority, so he began the implementation of all three assignments.

Morgan began calling himself COSSAC, taken from the first letters of his new title. This was meant as a joke. However the name stuck.[4]

The third assignment became the central focus of COSSAC. The most immediate issue was to select a suitable landing area for the cross-channel invasion. The Combined Operations Command (COC) headed by Lord Louis Mountbatten had experience with this problem, as it had been charged with launching multiple raids along the coastlines of Nazi-occupied Europe. The COC conducted missions of various sizes mainly designed to sabotage key enemy assets.

In 1942 a more ambitious operation was planned to determine whether it was possible to quickly capture a major port with its facilities largely remaining undamaged. The port of Dieppe in France was selected as the site for an exploratory foray that was supposed to be executed in less than one day.

On August 13, 1942, over six thousand troops, mostly Canadian forces but also Royal Marine Commandos and a small contingent of US rangers, stormed ashore at Dieppe in a dawn raid. By early morning half were dead, wounded, or captured. The rest withdrew after this humiliating defeat. Only about 2,500 returned to England.[5] It was an appalling slaughter.

Dieppe weighed heavily in the future calculations of both the German and Allied military planners. It convinced many of the German generals that the future invasion could be defeated at the water's edge. They also came to believe that the Allies' target of choice would be the capture of a major seaport in order to keep the invasion properly supplied. In their subsequent building of Festung Europa's (Fortress Europe) fortifications, the Germans tended to concentrate these defenses in regions around major channel seaports: Calais, Antwerp, Dunkirk, Le Havre, Boulogne, and others.

However, the Germans drew the wrong conclusions from Dieppe. This was only partially later rectified by Field Marshal Erwin Rommel's energetic defensive efforts that we will examine in a later chapter.

Morgan's COSSAC planners also learned important lessons from the Dieppe debacle and other amphibious operations in North Africa, Sicily, and Italy. First, they could not expect to capture a major port intact in an early assault. From Dieppe came the idea of constructing a portable harbor. Second, a massive air and naval bombardment was mandatory to soften up the German defenses. Third, a specially trained and equipped marine assault force was required to get and stay ashore. New tactics and techniques were proven under fire, and a new generation of landing craft and equipment for such operations was developed.[6]

## INVASION SITE DECISION

In the end the COSSAC planners winnowed the choice of an invasion site to two areas: the Pas-de-Calais and the coast of Normandy west of the Seine estuary. Pas-de-Calais was nearer to Berlin, but Normandy offered better anchorages. Both offered good inland-access roads and shorelines interspersed with wide, sandy beaches framed by a mixture of cliff and shingle.

But there was no clear-cut choice. Morgan feared that the inefficiency of the British planning machinery, interservice rivalry, and the dead hand of British bureaucracy would impose a crippling delay in reaching a decision.[7] As previously mentioned, Lord Mountbatten was head of the Combined Operations Command (COC) that had conducted British raids along the coasts of Nazi-occupied Europe. He was related to the royal family and was a close personal friend of Churchill. It was the prime minister's idea to establish the COC, and Churchill helped to ensure Mountbatten's appointment as its commander. Due to his political and social connections at the highest level, Mountbatten was able to assemble a formidable group of military commanders to attend a brainstorming program at his COC training headquarters at Largs in Scotland. What became known as the Rattle Conference (June 28–July 2, 1943) was intended as a COC training course for senior officers. Instead its seminar sessions mapped out the potential invasion points. It was chaired by Mountbatten with buoyant confidence and enthusiasm, and consensus was hammered out on the place and methods for the landing on the continent.

Rattle became known as the "Field of the Cloth of Gold Conference" because Mountbatten attracted so many high-ranking officers. There were twenty generals, eight admirals, eleven air marshals and air commodores, plus numerous brigadiers. Of those attending, five were Canadian and fifteen were American.[8]

Mountbatten interspersed these planning sessions with rousing pipe-band performances and champagne suppers. But Rattle got the job done.

The senior Anglo-American officers chose Normandy. This site offered the potential capture of two major ports—Cherbourg and Le Havre. It also included the possibility of capturing the ports along the coast of Brittany, just to the west of Normandy. Pas-de-Calais, though closer to the German border, offered none of these vital logistical plums in support of a long-term campaign to defeat Germany.[9]

Morgan's orders were to complete the monumental task of turning the voluminous plans and related memorandums into a detailed operational plan for the invasion by August 1, 1943. Before that deadline, Morgan was to present a preliminary report to the British Chiefs of Staff. But Churchill insisted on seeing the plan before anyone else![10]

The old American code name ROUNDUP had been discarded. Morgan sent one of his senior deputies, Major Roger Fleetwood Hesketh, to the Inter Services Security Board (ISSB) to assign a new code name. These code names were carefully collated to avoid duplication and compiled so no similar-sounding code names would be assigned to future operations. All this effort was to avoid confusion over the Allies' secret operations.

When Hesketh returned he reported to Morgan that the one code word then available was "Mothball." At that time the Allies had numerous European and Pacific military operations taking all the other potential names and only Mothball was left![11]

On hearing this, Morgan knew Churchill would rebel. He would never willingly swallow an "Operation Mothball."

When Morgan presented his plan and code word—Mothball—to the prime minister, Churchill went right through the roof. "Do you mean to tell me that those bloody fools want our grandchildren 50 years from now to be calling the operation that liberated Europe Operation Mothball? If they can't come up with a better code name for our landing than that, I damn well will pick the code name myself."[12]

Morgan said that Churchill "glowered for a moment" and then shouted, "Overlord. We shall call it Overlord." That is how the greatest D-Day of them all came to be known to posterity as Operation OVERLORD.[13] It was Churchill's most important personal contribution to the invasion plan.

## NEVER PREVIOUSLY ATTEMPTED IN HISTORY

In his newly titled initial report of July 15, 1943, Morgan wrote, "An operation of the magnitude of Operation OVERLORD has never previously been attempted in history. It is fraught with hazards, both in nature and magnitude, which do not obtain in any other theatre of the present world war."[14]

The COSSAC plan's mission was based on the directive from the Combined Chiefs of Staff: "You will enter the Continent of Europe and, in conjunction with other Allied Nations, undertake operations aimed at the heart of Germany and destruction of her Armed Forces."[15]

Throughout the spring and summer of 1943, a team of about forty British and American officers with the rank of colonel and above conducted a detailed analysis of every aspect of OVERLORD. Those continuous meetings were held at Norfolk House, the COSSAC headquarters.

The growing mutual trust among the members of the Anglo-American planning staff was apparent during a transatlantic telephone conference call from London with US military staff in Washington, DC. A small group participated at each site. At its conclusion a senior US Army general warned, "For Christ's sake, don't tell the British," regarding the information they had shared. Loud laughter broke out at the other end of the line. The general asked what was so funny. He learned that London group included two British generals and an admiral.[16]

After Morgan and his COSSAC staff finished the OVERLORD plan, they celebrated with a high-spirited party held on the top floor of the Norfolk House. To accommodate both British and American tastes, it featured an American swing band and a British dance orchestra. Morgan recalled, "All entered wholeheartedly into the occasion."[17]

Although Field Marshal Sir Bernard Montgomery and his staff later belittled the initial COSSAC plan, its research memoranda provides solid evidence of the broad range of challenges they screened and debated, and for which they actually conducted feasibility tests. For example, they sent Royal Navy canoeists close inshore by submarine and landed them to take surface samples of the proposed landing beaches. This was to determine whether the terrain could withstand the weight of landing craft, tanks, jeeps, and other vehicles to preclude them ending up bogged down in a mire as what happened at Dieppe.[18]

"The crux of the problem," wrote Morgan, "is . . . likely to be our ability to drive off the German reserves rather than the initial breaking of the coastal crust."[19] In formulating this plan, Morgan had to factor in many constraints. The size and scope of the initial and follow-up landings were limited by the available number of landing craft and supply ships available. His instructions were to plan an opening assault with only three divisions.

In order to fulfill the Combined Chiefs of Staff's prime directive, France and the Low Countries (i.e., Holland, Belgium, and Luxemburg) had to be cleared of German forces before the final drive into the heart of the Third Reich. Logistics were at the heart of the OVERLORD operation. The capture of major ports such as Antwerp, Brest, Le Havre, and Marseille were vital for mounting a successful invasion and sustaining the subsequent deployment of large numbers of troops. During the actual OVERLORD campaign, forty-eight million tons of supplies had to be delivered in order to sustain US forces in Normandy. To do this, these ports had to be quickly seized, cleared of obstructions, and opened to shipping.

Morgan envisioned a large buildup of forces in order to begin the liberation of all of France. The coastal area of Normandy could not physically accommodate all of the necessary forces. By ninety days after the invasion, a larger lodgment area bounded by the Seine River on the north, and the Loire on the south, would be needed. This included the ports of Cherbourg and Brest. The other component in the liberation of France was Operation ANVIL that the Allied invasion mounted in southern France, which included the objectives of seizing the ports of Toulon and Marseille. ANVIL's drive northward up the Rhone River valley would link up with OVERLORD forces advancing eastward with the aim of destroying German forces or forcing their rapid retreat into Germany. (See Map 1A.)

COSSAC proposed three landing beaches between Le Havre on the Seine and the base of the Cotentin Peninsula. British forces would land on the left to be supplied by Le Havre, Dunkirk, and Antwerp. The Americans would land on the right with their supplies coming through Cherbourg, Brest, and, with the success of Operation ANVIL, Marseille.

Morgan recognized that the Cotentin Peninsula itself gave the German defenders ample opportunity to stop the Allied invasion cold. Beyond the beaches of Normandy were thick woods, hedgerows (the "bocage"), and undulating hills. This whole area, Morgan stated, was "on the whole unsuitable for the use of large armored forces" because of "the marshy river valleys . . . steep hills and narrow valleys."[20]

That is why the COSSAC plan gave top priority to the rapid capture of Caen, Bayeux, and the road to St. Lo, on D-Day itself or shortly thereafter. Next the Americans would capture the port of Cherbourg, and the British would open the road to Falaise. This area north, northwest, and southeast of Caen was flat and open—ideal tank country. Here the Allies could deploy their numerous armored divisions to begin the liberation of France.[21] (See Map 1B.)

Morgan realized that the three-division size of the initial invasion force in the COSSAC plan was far too small, but his directives forced him to base the plan on the available number of landing craft. However, when not faced with such constraints, his projections regarding the total number of Allied divisions needed to win France and go on to conquer Germany were far from cautious, as he called for fifteen British and eighty-five US divisions (one and a half million men). During the entire Second World War the US Army deployed a total of eighty-nine divisions. Back in early 1942 at the Arcadia Conference, Churchill estimated that this campaign would require twenty British and twenty American divisions. Marshall's original Operation ROUNDUP called for forty-eight divisions (thirty US and eighteen British).[22]

The British Chiefs of Staff were not very enthusiastic when they reviewed the COSSAC plan in early August. They even refused Morgan's request to forward the plan to the American chiefs of staff.[23] The Combined Chiefs of Staff was soon meeting at Quebec (Quadrant Conference) to examine Morgan's plan.

Morgan outflanked his own chiefs by sending Major General Ray W.

Barker, his American second-in-command, to brief Marshall and Roosevelt before the Quebec meeting. Subsequently at Quadrant (August 17–24, 1943), Morgan's basic OVERLORD plan was accepted by the Combined Chiefs of Staff.[24]

COSSAC was only a rough draft for OVERLORD. However it did settle an important issue. Morgan's staff had formalized Normandy as the target landing area. What appears self-evident today was far from certain in 1943.

Morgan's planning accomplishments also highlighted the bumpy road of the Allied partnership. It showed there were significant cultural and institutional differences in British and American approaches to planning grand strategy.

In the US military planning, the senior officers would outline the objectives and provide a tentative timetable. Their staff subordinates were then charged with developing the detailed planning needed to attain the objectives.

The British strongly objected to this approach. They preferred to secure complete agreement throughout the chain of command for every detail of an operation. This obviously was more time-consuming, but it produced a more carefully written, analytical plan.

The Americans thought that this was a waste of time and effort. US plans often produced astounding numbers and almost impossible deadlines in the British view. They usually greatly underestimated America's production capabilities.[25]

Though the American enthusiasm as beginners was often counterbalanced by the five years of British war experience, this fundamental planning and operational conflict was never resolved. As we will see, this would repeatedly jeopardize vital battlefield decisions throughout the Normandy campaign thus ultimately extending the war in Europe.

The target date for OVERLORD of May 1, 1944, was also approved at the Quebec Conference. However, Morgan's planning dilemmas were far from over. The basic COSSAC plan was little more than an outline of a planned operation. Time was running out. A detailed plan was a necessity. A supreme commander needed to be appointed for OVERLORD. Throughout the autumn of 1944 Morgan remained frustrated in his role as COSSAC's interim commander without decision-making authority.

After World War II ended, Morgan wrote to British historian Liddell Hart about these and many other issues he faced during COSSAC's lifespan. One of his most unsettling comments might help us better understand some of the Normandy campaign's command dilemmas. Morgan observed that as the size of the US commitment to OVERLORD grew in manpower, aircraft, ships, etc., so did the signs that the British were developing an inferiority complex. He thought that this situation was "frightening."[26]

After OVERLORD's supreme commander was chosen, the COSSAC planners were absorbed into the Supreme Headquarters Allied Expeditionary Force (SHAEF). By January 1944 SHAEF had established itself at Norfolk House. It was headed by 489 officers, almost equally divided between the Americans and British, and included 614 staff members of lower rank, two-thirds of whom were British. Morgan was appointed as SHAEF deputy chief of staff for the war's duration. But who would be named as SHAEF's supreme commander?[27]

# CHAPTER 3
# "WHO WILL COMMAND OVERLORD?"

"His extraordinary generosity of spirit to his difficult subordinates proved his greatness as Supreme Commander."
—Max Hastings commenting on
Dwight D. Eisenhower[1]

At the Tehran Conference, less than a year before the actual Normandy invasion, Stalin asked Roosevelt and Churchill the critical invasion question: who will command OVERLORD? Incredibly, both responded no one would.

They tried to sidestep the issue. But Churchill reported that the Soviet leader became insistent: "Stalin declared it essential that a man should be appointed at once to be responsible, not only for the planning, but also for the execution."[2]

Actually a supreme commander shell game had been underway for quite some time. The two top candidates were the Anglo-American chiefs of staff—Alan Brooke and George C. Marshall.

## ALAN FRANCIS BROOKE

The seventh and youngest child of Sir Victor Brooke, a baronet from Ulster, Northern Ireland, Alan Brooke was born in 1883. Since his mother preferred warmer climes, he was raised in Pau, in the south of France, until he was sixteen. He was privately educated and spoke fluent French and German before learning English. Brooke also was a proficient hunter, fisherman, and horseman.

Fig. 3.1. Field Marshal Sir Alan Brooke. (© Imperial War Museums [TR 151])

Brooke entered the Royal Military Academy in Woolwich at the age of eighteen. Upon his graduation in 1902, he was commissioned as a second lieutenant in the Royal Regiment of Artillery with which he served in France during World War I. Most of his service was as a staff officer. At the Battle of the Somme he introduced the French "creeping barrage," a system designed to reduce casualties by covering an infantry advance with machine-gun fire. Brooke earned a reputation as an outstanding operational planner and by the end of the war was promoted to lieutenant colonel and was awarded the Distinguished Service Order.

After the war most of his service was as a staff officer. He attended the Staff College at Camberley and in 1929 was appointed commandant of the School of Artillery. That same year, he remarried. (His first wife had been killed in an automobile accident in 1925.) This second marriage has been credited with being a calming influence on his ego-driven personality.

Brooke was an instructor at the Imperial Defence College from 1931 to 1933 where Bertram Ramsay was his naval colleague. A close friendship developed between them. After commanding a mobile division that prefigured later armored divisions, Brooke was promoted to lieutenant general and in 1939 became commander in chief of Britain's antiaircraft command. As a result, he worked closely with Air Marshal Hugh Dowding, then commanding Fighter Command, in preparing for potential German Luftwaffe attacks.

In August 1939 Brooke became commander in chief of the Southern Command. At the outbreak of World War II, he was placed in command of II Corps in the British Expeditionary Force. In a decisive battle (May 28, 1940) on the road to Dunkirk, his troops held the German forces back long enough to allow over 300,000 British and French troops to be evacuated to England. After Dunkirk he again was sent to France, where upon his recommendation three additional combat divisions and other army units (140,000 men) were evacuated to Britain.

In July 1940, Brooke became commander in chief of the Home Forces, overseeing plans to defeat any potential German invasion of England after the fall of France. Due to his record as a superb field commander, Churchill appointed him chief of the imperial general staff in December 1941. Noted for his clarity of mind and unflinching realism, he became the master strategist of Britain's military effort. However, he could be highly critical and short-tempered if anyone disagreed with his decisions.

In March 1942, Churchill gave Brooke the additional post of chairman of the Joint Chiefs of Staff, thus making him his chief military advisor. As chief of staff he played a critical role throughout the war in effectively quelling Churchill's frequent—often last-minute—meddling in military decisions. In one episode after Brooke voiced his strong oppositions to one of the prime minister's pet projects, an outraged Churchill told his personal chief of staff, General Sir Hastings Ismay, that Brooke hated him and had to go. Ismay, who intervened to soothe Churchill's stressed ego, reported this to Brooke. Brooke replied, "I don't hate him, I love him, but when the day comes that I tell him he is right when I believe him to be wrong, it will be time for him to get rid of me."[3]

Under his chairmanship the chiefs of staff became a most efficient military machine shaping global strategy. Many military experts believe Alan Brooke was the most capable British general of World War II. General Douglas MacArthur wrote that Alan Brooke "is undoubtedly the greatest soldier that England has produced since Wellington."[4]

Through most of 1943, it had been assumed that OVERLORD's supreme commander would be British. It would provide a balance to Eisenhower's appointment in 1942 as TORCH's commander in the Mediterranean theater. Also Britain would be the launching point for OVERLORD. At least in its beginning phase, British and Commonwealth forces were to dominate on the ground. Churchill repeatedly assured Brooke that he had the cross-channel invasion command, and on June 15, he offered Brooke this appointment.

Then sometime during 1943, Churchill began to alter his perspectives on this issue. He appears to have realized that as OVERLORD advanced, the preponderance of troops would be American. Shortly before the Quebec Conference in August 1943, Churchill visited Roosevelt at this home in Hyde Park, New York. Historian Carlo D'Este suggests that Churchill proposed agreeing to an American as supreme commander for OVERLORD if he could appoint Lord Louis Mountbatten, his longtime protégé, as the new supreme commander in Southeast Asia.[5]

As a result of this meeting, after the end of the Quebec Conference Churchill broke the news to Brooke (August 15) that he would not be named the Allied supreme commander, claiming that Roosevelt and his chief adviser, Harry Hopkins, had strong-armed him into accepting an American to command OVERLORD. Brooke was acquiescent but crushed. Churchill presented it "as if it were one of minor importance!" Brooke later wrote, "It took me several months to recover from [it]."[6]

At that time both Churchill and Roosevelt had agreed on George C. Marshall's appointment to the supreme command of OVERLORD. Brooke clearly resented their choice, since he believed that Marshall lacked his in-depth command experience in the field and was an amateur in strategic planning.[7]

## GEORGE C. MARSHALL

Initially, President Roosevelt desired to reward George C. Marshall with OVERLORD's supreme command. At the time of Pearl Harbor Marshall was in a strong leadership position. Though he had never commanded a division during America's participation in World War I (1917–1918), he had been chief of operations for the First Infantry Division. As such he worked under his mentor, General John J. Pershing, commander of the American Expeditionary Forces. Marshall had been a key planner of American operations, including the Meuse-Argonne Offensive. After the war he was Pershing's aide-de-camp for five years before his appointment as assistant commandant of the US Army Infantry School at Fort Benning, Georgia. He was appointed as the army chief of staff on the same day (September 1, 1939) that Adolf Hitler began World War II by invading Poland.

Fig. 3.2. General George C. Marshall. (Wikimedia Creative Commons, source: Dutch National Archives; licensed under CC BY-SA 3.0 NL)

The US Army and US Air Force in the summer of 1939 had a combined strength of less than 200,000 men. That grew to over eight million by 1945. As the new chief of staff, Marshall was pivotal in ensuring that this gigantic force was well armed, equipped, and trained. He carefully selected able commanders whom he had often mentored at Fort Benning during the preceding decades. As *Time* stated, he "had armed the Republic."[8]

Marshall was often criticized for being aloof and overly rigid. But he exercised his leadership with discipline and tact. Churchill, who often crossed swords with him during the OVERLORD operation, called him "the noblest Roman of them all." At the war's end in 1945, Churchill also astutely titled him the "Architect of Victory."[9]

At the time of the Quebec Conference everyone in the British-American command circles assumed that Roosevelt would name Marshall as OVERLORD's commander in chief. Roosevelt thought that the general had earned his spurs as U.S. Army Chief of Staff and a member of the Combined Chiefs of Staff. In Roosevelt's estimation he merited this great opportunity to be remembered as "the Pershing of the Second World War." The US secretary of war Henry Stimson supported this general consensus when he wrote to Roosevelt, "General Marshall already has a towering eminence of reputation as a tried soldier and as a broad-minded and skillful administrator."[10] Even though no one had officially offered Marshall the appointment, he began to close his stateside home anticipating a move to England.

Back in Africa, Eisenhower (or "Ike") also heard after the Quebec Conference that he would trade commands with Marshall. He would chair the Joint Chiefs of Staff while Marshall would command OVERLORD. Ike had always thought that Marshall would lead the cross-channel attack, but he loathed the idea of again being stuck behind a desk in the Pentagon.[11]

Sometime between Quebec and the conferences held in Cairo and Tehran (November 22– December 1, 1943), the president began to hesitate. How good a substitute was Eisenhower for Marshall? Could anyone really replace him? Who could continue running the entire Pacific-European war while Marshall ran OVERLORD? How could Eisenhower as chief of staff become Marshall's theoretical superior? Could Eisenhower handle the personalities and issues already mastered by Marshall, including General MacArthur, Admiral King, Congress, the Pacific War, and all of the ramifications surrounding appropriations, war production, and the draft?

Members of the Joint Chiefs of Staff also objected, saying Marshall was essential in Washington. Some even suggested that the OVERLORD command was a demotion from chief of staff. Others were perhaps jealous of the supreme command appointment. However most of his contemporaries considered Marshall as the essential commanding personality whose direct and honest approach could successfully manage a politically influenced president. His role in this respect was similar to that of General Alan Brooke, who was adept at reining in his mercurial, often overly interfering prime minister.[12]

While Roosevelt vacillated over the supreme command appointment, on October 1, 1943, Eisenhower was told personally by Frank Knox, secretary of the navy, that Marshall had officially been named to command OVERLORD. Roosevelt's personal advisor, Harry Hopkins, also gave Ike the same news and said that he was to become the chief of staff. With these assurances, Eisenhower sent Major General Walter Bedell Smith, who was his own chief of staff in North Africa, to brief Marshall in Washington.[13]

It was not until December 5 in Tehran that the president, hating confrontation, finally talked to Marshall about the possibility of staying in Washington. Only the day before, Marshall had told Hopkins that he would "wholeheartedly" accept whatever decision Roosevelt made. A greatly relieved president finally told Marshall, "Well I didn't feel I could sleep at ease with you out of Washington."[14]

## DWIGHT D. EISENHOWER

With both Marshall and Brooke out of the running as supreme commander, there was little doubt about who would be appointed. The British high command was impressed with Eisenhower's likable personality and dedication to the Allied cause. Churchill had developed both respect and a genuine liking for this collaborative American, first as commander of US forces in England, then during his command of the Mediterranean campaigns. Churchill was impressed by Eisenhower's ability to smooth relationships between the British and American commands.[15]

Brooke thought along the same lines, seeing Eisenhower as a far better choice than Marshall. Although he saw Eisenhower grow in command abilities during the Mediterranean campaigns, Brooke still had reservations about his strategic abilities. What particularly impressed Brooke were Eisenhower's abilities to develop the alliance structure into a day-to-day workable, successful operations command.

On December 7, 1943, the second anniversary of Pearl Harbor, Roosevelt's plane stopped in Tunisia to refuel before flying on to Oran, where the battleship *Iowa* would take him home. Eisenhower met the president's party at the airport and walked alongside Roosevelt as the secret service escort wheeled him into Ike's waiting limousine. Without any prior warning a smiling president stunned Eisenhower by announcing, "Well, Ike, you are going to command OVERLORD!"[16]

## Background

Although Eisenhower's parents were pacifists, he had accepted an appointment to West Point in 1911. When the United States entered World War I in 1917, Eisenhower was promoted to captain. Though he saw no action in Europe, Eisenhower was recognized by his superiors as an officer possessing excellent organizational abilities.

After the war Eisenhower helped organize America's first tank units. At Camp Meade in Maryland Ike was assigned to tanks. There he met Colonel George S. Patton. They became lifelong friends. In 1922 Eisenhower, now a major, was sent to the Panama Canal Zone to serve as executive officer of the Twentieth Infantry Brigade under the command of Brigadier General Fox Conner, one of the US Army's leading thinkers and an expert on strategy and tactics. Impressed with Eisenhower's abilities, he organized an advanced course for Ike on military history and its lessons from the great past campaigns. In 1925 Conner helped Eisenhower gain admission to the Command and General Staff College at Fort Leavenworth, Kansas. He graduated first in his class in June 1928.

While serving as executive officer to the assistant secretary of war, General George V. Moseley, Eisenhower became known as an excellent staff officer in Washington, DC, military circles. This led to his appointment in 1932 as aide to General Douglas MacArthur, US Army chief of staff.

In 1935, Roosevelt sent MacArthur to reorganize the military forces in the Philippine Islands. Ike followed him as his chief of staff. There Eisenhower began questioning MacArthur's policy decisions, and a lifetime rift between the two men began that never closed. This precipitated Ike's return to the United States in December 1939. He first served at Fort Lewis where he was promoted to colonel and made chief of staff under Major General Kenyon Joyce. In June 1941 he was assigned to Fort Sam Houston in San Antonio, the Third Army headquarters, where he was chief of staff under Lieutenant General Walter Krueger.

As we have already noted, with his appointment as chief of staff in 1939, General Marshall began revolutionizing the army's structure in preparation to fight and win a global war. Among his many innovations was the creation of a board of retired generals, what he called the plucking committee. During the war's duration they put over seven hundred officers out to pasture. This gave Marshall the leverage to appoint to the upper ranks men he saw who had great command potential, with Eisenhower, George S. Patton, and Omar Bradley at the top of his list.[17]

Eisenhower and Marshall had only met twice. But Ike's army-wide reputation and his planning role in the defense of the Philippines brought him to Marshall's attention.

Five days after Pearl Harbor, Major General Walter Bedell Smith, Marshall's assistant, telephoned Eisenhower. "The chief," he said, "says for you to hop a plane and get up here right away."[18] Because of Eisenhower's knowledge of the Philippines, Marshall immediately appointed him head of the Far Eastern desk at the army's War Plan Division. Marshall increased his responsibilities rapidly, in March 1942 making him head of the newly formed Operations Division, which dealt with military plans and operations throughout the world.

By mid-1942 Eisenhower was promoted to major general and placed in charge of the US Army's European buildup in England. As we have seen, he then went on to command the Allied invasions of North Africa, Sicily, and Italy.

## SHAEF Commander in Chief

On January 17, 1944, Eisenhower arrived in London to assume command of the Supreme Headquarters Allied Expeditionary Force (SHAEF). COSSAC ceased to exist.

When Eisenhower began his duties most of the other OVERLORD top appointments to ground, air, and naval commands were already in place. By previous agreement these were not Ike's to make. The British had back-handedly agreed to a 1944 cross-channel invasion. They had done most of its planning and would supply the majority of initial assault divisions. Though the British agreed to make Ike SHAEF supreme Allied commander in chief, they had insisted that most of the other crucial OVERLORD command appointments would be British.[19]

General Bernard Law Montgomery had been named the overall ground commander of what was labeled the Twenty-First Army Group composed of all American, British, and Canadian forces. The air forces were placed under the command of Air Chief Marshal Sir Trafford Leigh-Mallory. Admiral Sir Bertram Ramsay was given the naval command for OVERLORD, code-named Operation NEPTUNE.

Aside from these senior appointments, Eisenhower had a free hand in selecting the other members of the SHAEF staff. As the top US general in Europe, he also appointed or vetoed all American army corps or division commanders, contingent on Marshall's approval.

Eisenhower selected British air marshal Sir Arthur Tedder as his deputy commander. Major General Walter Bedell Smith became chief of staff. Eisenhower made COSSAC's former chief general Morgan a deputy to Smith, managing SHAEF's large staff.

For US field commands, Eisenhower chose General Omar Bradley to head the US First Army. Later Bradley led the US Army group once it was activated. General Courtney Hodges then took over the First Army, and General George S. Patton was named the commander of the Third Army.[20]

In three short years, Eisenhower, now fifty-four, had risen from colonel to the general commanding OVERLORD. While still noted for his charm and diplomatic skills, the years had taken their toll. He was a chronic workaholic and chain-smoker, and late-night conferences, inspection trips, and endless meetings with truculent allies had etched deep worry lines into his face. The weight of supreme invasion commands had transformed Ike into a more restless, abrupt, far less approachable personality.

As supreme commander Ike learned that despite a lofty title his power was far from absolute. In reality he directly commanded very few people. In early 1943 Ike already understood that the British always considered the impact on their empire when making military decisions.[21] Eisenhower mastered how to best cooperate and compromise with outside forces, be they political, logistical, Allied, or members of his own army command.

Fig. 3.3. Meeting of the Supreme Command. Allied Expeditionary Force in London. February 1, 1944. Left to right (front row): Air Chief Marshal Sir Arthur W. Tedder, deputy supreme commander, Expeditionary Force; General Dwight D. Eisenhower, supreme commander, Expeditionary Force; General Sir Bernard Montgomery, commander in chief, Twenty-First Army Group. Back row: Lieutenant General Omar Bradley, commander in chief, US First Army; Admiral Sir Bertram Ramsay, Allied naval commander in chief, Expeditionary Force; Air Chief Marshal Sir Trafford Leigh-Mallory, Allied air commander in chief, Expeditionary Force; Lieutenant General Walter Bedell Smith, chief of staff to Eisenhower. (Collection of the Imperial War Museums)

Eisenhower's primary job was to keep the Allied OVERLORD ship afloat and on course to its final destination. He did not take sides. Bradley, Patton, and other Americans often complained that Ike was too pro-British.

After the landings, Eisenhower spent much of his time in Normandy. But he took no active command role. Part of Ike's personality and style of command was to delegate responsibility and scrupulously keep his hands off. Even after moving his headquarters to France, Eisenhower believed that he lacked the intelligence-gathering staff needed to direct events. Instead he visited commands, listened, encouraged, but refrained from issuing orders. As our subsequent analysis will illustrate, by electing to use such a very detached command style, Eisenhower ran the grave risk of failing to intervene effectively at critical moments during the Normandy campaign.[22]

His lack of battlefield experience and personal success inevitably aroused the jealousies of many other capable commanders. "Just a coordinator, a good mixer, a champion of inter-Allied co-operation, and in those respects few can hold a candle to him," wrote Brooke. "But is that enough? Or can we not find all the qualities of a Commander in one man?"[23] After the war Brooke offered his final judgment on Eisenhower: "My opinion, however, never changed much as regards to his tactical ability or his powers of command. . . . As Supreme Commander, what he may have lacked in military ability he greatly made up for by the charm of his personality."[24]

Eisenhower was very sensitive to his shortcomings as a general in the field. This might in part explain his command style. But for all the players available in 1944, he was unmatchable as a supreme commander. Historian Max Hastings comments that "he revealed a greatness of spirit that escaped Montgomery, perhaps every British general of the Second World War with the exception of [First Viscount General William] Slim [hero of the Burma campaign]."[25] Even his fellow American commanders often proved difficult. They were irked that all of the principal OVERLORD commanders were British. Eisenhower's extraordinary generosity of spirit during many moments of Anglo-American tension proved his greatness as supreme SHAEF commander.

## BERNARD LAW MONTGOMERY

Eisenhower first met Montgomery in late spring 1942 while in England to kick some urgency into the US contingent organizing the buildup of American forces in England. While there, he also met with Brooke and Mountbatten. Overall Ike found the English to be helpful, pleasant, and warm allies. Then he met Montgomery.

Ike and General Mark Clark motored to a British army training center in Sussex commanded by General Montgomery. "Monty" and his staff were briefing a group of American officers about lessons learned while fighting the Germans.

Clark recounted that Montgomery set the meeting's tone with this opening announcement. "I have been directed to take time from my busy life to brief you gentlemen." Montgomery then began a patronizing lecture, since he and Brooke both believed the Americans were inexperienced, a bunch of reckless newcomers, and, if not guided by a veteran British hand, might bring disaster to the Allies. Soon into the program Ike began to unobtrusively smoke a cigarette. Montgomery, wrinkling his dachshund-like nose, stopped speaking abruptly and demanded, "Who is smoking?" A startled Eisenhower responded, "I am, sir." "Stop it," Montgomery snapped. "I don't permit it."[26] Ike turned crimson and meekly snuffed out his smoke.

On the trip back to London his driver Kay Summersby recalled that Eisenhower was "furious—really steaming mad," overhearing the words, "Montgomery" and "son-of-a-bitch" as Ike's temper flared.[27] He hoped never to encounter this arrogant general again. Unfortunately their association was to be long and filled with many troubling encounters throughout the war.

## Background

General Sir Bernard Law "Monty" Montgomery, the hero of El Alamein, was the son of an Anglican Church of Ireland (Northern Ireland) missionary bishop. Although he was born in England, he spent most of his unruly and difficult childhood in Tasmania. Monty's many adult eccentricities were apparent earlier. He freely admitted, "I was the bad boy of the family."[28]

In 1902, the family returned to England. Bernard was enrolled as a day student at St. Paul's School in London. His last report described him as "rather backward for his age."[29] At home he was moody and silent.

Monty was nineteen when he entered the Sandhurst Royal Military College in 1907. Slightly older than his Sandhurst colleagues, he was outwardly less mature. His undisciplined behavior almost caused him to be expelled from Sandhurst.

When World War I began, Montgomery was a twenty-six-year-old platoon leader. In its opening days he was severely wounded. For his gallantry he received the Distinguished Service Order. Montgomery did not return to France until 1916 as a brigade staff officer. By 1918 Monty had risen to a lieutenant colonel and the chief of staff of the Forty-Seventh Division.[30]

After the war, Montgomery applied for the course at the Staff College at Camberley, regarded as an essential step for reaching the highest army ranks. After he was turned down in 1919, Montgomery, a good tennis player, got himself invited to play tennis at the house of Sir William Robertson, his commander in chief. There he pled his case so well that shortly afterward he was ordered to report to the Staff College. In spite of his arrogant attitude that he knew more than his instructors, Montgomery must have distinguished himself, as in January 1926 he received a three-year appointment to the Staff College faculty.

In the 1930s Monty was also a senior instructor at the army Command and Staff College in Quetta, India, with the rank of full colonel. In the summer of 1937 he returned to England and was promoted to the rank of brigadier, commanding the Ninth Infantry Brigade, Portsmouth. It became the star brigade of the British army. It was selected for special exercises in 1937 and 1938. At their conclusion, General Wavell, commander in chief of the Southern Command, commented, "Brigadier Montgomery is one of the cleverest brains we have in the higher ranks, an excellent trainer of troops and an enthusiast in all he does."[31]

When his wife, Betty, died in October 1937 from blood poisoning, David, his then nine-year-old son, was away at preparatory school. Monty never allowed his son to visit her. Nor was her son at the funeral. Only after it was over did he tell David. The impact must have been crushing, because David was very close to his mother. Monty then compounded this highly questionable treatment of his son by refusing his own sister's offer to let David live with her family. Instead the boy was consigned to some of Montgomery's friends in Portsmouth. He saw little of his son during the next ten years.[32]

Needless to say, David did not follow in his father's footsteps. He attended schools at Winchester and Trinity College, Cambridge. Montgomery disapproved of David's career in international commerce, regarding it as bizarre and even fairly disreputable.[33]

In October 1938, Montgomery was selected to command the Eighth Division in Palestine and was promoted to the rank of major general. The following May, Montgomery became seriously ill from suspected tuberculosis. After his arrival in England that summer, he was found to have an infection from a World War I bullet wound.

Montgomery had arrived home at a very opportune moment. On August 28, 1939, he was appointed to command the Third Division. Less than a week later, Britain was at war with Germany.

Montgomery seemed to be well educated and positioned for higher command at the opening of World War II. However, he had been denied a virtual component of a British senior officer's higher education—attending the Imperial Defence College in London. Opening in 1927, a group of twenty to thirty-six select army/navy officers attended a year-long course. Other officers eventually came from the Royal Air Force (RAF), the British Territorial Army, the United States, and even industry and government. From 1931 to 1933 Admiral Bertram Ramsay and General Alan Brooke had helped direct the staff. They stressed its importance as an arena for learning the value of networking with all branches of the armed services. Many of Monty's contemporaries were selected. Among them were General Claude Auchinleck (1927), Air Marshal Arthur Tedder (1928), Admiral Andrew Cunningham (1929), General Harold Alexander (1930), Air Chief Trafford Leigh-Mallory (1934), General Henry Crerar of the Canadian army (1934), General Richard O'Connor (1935), and General Bill Slim (1937).

The peculiar omission from this pantheon of attendees was Monty. His three OVERLORD fellow commanders had all attended or directed staff. Even Eisenhower had attended the US equivalent of the Imperial Defence College. Cunningham commented that his year at the college was "one of the most interesting and valuable I have ever spent."[34] The decision not to send Montgomery was a possible War Office judgment on his suitability for higher command. An Imperial Defence College year might have exposed him to the necessity for collaboration at high command levels during coalition warfare.

At the end of September 1939, the British Expeditionary Force landed in France. General Alan Brooke was Montgomery's corps commander. Before the German offensive began, he had identified Montgomery as an eccentric but also inspiring division commander. Brooke particularly noted Monty's division exercises as "an eye-opener to me as to his ability as a trainer." Taking the measure of the man Brooke appointed himself Montgomery's guardian.[35]

It was a good thing he did. At the end of November 1939, Monty issued a divisional order to his troops on the prevention of venereal disease. Its explicit vulgar language showed a remarkable lack of judgment and sensibility for a British general. The Third Division chaplain filed a complaint that eventually reached Field Marshal John Gort, commander in chief of the British Expeditionary Force.[36]

Brooke saw the circular and told Monty "he had inevitably undermined the respect and esteem of the division for him."[37] Brooke realized that this might cause Montgomery to be relieved of command and sent back to England.

To head off this disaster, Brooke directly intervened with Gort. He promised to deliver a severe reprimand to Montgomery regarding this obscene language and to express the commander in chief's displeasure warning that he "could certainly not withstand any further errors of this kind." Montgomery, sensing the importance of Brooke's mentorship, expressed his deep remorse. Monty's reaction to past criticisms had been cavalier and belligerent. Instead, Brooke relates, "He took it wonderfully well." Brooke concludes the strange incident by writing in his diary, "It is a great pity that he spoils his very high military ability by a mad desire to talk or write nonsense."[38] Unfortunately Brooke would have many more opportunities in the future to intervene in order to overcome more of Monty's "nonsense."

On May 10, 1940, the Germans launched the Ardennes offensive, splitting the Allied front. Fearing encirclement the British Expeditionary Force and French armies, a total of over 300,000 troops, were forced back to the port of Dunkirk and evacuated back to England by June 1, 1940.

During this retreat General Harold Alexander, Brooke, and Montgomery emerged for the first time as a fighting team. Alexander was commanding the First Division of I Corps. During these operations he was placed temporarily under Brooke's command. It was during these critical days that Brooke gained an appreciation of these two commander's strengths, which led to their future command appointments in the North African Campaign.

Monty's Third Division survived and was immediately reequipped to defend the Sussex coast. He then was promoted to command V Corps in Dorset and Hampshire, then XII Corps in Kent (April 1941), and finally South-East Command (December).[39]

During 1941 to 1942 the British military campaign in North Africa had swung from early victory over the Italian armies to disastrous defeat at the hands of the Germans with the fall of Tobruk in June 1942. Field Marshal Erwin Rommel's Afrika Korps and the allied Italian forces continued their advance toward the Suez Canal only to be halted by the British at El Alamein in July.

On August 3, 1942, Churchill flew to Egypt to make a major change of command in what became known as the "Cairo purge." The post of commander in chief of the Middle East Command was given to General Harold Alexander, who had just returned from a command in Burma. Lieutenant General William Henry Ewart Gott was named to command the British Eighth Army. Fate then intervened. On August 7 while flying to Cairo, Gott was killed when his plane was shot down by a flight of Messerschmitt 109s. A 2005 interview with one of the German pilots revealed that their intended target had been Churchill, not Gott.[40] That evening Churchill appointed Montgomery to take Gott's place. He had been slated to command the British First Army in the forthcoming TORCH operation.

The next morning Monty got the orders for Egypt while still shaving. He bolted out of England and arrived in Cairo on August 12. The following day he addressed his new staff by telling them, "We will then work together as a team, and together we will gain the confidence of this great army and go forward to final victory in Africa."[41]

Sir Anthony Eden was secretary of state for foreign affairs. Oliver Harvey, his private secretary, recorded this reaction to the news on August 10 in London: "What frightful luck pursues us! . . . It is now decided that Montgomery is to be the General to take his place. He has the reputation of being an able and ruthless soldier and an unspeakable cad."[42]

After Monty's defeat of Rommel in North Africa, he acquired the title "Montgomery of Alamein." His swaggering image was used effectively as a propaganda tool to boost the British people's morale, just as Rommel "the Desert Fox" had been similarly used in German propaganda. Following the Afrika Korps' surrender, Montgomery's participation in the assaults on

Sicily and the Italian mainland further strengthened his reputation as the war's leading British commander.

## SHAEF Ground Command

By the time of Eisenhower's OVERLORD appointment, there were only two serious British candidates to lead the Normandy invasion ground forces: Alexander and Montgomery.

General Sir Harold Alexander had been the Allied theater commander in chief for the North African Campaign and was then leading the Italian Campaign. He was Churchill's favorite general—a commander in the tradition of great Anglo-Irish military gentlemen. Since the war's early days, Churchill's admiration had grown to the point that he considered him a paragon among soldiers. Alexander was popular with almost everyone in both Allied camps. He had experience of commanding army groups in the Far East and North African campaigns where he succeeded in getting people from different national backgrounds to work together. Montgomery had commanded only a single army. While Montgomery was often high-handed, arrogant, and difficult to handle, Alexander possessed immense natural charm and was without pretension. It was not part of his personality to become offensive to get his way.

When talking to Eisenhower in early December 1943 about the appointment, Brooke discovered Ike preferred Alexander. "He also knew he could handle Alex, but was not fond of Monty and certainly did not know how to handle him."[43]

Eisenhower had drawn up a list of top British and American commanders whom he wanted with him. Alexander was at the top of this list. Ike greatly admired his low-key manner and ability to get along with generals under his command. Other British and American commanders alike believed these personality traits were essentially for overcoming the major battlefield obstacles ahead.

Among them was American general Omar Bradley who wrote that if Alexander had commanded the overall Normandy invasion land forces, "we could probably have avoided the petulance that later was to becloud our relationships with Montgomery." Bradley contrasted Monty's "rigid self-assurance" to Alexander's "reasonableness, patience, and modesty of a great soldier."[44]

Bradley had personally worked with both Monty and Alexander in the North African and the Sicily campaigns. After Operation TORCH had successfully positioned American troops in North Africa, they joined with Montgomery's Eighth Army to form the Eighteenth Army Group commanded by Alexander. He in turn reported to Eisenhower who was appointed the supreme Allied commander in the Mediterranean. Bradley commended Alexander's forbearance and maturity as a leader in guiding the new American "field command to mature and eventually come of age."[45]

Eisenhower badly wanted Alexander appointed by the British. He went so far as to tell Churchill he would place all of the ground forces temporarily under Alexander's command until he personally took overall control of all Allied forces in Europe after D-Day. Later during the Normandy campaign Eisenhower offered this summary of Montgomery's personality: "Monty is a good man to serve with, and an impossible man to serve over."[46]

Even Brooke, shortly before the Allied invasion of Sicily, wrote in his diary, "He [Montgomery] requires a lot of educating to make him see the whole situation, and the war as a whole outside 8th Army orbit. A difficult mixture to handle, brilliant commander in action and trainer of men, but liable to commit untold errors in lack of tact, lack of appreciation of other people's outlook. It is most distressing that the Americans do not like him and it will always be a difficult matter to have him fighting in close proximity to them. He wants guiding and watching continually."[47]

With all of this backing for Alexander, why was Montgomery selected? The support of one man, his mentor Brooke, had elevated Montgomery to army command and finally to the lead British role in OVERLORD. For all his previous misgivings he still believed that Montgomery was a superior general to Alexander. Brooke had in fact earlier written (September 1943), "I am afraid that neither Eisenhower nor Alexander will ever have sufficient vision to be big soldiers."[48]

Historian Russell Weigley states, "There is every reason to believe in retrospect as Brooke believed then, that Montgomery not only surpassed Alexander as an operational commander, but was altogether Britain's ablest general of the war."[49] This judgment is today open to serious debate.

Churchill might have fought Brooke successfully over this key appointment. But at that time he lay exhausted in a sick bed in Tunisia. After the Tehran and Cairo conferences, Churchill was stricken with pneumonia and was bedridden for several weeks. At the end of December 1943, Churchill's doctor insisted on the prime minister taking another three weeks' convalescence. Churchill decided to recuperate in Marrakech, where he had stayed after the Casablanca Conference.[50]

As a result, Churchill was absent from the War Cabinet meetings in London when the key British OVERLORD appointment was made. Initially the cabinet was also in favor of Alexander. Churchill thought that Alexander approached military operations in the same swashbuckling spirit as his own. He also wanted to support Eisenhower's strong preference.[51] However, Eisenhower's selection as OVERLORD's supreme commander surprised the War Cabinet and might have unsettled British public opinion, since many thought a Brit would be the overall commander.

Both Brooke and Sir James Grigg, the secretary of state for war, and Clement Attlee, the deputy prime minister, told the cabinet that Montgomery was a better general than Alexander. Attlee, a socialist, objected to appointing a son of an earl. Also lending support was the OVERLORD planning staff request for "the early appointment to the British Army in England of some colorful personality who might impart the dynamism that we judged to be in short supply, through the Army to the people."[52] Who better than the "hero of El Alamein"?

A weakened Churchill finally acquiesced to the War Cabinet's choice of Montgomery as OVERLORD's general commander, with Alexander remaining in Italy. On December 18, in a telephone call, he told Roosevelt, "The War Cabinet desires that Montgomery should command the first expeditionary group of armies. I feel the Cabinet are [sic] right as Montgomery is a public hero and will give confidence among our people, not unshared by yours."[53]

Incredibly even at this late date, Churchill still had high hopes that Alexander also could persuade the Americans to launch a major Allied offensive through the Balkans in the direction of Vienna. Such a campaign had always been the ultimate part of Churchill's "soft underbelly" strategy for winning the European war. Politically it might have forestalled the postwar Soviet domination of Eastern Europe. Militarily it might have delayed or even canceled out a major head-to-head confrontation with the German army in northwestern Europe, eliminating the need for OVERLORD.

On December 24, Montgomery received his OVERLORD appointment and was ordered to London to assume his new command. After his successes in North Africa and the Mediterranean he had become an international star. Monty with his trademark sweater and beret had become widely known and beloved, particularly in England. Many saw him as the savior of the Allied cause. King George VI summarized a popular British viewpoint: "How nice to have Eisenhower in nominal command with Monty at his side."[54]

## TRAFFORD LEIGH-MALLORY

A World War I fighter pilot, Trafford Leigh-Mallory attended the RAF Staff College in 1925. He was appointed to command the School of Army Cooperation in 1927 and then was posted to the Army Staff College. In 1937 he was promoted to air commodore and made commander of No. 12 Group, Fighter Command.[55]

During the Battle of Britain, Leigh-Mallory quarreled over tactics with Air Vice Marshal Keith Park, the commander of 11 Group, and Sir Hugh Dowding, head of Fifteen Command. After the Battle of Britain he used political influence to have Park and Dowding removed, and he was named the commander of 11 Group. This aroused considerable animosity within the RAF ranks. The official history of the Battle of Britain did not even mention Dowding's name. This led Churchill to comment, "This is not a good story. . . . The jealousies and cliquism which have led to the committing of this offense are a discredit to the Air Ministry."[56]

In November 1942, Leigh-Mallory became head of fighter command. After COSSAC was organized by General Morgan, Leigh-Mallory became the leader of a small Anglo-American staff planning air support for OVERLORD. As a result of his role in COSSAC, in August 1943 the Combined Chiefs of Staff selected him as the SHAEF air commander in chief.[57]

Eisenhower was frustrated by this appointment. He wanted an air commander who understood the importance of air support for ground operations. Leigh-Mallory had no experience with heavy bombers or airborne transport operations, having been in fighter command his entire career. This placed him at a distinct disadvantage in his future dealings with both the heads of British and American strategic bombing forces.

Moreover, Leigh-Mallory was not a popular figure. He did not get along with other people. Leigh-Mallory was described by one British officer as a man with a "peculiar knack of rubbing everybody up the wrong way."[58] American Air Force General Elwood R. Quesada noted, "I just didn't know people at that level behaved like that. Nobody wanted to be under Leigh-Mallory, even the British."[59] Many Americans disliked him as well due to his pessimism and indecision.

Eisenhower, upon his appointment as OVERLORD's supreme commander, was convinced from his prior invasion experiences (TORCH, North Africa; HUSKY, Sicily; AVALANCHE, Salerno, Italy) that the close coordination of air and ground forces during the invasion was essential. For that reason he chose as his deputy commander a second airman, Chief Air Marshall Arthur Tedder. It was lucky he did.

## ARTHUR TEDDER

In World War I, Arthur Tedder commanded several different fighter squadrons in France. After the war he became the commandant of the No. 2 Flying Training school (1924). Tedder attended the Imperial Defence College in 1928, and then became assistant commandant at the RAF Staff College in 1929. By 1934 he was director of training at the Air Ministry and was promoted to air commodore. Tedder in 1936 became the commander of the RAF Far Eastern Forces (Burma, Hong Kong, and Borneo).[60]

In 1938 he was named the director general for research at the Air Ministry. At the outbreak of World War II, Tedder's department was moved into the new Ministry of Aircraft Production. There he clashed with its head, Lord Beaverbrook. This also resulted in frosty relations with Churchill.

As a result in June 1941, Tedder was transferred to the post of commander in chief of RAF operations in the Mediterranean and North Africa. His success in upgrading RAF operations was a key factor in the British victory of October 1942 at El Alamein. However, Tedder came to loathe Montgomery during this campaign.

After the 1943 Casablanca Conference, Tedder was appointed the overall Allied air commander throughout the Mediterranean. It was then that he began to collaborate with Eisenhower. Their joint staffs worked well together better integrating the land, sea, and air elements for the invasions of Sicily and Italy.

Upon his appointment to command OVERLORD, Eisenhower selected then air marshal Tedder as his deputy commander due to the companionable relationship that had developed between them. Tedder, like Eisenhower, saw OVERLORD as an Allied rather than a British or American operation.[61]

In a February 1943 speech to a group of Allied officers Tedder vowed never to use "us British" and "you Americans." "From now on it is 'we' together who will function as Allies, even better than either of us alone."[62] Tedder's resolve would be stretched to the limits over the coming months.

## WALTER BEDELL SMITH

The appointment of Walter Bedell Smith as SHAEF chief of staff was due to his prior efficiency as a staff officer under both Marshall and Eisenhower. After serving as an officer in World War I, Smith was appointed as a staff officer and instructor at the US Army Infantry School at Fort Benning, Georgia, where then lieutenant colonel George C. Marshall was the assistant commandant. When Marshall was appointed as the US Army chief of staff in 1939, he secured the post of secretary of the general staff for Smith. After the Combined Chiefs of Staff was created in 1942, Smith was named its secretary and promoted to the rank of brigadier general. He then moved to London as Eisenhower's chief of staff and continued in that position when Eisenhower was made supreme commander of TORCH in North Africa and other later operations in the Mediterranean.

Often typified as Eisenhower's "pit bull," Smith was to handle the press and delicate political and diplomatic tasks. Smith, whose nickname was "Beetle," became both Eisenhower's "primary shock absorber" and "hatchet man" in dealing with the difficult personalities of other commanders and as the bearer of bad tidings. Despite a reputation for toughness and irascibility, Smith managed to handle the sensitive egos of Montgomery, Patton, Bradley, and other commanders in a reliable and discreet manner. He worked hard behind the scenes to help Eisenhower foster the close Allied cooperation needed for the success of OVERLORD.[63]

## OMAR BRADLEY

Omar Bradley's origins were humble. He was born in 1893 in a three-room log house on a Missouri sodbuster farm. West Point was a key early stepping-stone. His graduating class of 1915 became known as the "Class the Stars Fell On." It produced a prodigious number of generals—59 out of 164 graduates. Bradley and fellow classmate Dwight Eisenhower both became five-star generals.[64]

He was not sent to Europe during World War I, but instead was assigned to the Mexican border patrol conducting troop basic training. After the conflict Bradley taught math at West Point (1920–24) and attended the Command and General Staff College at Fort Leavenworth, Kansas (1928–29).[65]

Another big break came in 1929 when Bradley became an instructor in tactics at the Infantry School at Fort Benning, Georgia. His abilities brought him to the attention of Colonel George C. Marshall whose influence would propel Bradley's future career. Marshall noted that Bradley "was conspicuous for his ability to handle people and his ability to do things simply and clearly."[66]

In 1934 Bradley attended the US Army War College in Washington, DC, and then worked at the War Department. When Marshall was selected as army chief of staff in 1939, he selected Bradley to be one of his two assistants.

Early in 1941 Marshall appointed him the commandant of the US Army Infantry School at Fort Benning with a promotion to brigadier general. Bradley replaced Courtney H. Hodges, who became chief of infantry. They had been classmates at the Army War College. Later Hodges would become Bradley's deputy during the Normandy campaign, commanding the US First Army. Bradley admired Hodges as a modest gentleman, two personality traits they jointly shared.[67]

After Pearl Harbor, Bradley trained the Eighty-Second Infantry Division and shaped up a slack Twenty-Eighth National Guard Division. In February 1942 Marshall sent him to Algiers to assist Eisenhower, the supreme commander of Operation TORCH, in beefing up the US divisions in North Africa. The Germans had just soundly defeated the American army at Kasserine Pass.

Except for several social occasions, Bradley had not seen his former classmate since West Point. Eisenhower took him to the map showing the US retreat in Tunisia and told him, "I want suggestive corrections."[68] At the time both British and American sources were questioning Eisenhower's fitness to command TORCH.

Bradley went on a fact-finding mission where he found that the commander of the II Corps divisions had lost the confidence of his men and morale was low. In early March Eisenhower appointed General George S. Patton to command II Corps, the American forces in Tunisia. Patton promptly asked Eisenhower to name Bradley as his deputy commander, a move Ike had told Bradley was coming. Patton already had been preparing for the future invasion of Sicily. If all went well once Bradley had commanded troops in the field, he would get the command of II Corps and Patton would go to Sicily.

Bradley became a very active deputy commander. He played an important role on the battlefield and in logistics. Patton respected Bradley's judgment and used him as a sounding board for his decisions. After Patton left in mid-April, Bradley took over II Corps for the final battles in the Tunisian campaign.

Bradley's skills as a tactician seem linked to his mathematical bent. He was a mathematician who enjoyed playing poker. Bradley developed a system to mentally determine the winning odds on each hand. He folded at less than 70 percent. He used the same strategy on the battlefield. Bradley bet heavily on a big battle he thought he could win, trusting that the math would prevail if he persevered.

For the follow-up invasion of Sicily (Operation HUSKY), Bradley again commanded II Corps with distinction in Patton's Seventh Army. Professionally Bradley had stood by Patton during both these campaigns, even though on a personal level they were very different.

Bradley has been characterized as quiet, somewhat dull, steady, industrious, careful, apparently unambitious, neither flamboyant, nor ostentatious, and never raising hackles. Perhaps Eisenhower best summed it up in the tribute he wrote in Bradley's West Point yearbook: "True merit is like a river, the deeper it is, the less noise it makes."[69]

After the Sicily operation ended, Patton sent Bradley a formal letter offering his "admiration for and appreciation of the magnificent loyalty and superior tactical ability you have evinced throughout the Campaign of Sicily."[70] It seems that loyalty may have motivated Bradley to attempt to cover up Patton's slapping of two hospitalized soldiers he thought were cowards. When he received a detailed medical report and complaint protesting this abuse, Bradley locked them in a safe and said nothing. The doctors involved then complained directly to Ike who reprimanded Patton. (More details in the next section.)

But Bradley's loyalty had its limits. During the Sicily campaign Patton and Montgomery's great egos had clashed. This rivalry culminated in their so-called race to be the first to take Messina, the key seaport and jump-off point for the invasion of the Italian mainland. Patton narrowly beat the Brit. He then staged a parade to celebrate this victory. Bradley refused to participate and later said, "His . . . parade plans into Messina sickened me and soured me on Patton."[71]

What ruptured their relationship at that time was Patton's faulty judgment. Bradley's own conduct toward his subordinates and enlisted men was often more like a benign father. Dubbed a "soldier's soldier" by war correspondent Ernie Pyle, the "GI General" by others, Bradley was often turned off by Patton's flamboyant style, as were many others.[72]

When it came time for Marshall and Eisenhower to appoint the American ground commander for the invasion of France, the final choice narrowed down to Patton or Bradley. Although Bradley was relatively junior by rank and time in service, both men favored Bradley. They saw that an army group commander required strategic farsightedness, diplomatic skill, and the ability to balance contending issues and people. Bradley was the far better choice.

On September 2, 1943, Eisenhower met with Bradley at General Alexander's headquarters outside Messina and told him he had been selected to lead an army in the invasion of France."[73]

## GEORGE S. PATTON

> With sirens shrieking Patton's arrival, a procession of armored scout cars and half-tracks wheeled into the dingy square opposite the schoolhouse headquarters of II Corps. . . . In the lead car Patton stared liked a charioteer. He was scowling into the wind and his jaw strained against the web strap of a two-starred steel helmet.[74]

Some officers called him "picturesque," and others said, "Patton sure scares the shit out of me."[75] After the war when his enemy, German field marshal Gerd von Rundstedt, was asked to name the most impressive American commander, he declared, "Patton was your best." Others have called him "America's Warrior" because he had a "genius for war."[76] The personification of flamboyance, Major General George S. Patton Jr. was acclaimed for his mad-dashing military exploits, but also censured for his unbelievable lapses in judgment. Yet his brilliance in pursuit made him irreplaceable as America's top offensive general of World War II.

## Background

Born in San Gabriel in 1885, near Pasadena, California, on the 1,800-acre Wilson-Patton ranch, Patton had a privileged childhood in a family with a rich military tradition. He attended Virginia Military Academy before entering West Point. Patton graduated in 1909 and saw his first combat in the Pancho Villa Mexican Expedition in 1916 as a member of General John J. Pershing's staff. During World War I he was assigned to the new US Tank Corps.[77]

In August 1918 Patton took command of the American First Tank Brigade. During the Meuse-Argonne Offensive at Cambrai, France, together with British forces, he led his men to victory on September 26, during the world's first major tank battle. The general commanding the Tank Corps told Patton, "[Y]ou had a very great, far-reaching and disastrous effect on the enemy."[78] He was promoted to colonel and awarded the Distinguished Service Cross.

After the war ended Patton was assigned to ten different staff postings in Washington, DC, Hawaii, and elsewhere. He attended the Command and General Staff College (1923–1924) and later the Army War College (1932).[79]

During the interval between the wars, Patton had kept up with the latest thinking on armored warfare. Much of this came from abroad. From Germany came General Heinz Guderian's *Achtung Panzer!* and General Erwin Rommel's *Infantry in War*. Liddell Hart and J. F. C. Fuller were the British apostles of mobile warfare, and Colonel Charles de Gaulle wrote about the modernization of the French Army.

Before and after the German conquest of Poland, Patton read and reread the German officers' book translations and US Army G-2 intelligence analysis from reports by observers. This information confirmed many of the tactics that Patton earlier had considered possible for armored forces.[80]

A major turning point in his army career occurred in December 1938 with his promotion to colonel commanding the Third Cavalry at Fort Meyer, Virginia. General Marshall had been appointed army chief of staff on September 1, 1939. His official residence was at Fort Meyer.

Patton hosted Marshall at his personal quarters while Marshall's own lodging was being remodeled. He did not have to make much of an effort to convince Marshall about the future importance of armored warfare, or his role in it. Marshall already considered Colonel Patton as an outstanding combat leader, and he knew his eccentricities. He had earlier written to another officer in the War Plans Division, "Patton is by far the best tank man in the Army. I know this from the First World War. I watched him closely when he commanded the first tanks we ever had. I realize that he is a difficult man but I know how to handle him."[81]

Patton created a larger-than-life persona. He projected masculinity and toughness with his scowling face. He had a deep well of energy and an unquenchable desire to win. Patton was unorthodox in both his military methods and beliefs—including reincarnation. Patton's unpredictable highs and lows, and displays of violent temper, were punctuated with trademark streams of profanity. He sported a custom-made uniform, ivory-handled pistols, and he affected other conspicuous displays of rank and power. Fellow officers were often uncomfortable with Patton's posturing and personality. He loved publicity, and was often his own worst enemy due to his propensity to act precipitously and to make ill-judged public statements.

But Marshall was willing to overlook these personal limitations because he saw in Patton a potential military genius as a commander who could lead a relentless offensive. While at Fort Benning, Marshall had begun making a list of junior officers' strengths and weaknesses. The legend arose that this evolved into Marshall's "little black book" as a way to evaluate future potential army leaders. Many of these men passed through Marshall's staff in Washington. They became "Marshall's men" whom he mentored and promoted to senior rank—Eisenhower, Bradley, and Patton among many others were placed at the top of his list.[82]

Marshall appreciated Patton's thorough mastery of the technology, tactics, and doctrine of armored warfare as it evolved before and during World War II. His strength was not just in theoretical matters. Patton led from the front often advancing on foot, even leaping from tank to tank. He openly defied superiors and braved mortar/machine-gun fire to provide the impetus for keeping his armored offensive moving forward. This was the military genius Marshall had bet on and hoped to channel and control for achieving battlefield victory.

## World War II Commands

Almost immediately after the attack on Pearl Harbor, Patton was given the command of I Armored Corps. In February 1942, he established the Desert Training Center on ten thousand acres of the Mojave Desert, fifty miles east of Palm Springs, California. During the course of the war over one million soldiers received armor and infantry training at Camp Young and the other training facilities scattered across the desert.[83]

After Eisenhower's appointment to lead Operation TORCH, he summoned Patton to Washington (July 30) to command the Western Task Force that would invade Morocco. The initial landings of thirty-five thousand men took place on November 8, 1942. Casablanca fell three days later, and Patton negotiated an armistice with the Vichy French forces.[84]

Then Patton finally got the fighting command he had been waiting for. On March 5, 1942, he took over a disorganized II Corps, with Bradley as his deputy. By April 15 after pushing the Germans back, Patton was able to hand over the Tunisian command campaign to Bradley while he moved on to overseeing the planning for Operation HUSKY, the invasion of Sicily.[85]

Patton's Seventh Army invaded southern Sicily on July 10, while Montgomery's Eighth Army attacked in the west. British general Alexander was the overall ground commander. Initially Patton's assignment was to protect Montgomery's left flank. But after the British got bogged down in their advance on Messina, Patton got approval to take Palermo on Sicily's northern coast. He then raced to Messina to beat Montgomery by only a few hours on August 16.[86]

The two military prima donnas—Patton and Montgomery—had first met in February during the Tunisian Campaign. Being two extremely ego-driven personalities, they developed an intense loathing of the other. After the campaign Montgomery heard that Patton was ridiculing his battlefield performance. Monty reportedly replied that he had three messages for Patton: "Get out of my way, train your men, and leave me your petrol."[87] If he heard it, Patton must have been doubly gleeful in beating Monty to Messina. Though rivals, they did share some common perspectives. Patton once complained to Montgomery about an order from Alexander's headquarters. "George," an amazed Monty told him, "let me give you some advice. If you get an order from Army Group that you don't like, just ignore it. That's what I do."[88]

Patton's most serious professional setbacks did not occur on the battlefield, but in a hospital. The infamous slapping incidents of two soldiers suffering from "battle fatigue" in August 1943 came very close to ending his military career. Only Eisenhower's direct intervention with Marshall saved his friend from oblivion. Patton was ordered to personally apologize to both men, to the doctors, and to the Seventh Army. Patton thought both men were cowards and even had threatened to shoot them. Afterward he told a friend that if he had to do it over again, he would not have changed a single thing![89]

Patton's conduct in Sicily undermined his chances for the American ground command of OVERLORD. An exasperated Eisenhower wrote, "Georgie is one of the best generals I have, but he's just like a time bomb. You can never be sure when he's going to go off. All you can be sure of is that it will probably be at the wrong place at the wrong time."[90] Patton did not command another army in combat for the next twelve months.

After Sicily Marshall wanted Eisenhower's recommendations to plan and head the invasion of France. At the beginning of the Sicily operation, Patton had been his clear choice. Ike thought that "Patton's methods were deplorable but his result was excellent."[91] He saw in Patton an "enfant terrible" who needed to be kept on a tight leash. Once Patton was ruled out, Ike turned to Mark Clark and Omar Bradley. Clark had experience at planning amphibious operations, and was the US ground commander in Italy. Clark might have been a clearer choice over Bradley, but he too had a reputation for being difficult and having a large, overriding ego.

Bradley's performance in Sicily had been excellent. He now had corps command experience in two major campaigns and showed a superior ability in tactics and logistical operations. In the final analysis Bradley's personality was his greatest asset. Marshall and Eisenhower thought his adeptness at handling people and diplomatic ability was more important for this command than aggressiveness and bravado.

However, Ike came to realize that he still needed Patton's tactical genius and drive on the command team to lead the Normandy bridgehead breakout and the charge across France to victory. Eisenhower wanted Bradley as army group commander and Bradley to work with Patton. They would make an unbeatable team. With Patton as the spark plug and Bradley as the regulator, he could get more out of Patton than anybody else.

But Bradley objected to this proposal. He told Eisenhower that Patton would be uncomfortable as his subordinate, a reverse of their roles in two prior campaigns. Privately Bradley also thought Patton was too emotional and impulsive and found his staff work often inadequate.[92] Even so Bradley did consider Patton a highly effective commander. His unorthodox methods did work—at least for Patton.

When Eisenhower offered Patton command of the Third Army as part of Bradley's US Army Group, Patton swallowed his pride and accepted. He was disappointed and hurt. However, the opportunity to participate in this crucial campaign provided him with the chance for fame that he so persistently sought. The reversal of authority would be difficult for both of them, but they would make it work.[93]

## BERTRAM RAMSAY

Of all the major Allied commanders of OVERLORD Admiral Sir Bertram Ramsay is among the least well-known. Perhaps one of the reasons why he has attracted so little controversy or criticism, in contrast to the other talented but often abrasive brotherhood of D-Day commanders, is that he was killed in January 1945 when his plane crashed after takeoff near Paris, en route to meet Montgomery in Brussels.

As Allan Packwood, director of the Churchill Archives Centre, Cambridge, which holds his papers, noted, "Sadly, because of Admiral Ramsay's untimely death, his undoubtable contributions to the Second World War has been somewhat overshadowed by those who lived and were able to write their memories and receive their honors."[94]

Considering all the factors that contributed to the successful Normandy amphibious invasion, the critical one was command and control. Without superb orchestration, this massive, complex invasion would have failed. Ramsay prepared a logistical plan in the most staggering detail. His amphibious invasion plan provided every ship captain and every divisional commander with his own briefing book. Nothing was left out. The man who retrieved a defeated army from Dunkirk masterminded a triumphant Allied return to Europe on D-Day.[95]

## Background

Ramsay was born in 1883 at Hampton Court near London, where his father, then major William Alexander Ramsay, was posted in command of the Fourth Hussars. He was the third son of a Scots family with a long tradition of military service who later was appointed commander of this regiment with the rank of brigadier general. As military pay was hardly munificent, William encouraged his son to take the Admiralty entry examination, which paid the sum of one hundred pounds (the equivalent of ten thousand pounds in today's currency) to the family of a cadet who sat for and passed this test. Fifteen-year-old Bertram Ramsay passed with flying colors.

During World War I he served aboard the HMS *Dreadnought* in the Dover Patrol and the Grand Fleet. By 1917 he was in command of the destroyer HMS *Broke*. He took part in the Second Ostend Raid in 1918.

Following the war, he served as a staff officer for every senior commander. Ramsay had specialized in signals that sharpened his capacity for lateral thinking. He was a flag lieutenant to the admirals commanding both the Atlantic and Mediterranean fleets. Ramsay accompanied Lord Sir John Jellicoe, admiral of the fleet, as his flag commander during an around-the-world cruise. From 1927 to 1929 Ramsay was on the staff of the Royal Naval War College. In 1929 he served as chief of staff to the commander in chief of the China Squadron, and in 1931 he was appointed to the staff of the Imperial Defence College. His opposite numbers in the army and air force were Alan Brooke, Arthur Tedder, and Trafford Leigh-Mallory, all of whom were to become his fellow OVERLORD commanders.

Ramsay's career thus far had been propelled by a strong work ethic and high personal standards. He faulted himself in trying to apply these perfectionistic traits to the other officers around him. Ramsay wrote in his diary, "My faults are that I can't sit still and see things done in an antiquated and un-progressive way."[96]

Ramsay by temperament expected the highest standards from his officers and crew. Though sometimes one officer recalled that "he carried the aura of vinegar." But overall he was considered fair and polite. In a crisis Ramsay exuded confidence and calm. He always knew the name of his staff and more than amply recognized their hard work. Both senior and junior officers grew to respect and trust him. A junior officer commented, "He was a good man and a very good boss. . . . What was superb was the lead he gave to his staff, and his tolerance and kindness. I never met anyone like him."[97]

Ramsay exemplified a younger generation of highly professional British naval officers. Naval historian Correlli Barnett believed that he "combined austere personal integrity, high professionalism, and a personal warmth which won the enthusiastic loyalty of his subordinates."[98]

In 1935 then rear admiral Ramsay was made chief of staff under Home Fleet admiral Sir Roger Backhouse. Backhouse was one of the old school, do-it-all-yourself admirals who disdained the modern staff system and insisted on exercising a tight personal command down to the minutia of dealing with all incoming fleet signals and business. As he was not being allowed to do his job, Ramsay rebelled against this giant step backward and asked to be relieved of his position after only four months on the job. Their parting was amicable with Backhouse feeling no ill will toward him. However, this cast a shadow on Ramsay's career moving him to the retired list for the next four years.[99]

When Backhouse unexpectedly became first sea lord during the 1938 Munich crisis, he appointed Ramsay vice admiral in charge at Dover, even though he was still on the retired list. Some have speculated that Backhouse was motivated by remorse over his previous role in short-circuiting Ramsay's highly professional career record.[100]

The Dover Command was the most ancient in all the Royal Navy. Ramsay's headquarters were located in galleries and chambers deep down in the chalk behind the famous white cliffs of Dover. The principal gallery had a window in the cliff face with a vista of the harbor and English

Channel. A large chamber called the Dynamo Room served as the headquarters' nerve center.

## World War II Commands

Germany's successful attack in May 1940 on France, Belgium, the Netherlands, and Luxemburg trapped the British Expeditionary Force (BEF) and their French allies at the port Dunkirk. On May 26, Ramsay was ordered by the Admiralty to implement an emergency evacuation of these troops (Operation DYNAMO). Ramsay mobilized 933 small craft and naval vessels into a massive amphibious operation that afterward would be called the "miracle of Dunkirk."

Ramsay had initially estimated that only forty-five thousand of the BEF could be evacuated. However, when the destroyer *Shikari*, the last ship evacuating soldiers, sailed from Dunkirk shortly before 4:00 a.m. on June 4, an astounding 338,226 troops had been rescued. Ramsay and his staff's organizational feat of turning this motley fleet into a coherent operation on such short notice was truly an outstanding achievement. Dunkirk was a masterpiece of damage control and interservice cooperation. Ramsay had proven himself to be the right man in the right place at the right time. His services were recognized when he was knighted on June 7.[101]

In April 1942 Ramsay was appointed naval commander in chief for the invasion of northwestern Europe (Operation ROUNDUP). As we have seen that operation was postponed in favor of Operation TORCH, the invasion of North Africa, for which Ramsay was the chief amphibious naval planner. Ramsay afterward led the British Task Force (July 1943) for the invasion of Sicily (Operation HUSKY).

As the expert who had masterminded all of these amphibious operations, Ramsay was the obvious choice in October 1943 for appointment as the commander of the Allied Naval Expeditionary Force for Operation OVERLORD. As Allen Packwood has commented, "He eschewed normal career advancement to specialize in logistics but these are exactly the skills needed when we get to the Second World War. . . . So by the time we get to June 1944, he is the go-to man for complex naval operations; although nothing he had done was anything as complex as D-Day itself."[102]

## THE MELTING POT OF COMMAND

Both political necessity and the personal assessments and biases of Roosevelt, Churchill, Marshall, and Brooke largely determined the makeup of the OVERLORD command structure. This chapter has explored the backgrounds and the personality traits of the major OVERLORD commanders and the relationships and rivalries that preceded their appointments to this campaign. Previously we have also shown that the British and Americans had very different perspectives on when the invasion of northwestern Europe should be launched and who should be the supreme commander. Subsequent chapters will show that all this lack of a shared vision only grew throughout the Normandy campaign and served to seriously lengthen the war in Europe.

CHAPTER 4

# THE OVERLORD GAMBLE

"The greatest amphibious operation of all time."
—Admiral Sir Bertram Ramsay

## MUDDLED COMMAND

When Eisenhower arrived in London in mid-January 1944 his position as "supreme commander" remained nebulous at best. Though the British had agreed to an American having the top command position, they could take comfort in knowing that they had operational control of all Allied air, land, and sea forces. (See chart 1.)

This had been the modus operandi that evolved in the Mediterranean theater when British forces predominated. During both Operation TORCH and Operation HUSKY Eisenhower was essentially a figurehead political commander.

But Operation OVERLORD was a world apart. Though his boss Marshall told Eisenhower he must get along with his allies, he was determined this time to retain control. He was the man who had to make OVERLORD work. If the cross-channel invasion failed, it would rest squarely on his shoulders.

This real possibility of a German victory created an atmosphere of intense Allied cooperation. It did not however prevent individuals grasping for power.

In the proposed OVERLORD command, General Montgomery was to serve in two positions: commander of all Allied land forces and commander of the British Twenty-First Army Group. The British provided the majority of naval shipping and enjoyed approximate parity in ground forces until early July.

In July 1944 additional US divisions would begin tipping the balance of forces. At that time Eisenhower was to assume the position of Allied general forces commander, with General Bradley taking command of the new Twelfth US Army Group made up of the First and Third armies. Montgomery was to retain the command of the British Twenty-First Army Group. However, that command arrangement did not suit Montgomery.

On January 20, the day before the first full-blown OVERLORD conference, Montgomery made a demand for his own separate headquarters as ground commander in chief, distinct from his Twenty-First Army Group staff. Walter Bedell Smith as SHAEF chief of staff torpedoed Monty's request. He adamantly took the stand that no additional command structure could exist between Eisenhower and his commanders. Instead he forcefully made the case for Eisenhower to assume direct control of the two army groups when they began forming for Normandy.

As we will see, that handoff was delayed from July to September 1944 largely for political reasons. Even then, Eisenhower did not insist on implementing his own Allied ground force operational plans until March 1945.[1]

This confusion over final authority continued to dominate critical decisions during the OVERLORD operation. In hindsight Smith bitterly concluded, "We would have saved a lot of trouble if we had started off with Montgomery and Bradley as equals."[2]

## CHANGING THE PLAN

Eisenhower read the preliminary OVERLORD plan in Algiers (October 1943). He questioned the strength of the initial assault as "too weak in number and frontage."[3] He wanted to increase the assault force from three to five divisions with two more in reserve. This would broaden the invasion front and enlarge the size of the initial bridgehead.

At a meeting in Algiers on December 27, 1943, Eisenhower, Montgomery, and Smith met to review the OVERLORD plans. They all agreed with Eisenhower's initial analysis on the need to strengthen the invasion forces. On December 31, Montgomery visited Churchill at Marrakech. Monty wrote in his diary, "He then said he was very anxious to have my first impressions of OVERLORD, which I had never seen." This is where Montgomery had his first real glimpse of the existing plans. Later in his memoirs Montgomery incredibly omits his earlier meeting with Eisenhower and claims all the credit for himself on the overhaul of the OVERLORD operational plans.[4]

At the Algiers meeting, Eisenhower asked Montgomery to act as the temporary Allied ground forces commander during the first stage of the invasion. This seemed to confirm Montgomery's perception that Eisenhower lacked confidence as a field commander. As planning rolled forward during the next seventeen weeks, Montgomery made substantial contributions to OVERLORD. This led him to leap to the assumption that he alone commanded OVERLORD.[5]

During this planning phase Montgomery and all the other commanders had a great advantage stemming from the three very large-scale amphibious invasions launched between July 1943 and January 1944 (Operations HUSKY-Sicily, AVALANCHE-Salerno, and SHINGLE-Anzio). They better prepared the Allies for the biggest assault of all time—Normandy. None of those landings had been perfect, but they provided the Allies with an excellent rehearsal for OVERLORD.[6]

COSSAC bequeathed to SHAEF two important legacies: a clearly outlined plan and a functioning planning staff. In many ways the OVERLORD operation was a complex logistical plan. Logistical experts teamed with the operational planners because logistical constraints, both in manpower and supplies, dominated operational planning calculations. Even with this emphasis, logistics became the Achilles' heel of the OVERLORD campaign.[7]

## NEPTUNE

The first phase of OVERLORD that included the amphibious assault and the establishment of a secure bridgehead was code-named Operation NEPTUNE. Although still on the retired list, in October 1943 Admiral Sir Bertram Ramsay, the hero of the Dunkirk evacuation, entered Norfolk House, headquarters of COSSAC, to take up the post of Allied Naval Commander (Normandy) Expeditionary Force (ANCXF).

Ramsay had served as second-in-command to Admiral Sir Andrew Cunningham in TORCH, and then was British supreme naval commander for HUSKY. Thus, he had established an unrivalled track record for organizing large-scale joint and combined amphibious landings. No one got on better with the Yanks in general and Eisenhower in particular than Ramsay. Within the OVERLORD command he faced the greatest challenge of his career that would test to the utmost his resourcefulness and organizational abilities.

Fig. 4.1. General Dwight D. Eisenhower and Admiral Sir Bertram Ramsay at Southwick House. (© Imperial War Museums [H 39152])

Ramsay had to transport the world's largest invasion fleet across the English Channel and successfully land it on D-Day. He then had to keep it well supplied by sea, as it advanced inland. NEPTUNE had no precedent in terms of scale, risk, and strategic importance. This operation was the Allies' first and possibly only chance of reestablishing a western front, defeating the German army, and advancing into the Third Reich. The outcome of the war in Europe was largely staked on NEPTUNE.[8]

The success of the Normandy gamble depended on Ramsay's ability to evaluate and synthesize the information gathered by the General Staff Intelligence section of British General Headquarters. In 1943 it was renamed the Theatre Intelligence Section with the responsibility of providing Ramsay with the information he needed for planning a cross-channel invasion.[9]

On March 2 Ramsay issued the naval plan for NEPTUNE.

> The object of Operation NEPTUNE is to carry out an operation from the United Kingdom to secure a lodgement on the Continent from which further operations can be developed. This lodgement area must contain sufficient port facilities to maintain a force of 26 to 30 divisions and enable this force to be augmented by follow-up formations at the rate of three to five divisions in a month.[10]

Ramsay emphatically warned that adequate logistical planning was the vital lynchpin for ensuring the Normandy campaign's ultimate success.

> It is important that the military plan for the subsequent land campaign should be worked out first. . . . There is a danger that . . . an assault plan . . . will not give effect to the military requirements for the land battle. . . . In general it is the responsibility of the Navy to land the Army as they require, but as the plan develops Naval considerations will arise which must be discussed and agreed upon.[11]

Ramsay at this time was joined by other SHAEF logistical planning experts in issuing the same warning to all the Allied commanders. They emphasized that once the Allies had broken out of the Normandy bridgehead, no major advance into Germany was logistically possible with the opening of the Port of Antwerp to Allied shipping. Unfortunately as the OVERLORD operation progressed, Ramsay's repeated warnings regarding this key port fell on deaf ears. Ramsay's logistical task was to build what he metaphorically termed a two-way bridge to France. This "bridge" must carry inbound and outbound traffic at a steady speed, each "vehicle" (ship) carrying a similar load made a delivery every fourth day. The aim was to make traffic control as simple as possible.[12]

Between March and June 1944, Ramsay and his staff prepared detailed operational orders to carry out the final OVERLORD plan. This formidable package offered encyclopedic coverage for all of the ships in the D-Day and subsequent operations.

The naval element of NEPTUNE was divided into four phases:

1. In the "prestowed phase" from D-Day to D+8, mechanized transport ships, small coastal vessels, barges, and landing craft were to move preloaded cargo and troops to the beaches as quickly as possible.

2. During the "buildup phase" from D+9 to D+21 the same mix of vessels would pick up additional loads.
3. The "maintenance movement period" from D+22 to D+41 would employ commodity-loaded deep draft vessels to augment the buildup.
4. A final "change-over period" from D+42 onward would use primarily deep draft vessels directly from the United States whenever possible.[13]

Some officers thought this NEPTUNE preplanning was too detailed. Ramsay understood that in the US Navy the command orders were largely limited to the definition of tasks and issuance of directives. He believed, however, that a complex operation of this magnitude, using combined US and British ships attacking on a narrow front, required much more detailed ship choreography.

On June 6, 1944, Ramsay's detailed operational orders were executed as planned. "They stand to this day," says naval historian Correlli Barnett, "as a never surpassed masterpiece of planning and staff work."[14]

On April 26, 1944, Ramsay moved with his staff to a new headquarters at Southwick House. Placed on a ridge seven miles from Portsmouth, Eisenhower's formal command post and Montgomery's tactical headquarters already had been erected amid a maze of truck caravans and huts scattered throughout Southwick Park. Henceforth Southwick became OVERLORD's nerve center. On that same day Ramsay was restored to the Active List of the Royal Navy.[15]

One of Ramsay's first actions was the addition of Vice Admiral Sir Philip Vian as his deputy commander. However, the expansion of the cross-channel operation from three divisions to five, which meant the need for five landing beaches, necessitated the creation of two naval task forces to cover them. Vian was appointed commander of the Eastern (British) Task Force rather than second-in-command of the whole invasion fleet.

Vian had a reputation as a "fighting admiral." This new command seemed ideal. But the new diversity of shipping made him uneasy, as he was faced with administering a task force of cruisers, destroyers, minesweepers, and a strange conglomeration of hundreds of specialty landing craft and landing ships (i.e., larger ships that could land troops, supplies, and equipment right on the beach) including the following:[16]

LCVPs—Landing Craft Vehicle and Personnel (Higgins boats)
LCMs—Landing Craft Mediums
LSTs—Landing Ship Tanks
LSIs—Landing Ship Infantry
LCUs—Landing Craft Utility
LCTs—Landing Craft Tanks
LCI (L)—Landing Craft Infantry Large

Ramsay had to help Vian overcome a sense of "being a little helpless,"[17] in organizing this disjoined assemblage of shipping.

Ramsay appointed Rear Admiral Alan G. Kirk to command the Western (American) Task Force. He had known Kirk as the American naval attaché to Britain. Unfortunately Kirk disliked the British and particularly Ramsay. Kirk, a product of US Navy culture, bristled at the command and control structure of the Royal Navy. Kirk constantly overstepped his bounds by challenging all the minute planning that came down from Norfolk House. But his superior, Admiral Harold R. Stark, commander of US Naval Forces Europe, gave Ramsay the full support he needed. Stark played a key role in the naval buildup for NEPTUNE. He was exactly the team player the Normandy invasion needed.[18]

Despite these varying tensions with his two task force commanders, Ramsay maintained a fully integrated naval command following his overall NEPTUNE plan. Each of his admirals was in charge of all the ships within their task force areas.

The case for an extensive naval bombardment in Normandy had been strengthened by previous Allied amphibious invasion experiences in the Mediterranean and the Pacific. Admiral Cunningham, now the British first sea lord, recognized that three phases of bombardment were necessary: First, German coastal defenses and mobile batteries had to be silenced. Second, immediately before the actual landings, saturation bombing was required until it became too dangerous for Allied troops. Third, the armies needed fire support to help expand the beachhead using air spotting or land-based fire control units in communication with the battleships and cruisers.[19]

To accomplish these bombardment assignments, Ramsay wanted to augment his naval forces by one battleship, seven cruisers, and fourteen destroyers. This would enlarge the final NEPTUNE fleet to six battleships, twenty-five cruisers, and fifty-six destroyers. Ramsay saw this as "a huge force but not great in respect for the issues at stake."[20]

Ramsay also knew that the Royal Navy could not provide this expanded naval force due to its many other war theater commitments. When Ramsay turned to Admiral Ernest J. King, the chief of staff of the US Navy, he was reluctant to part with the requested ships. King commented, "There are so many craft involved now that one could almost walk dry-shod from one side of the channel to the other."[21] Some analysts attribute this to King's anti-British prejudices, while others believe that he felt that the Pacific theater took precedence over the needs of the war in Europe. Finally a month after the Joint Chiefs of Staff in Washington were notified, King responded by handing over three old battleships, three cruisers, and thirty-one destroyers, a more powerful flotilla than Ramsay had requested. This failed to change King's Anglophobic attitudes.[22]

Admiral Cunningham also pointed out to Ramsay that German mining of the shallower waters off the Normandy coast posed a great danger to capital ships during NEPTUNE. Ramsay formulated a minesweeping plan with Vian and Kirk for overcoming the German minefields—especially a main barrier within seven to ten miles off the Normandy coast. Their plans amounted to the largest single minesweeping operation of World War II.[23]

One safe channel, two miles wide, was swept simultaneously through the main German minefield for each of the five assault forces. This was to be accomplished by one fleet minesweeping flotilla of 255 vessels. Kirk who had previously criticized Ramsay's overly detailed plans now acknowledged "that minesweeping was the keystone of the arch of this operation. . . . The performance of the minesweepers can only be described as magnificent."[24]

The NEPTUNE phase of the OVERLORD operation was a vast and intricate undertaking. Personality differences caused relatively little friction. Ramsay's ability to forge a single NEPTUNE team structure was facilitated by its daunting scope and extreme urgency. This rarified atmosphere served to impose the discipline and unity needed for producing a final magnificent NEPTUNE operational plan.[25]

## JANUARY 21—FIRST SUPREME COMMANDER CONFERENCE

The initial meeting of Eisenhower and his staff with the OVERLORD commanders at Norfolk House on January 21, 1944, had great historical significance. First, it confirmed Eisenhower's important decision as supreme commander to expand the beachhead from three to five landing zones. It was agreed that a three-division assault lacked effective sustainability as the Germans could more easily contain such a narrow beachhead, and readily concentrate a large counterattack to smash it.[26] This became one of the key decisions for winning the war in Europe. Recalling the immediate past record of Allied collaboration, it proved little short of a miracle that this cornerstone decision gained approval almost by acclamation.

Secondly, the conference produced Montgomery's first outline as overall ground commander of the strategy for D-Day and the subsequent Normandy campaign. Montgomery's conception of D-Day was to use overwhelming and focused air and naval bombardments to get the infantry ashore and penetrate the German Atlantic Wall. This would enable British and later American armored units to land and quickly fan out into an initial Caen-Bayeux bridgehead. This lodgment would be about eighty miles long and twenty miles deep from the neighborhood of Caen to the base of the Cherbourg peninsula. (See Map 2.) The Bayeux River would be the separation point with the American army on its right and the British army on its left.

Caen was to be taken by the British on the first day. It was Monty's number one priority. This would aid in consolidating the beaches and set the stage for the armored units advance to the east. Caen was an excellent hub with good roads in all directions, including Bayeux to the west, another D-Day objective. Taking Caen was also the key to a war of tank maneuver, allowing the Allies to rapidly exit the beaches and move beyond the confining bocage (hedgerows) that checker-boarded the Normandy area.

The American army's primary objectives were to take Bayeux and ultimately Cherbourg; then moving south and west out of the Normandy region, General George S. Patton's Third Army would march into Brittany and seize Brest and other vital ports. With their supply lines secured, the combined Anglo-American armies would advance from Caen to the northeast toward Paris and the Seine River. After defeating the Germans on the Seine, the Allies would pour through northern France until they reached the German border in the regions around Belgium and Luxemburg. (See Map 1A.) The last objective was to be reached ninety days after D-Day.

Throughout that day's conference Montgomery emphasized the necessity for a rapid advance to seize Caen and other key British objectives. Monty planned to immediately deploy a British armored thrust from the beachhead to take the city and related objectives, thereby unbalancing the German counterattacks. He stressed that a rapid victory hinged on following a surprise amphibious assault with a lightning armored advance.[27]

Montgomery declared,

> In the initial stages, we should concentrate on gaining control quickly of the main centres of road communications. We should then push our armoured formations between and beyond these centres and deploy them on suitable grounds. In this way it would be difficult for the enemy to bring up his reserves and get them past these armoured formations.[28]

A major change to the OVERLORD plan that Montgomery initiated was the deployment of several airborne divisions on both flanks of the five invasion beaches. Their mission was to weaken German counterattacks during the initial Allied beach-assault phase. Two British divisions were also to seize the bridges over the Orne River and Dives River that led into Caen, enabling armored units to link up and seize Caen on D-Day. But Eisenhower, Bradley, and Montgomery also wanted to use these airborne divisions to cut the neck of the Cotentin Peninsula and protect the landings at the western-most American beaches.[29]

Two days later, on January 23, Eisenhower formally accepted Montgomery's initial operational proposals. From that day on, the herculean efforts began to convert these ideas into a successful written operational plan. Of all the challenges OVERLORD now faced, the vital necessity for a dramatic increase in landing craft topped Eisenhower's to-do list.

## LANDING CRAFT SHUFFLE

The day after this initial OVERLORD commanders' conference, Ramsay presented Admiral Cunningham with the new shipping requirements for an expansion to five invasion beaches. While Ramsay endorsed the proposal, he pointed out that the Allies did not have enough landing craft within the European theater to cover all their diverse offensive operations.

Much of this shortage problem stemmed from the decision that had been approved at the Quebec Conference to launch a diversionary landing in southern France (ANVIL) simultaneously with OVERLORD. Once SHAEF had agreed to a five-division initial Normandy assault, pressure began to build to cancel ANVIL and thus resolve the landing craft problem.

Eisenhower was reluctant to do so because he thought that forcing the Germans to fight on two fronts would optimize OVERLORD's chance of success. American naval production schedules had been disrupted in April 1942 to give top priority to landing and beaching craft for an earlier cross-channel invasion that was then canceled. The schedule was further upset in January 1943 when building ships for anti-submarine warfare was given top priority.[30]

Eisenhower's solution was to request 271 more landing craft and forty-seven additional LSTs from the Combined Chiefs of Staff in Washington. This move upset Ramsay who thought "the five division assault must stand and ANVIL must be cancelled in order to make it possible to mount it. . . . Ike must definitely arrive at a final decision . . . without any more waffling."[31] Ramsay believed that operational planning had to adjust to the actual logistical reality.

As late as February 6, Eisenhower still advocated launching both military operations simultaneously. For months pro versus con ANVIL constituencies continued this landing craft and LST dispute. By March Eisenhower was vacillating. Finally on March 20 Eisenhower broke the impasse when he announced that ANVIL would not be launched concurrently with OVERLORD. The lack of sufficient sealift also caused the postponement of the Normandy invasion until June 5, and ANVIL was moved back to late summer.

American shipyards began a crash LST construction program. They turned out fifty vessels in April and eighty-two in May. The United States Pacific Fleet also reluctantly gave up 2,483 additional landing craft for OVERLORD. These efforts combined with the dual postponements made a more robust OVERLORD possible.[32]

The Americans at last accepted the fact that in some instances logistics do trump strategy. Ramsay expressed his sincere relief: "[I] am feeling more comfortable about the state of things. Heard (March 25) that ANVIL is at last 'off'. Thank goodness. It only shows how cumbersome is the machine which wields the power.... 6 weeks ... it has taken till now to get the decision."[33] This delay in resolving important issues continuously plagued the entire Normandy campaign.

## THE "PORTABLE PORT"

As Montgomery outlined his operational plans on January 21, he also emphasized the crucial importance of seizing ports. Logistics were the key to the invasion's success. Once ashore the attacker had to be able to reinforce his bridgehead faster than the defender could bring up reinforcements to drive him back into the sea.

The important lesson of the Dieppe disaster was that the Allies were not going to rapidly capture a major port. Furthermore, they could not prevent the Germans from destroying a port's shipping facilities.[34] "Well, if we can't capture a port, we will have to take one with us," said Captain Hughes Hallett on Mountbatten's COC staff as he returned from the Dieppe raid.[35]

Mountbatten first suggested this solution for OVERLORD at the Rattle Conference (June–July 1943). In fact, it was not a novel idea. In early 1917, the British War Office had drawn up plans for building floating docks and breakwaters. During the late 1930s, the Royal Navy had towed such an enormous floating dock complex over ten thousand miles to strengthen Britain's Far Eastern fortress at Singapore.

In August 1943, General Morgan in his role as commander of the preliminary COSSAC planning convinced the Combined Chiefs of Staff that two artificial harbors, which were code-named Mulberries, were indispensable to OVERLORD. Plans moved forward for the Royal Navy to construct one full-scale harbor in the British invasion sector at Arromanches. A second Mulberry was to be installed for the American sector at St. Laurent. Once in place the two harbors would eventually develop the capacity to receive twelve thousand tons of supplies per day, equal to the seaport of Dover.

These plans were already underway when Ramsay assumed command of NEPTUNE. At first skeptical about the feasibility of the Mulberries, he became much impressed by what he saw after their installation off the Normandy beaches by mid-June.

In the end, the biggest headache with the Mulberries was coping with their size. These harbors were so enormous that all of the tugboats in Britain were too few to move them from Scotland's shipyards to Normandy. Additional tugs had to be brought across the Atlantic from the US Eastern Seaboard to complete the pool of over two hundred tugs needed for towing the Mulberries to the Normandy coast.[36]

Providing the fuel supply required by a modern mechanized army was another major logistics problem. How was fuel to be delivered without a large port oil terminal? In the spring of 1942, Commander Thomas Hussey, RN, part of Mountbatten's Combined Operations Command, suggested a fuel pipeline running across the bed of the English Channel.

In December 1942 a trial line was laid across the Bristol Channel. Motor fuel was successfully pumped through it for two and a half months. In June 1943 Geoffrey Lloyd, the minister of fuel, ordered the preparation of two alternative versions now named "Pluto" (Pipe Line under the Ocean). The Admiralty was given the task of laying the pipeline. Ramsay organized a new command—Force Pluto. One hundred officers and one thousand merchant marine sailors installed Pluto and after D-Day kept gasoline products flowing to the growing Allied armies in France.[37]

## DOUBTING THE MESSENGER

On February 11, 1944, General George S. Patton picked up General Bradley and drove him to St. Paul's School in West Kensington, Montgomery's London headquarters. There they met with Monty, Lieutenant General Miles Dempsey, who was to command the British invasion army, and Major General Francis de Guingand, Montgomery's chief of staff.

All five commanders realized the opening days of OVERLORD were the most critical. Will the objectives be reached? How fast can all the beaches be linked up for the move inland? Will the initial bridgehead be strong enough to survive the panzer counterattacks that Field Marshal Erwin Rommel, the German Normandy commander, was sure to mount?

Montgomery asked his biggest rival, "You've seen the Plan, Patton?"[38]

"I've seen it but did not have much of a chance to study it yet," Patton answered.

"Did you like what you saw of it?" Monty inquired.

"No," Patton said grinning.

"It doesn't give me anything to do!"

Montgomery ignored Patton's deeply felt objection and delved into the plan's details. He lectured Patton on using aggressive tactics. "We must aim at success in the land battle by the speed and violence of our operations."[39]

Though Patton appreciated Monty's new aggressive spirit, he knew from past experience that they were at odds with his battlefield tactics. Immediately after the Battle of El Alamein (October 1942), Montgomery failed to pursue Rommel, although he knew from Ultra intelligence that the Germans had only eleven serviceable tanks with enough fuel for four days. His failure to act immediately meant that he missed the ideal opportunity to destroy the Afrika Korps.[40]

Rommel wrote in his diary, "Their command was as slow as ever in reacting. When we embarked on our retreat on the night of the 2nd November, a long time elapsed before the British forces started their pursuit. . . . Their command continued to show the customary caution and lack of resolute decision."[41]

Montgomery continued his failure to aggressively pursue German forces on the battlefields of North Africa, Sicily, and Italy. He repeatedly became bogged down in a succession of encounters. Thus Patton had good reason to doubt that Montgomery now had the key attribute for winning the Normandy campaign—audacity. Six months before the start of the Normandy invasion, Patton thought it was "highly probable" that the British would get "boxed in" in their area of operation and drag the whole operation into stalemate or even defeat.[42]

Montgomery's "plan" called for the capture of Caen, about seven miles inland from the Sword invasion beach, on the first day. As Ladislas Farago, Patton's biographer, recounts, Patton believed without any reservation that "[t]his would be too tough a nut for Montgomery to crack." Patton told Bradley, "I think he's the best general the Limeys have. But he is not a man for fast and bold action. He is a master of the set battle. . . . Monty is supposed to take Caen on D-Day. . . . Well Brad, he won't take it. . . . He'll take his time and meantime the Germans will get ready for the counterattack."[43]

Montgomery's basic challenge was taking Caen to securely anchor the invasion's east flank bridgehead in order to prevent a counterattack by Rommel. As long as the Germans controlled Caen, the British could not bypass the city to gain access to the open Caen–Falaise plain and its two rivers, the Odon to the south or the Orne to the north of the city.[44] (See Map 2.)

Over the next several months, Bradley often met with Montgomery to solve operational details for OVERLORD. Montgomery's emphasis on the necessity for rapid thrust and maneuver appealed to Bradley. Even though these meetings were stiff and formal as Monty was withdrawn and not usually open to his suggestions, Bradley remained impressed by the "plan."

Yet Bradley recognized that it had a number of flaws. He disagreed with Montgomery's analysis that the beach defenses and German counterattacks in the hinterland would be light. Like Patton, Bradley thought that Montgomery was hopelessly optimistic about reaching his first-day objectives. Incredibly, Montgomery even told Bradley that the British tanks would reach Falaise before the end of D-Day![45]

## AIR TURBULENCE

Given the vast scale of OVERLORD, operational tensions were inevitable. However Eisenhower was generally able to secure multinational cooperation in most areas. The one major exception was the Allied air forces.

At the January 21 meeting of OVERLORD's commanders, Eisenhower requested that parts of British air marshal Sir Arthur Harris's Bomber Command and General Carl Spaatz's US Army Air Force Command in Europe be placed under the control of SHAEF to support OVERLORD. They both objected immediately because it would weaken the strategic bombing offensive against Germany, which they viewed as a decisive factor in the total Allied war effort. In some quarters it was believed that air power alone would bring Nazi Germany to its knees.

To Harris and Spaatz even temporarily allowing their bomber forces to be deployed in tactical operations headed by Air Chief Marshal Trafford Leigh-Mallory was anathema. Mallory's main command experience had been with fighter operations. Moreover, due to his prior conduct during the

Battle of Britain, Leigh-Mallory was not liked or respected by his British colleagues.[46]

British air chief marshal Arthur Tedder was the key person for resolving this impasse. His earlier command of Allied air forces in the Mediterranean had given him both strategic bombing and tactical air experience. He ultimately was acceptable to Harris, Spaatz, and the fighter commanders as Eisenhower's deputy.

His Mediterranean experience led Tedder to conclude that the most effective tactics for supporting an amphibious landing was isolating the bridgehead battlefield by bombing the enemy's railroad marshaling yards, thus disrupting their ability to reinforce and successfully counterattack. Tedder named this concept the "Transportation Plan." In February Leigh-Mallory proposed implementing this plan to disrupt enemy logistics by bombing the rail centers for the Normandy area shortly before and after the invasion.

Initially both Harris and Spaatz, supported by Prime Minister Winston Churchill, virtually declared war on the Transportation Plan. They saw it as a major interference with Harris's night saturation bombing and Spaatz's effort to devastate Germany's oil production.

Tedder was able to persuade Air Chief Marshal Sir Charles Portal, RAF chief of staff, to authorize a trial raid on a French railyard. On the night of March 6, Bomber Command launched a devastating attack on the rail center at Trappes that kept it from properly functioning for a month. The Transportation Plan was shown to be feasible.

In mid-April 1944 after months of arguing, Eisenhower threatened to resign. Instead a compromise was finally reached by giving "direction" of the strategic air forces to the supreme Allied commander. In effect, direction was given to Air Marshal Tedder to liaison with Harris and Spaatz who remained in command of their bomber forces and continued the strategic bombing of Germany. Thus SHAEF was able to largely resolve the OVERLORD plan's ambiguities and the impasse over its bombing strategy. Tedder was able to direct specific requests to the bomber forces by selecting limited targets with high strategic priority.[47]

While controversy raged over the OVERLORD Transportation Plan, in early 1944 the Allied air forces began a new phase in their offensive. During "Big Week" fleets of Flying Fortresses and Liberators were escorted to and from their targets by the long-range Mustang fighters now equipped with Merlin engines. They pounded German aircraft factories across Europe. Over six hundred German fighters were shot down, thus showing the superiority of the P-51 Mustang to anything in the enemy's air force. Though Allied bomber losses were high, the Luftwaffe lost many of its best fighter pilots. There were no replacements to fly new aircraft, even if they were delivered. After Big Week, the quality of German pilots began to decline. A combination of high pilot attrition and insufficient fuel for new pilot training gutted the Luftwaffe pilots' proficiency. By June 1944 this effective air campaign reduced the Luftwaffe to a small and declining defense force.[48]

General Adolf Galland who commanded German fighter operations agreed that by D-Day, "The Luftwaffe was not in a position to interfere with all these operations. . . . In France we still had only two fighter wings."[49]

The addition of Mustang fighters to the Allied air arsenal gave the Allies mastery of the skies over the English Channel and the Normandy invasion area. Heavy bombing did reduce German aircraft and oil production, but more importantly the Mustangs killed off the cream of German pilots. When D-Day began, the Allies had a thirty-to-one superiority over the Luftwaffe. On D-Day Ike could reassure his troops, "If you see fighting aircraft over you, they will be ours."[50]

One thing that was not achieved by D-Day was harmony in the Allied air command. The Allied air chiefs fought over their role and deployment, disputed Leigh-Mallory's orders, and did not have sufficient forward air controllers for close ground-air support. Throughout the Normandy campaign it took the combined prodding of Tedder and Montgomery to obtain the assets requested by Leigh-Mallory to provide air support for such ground offensives such as CHARNWOOD, GOODWOOD, TOTALIZE, COBRA, and the Falaise Pocket.

Allied airpower was indeed critical before and during the entire OVERLORD operation. But as Max Hastings points out, an end to the squabbling between senior American and British airmen might have considerably eased the problems of the ground battle.[51]

## DECEPTION AND SECRETS

The fate of D-Day largely rested on three factors: surprise, speed, and concentration of force. Operation JAEL (named after an Old Testament heroine who killed an enemy commander through deception) was the Allies' overall plan to surprise the Germans on the day, time, and place for the invasion of Western Europe. The overall deception plan was code-named Bodyguard. One part of this plan was Operation ZEPPELIN. It was designed to convince the Germans that the Allies would launch an invasion in the Balkans and Greece and then press their attack through central Europe and Austria into southern Germany.

Cicero was a Turkish agent who worked in the British embassy in Istanbul. He somehow obtained keys to dispatch boxes and photographed highly classified documents that he sold to the Germans. British intelligence seeded the boxes with false information. This influenced Hitler to reinforce the Balkans with twenty-five divisions that could have been in France for D-Day.[52]

The other half of the deception campaign had three parts: Fortitude North, Fortitude South, and Bodyguard. Fortitude North was designed to convince the Germans that the Allies would invade Norway and that neutral Sweden would then join them. Next the Allies would take Denmark and invade northern Germany. Hitler was already obsessed with Norway. Two hundred thousand troops occupied the country. In May 1944, Rommel convinced Hitler to transfer five infantry divisions in Norway to France. The Abwehr (German Army Intelligence) intercepted a Fortitude North message that threatened Norway. Hitler stopped the reinforcements moving to Normandy.

The objective of Fortitude South was to persuade the Germans that the D-Day landings would occur in the Pas-de-Calais sector, the narrowest part of the English Channel opposite Dover, England. It made the major ports of Boulogne, Dunkirk, and Calais within easy reach and offered the shortest land route to Germany. Also it was closer to the airfields in England, giving Allied fighters extended flying time. Because the German general staff believed this to be the most likely site for the invasion, the largest concentration of German troops and fortifications were placed in this coastal area of France.

A key part of this deception was the creation of a fictional First US

Army Group (FUSAG) under the command of General George S. Patton. It sought to convince the Germans that Patton's army would invade the Pas-de-Calais in July. To provide false information to German air reconnaissance, dummy invasion craft, tanks, trucks, and aircraft were lined up on Britain's east coast roads and ports.

Britain's Ultra code-breaking program at Bletchley Park had cracked the German Enigma ciphers in 1940. These Ultra intercepts revealed that the Germans believed that there was a real First US Army Group (FUSAG).[53]

Patton appreciated the importance of Fortitude South but did not enjoy his role in it. In a letter to a friend, he wrote, "I had some very interesting trips while I was working as a decoy for the German divisions, and I believe that my appearances had a considerable effect."[54] By May the Germans' attention was firmly fixed on the Calais area.

Bodyguard was directed at Hitler personally. It played on his rising paranoia. The Allies wanted Hitler to believe they would invade at Calais with a diversionary attack in the Balkans or Norway.

Bodyguard's objective was to get Hitler to spread his armies throughout Fortress Europe. It succeeded. Field Marshal von Rundstedt, commander of German forces in Western Europe, complained that in trying to hold on to everything, Hitler would lose everything.[55]

Unbelievably the secrets of D-Day were kept even though about 189,000 invasion maps were prepared for the OVERLORD operation. There were many gaffes. On one occasion twelve copies of the OVERLORD orders were blown out of Norfolk House, falling among the crowd in St. James Square, London. All the staff ran out of the building and quickly recovered eleven copies. Two tense hours elapsed before a Londoner handed the missing copy to a sentry across from the War Office. His identity was never discovered.

In another incident a truck full of invasion maps overturned on a highway near Salisbury. In both incidents all the maps were retrieved before any unauthorized individual saw these top secret D-Day maps.[56]

Innocent mistakes can happen. Sergeant Thomas P. Kane, an American soldier of German descent, worked in London's Ordinance Supply Section of SHAEF. By mistake he sent classified documents to his sister in Chicago. The package burst open in an Illinois mail-sorting office. Although they were shown to be innocent, all people in this classified secret drama were kept under close surveillance until after the invasion.[57]

People lose things every day. A British staff officer traveling in a taxi left behind his briefcase containing Operation NEPTUNE's communication plan. A conscientious driver soon turned it in to the Lost Property Office intact.

In early June an American air force major general who was a friend and West Point classmate of Eisenhower announced during a reception at Claridge's that D-Day would occur before June 15. He compounded his stupidity by offering to take bets on his accuracy. Eisenhower demoted him and sent him back to America. Because of the officer's outstanding service record, he was not court-martialed.[58] Luckily his bragging did not reach German intelligence.

The invasion's most frightening potential security breach occurred when a senior British officer who worked on the *Daily Telegraph* crossword puzzle each morning began finding they included some of the invasion's most secret code words. Between May 2 and June 2, five crosswords included the words Overlord, Neptune, Mulberry, Gold, June, Sword, Utah, and Omaha. MI5 discovered that two schoolmasters in Surrey compiled the crosswords. The senior compiler had been authoring the puzzles for twenty years; his associate was a longtime friend. After a stringent examination they were found to be innocent. The episode was considered a bizarre coincidence. That changed in 1984 when Ronald French, a fourteen-year-old pupil of one of the crossword puzzle's authors, claimed he had helped insert the code words into the puzzles. French had heard them used by American soldiers stationed in Surrey while they were talking about the invasion. Fortunately, German intelligence did not study British crossword puzzles.[59]

## APRIL 7—EXERCISE THUNDERCLAP

A comprehensive review (Exercise THUNDERCLAP) of OVERLORD planning was held on April 7 at St. Paul's School. A series of briefings by Montgomery, Ramsay, Leigh-Mallory, Bradley, Dempsey, and even the corps commanders covered the ground, naval, and air operations. Eisenhower and his planners were present, as was Churchill and Patton.

Standing in front of a large Normandy map, Montgomery led off using a sixteen-page outline on D-Day and the subsequent OVERLORD campaign. (See Map 2.) Lieutenant General Sir Miles Dempsey had the command of the British Second Army, composed of British and Canadian troops. They would land at three beachheads: Gold—British Fiftieth Infantry Division, Juno—Third Canadian Division, and Sword—British Third Infantry Division. Elements of the Seventy-Ninth Armored Division would land on all three beaches.

General Omar Bradley had the command of the American First Army. It would land at two beachheads: Utah Beach (the Fourth and Ninetieth infantry divisions) and Omaha Beach (the First and Twenty-Ninth infantry divisions). In the early-morning hours of D-Day, the British Sixth Airborne Division and the American Eighty-Second and 101st Airborne Divisions would arrive by parachute and gliders to help secure the territory immediately behind these beachheads.

Montgomery's whole presentation stressed offensive action. The British and Canadian objective of Caen, seven miles inland from Sword, was to be secured on D-Day. These forces would then move south and southeast of the city and take its Carpiquet Airfield. Soon afterward they were to take Falaise, twenty miles south of Caen.

Meanwhile the Americans would take Cherbourg, capture St. Lo, and then advance thirty miles farther south to Avranches. (See Map 1B.) This would open the door to Brittany and its ports. The American forces would then wheel to the east toward the Seine River and Paris.

Sometime during these operations, the First Canadian Army under General Henry Crerar would land and cover the British left flank, and then advance to the seaport of Le Havre. Meanwhile, the Third US Army, under the command of General Patton, would help clear Brittany, seize seaports, and then cover the First US Army's right flank on the march to Paris.

In his April 5 presentation, Montgomery envisioned attaining all OVERLORD objectives in ninety days. (See Map 1B.)

Through Ultra intelligence intercepts, the Allies estimated that on D-Day the Germans would have fifty-five divisions in Western Europe. The Allies could put ashore a little over seven divisions on D-Day. It was estimated that two panzer divisions could be mobilized against the invasion by that night, and that in five days, Rommel might have six panzer divisions to strike against the Allies.

In the race to reinforce the bridgehead, the Allies planned to have over ten divisions onshore on D-Day+1, fourteen by D+4, and twenty-four by D+20. By ninety days after D-Day, all forty-five Allied divisions in Britain would be on the continent. This slow, methodical buildup of ground forces was made possible by total Allied air supremacy that could stop or significantly slow the rate of Wehrmacht reinforcements into the Normandy bridgehead. Eisenhower's support of the Transportation Plan, begun a week after the St. Paul briefing, was an essential element in making this strategy work.

Neither on that day nor in his master plan did Montgomery call for building a defensive posture around Caen or making the city a hinge for the entire front. Instead he insisted that on D-Day he would take Caen and moving onward deploy British armor on the Falaise plain in a strong, aggressive offensive to firmly anchor the British flank and unbalance the German response.[60]

Later Bradley and others present on April 7 agreed that Montgomery's concept of the Normandy campaign was not defensive. The capture of Caen by British and Canadian forces was never termed a holding action or a deliberate strategy for drawing in Rommel's reserves.[61]

Montgomery's program on April 7 also correlates with General Dempsey's published operational plan for the divisions under his command. The entire campaign in Normandy's eastern bridgehead sector rested on this "fragile reed." As historian Carlo D'Este states, "All future actions envisioned that day and noted in later documents and orders were predicated upon the successful capture either of Caen itself or of the Orne-Odon river crossings in the West."[62]

Historians Nigel Hamilton and Max Hastings concur that Montgomery's overambitious plans were designed to convince his fellow commanders and Churchill that he was capable of mounting an aggressive offensive campaign. At the very least, Montgomery was guilty of overreach. In the end his operational plans produced a muddled campaign and great discord among the other commanders.[63]

## PREPARING THE FORCES

Until the fall of 1943, most American troops were dispatched to staff US Army Air Force units in England. The buildup of forces for OVERLORD began in October 1943 and continued until May 1944, with more than 100,000 troops arriving each month. The success of the naval war of the North Atlantic made this massive troop buildup possible. The defeat of German U-boat forces was largely due to the introduction of 260 new American escort destroyers, jeep escort aircraft carriers, new electronic anti-submarine/air defenses, and the Ultra intercepts that identified lurking German wolf packs that were then hunted down. No troopships escorted by the US Navy were ever lost.[64]

On D-Day the Americans landed 130,000 men in Normandy; another 1.2 million followed by D-Day+90. With them came an endless river of equipment, including 137,000 wheeled and semi-tracked vehicles, 4,217 full-tracked vehicles, and 3,500 artillery pieces. Month after month, a ceaseless flow of transatlantic convoys unloaded an ever more massive stockpile of K-rations, petroleum, ammunition, blood plasma, tents—the endless variety and quantity of equipment needed to support the invasion. The average soldier in Normandy received six and a quarter pounds of rations a day.[65] This logistical triumph was due to Ramsay's meticulous planning of Operation NEPTUNE.

By D-Day the British assembled with nearly sixteen divisions, slightly over half a million men. This included some of their best battle-hardened men from the Mediterranean. Additionally the Royal Navy provided the majority of D-Day naval escorts, while the RAF contributed about four thousand first-line aircraft.

Across Britain great tent encampments arose as troop assembly areas. Carefully camouflaged to render them unobtrusive from ten thousand feet, each was equipped with field bakeries/messes, water/bath facilities, and post offices.

To properly prepare and train over a million men for the amphibious assault and subsequent battles, the entire local population in twenty-five square miles of west Devon was evacuated. Here the assault forces rehearsed with live ammunition. Other troop field exercises were held all over the United Kingdom. They were given odd code names, such as BEAVER,

FABIOS, DUCK I, II, III, or TIGER. These war game participants ranged from special forces to entire divisions.[66]

By May 1944 this great Allied army that was to crack Fortress Europe had become one of the best prepared invasion forces in history. All units studied and practiced how to effectively fight in a wide variety of battlefield conditions and terrains. Cooperation was stressed—both among naval, air, and ground units and the Allied forces of different nations. Yet, there were some notable glitches in this preparation.

After the beach assault, the British faced defeating German forces around Caen. The American inland offensive operations were confronted with areas that the Germans had flooded and hedgerows ("bocage" to the French).

The dictionary definition of a "hedgerow" is a simple row of trees or bushes that separate one field from another. What the Americans actually found in Normandy were six- and even eight-feet-high hedgerows trapped by a row of trees that added an impenetrable layer anywhere from six to twenty feet high. Tanks could not break through them and had to expose their vulnerable undersides to climb over them, thus making their guns useless. The bocage offered the Germans ideal defensive positions. "I couldn't image the bocage until I saw it," said Bradley after the war.[67]

In preparing the original COSSAC invasion plan, General Morgan had alerted the British Chiefs of Staff to the difficulties posed by the bocage. General Alan Brooke, one of their members, was also very much concerned about this bocage country. He had spent many summers there as a boy. In July 1940, he had led Anglo-French forces across this terrain before the Dunkirk evacuation. Similarly, Patton had also traveled extensively in this area as a soldier in World War I. He understood how disruptive it was for offensive warfare.

Allied planners, however, failed to prepare the troops and equipment to meet the bocage challenge—a major gaffe. Aerial photos clearly identified an eight-square-mile hedgerow area behind the American beaches, divided by four thousand bocage enclosures. A battalion commander lamented, "We were rehearsed endlessly for attacking beach defenses, but not one day was given to the terrain behind the beaches, which was no less difficult and deadly."[68] This training failure greatly delayed the Allied breakout from the Normandy bridgehead.

In March and April, all five Allied assault forces participated in the culmination of the joint army/navy training program with full-scale rehearsals of the beach landings. Troops and their assault equipment were loaded on the same ships and mostly the same ports that would be used for embarkation on D-Day.

On April 27 Eisenhower, Ramsay, Montgomery, and the other principal commanders watched the first day of Exercise TIGER. It was staged at Slapton Sands Beach in Lyons Bay in the southwest of England, a site that was chosen for its similarity to Utah Beach. The plan was for Rear Admiral Don Pardee Moon's amphibian command to put most of General Joseph Collins's Fourth US Infantry Division ashore. They would then advance twenty-five miles inland and "capture" the city of Okehampton. The beaches were mined and strewn with barbed wire and steel boat obstacles. Moon's landing force consisted of twenty-one LSTs, twenty-eight LCI (L)s, sixty-five LCTs, and almost one hundred other smaller ships with a warship escort.[69]

In the first wave due to part of the flotilla's late arrival, a signal mix-up caused the British heavy cruiser *Hawkins* to open fire on the beach among the American landing craft. This resulted in a number of friendly-fire casualties. This communication breakdown was soon remedied, and the amphibious assault proceeded. Ramsay commented, "It was a flop . . . much to criticise but the main thing was the lack of senior naval or army officers on the beach to take charge and to supervise."[70] A greater disaster was to follow.

The next morning (April 28), eight LSTs and two pontoons escorted by only one British corvette set out for the second wave of the exercise. Prior to the departure for the exercise, the *Scimitar*, an older destroyer, was struck by an American landing craft while inside Plymouth Harbor. Though the damage was minor, the British commander in chief of Plymouth ordered the *Scimitar* into the repair yards. Unfortunately, no one communicated this information to the US Navy Commander Bernard Skahill, the commodore of the convoy, because he was not in the Royal Navy chain of command. The convoy was down to only one escort.[71]

British radar noted the departure of German E-boats from Cherbourg. But due to the two separate communication systems, Skahill was not warned. It was not until after midnight that the single British escort was even notified. By then the British Admiral commanding in Plymouth belatedly dispatched a second destroyer as a relief escort, but was too late to intervene.

Nine E-boats closed in on the Allied convoy. Each was armed with 40mm guns and four torpedoes. About 2:00 a.m. the first torpedo was launched. "All of a sudden, the whole sky is lit up [tracer rounds]," wrote Andy Korosi assigned to LST-511. "Shortly after that, we heard another explosion. The [LST] 507 got torpedoed. Another one got hit with two torpedoes—that one sunk in seven to ten minutes. . . . Two other LSTs caught fire—one was abandoned and the other limped back to the shore."[72]

Both LST-507 and LST-531 were sunk, and LST-289 was damaged. The final death toll from Operation TIGER was 198 sailors and 441 soldiers killed, which paradoxically was more than died five weeks later during the landing of American forces at Utah Beach on D-Day.[73]

The news of this disaster was withheld from the public for fear that it might undermine public support for the actual D-Day invasion. The full story of this tragedy was not revealed until many years after World War II.

Rear Admiral Moon began an investigation immediately after the event. Ultimately his recommendation for future exercises was that "at least" four escorts should be assigned to any convoy or even more for longer convoys.

The British naval commanders on the scene had a major responsibility for the communications failure that caused the Slapton Sands tragedy. However in a broader view of the OVERLORD operation it shows how difficult it was for the separate Allied army, navy, and air services to achieve a seamless level of communications and cooperation on an operational level that might have prevented the many other strategic and tactical errors that occurred throughout this campaign.

As a result of Slapton Sands, Admiral King ordered eight more US Navy destroyers to bolster Ramsay's command. Many operational lessons were learned from this incident, and corrective measures were implemented that did save lives the day of the actual invasion.

About a week later on May 3, the Allies began FABIUS, a final series of training exercises. Dempsey's Second British Army practiced landings on the beaches east of Portsmouth. Everything went smoothly, with no E-boat attacks. Ramsay communicated to Eisenhower that the NEPTUNE force was now ready for action.[74]

## DRESS REHEARSAL—MAY 15

On May 15 at St. Paul's School in Hammersmith, West London, a dazzling array of commanders and leaders gathered for OVERLORD's final full-scale briefing. It was the largest meeting of Allied military leaders ever assembled during the entire war. Those present included King George VI, Churchill, Eisenhower, Tedder, Montgomery, Ramsay, Leigh-Mallory, Brooke, Dempsey, and the other British Chiefs of Staff; the major American commanders, Bradley, Patton, Hodges, Smith, and Simpson; the top Canadian commander Crerar; other British, Canadian, and US corps and division commanders; naval and air task force commanders; and a multitude of SHAEF and Whitehall senior officers. One hundred forty-six engraved invitations and security passes had been distributed a month earlier.[75]

At 10:00 a.m., Eisenhower introduced the program to the leaders who would soon assault Nazi Fortress Europe. He had just chosen June 5 as D-Day. Behind him was a huge top secret three-dimensional plaster relief map of the invasion beaches on the Normandy coast. Thirty feet wide, it was on a tilted platform visible throughout the room. This model of what would become one of the world's best-known battlefields was on a scale of six inches to the mile and showed Normandy's cities, towns, rivers, beaches, and upland features in bright colors. As each commander spoke, he walked around the display, pointing at key features.[76]

Eisenhower was brief, stating, "We are here to get the best possible results." Then he called on General Montgomery to begin thc briefing.[77]

As Montgomery rose to speak, pointer in hand, a loud pounding started at the door. The hammering grew louder. Monty angrily ordered the door opened. In marched General Patton. Ignoring Monty's withering gaze, he sat in the second row. Another concession forced upon Monty was allowing those in attendance to smoke. This announced concession brought muffled gasps from some in the room. Perhaps he remembered chain-smoking Eisenhower from two years prior, and of course, there sat cigar-puffing Churchill.[78]

In forceful tones, Montgomery then outlined the entire NEPTUNE-OVERLORD operation. The invasion plan has been previously covered in this chapter. Patton's Third Army was to land between D-Day+15 and

D-Day+60. Its mission was to capture the Brittany region and its important seaports. Later it would support the advance of the First US Army toward Paris.

The OVERLORD operation was planned for ninety days. After the breakout from the invasion lodgment area itself, OVERLORD planning was very minimal. On May 3 SHAEF planners presented Eisenhower with several alternative courses of action. These included the capture of Germany's industrial Ruhr or the capture of Berlin. Eisenhower rejected the Berlin option and considered seizing the Ruhr through either a frontal assault or a double envelopment. However, no specific operational plan was prepared.[79] (See Map 3.)

Montgomery's presentation offered a very accurate prediction of Rommel's potential counterattack plan. The greatest danger was that the panzer divisions close to the coast would be used by the Germans to throw the Allies back into the sea during the first days of the invasion.

In this presentation and in his May 8 planning document, Monty emphasized that the Allies must quickly move forward and keep the initiative:

> We must blast our way on shore and get a good lodgement before the enemy can bring sufficient reserves to turn us out. Armored columns must penetrate deep inland, and quickly, on D-Day. This will upset the enemy plans and tend to hold him off while we build up strength. We must gain space rapidly, and peg out claims well inland.[80]

He stressed that the main D-Day objective of the Second British Army was to take Caen. "Once we can get control of the main enemy lateral [corridor], Granville-Vire-Argentan-Falaise-Caen, and the area enclosed in it is firmly in our possession, then we will have the lodgement area we want and can begin to expand," he assured his audience.[81]

The army that quickly gained control of this Caen-Falaise corridor would control the battle. This was borne out by subsequent events. A slow, safe advance would give Rommel the time he needed to reinforce and shift his troops across the battlefront to keep the Allies contained inside their bridgehead. That is exactly what Rommel did!

In rapid succession Omar Bradley, Carl Spaatz, Bomber Harris, and Bertram Ramsay laid out the roles of their forces. All made clear their complete determination to win the war in Europe beginning with an OVERLORD victory.

The question not answered that day was, "What then?" OVERLORD assumed that on reaching the Seine River the Allied armies would pause and regroup. What actually occurred was that the Germans confined the invasion bridgehead longer than expected, and then collapsed rapidly, catching the Allies by surprise. Other than targeting the German Ruhr industrial heartland using a broad-front advance on the road to Berlin, SHAEF's post-OVERLORD scheme was a vague outline. This failure would cause a number of major operational disagreements among the commanders that helped to delay ending the war in Europe.

In his diary entry for that day Alan Brooke made one of the more perceptive evaluations of the plans outlined in the May 15 briefings:

> The main impression I gathered was that Eisenhower was a swinger and no real director of thought, plans, energy or direction! Just a coordinator—a good mixer, a champion of inter-allied cooperation, and in those respects few can hold a candle to him. But is that enough? Or can we not find all qualities of a commander in one man? Maybe I am getting too hard to please, but I doubt it.[82]

Even accounting for Brooke's frustration at not being named OVERLORD's supreme commander, his impressions proved on target regarding Eisenhower's relationships with his principal commanders during the Normandy campaign.

Ultimately the Allies would discover four major flaws in their overall OVERLORD invasion planning:[83]

1. They overestimated their ability to quickly establish a substantial bridgehead, particularly in the failure to seize Caen.
2. Training was defective especially in not preparing tactical measures to deal with the difficult bocage terrain.
3. The troops were not prepared to cope with the intense German resistance that caused a stalemate in the Allied advance.
4. After the Allied breakout, they lacked the command ability for quickly formulating action plans that took full advantage of battlefield opportunities.

## COUNTDOWN TO D-DAY

As D-Day neared, tensions among its leaders rose to high levels. Eisenhower knew that the D-Day operation in its present form could be undertaken only one time. American resources were sufficient to bear the consequences of a defeat in Normandy, but Britain's physical and political capital was stretched to the limit. An OVERLORD failure would threaten Churchill's government and the future careers of the OVERLORD commanders. A defeat might significantly lengthen the Nazi occupation of Continental Europe. Events both planned and unforeseen heightened the war of nerves in the countdown to D-Day.

### MAY 25—WHERE IS MONTY?

Operation COPPERHEAD was one of FORTITUDE's deception plans. Meyrick Clifton James was a member of the British Army's Pay Corps Drama and Variety Group who was given the starring role of playing Monty's double.

On May 25 in an attempt to divert German attention away from northwestern Europe, James flew from England to Gibraltar on Churchill's private plane. The British spread false rumors that Montgomery was traveling to Gibraltar and North Africa to prepare for a major Allied invasion of southern France.

On May 26, "Monty" was dutifully greeted by Gibraltar's governor Sir Ralph Eastwood. Later a reception was held at the governor's house. "Plan 303," the landings in the south of France, was a topic of conversation heard by Ignacio Molina Perez who was the liaison officer between the Spanish government and the British and also a Nazi spy code-named Cosmos.[84]

At just the right moment Perez saw "Monty" get into his car. The Spaniard was told it was the commander in chief on his way to Algiers. Perez dutifully reported the incident to Berlin.

James then flew to North Africa where for several days he made a number of appearances as Monty with General Maitland Wilson, the Allied commander in the Mediterranean theater. He was then flown to Cairo, where he remained hidden until after D-Day.

Though German intelligence was fooled into believing it really was Montgomery, they still guessed that "Plan 303" was an Allied deception. British intelligence MI5 only declassified the full details of this deception operation in 2010.[85]

## MAY 26—UNNERVING NEW INTELLIGENCE

Ramsay noted in his diary, "Disturbing features of Overlord have arisen in the strengthening of German divisions in the Neptune area, particularly opposite the west flank of the Americans. This makes their task very much more difficult & particularly that of the Airborne Divs & may necessitate a change of plan."[86]

Over the past three weeks Allied intelligence had learned of German reinforcements that shifted the Ninety-First Infantry Division to a position behind Utah Beach. This necessitated a change in the drop zones of the US Eighty-Second and 101st Airborne Divisions.

Also the Twenty-First Panzer Division was moved to an area south of Caen. However, Montgomery did not make any new provisions for ensuring that the British could take Caen on D-Day as he planned by either briefing the officers involved or reinforcing the thrust to take this city.

Unfortunately the intelligence services failed to discover that part of the battle-hardened German 352nd Infantry Division had been relocated to a position just behind Omaha Beach. This had near disastrous consequences for D-Day that we will discuss in the next two chapters.

## MAY 28—NEPTUNE UNLEASHED

On a glorious hot summer day Ramsay flashed out the order, "Carry out Operation NEPTUNE."[87] A huge fleet of warships, landing craft, and landing ships sailed from harbors throughout the United Kingdom to their assigned invasion embarkation ports. There they rendezvoused with the million-man army that had been streaming into southern England. In eight days they planned to be in France. All the crews were now sealed in their ships

## MAY 29—A "FUTILE SLAUGHTER?"

This was one of Eisenhower's worst days before the invasion. Leigh-Mallory, his air chief, sent a hand-delivered letter challenging the paratroop drop. Because of the German Ninety-First Infantry's shift in location, Leigh-Mallory feared the airdrop of both the Eighty-Second and 101st Airborne would be a "futile slaughter" and should be canceled.[88]

Under the OVERLORD plan, prior to the beach landings, two American and two British paratroop divisions were to be flown to Normandy for an early-morning drop. On the eastern end the initial American objective was the little hamlet of Sainte-Mere-Eglise due to its location along the main road, Route Nationale 13, that connected Cherbourg to Bayeux, an important axis for German reinforcements.

Meanwhile at the western end of the bridgehead, the British were to seize important bridges for the armored advance into Caen later that day. The airborne divisions were to blow up key bridges, mine the appropriate roads, and prevent the German counterattack from reaching the troops arriving by sea.

That night Eisenhower dictated a formal letter confirming his decision for the airborne assault to go forward. Both Bradley and Montgomery concurred with Ike's decision.[89]

## MAY 30—"NO ILLUSIONS"

On this day over two thousand aircraft destroyed every bridge over the Seine River between Paris and the coast. Also smashed were railroad lines, airfields, radar/radio installations—any target that might impede D-Day.

Rommel saw the staggering results. When he returned to his headquarters at La Roche-Guyon that night after a rocket launcher demonstration, Rommel had to cross the Seine by boat. He harbored no illusions about the potential effects of Allied air power.[90]

## JUNE 1, A.M.—VISIT TO THE BEACH?

Churchill wanted to be part of D-Day's historic movement. "I thought it would not be wrong for me to watch the preliminary bombardment in this historic battle from one of our cruiser squadrons, and I asked Admiral Ramsay to make a plan."[91]

Upon hearing of this request, Eisenhower told Churchill it was a crazy idea. Churchill defied him. No American general had the power to prevent the prime minister from viewing D-Day from the deck of a Royal Navy ship that in effect was British soil. Ike backed down. When Montgomery heard of this controversy, he was apoplectic. He exploded, "Why in the hell doesn't he go and smoke his cigar at Dover Castle and be seen with the Lord Mayor? It would fix the Germans' attention on Calais."[92]

On June 1 Ramsay went to the Cabinet Office to see Churchill. To his astonishment there with the prime minister was King George VI. "The P.M. [prime minister] explained that H.M. [His Majesty] wished to embark on the same venture as the P.M. namely to go over with the Assault Forces. . . . I said that I considered the risk was unacceptable." The king agreed to this, but Churchill said Ramsay's ban didn't extend to him. Ramsay told Churchill "he had no job over there."[93] They left it that he would think it over.

Fortunately the king stopped Churchill's embarkation with a skillful June 2 letter:

> My dear Winston, I want to make one more appeal to you not to go to sea on D-Day. Please consider my own position. I am a younger man than you, I am a sailor, and as King I am the head of all the services. There is nothing I would like better than to go to sea but I have agreed to stay at home; is it fair that you should then do exactly what I should have liked to do myself?
>
> Your very sincere friend, George R.I.

Definitely outmaneuvered, Churchill peevishly replied the next day:

> I must defer to Your Majesty's wishes, and indeed commands. It is a great comfort to me to know that they arise from Your Majesty's desire

to continue me in your service. Though I regret that I cannot go, I am deeply grateful to Your Majesty for the motives which have guided Your Majesty in respect,

Your Majesty's humble and devoted servant and subject,
WINSTON S. CHURCHILL[94]

The king did visit the Normandy bridgehead on June 16, ten days after D-Day, while Churchill landed in Normandy on June 12.[95]

## JUNE 1, P.M.—END OF THE WAR?

That night Bradley and Patton had dinner at Montgomery's headquarters near Portsmouth with his two commanders, Crerar and Dempsey. The mood became congenial. Finally Montgomery predicted that "if it all goes as planned," the war would be over by November 1.[96]

## JUNE 2–3—A LOFTY PERCH

On June 2 Eisenhower went to his war camp code-named SHARPENER five miles northwest of Portsmouth Harbor. Nearby was Montgomery's headquarters. A mile down a cinder path from Eisenhower's camp stood Southwick House, Ramsay's headquarters. Southwick's lofty hilltop perch was a short distance from the naval might assembled in Portsmouth Harbor—a thousand-ship fleet waiting to be launched. The rest of the OVERLORD armada, a total of nearly seven thousand ships and craft of every type, filled Great Britain's ports on the English Channel and the North Sea and even extended to Wales and Glasgow and Belfast.[97]

On June 2 Admiral Sir Bertram Ramsay gathered a group of his captains. He proclaimed that it was going to be "the greatest amphibious operation of all time."[98]

## JUNE 3—A "D-DAY SURPRISE"

Eisenhower had already experienced enough last-minute pre-invasion jolts. Then on June 3 at 4:39 p.m. Eastern Time across the Atlantic came this news flash: "Eisenhower's HQ Announces Allied Landing in France!"[99]

This message was immediately sent by the CBS, NBC, and ABC networks to over five hundred radio stations. It then spread to stations in Moscow, Cuba, and Chile. In New York at the Polo Grounds, the Giants vs. Pirates baseball game was interrupted for a minute of prayer. At the Belmont Racecourse officials prepared to cancel the remaining races that day.

Five minutes after this "D-Day" announcement, the Associated Press (AP) issued an urgent retraction. Had the false broadcast been a FORTITUDE deception or a secret Nazi plot to unhinge the invasion? It was discovered that it happened because of a twenty-three-year-old teletype operator's slipup at the AP's London Fleet Street office. While making a practice run of the D-Day release sent by SHAEF, she accidently left her machine switched to the "on" position for a transatlantic linkup and then hit the teletype keys too hard. By the time Eisenhower heard about this false invasion announcement, he was too worn out by other invasion gaffes to respond. What the Germans thought of the announcement remains unknown.[100]

## JUNE 3–5—THE WEATHER GODS' DICE ROLL

When planning any amphibious assault, weather is all important. Eisenhower had personally fixed a June 5 D-Day back in mid-May after a careful consideration of the tides and moon. A successful landing on the Normandy beaches had to satisfy five complex and demanding tidal- and weather-related conditions:

1. The landing craft needed to reach the shore at low tide so that the destructive German underwater beach obstacles would be exposed.
2. The bombers and naval ships that were to rake the beaches with gunfire needed an hour of daylight before the low tide in order to launch attacks on the German defensive positions.
3. A second low tide was necessary before darkness fell to land the Allied second wave of troops.

4. The airborne troops needed a late-rising full moon to guide their early-morning night drops that were to precede the beach landings.
5. It was essential for the landing craft to have a reasonably smooth sea and good visibility.

The tidal and moon-phase requirements were met between June 4 and June 7, but the weather would be the crucial factor in determining the final date. Very few people knew the secret of the date and place. They had a special security classification higher than top secret; the code name chosen was BIGOT. A chosen few were BIGOTed on the ultimate secret of D-Day.[101]

But all now hinged on the weather. After midnight on June 3, several of NEPTUNE's tightly scheduled elements were to be set in motion. At 9:30 p.m. Eisenhower and his principal commanders met at Southwick House to hear the latest weather report from Group Captain James M. Stagg, Royal Air Force, Ike's chief meteorologist. The day before, Stagg had told Eisenhower that the weather outlook for a June 5 invasion was "full of menace" and that the weather was probably going to get worse before it improved. Ike opted to wait until the next morning and hear one more weather report before he decided on a postponement.[102]

The next morning, June 4, the SHAEF chiefs gathered again at 4:30 a.m. Stagg advised them that the weather would deteriorate over the course of that day. "Do you foresee any change?" inquired Eisenhower. "No" was Stagg's response.[103] The other commanders were all against an invasion launch except Montgomery, who was usually overcautious. He was prepared to go in even without a guarantee of air cover. This shocked Air Chief Marshal Tedder who wrote that Monty "amazingly asserted his willingness on the part of the army to take the risk."[104] Later in his memoirs Montgomery admitted his mistake. "It was clear that if we had persisted with the original D-Day of the 5th June, we might have had a disaster."[105]

Eisenhower delayed the invasion for twenty-four hours. The earliest departing naval task force already at sea was able to hold up while the other invasion components remained in port.[106]

While waiting for a break from the weather gods, the supreme commander knew that any postponement beyond June 6 would have immeasurable political and strategic outcomes. Ironically, his son John was to graduate from West Point on June 6. Eisenhower's wife, Mamie, would attend while he presided over the day that would largely make or break his future reputation as a great commander.[107]

At 9:00 p.m. on June 4, the SHAEF commanders met again. But this time Stagg held out a ray of hope. The meteorologists had detected a lull between two storms. On the morning of Tuesday, June 6, the wind would fall, seas become calmer, and clouds dissipate. "Not great weather, but adequate."[108]

A cheer went up. In this tense and grave atmosphere, the commanders weighed the consequences. A further postponement meant a two-week delay for the right tidal and moon conditions. Though it still remained a big gamble, Eisenhower finally gave the order. "I don't like it, but there it is. Let's go."[109]

The next morning at 3:30 a.m. June 5, Stagg reconfirmed that "no substantial change has taken place." It was 5:00 a.m. when Eisenhower made the June 6 decision irrevocable: "OK, we'll go."[110] Eisenhower had made what many believe was the most significant decision of OVERLORD. Landing in bad weather on the Normandy coast caught the Germans off guard and contributed to the success of D-Day.[111]

## NEPTUNE UNLEASHED

When Eisenhower gave the final okay, a vast air and sea armada thundered into life. The last successful cross-channel invasion by the Normans in 1066 (though going in the opposite direction) paled in comparison with this modern aggregation of personnel, weaponry, and equipment. From England's ports and air fields, an unparalleled invasion force moved toward France.

Of the seven thousand Allied ships, 138 were major warships including six battleships (three US); two monitors; twenty-three cruisers (three US, two French, one Polish); eighty-one destroyers (thirty US, two Polish, one French, one Norwegian). Also in the NEPTUNE armada were 221 escort vessels, 287 minesweepers, 805 cargo vessels, 495 light coastal vessels, and over 4,000 landing ships and craft that fell into 46 distinct specialized categories.[112]

The flotilla of battleships and cruisers was flanked by the destroyers.

These warships passed through two huge troop transport convoys with sixty barrage balloons flying over them. Immediately after was a convoy of landing craft carrying tanks formed in a row of four ships in width and extending five and a half miles in length. Seventy-nine percent of all the vessels were British. After almost four years at war, this was the greatest display of naval military might that the United Kingdom and its empire had mustered.

From overhead came the unremitting roar produced by the Allied air force of 1,400 troop transports, 11,590 military aircraft of various types, and 3,700 fighters—almost 17,000 aircraft positioning to support the landings.[113]

On June 6 Captain Frank Dillon of the US Army Air Force (USAAF) was sent on a reconnaissance mission in his P-51 fighter to determine the height of the waves on the Normandy beaches. By 5:30 a.m. he was flying back at three thousand feet over the English Channel.

> I saw the nose of the ships coming in to make the invasion. . . . I saw this armada . . . there were battleships, cruisers, destroyers and assault craft all lined up. . . . I looked, and I looked and there was no end. Big ships leading the way. Ships and ships and ships as far as I can see. . . . I can only say the view was awesome.[114]

OVERLORD was poised to strike. What were the chances of success for the Allied invasion? To find out, we need to examine the state of the German preparations to repel OVERLORD.

# CHAPTER 5
# CRACKS IN FORTRESS EUROPE

"It's really sad to see these children's faces in grey uniforms."
—Heinrich Boll, NCO, 348th Infantry Division

## BIRTH OF THE ATLANTIC WALL

In June 1940 the surrender of France made Nazi Germany the virtual masters of Western Europe. From the perspective of Herman Goring and the other German officers standing on the cliffs at Calais with Dover in sight across the narrow English Channel, Hitler had won the war.

Most Europeans and Americans agreed with one notable exception—Winston Churchill. Unwilling to negotiate an armistice during the summer and fall of 1940, the United Kingdom suffered through the Battle of Britain from the air, and the threat of a German amphibious invasion that in the end was indefinitely postponed by Hitler.

The British began retaliating with pinprick air raids, small parties of naval raiders, and support for resistance movements across occupied Europe. Only at the end of 1941 did Hitler begin seriously devoting attention to building Atlantic coastal defenses.

In March 1942, the Germans began planning how to defeat any Allied invasion of Western Europe. Field Marshal Gerd von Rundstedt was appointed commander in chief in the West. He had been a staff officer in France during World War I. In 1939 Rundstedt commanded an army group for the invasion of Poland. He then led major forces in the attacks on France (1940) and Russia (1941). Dismissed for retreating in Russia, the führer gave him command of forces for the defense of the Netherlands, Belgium, and the occupied regions of northern France.

Fig. 5.1. Gerd von Rundstedt. (Sueddeutsche Zeitung Photo/Alamy Stock Photo)

On March 28, 1942, British Combined Operations Command under the command of Admiral Lord Louis Mountbatten launched on a highly successful large-scale raid against the Nazi naval base at St. Nazaire, France, on the Loire River. British ships and troops inflicted extensive damage on it. On August 19, a division-sized Allied raid on the port of Dieppe included heavy naval and air support. It was overwhelmingly defeated by the local German defenders. These and other raids convinced the German high command on the value of building extensive defensive works particularly around the major seaports that would be key logistic points for supporting a major Allied invasion.

On September 29, 1942, Hitler convened a major conference to consider Germany's defense of Western Europe. It resulted in the order for the immediate construction of the Atlantic Wall, a barrier of concrete stretching from Norway to Spain defended by 300,000 troops. Hitler also envisioned the building of fifteen thousand permanent defensive positions, many of which he would design himself. These fortifications were to be built by the German agency for military works, Organization Todt. The heaviest construction was concentrated along the narrowest part of the English Channel, around Pas-de-Calais. For two years, 225,000 men worked around-the-clock using more than a million tons of steel and over twenty million cubic yards of concrete. Hitler ordered that this West Wall be finished by March 1, 1943.[1]

On October 25, 1943, Rundstedt issued a comprehensive report on the state of the West Wall defenses from his headquarters in the West at St. Germain, just outside Paris. He pulled no punches. The fortifications were half-completed and lacked defensive depth. The Germans in Western Europe lacked an effective mobile reserve to launch counterattacks. The forces looked strong around the major ports, but were weak to nonexistent elsewhere.

Hitler studied this report carefully and on November 3, 1943, ordered a massive shake-up of the defensive programs. More troops, labor battalions, and weapons were to be deployed to defeat the menace of an Anglo-American invasion. In addition, Hitler ordered Field Marshal Erwin Rommel to take command of the most threatened coastal areas in France and provide the spark to complete the building of the West Wall.

Erwin Rommel was an officer in World War I. He taught tactics at the Infantry School in Dresden where he wrote a notable book on infantry tactics. Rommel was the commander of the Führer Headquarters for the invasion of Poland. In 1940 he commanded the Seventh Panzer Division on its dash to the English Channel during the invasion of France. From 1941 to 1942 he led the Afrika Korps. His first success in North Africa was seizing Tobruk, which led to his promotion to field marshal. Rommel then launched a further offensive to take the strategic Suez Canal but was first checked and later decisively beaten at El Alamein by General Montgomery. After the Allied TORCH invasion, the Afrika Korps was increasingly plagued by supply shortages, and in March 1943 while Rommel was on sick leave in Germany, he ineffectively sought to gain priority status for supplying his forces. The Afrika Korps was then turned over to the command of General Arnim, was trapped between the Allied armies in Tunisia, and forced to surrender in May 1943.[2]

Fig. 5.2. Erwin Rommel. (Pictorial Press Ltd./Alamy Stock Photo)

## COMMAND STRUCTURE FROM HELL

Hitler, Rundstedt, and Rommel all believed that victory in the West depended on throwing an Allied invasion back into the sea at all costs. But there was strong disagreement on the strategy for achieving it.

If the Allied OVERLORD command structure showed deficiencies during the Normandy campaign, the German chain of command in Western Europe (see chart 2) was a recipe for disaster. On December 30, Hitler accepted Rundstedt's proposal that integrated Rommel and his Army Group B into the German command. Rommel, though nominally subordinate to Rundstedt, became responsible for Holland, Belgium, and northern France south to the Loire River. He was given the command of the troops in the Netherlands, the Fifteenth Army defending Pas-de-Calais, and the Seventh Army defending Normandy and Brittany. But Hitler also appointed Rommel as inspector general of defense in the West, reporting directly to him. This reduced Rundstedt's overall authority.

Though not a big fan of the Desert Fox, Rundstedt was pleased to get reinforcements from Hitler, so he played along and offered the junior field marshal his full cooperation. Rommel respected the Prussian Rundstedt and tried not to overstep his authority. They both had to contend with a command system that Hitler had fouled up beyond belief. Within weeks of his appointment senior German officers began asking, "Who really is in command?"

After 1941 Hitler had dropped his role as the nominal commander in chief of the German armed forces and became its actual supreme commander. He determined the overall strategy on every front. The führer daily supervised the execution of plans and sometimes even tactical operations. These orders were handed down through the armed forces high command (OKW) under General Wilhelm Keitel, chief of staff, and Colonel General Alfred Jodl, chief of operations.

Rundstedt had no control over the Luftwaffe or the navy in the OB West area. He could ask Field Marshal Hugo Sperrle, commander of the Third Air Fleet, for his cooperation, but Sperrle took his orders only from Hermann Goering, the commander in chief of the Luftwaffe. They might ignore Rundstedt's requests. The same was true for the German Naval Group West. Both the air force and navy acted as independent, not integrated commands. Even the military governors of France, Belgium, and the

Netherlands who followed OB West in tactical matters followed OKW dictates on administrative matters and internal affairs. The SS forces took orders from Reichfuehrer Heinrich Himmler, and the Todt construction organization worked directly for Albert Speer.

The principle of divide and rule worked well for Hitler in the political sphere, but this extreme fragmentation of command proved disastrous for German military effectiveness. For example, on the tactical level the naval coastal guns remained under naval command until the moment the Allies landed, but then command of the coastal batteries reverted to the army. The German command structure became a formula for defeat even before the Allied Normandy armada sailed.[3]

## "WHO IS ON FIRST?"

It comes as no surprise that the German high command was equally divided on the strategy for meeting and defeating an Allied invasion.

Rundstedt envisioned a classic counterattack once the exact location of the invasion was clarified. He wanted a strong, mobile panzer reserve centrally placed to launch a rapid, vigorous assault that would drive the invaders back into the sea before their bridgehead could be reinforced. Rundstedt's strategic vision rested on defense in depth, a swift panzer counterattack, and the utter collapse of the Allied invasion.[4]

Rommel previously had firsthand experience in North Africa with the devastating effectiveness of Allied air and naval campaigns. He saw little possibility of rapidly moving panzer reserves to meet the landing forces without sustaining significant casualties. "British and American superiority in the air alone has again and again been so effective that all movement of major formations has been rendered completely impossible," Rommel wrote.[5]

In his view the Wehrmacht had to stop the invasion at the water's edge, on the landing beaches. Rommel proposed a strong static linear defense of concrete fortifications. "This will require the construction of a fortified and mined zone extending from the coast five or six miles inland."[6]

Rommel also wanted the panzer divisions to be placed near the coast where the Allies were most likely to land. They would then launch the decisive counterattacks within the first forty-eight hours of the invasion. The German tanks were meant to counterattack in small packets deployed from behind the beaches. The panzers would attack once the Allies had landed with close encounters to mix in and break up the seaward assault. With this deployment Rommel hoped to avoid being blasted by Allied destroyers firing at point-blank range as previously occurred at the Sicily and Salerno landings. It would be on that "longest day" that the battle would be decided.[7]

Hitler saw advantages in both strategic plans. He kept vacillating, and his lack of decision ultimately doomed the German defense.

Rommel's worst critic was not Rundstedt but Field Marshal Leo Geyr von Schweppenburg. He was appointed commander of Panzer Troops West in July 1943. His command was positioned near Paris for a potential large-scale counterattack in either Normandy or Pas-de-Calais. Geyr advocated large-scale counterattacks in divisional strength, not Rommel's battle group tactics. Commit the panzers in mass was his guiding principle. Allied air power might delay movement but not stop them. Properly trained units under aggressive officers will arrive in time at the right location to drive the Allies back.[8]

Rommel knew that control of the armored and motorized units during the critical twenty-four hours after the landings was vital. Northern France had relatively few roads, and many rivers and bridges offered inviting targets for Allied air interdiction. The days of the German Blitzkrieg were over. Geyr, Rundstedt, and the other German commanders learned to regret their failure to support Rommel's strategy.

Part of their opposition stemmed from the fact that Geyr and Rundstedt were aristocrats with long family military lineages. Rommel was only a commoner, from a family of schoolteachers. Rundstedt also believed Rommel was overrated, one of "Hitler's officers" who had been overpromoted by the Nazi propaganda machine.[9]

This continuing controversy came to a head on March 19, 1944, when Hitler ordered his generals to attend a conference at his Eagle's Nest mountaintop hideaway in Obersalzberg. It was preceded by a dramatic procession of field marshals and generals with Erwin Rommel and Gerd von Rundstedt arriving in a 2.3 liter Mercedes-Benz Cabriolet 230 Open Horch command car.

Hitler greeted each commander individually and then ushered them all into lunch. Afterward, over Arabian coffee shipped in at great risk by submarine through the British-held straits of Gibraltar, he began his strategy review.

Hitler had long shared these generals' opinions that the Allies would land in the Pas-de-Calais sector. Now, without any warning, he changed his view, stating that they were all captives of rigid Clausewitzian military theory. In a prediction that proved amazingly accurate, Hitler contended that the Allied real targets "are the two peninsulas, Brittany and the Cotentin [in Normandy]."[10] These would be the invasion sites since they provided "the best possibilities" for successful bridgeheads serving as a base for their offensive drive through France into Germany.

The Cotentin Peninsula was the probable first choice. The Normandy beaches and hinterlands were more suitable than Brittany's harsher landscape. They would offer a shorter route for the Allied offensive thrust into Germany's industrial Ruhr. Hitler appeared to be siding with Rommel's views when he concluded that wherever the Allies invaded, destroying the landing would be the sole decisive factor in the whole conduct of the war and hence the war's final result.[11]

Rommel must have been delighted by what he heard, and he again asked that the armored divisions be placed under his command. At first Hitler agreed. Then twenty-four hours later after a protest from Rundstedt, Hitler reversed himself. On March 21 as a compromise, he transferred only three panzer divisions, the Second, Twenty-First, and Sixteenth, to Rommel's Army Group B as a mobile reserve. Four other divisions, the First SS, Twelfth SS Panzers, Seventeenth SS Panzer Grenadier, and Panzer Lehr, were placed under the direct control of OKW as a central mobile reserve to be released only by Hitler. No one was satisfied by Hitler's "compromise."

By April only the Twenty-First Panzer Division had been shifted to the Normandy sector near Caen. Rommel increasingly suspected that the invasion would land in Normandy, at least as a diversion. On May 6 he again requested the release of more panzer divisions but was refused by Rundstedt and OKW. Hitler had thrown away his best chance for victory in the West.[12]

## HITLER'S NORMANDY LEGIONS

On a promontory high up over the River Seine stands the Chateau de La Roche-Guyon and its pretty local village. Here Rommel made his headquarters. Nearby at Giverny, Monet had painted his numerous studies of water lilies. Forty miles from Paris, the chateau was centrally located between Pas-de-Calais and Normandy. It was the ancestral home of the Rochefoucauld family, and to maintain cordial relations, Rommel allowed the duke and his family to continue occupying their private quarters. Thomas Jefferson had been a guest there when he was the US ambassador to France.

Tunnels were cut in nearby cliffs to accommodate his officers and staff. Rommel's rooms looked out on a rose garden, where after a hard day inspecting invasion defenses, he strolled with his chief of staff, Lieutenant General Hans Speidel. Rommel liked being in France. He appreciated its wine, food, people, and scenery. But he was not oblivious to the mood of occupied France as he observed, "What hatred there is against us."[13]

Rommel also could not ignore the sad state of the Wehrmacht in France. On paper the German army in Western Europe numbered 1,500,000 men, including naval and air force units. The army units totaled 850,000 soldiers—fifty-eight combat divisions, including thirty-three static, reserve, or training divisions (ten thousand men). Most had no transport or mobile artillery. They were assigned mainly to provide coastal defense. For years France had been used by the Wehrmacht as a rest and refitting area mainly for divisions recovering from service on the Russian front. Here they could be reequipped and trained. Some divisions included "ear and stomach battalions" composed of older soldiers who had lost their hearing or men recovering from stomach wounds. Many of these German infantry divisions were either older or younger than the norm. The average age in the 709th division was about thirty-six. Heinrich Boll, an NCO in the 348th Infantry Division, wrote, "It is really sad to see these children's faces in grey uniforms."[14]

A group of twelve first-class infantry divisions were also deployed along the coast. By 1944 these stronger divisions had almost thirteen thousand men. (American infantry divisions contained over fourteen thousand troops). Unlike most of the British and American formations, all of these static and first-class infantry units were staffed with a high proportion of combat-experienced officers and NCOs. They had been tested on the battlefield and readily passed on their knowledge and practical fighting skills to many of these inexperienced soldiers.[15]

There were two different types of Luftwaffe ground units. Parachute divisions (sixteen thousand men) were volunteer infantry units of high quality. Luftwaffe field divisions (12,500 men) were surplus personnel from antiaircraft, signal, maintenance, or administrative units that were weaker than regular infantry.[16]

There was also significant variation in the makeup of the German armored units. In June 1944 nine panzer divisions were in Normandy with two additional on temporary detachment to the eastern front. However, even these divisions were not uniform in tank numbers or troop strengths and quality. They ranged from the 21,386 men in the First SS Panzer, down to the Ninth Panzer with only 12,768. The Seventeenth SS was a panzer/grenadier formation (fourteen thousand men), which meant it had half-tracks but no tanks and only one armored battalion equipped with assault guns. The 116th, Twenty-First, Second, Ninth, and Eleventh Panzer Divisions' tank strength was less than a hundred, about half of British or American equivalents.[17]

On the other hand, the Panzer Lehr Division was manned by soldiers taken from the German armored training schools. They had the best equipment with tank and troop numbers at full strength. The quality and motivation of personnel were very high. General Fritz Bayerlein, an officer from Rommel's Afrika Korps, was in command. He was told, "With this division on its own you must throw the Allies into the sea. Your objective is the coast, no, not the coast—it is the sea."[18]

The same high quality of equipment and men were to be found in the First, Second, and Twelfth SS Panzer Divisions. The best recruits were placed in the SS panzer corps. Bayerlein observed, "No good replacements were ever sent to the infantry divisions."[19]

The SS panzer divisions were larger than their Allied counterparts. The First SS Panzer (Leibstandarte Adolf Hitler) was twice as large. But as noted earlier, they too had fewer tanks than the Allied formation. These SS units were composed of six motorized or mechanized infantry battalions, in contrast to only four in the Wehrmacht's armored divisions. This made all of these SS units larger than their army equivalents.[20]

By June 6, 1944, the Germans had deployed fifty-eight divisions spread from Norway to the Mediterranean to defend Hitler's Atlantic Wall. (See Map 4.) When the invasion came, most were in the wrong place.

The brunt of the attack was borne by the Seventh Army of Colonel General Friedrich Dollmann and portions of the Fifteenth Army, Army Group B commanded by Rommel. The German forces that were available included four coast-defense divisions manning fortifications, two infantry divisions, the garrison of Cherbourg, and three panzer divisions in reserve, only one being adjacent to the coast.

About 20 percent of the troops in the Seventh Army were foreign volunteers—Osttruppen. Many had volunteered for the Wehrmacht to escape starvation or disease in German slave labor camps. They included Poles, White Russians, East Indians, Ukrainians, Cossacks, and Hungarians. There was even a contingent of Korean soldiers whose unbelievable odyssey included being forcibly conscripted—captured—and recruited again and again by the Japanese, Russian, and German armies, before finally surrendering to the Americans on D-Day. The German officers and NCOs who commanded these units feared being shot in the back once the invasion began. Some of these Osttruppen deserted to the French resistance. While many surrendered early in the invasion, some of these foreign units fought well during the entire Normandy campaign.[21]

The Twenty-First Panzer Division was close to the British beaches near Caen. It tried to stop the British advance with lighter Mark IV tanks, instead of the larger gunned and heavily armored Panther or Tiger tanks. Many of its soldiers were "foreign volunteers" who could hardly understand orders in German or respond in kind to their NCOs and officers.

To resist Allied airborne assaults, the Germans positioned the Ninety-First Air Landing Division and Sixth Parachute Regiment on the Cotentin Peninsula behind the beaches assigned to the Americans, code-named Utah and Omaha.[22] In the Allied landing zones General Marcks's LXXXIV Corps deployed two third-rate coastal divisions, the 716th and 709th.

On March 15 Rommel was able to order the first-class 352nd Infantry Division stationed in St. Lo to the coast. They took over the defense of a thirty-mile coastal sector. In its center were the American invasion beaches. Luckily for the US troops, the German division commander, General Dietrich Kraiss, positioned only one artillery battalion and two infantry battalions on Omaha Beach. He then deployed a large reserve battalion twelve miles inland.

In May Rommel visited the 352nd Division and was not pleased with what he saw. He criticized Kraiss for dispersing his troops over a wide front and not placing enough troops in the most threatened shoreline sector in order to enable them to concentrate their fire on the landing zones.

As Kraiss was not one of Rommel's disciples, he refused to redeploy his division and instead straddled the front. If he had supported Rommel's tactical ideas, Kraiss would have placed a greater concentration of men on Omaha Beach and moved the division's reserves closer to the coast. Had he done so, D-Day might have turned out very differently.[23]

Not only were many of Rommel's units badly positioned, but also overall Hitler's forces in France were poorly armed to resist the invasion. The Seventh Army's equipment made it a largely make-do outfit. A hodgepodge of captured enemy equipment tanks, trucks, and artillery led to severe spare parts shortages. All the German units lacked sufficient antitank guns and self-propelled assault guns. Even proper caliber ammunition and artillery shells were in short supply.

Moreover, fuel shortages limited the mobilization of the few German motorized vehicles. Regimental commanders used their cars once a week. To make the Seventh Army more mobile, troops were given bicycles. French vehicles with French drivers proved unreliable since the Frenchmen often vanished during air raids.[24]

Only the German ground forces were somewhat competitive with the forces landed by the Allies. On June 1, 1944, the entire Luftwaffe Third Air Fleet in France had only ninety bombers and seventy fighter aircraft. The German air force in Western Europe on D-Day could only muster three hundred planes. The day of the invasion the Allied pilots flew 14,674 sorties, the Germans about 319. Few soldiers knew the situation was so bad. Walter Schwender, a German soldier in an army repair shop, recalled, "We often discussed the Allied landing. . . . We genuinely believed . . . that we were strong, we would throw them out in no time. But then we also thought there were several thousand German aircraft ready to come and give us support. We firmly believed that."[25]

The German Kriegsmarine's Navy Group West was too weak to stop the Allied cross-channel attack. Its fleet was composed of twenty destroyers, fifty to sixty E-boats (a motor torpedo boat), and twenty-five to thirty minesweepers and submarines. Grand Admiral Donitz, commander in chief of the German navy, had E-boats in France, but only thirty-five ready to sail. He realized that the entire German naval force could inflict "only fleabites" on the Allied invaders.[26]

## THE "ZONE OF DEATH"

In early 1944 when Rommel took command, the Atlantic Wall was more myth than reality. Even if the proposed fifteen thousand strongpoints had been built, there would not be a continuous line of fortifications across the three thousand mile coastline. The major ports had been fortified, but Rommel found that the Normandy coast was practically naked. Defenses were almost as bad everywhere else. A shortage of construction materials and the lack of a determined leadership with an overall vision undermined its effectiveness as a defensive system.

The 850,000 German soldiers guarding the Atlantic Wall were insufficient to the task. During World War II a division could successfully defend about six miles of frontage against a determined attacker. Rommel's proposed solutions to these multiple defensive shortcomings were elaborate defensive obstacles and extensive minefields of considerable depth. His orders included his own sketches for the design of these new defenses. Rommel's orders included the following:

> Between . . . strong points . . . and resistance nests, minefields of great depth will be laid. . . . The enemy . . . will have to fight his way through the zone of death . . . not only on the coast . . . [but also through] numerous and extensive minefields . . . in the rear areas. . . . Any airborne troops who attempt to penetrate to the coast from the rear will make the acquaintance of this mined zone.[27]

On January 13 Rommel initiated a plan calling for two million mines to be laid each month. Ultimately he wanted a mine every ten yards inland, requiring a minimum of twenty million mines. Because the Nazi Organization Todt was overwhelmed with port fortifications and repair of railroads bombed by the Allies, Rommel put his own soldiers to work laying these minefields as well as numerous barriers, obstacles, and antitank devices. Yet by May 20, 1944, only 4,193,167 mines had been put into place to defend the coast.[28]

Rommel also called upon the German navy to construct extensive naval minefields in the English Channel. However, little was done to expand the extent of the minefields in 1944. The Kriegsmarine had too few vessels to successfully mine the potential invasion routes.

The German defense was based on the expectation that the Allies would land at high tide. At high tide the Allied soldiers would have only a short stretch of beach to traverse. The alternative low tide landing exposed the soldiers up to a seven-hundred-yard dash across an open beach. German machine guns sited above the beach had interlocking zones of fire to cut them down.

With this in mind Rommel devised an ingenious dense belt of gruesome beach obstacles designed to rip the landing craft to shreds. It was an expanded version of the defensive works that he had deployed at El Alamein.

Fig. 5.3. German beach defenses, Pas-de-Calais. (Bundesarchiv, Bild 101I-719-0240-05/photo: Jesse)

The simplest beach obstacle placed for high tide was the "Czech hedgehog" or "horned scully." This was built with three steel or wooden four/five-foot-long rails, welded together at crazy angles and primed with mines or shells. These hedgehogs were taken from the Germans' West Wall bordering France and hauled to the beaches.

The low tide obstacles were also formidable. The so-called "Belgian Gates" were about seven by ten feet in dimension. Similar to large wire gates, they were supported by steel girders and topped with mines to lethally ensnare landing craft. Additional obstacles included "dragons-teeth"—four-foot-high concrete pyramids draped with barbed wire, and thousands of sharpened wooden stakes covered with mines. By the middle of May, more than 500,000 of these deadly passive defenses were imbedded across all the beaches, but only thirty-one thousand were attached to mines.[29]

Then came the actual fortifications. Spaced along the coast about one mile apart were steel-reinforced concrete bunkers equipped with hidden machine-gun posts and anti-tank guns. Between these fortified positions were machine-gun and flamethrower positions to sweep the beaches with a hail of shot and fire. Rommel had many of these positions reengineered to offer troops significant protection from aircraft and naval gunfire. Spaced farther apart were larger bombproof artillery bunkers able to cover many miles of open beach. Behind all of these fortifications were large-caliber coastal artillery batteries housed in bombproof bunkers capable of shelling Allied ships up to ten miles off the coast. He also ordered the beaches to be floodlit by searchlights to dazzle the enemy if they landed at dawn or at night.

Fig. 5.4. Bombproof artillery bunker on the German Atlantic Wall. (Wikimedia Creative Commons, author: Jebulon)

The Germans erected anti-paratroop defenses behind the fortified zone. "Rommel's asparagus" were anti-glider poles that were combined with other obstructions and minefields to disrupt landing sites. Rommel ordered these stakes to be fitted with artillery shells and interconnected by trip wires. A few days before D-Day he obtained a million captured shells, but they were not installed at the time of the invasion.

Rommel used deception to confuse the Allies about his real strength. False orders regarding troop dispositions were passed on to French railway officials. The Germans established dummy headquarters and moved advance personnel around the countryside. Fake gun positions and dummy railheads were built. Motor transport was moved around by day and night to confuse the enemy.

Rommel also flooded the low tidal marshlands behind Utah Beach. German engineers dammed rivers and streams, thus turning river valleys into lakes and swamps. Though most of these water obstacles were shallow, paratroopers overloaded with equipment could easily drown.

Even though shortages of manpower and equipment prevented Rommel from completing all the planned components of the Atlantic Wall, the Allied invasion forces faced a formidable combination of defenses. However, Hitler's vaunted Festung Europa or Fortress Europe was not impregnable.[30]

## INVASION CONFUSION

By the end of May 1944, the Allied FORTITUDE deception plan had succeeded in convincing the intelligence service of German high command West that the Allies had eighty-nine divisions in the British Isles and there were enough landing craft for twenty divisions to land in the invasion's first wave. The real numbers were forty-seven and six, respectively.[31]

FORTITUDE also had succeeded in deceiving the German high command into believing that Pas-de-Calais was the probable invasion site. Because of this Rommel concentrated more of his available units around Calais, though he also wanted to reinforce Normandy.

In late May, Hiroski Oshina, imperial Japan's ambassador to Germany, visited Hitler at the Eagle's Nest in Berchtesgaden. He asked Hitler where the Allies would attempt their invasion. The führer told the ambassador that the Allies had assembled "about 80 divisions in the British Isles." First they would invade in Normandy and Brittany. Then having attracted the German forces, "they will come forward with an all-out second front across the straits of Dover."[32] The Japanese radioed Hitler's predictions back to Tokyo. The Americans intercepted and decrypted the information.

By D-Day German troop strength in the most threatened sectors revealed the degree of FORTITUDE's overall success. The Fifteenth Army at Pas-de-Calais had grown to eighteen infantry and two panzer divisions. It had an interlocking fixed defense system, making it a true fortified zone. In contrast, the Seventh Army in Normandy and Brittany had fourteen infantry divisions and a single panzer division. Normandy was defended by a limited network of isolated, weakly manned strongpoints. The Twenty-First Panzer Division was its sole mobile reserve partially equipped with the French tanks captured in 1940.[33]

## THE PIGEON SHOOT

Carrier pigeons played an important role in Allied intelligence. They were fitted with tiny metal capsules in which coded messages on tiny pieces of ultra-thin rice paper were inserted. They carried French underground messages disclosing the locations of German fortifications and army units to the British Intelligence Service.[34]

The Germans knew that these pigeons were used for communications. Pigeon shooting was a favorite sport of German military personnel along the entire length of northern France in 1944. While thousands of Allied homing pigeons made it safely back to their roosts along the English coast, some did not. In the spring of 1944 sharpshooters in the 352nd Infantry Division bagged twenty-seven carrier pigeons in April and May before D-Day. As a result, Allied intelligence failed to learn about the 352nd Division's relocation to the coast. Thus when the Americans landed on Omaha Beach, they were surprised to find that the original second-rate defenders of the 716th Division had been reinforced by the battle-hardened veterans of the 352nd.[35]

## JUNE 4–5, THE ULTIMATE DECEPTION

On June 4 and June 5, a strong storm blew in over the English Channel and northern France. Unlike the Allies, the Germans had no meteorological stations in the western Atlantic. Their attempts to establish such facilities along the coast of southern Greenland had been terminated by Allied naval force raids in 1943.

Allied air and naval superiority frustrated German attempts to penetrate invasion preparations. During the first five days of June, the Germans gained no information from their reconnaissance sources. On June 4 German naval headquarters reported, "The enemy has [not] yet assembled his invasion fleet in the required strength" for landings.[36]

On June 5 a total of five German reconnaissance flights searched the English Channel. They found nothing. German Navy Group West reported, "Rough sea, poor visibility, Force 5–6 wind, rain likely to get heavier. . . . There is little prospect of short-term changes in the weather during the next few days."[37] The navy canceled its channel patrols for the night of June 5.

On that day Rundstedt's Paris headquarters told all German field commands, "There is no immediate prospect of the invasion."[38] As a result many German officers were not in Normandy on D-Day. Instead they had left their posts for army war games scheduled on June 6, 1944.[39]

## ROMMEL'S BIRTHDAY SURPRISE

By early June the strain of endless daily inspections and anticipation of a battle that could break out at any moment was taking its toll on the Desert Fox. Rommel wrote his wife that he was thinking about a surprise visit for her fiftieth birthday on June 6. The field marshal was even more focused on an important meeting with Hitler to ask for panzer reinforcements in Normandy.

Rommel noted in his diary that "fears of an invasion" between June 5 and June 8 were rendered less because the tides were "very unfavorable" (he expected the Allies at high tide) and that Germany's reconnaissance had not given "the slightest indication that a landing was imminent." After getting Rundstedt's approval for the trip, he telephoned Hitler's assistant for an appointment on June 7.[40]

At 7:00 a.m. on June 5, Rommel headed for his hometown of Herrlingen near Ulm in southwestern Germany (an eight- to ten-hour trip by car) to celebrate his wife's birthday on June 6, bringing a pair of fine leather shoes he bought in Paris for her. The next day he would drive to Berchtesgaden and press his requests for two panzer divisions, the Second SS and the Ninth Panzer, to be moved south and west of Caen where they could readily intervene in the first twenty-four hours of a landing in Normandy. Rommel was confident he would get them.

On May 1, Hitler's headquarters (OKW) had called Rommel at Chateau de La Roche-Guyon and spoken to General Speidel, his chief of staff. They wanted to know if the forces in Normandy could definitely defeat an Allied attack. Without waiting for a reply, the next day Hitler moved the Ninety-First Luftwaffe Airborne Division and several anti-tank and armored battalions into the Normandy region as reinforcements.[41]

A week later Hitler sent Rommel an urgent telex warning him to expect an Allied landing "in the middle May . . . point of concentration: first and foremost, Normandy."[42] On the evening of May 15, a skeptical Rommel called General Alfred Jodl, Hitler's chief of staff, to find out the source of Hitler's invasion warning. Jodl did not know. After the war, a search of German archives and German staff interrogations failed to reveal the source of Hitler's accurate invasion assessment.

Because Rommel's query was not answered, on May 17 he decided to make another inspection of the Cotentin Peninsula with his naval aide, Admiral Friederich Oskar Ruge. Ruge recalled that Rommel stood for a long time on what would soon be Utah Beach staring out to sea.

> "So," he asked Ruge, "this is where you think they'll land?"
>
> Ruge as a sailor told Rommel that the Cotentin land mass helped shelter those waters from the Channel's winds.
>
> "No," Rommel insisted, "they will come where their fighter planes will be closest to their bases."[43]

But Rommel took no chances. It was then he decided to make his June 5 to June 7 trip. Hitler recently had once again declined his pleas for more panzers in Normandy. But now Normandy had become Hitler's new invasion fixation. As the führer's favorite field marshal, Rommel was confident that a private meeting with Hitler would net him the two panzer divisions for Normandy. He had telephoned Hitler nearly every day.

By June 20 Rommel planned to position this armor behind what soon became the five Allied invasion beaches. With the additional tank divisions and the Twenty-First Panzer near Caen, Rommel believed that in two more weeks Normandy would be impregnable. Unfortunately for Germany, they would be two weeks too late.[44]

In yet another uncanny invasion prediction, Rommel was proven correct. On one of his numerous inspection tours, he told a group of his soldiers in Normandy, "Do not look for the enemy by daylight when the sun is shining. They will come at night in cloud and storm."[45]

## HITLER'S LUCK ENDS

The Germans were unlucky in Normandy. They were tricked by Operation FORTITUDE, deceived by the weather, and handicapped by the führer's inane command system. Even though the Germans had years to prepare, they lacked the well-equipped and well-trained army, navy, and air force units needed to decisively defeat an Allied invasion. Hitler also subverted any unified defensive/offensive strategy, thus adding confusion to Germany's preparations. Unlike the earlier days of World War II, Hitler's luck had ended. D-Day would take the Germans completely by surprise. The time, day, and place were almost totally unexpected.[46]

We have examined both the offensive and defensive preparations for the invasion of northwestern Europe. Yet the actual battlefield operations seldom take place as planned. June 6, 1944, proved to be no exception.

## CHAPTER 6

# THE "LONGEST DAY" COMES UP SHORT

"The challenge is not to fight to survive, but to fight to win the final victory."

—George VI[1]

After Eisenhower issued the go-ahead invasion order on June 5 at 5:00 a.m., four hours later Rear Admiral A. G. Talbot pulled the cork out of the D-Day invasion bottle when he had his ship's flag signal "Good luck: drive on."[2] Admiral Ramsay issued his "Special Order of the Day" as commander in chief of the world's largest expeditionary force: "I count on every man to do his utmost to ensure the success of this great enterprise which is the climax of the European war. Good luck to you all and God speed."[3]

For the rest of that day a teeming mass of assorted shipping in the rivers and bays of southern England gradually formed into the NEPTUNE armada. All five lead invasion forces rendezvoused slightly south of the Isle of Wight (Area ZEBRA). This congested mass of ships became known as "Piccadilly Circus," after London's perpetually snarled traffic crossroad. Each flotilla split off to its landing beach preceded by minesweepers and flanked by destroyers. Ships of all classes stretched from horizon to horizon. The different assault and bombarding units sorted themselves out and sailed in due course according to Ramsay's detailed NEPTUNE orders. Follow-up waves and reinforcements sailed afterward.

The storm that had almost canceled the June 6 D-Day became a blessing in disguise. The Allies had always believed that the invasion fleet would be discovered by the Germans midway to its destination. Instead the bad weather covered the fleet's presence from detection. Ramsay's greatest concern, a mass attack on the NEPTUNE fleet, never happened. Allied naval and air support effectively protected the fleet.

A few ships' mechanicals failed; others had engine problems. Some experienced fuel problems or water leaks. These returned to England. But only one D-Day ship was lost crossing the channel that night.

While the NEPTUNE invasion fleet peacefully proceeded into position off the Normandy coast, Operation FORTITUDE launched its own diversionary fleet toward Pas-de-Calais. Two small flotillas of British motor boats headed across the channel. Each boat towed two twenty-nine-foot-long balloons as part of a massive Allied electronic conjuring trick. One balloon sailed overhead while the other one was tethered to a raft. The nine-foot reflector attached to each of these balloons sent out a misleading radar echo of a ten-thousand-ton troop ship. In the skies overhead, Royal Air Force (RAF) bomber squadrons dropped thousands of aluminum foil strips to simulate hundreds of aircraft on German radar screens.[4]

The subterfuge worked as German radar stations began reporting a massive air and sea armada heading for Pas-de-Calais. Most of the small number of Luftwaffe fighters available headed northward, clearing the air space over Normandy for the Allies.

## "SAY HELLO TO FRANCE!"

Around 1:00 a.m. on June 6 thousands of soldiers on troop transports looked skyward at the more than 1,200 aircraft on their way to Normandy. These C-47 transport planes, many towing gliders, were filled with over twenty thousand British and American paratroopers. It was their first combat-mission drop for most of the C-47 pilots based in England. The Eighty-Second and 101st US Airborne Divisions dropped their men on the west end of the invasion zone behind Utah Beach; the British Sixth Airborne Division parachuted behind Sword Beach on the east end. (See Map 5.) These troops were to isolate the beach landings and prevent German reinforcements from launching a successful counterattack. June 6, 1944, was the 1,453rd day of the German occupation of France.[5]

Soon after 1:00 a.m. an American captain standing in an open air transport door saw the surf hitting the Normandy beaches. He shouted to his paratroopers, "Say hello to France!"[6] This was the start of the most carefully chronicled day in the history of warfare.

Low clouds swallowed the incoming airborne fleet, and German antiaircraft fire scrambled the formations. Only 4 percent of the Eighty-Second landed in their target zones. They would fail to secure all the causeway bridges leading to the beaches. Only 1,000 men out of 6,400 of the 101st landed near their objectives. Many parachutists landed in flooded fields. Encumbered by their heavy equipment, they sank in the mud and water, and many drowned. However the 101st was able to stop the Germans from counterattacking during the beach landing.[7]

Brigadier General James M. Gavin, assistant division commander of the Eighty-Second, successfully mustered one thousand troops near the target of St. Mère-Église. Unfortunately one of his regiments (505th) landed right on top of the village. They were shot out of the sky by the Germans. Garvin rallied his remaining forces for the attack that by dawn made St. Mère-Église the first town in France to be liberated by the Allies. The Germans, however, still shelled the town for two days, killing many inhabitants.

Gliders with additional men and heavy equipment made crash landings that were more chaotic than the initial paratroop drops. However despite the scattering of these units, the US airborne achieved most of their night and early D-Day morning objectives. At dawn 816 planes and 100 gliders had placed 13,000 Americans into Normandy. Only twenty-one aircraft were shot down, so few that Leigh-Mallory sent a written apology to Eisenhower for his earlier prediction of disaster.[8]

Meanwhile to the east, the British Sixth Airborne Division was hampered by landing at night in the wind and rain. The fact that most succeeded is in itself a miracle. The British paratroopers' objectives were to either seize or destroy bridges over the Orne and Dives Rivers in a five-mile area in order to shield the beach landings from German panzer attacks emanating from around the city of Caen. (See Map 5.)

High winds blew a number of these gliders off course and landed many parachutists up to seven miles from their targets. They were the lucky ones. The tow ropes of some gliders snapped in the gale, causing them to founder in the channel.

An important objective was the Caen Canal Bridge—code-named

Pegasus Bridge. One of the British gliders landed with its nose inside the bridge's barbed wire defenses due to poor visibility. The single German sentry on duty thought it was a bomber crash landing. Paratroopers jumped out of the wreck, and in three minutes the British had taken the vital bridge. Five other bridges were also taken or blown up, thereby stopping effective German counterattacks.

The Sixth Airborne also targeted the Merville coastal battery. Its two artillery pieces and ten heavy machine guns threatened the British invasion beaches and Allied fleet. One hundred Lancaster heavy bombers attacked the battery on the night of June 5, causing little damage. A naval bombardment was scheduled for 5:15 a.m. on June 6 in a forlorn hope to silence the guns.

The Ninth Parachute Battalion commanded by Lieutenant Colonel Terence Otway was to be dropped nearby at 12:50 a.m. If these troops succeeded in silencing the battery, he was to signal the fleet. His men were badly scattered by heavy antiaircraft fire. By 2:30 a.m. he had only 150 out of 650 men at the assembly point. With only one hour to spare, Otway's men infiltrated the German defenses and poured machine-gun fire through the artillery embrasures. The Germans surrendered only fifteen minutes before the fleet bombardment was to begin.[9]

At the same time that the Anglo-American paratroops hit the ground, a pair of RAF Stirling bombers began Operation TITANIC, dropping two hundred dummy paratroopers at St. Valéry in the upper Normandy toward Pas-de-Calais and other locations. These rubber "Rupert" dolls were intended to simulate large-scale parachute drops, thus deflecting German forces away from the genuine airborne operations in Normandy. When the Ruperts' parachutes opened, firecrackers began exploding in midair like gunfire. Also Special Air Service Brigades of the British army, equipped with special gramophones that played bursts of small-arms fire mixed with soldiers giving orders and battle cries, were dropped along with the Ruperts.[10]

There is little doubt they helped add confusion to the enemy's response that night. German general Max Pemsel, Seventh Army chief of staff, sent an entire brigade in a futile search for these bogus paratroopers.

## GERMAN WAKE-UP CALL

Because the Allied airborne landings were scattered and chaotic, the Germans were almost totally confused about what was happening. The paratroopers spread more chaos by disrupting German communications. Telegraph poles were blown up, telephone cables cut. German units became isolated from their command posts. The unintended dispersal of the three airborne divisions actually led to the Germans becoming more mystified about the Allied targets and wider mission.

The Allied airborne troops on the ground outnumbered the Germans two to one. Along with the massive air operations, they helped overawe many of the inexperienced German defenders.

German military intelligence, the Abwehr, had learned of the coded radio messages that the Allies would broadcast signaling the French underground to begin widespread covert action supporting the D-Day landings. When the Abwehr heard the messages before midnight, they informed the Wehrmacht high command in the West that the invasion was imminent. Unbelievably Rundstedt and most other senior commanders discounted this action as only Allied disinformation. Ironically only in Pas-de-Calais did its Fifteenth Army commander respond by placing his forces on high alert. No one in Normandy was notified.

The absence of so many senior German commanders from their headquarters only added to the night's confusion. Rommel had left for Germany. General Friedrich Dollmann, commander of the Seventh Army, was at the war game in Rennes. General Fritz Bayerlein, commander of the crack Panzer Lehr Division, was with his mistress in Paris. General Edgar Feuchtinger, commanding the key-positioned Twenty-First Panzer near Caen, was believed to be somewhere incommunicado with female company. Both Rundstedt in Paris and Hitler at Berchtesgaden were asleep.[11]

However, General Erich Marcks, commander of the LXXXIV corps in Normandy, did respond quickly to the events in the early hours of June 6. At midnight several of his officers at his St. Lo command post gave Marcks a surprise party for his fifty-third birthday (June 5). After a glass of Chablis and a short celebration, Marcks and his officers began receiving scattered and fragmented reports that led them to conclude that something serious was afoot. Ironically, on June 5 Marcks had participated in a war game at his headquarters. He had taken the role of Eisenhower and had launched his "attack" into Normandy.

At 12:40 a.m. on June 6 elements of the German 242nd Infantry Division clashed with enemy paratroopers of the US Eighty-Second Airborne north of St. Mère-Église at Mountebourg. (See Map 5.) A few minutes later Marcks learned that British parachute units had seized the Caen Canal crossing at Bénouville and blew up the bridge over the Dives river. At about 1:45 a.m. Marcks was informed that the 711th Infantry Division near Cabourg had made enemy contact. Major General Josef Reichert had been playing cards with his staff members when two British paratroopers landed on the front lawn of his headquarters and were taken prisoner by the Germans. Reichert concluded that the Allies were about to land on the Cotentin Peninsula and the paratroops were designed to secure the far eastern flank of the seaborne assault.[12]

Other reports flooded into Marcks's command post. All this news convinced him to put the LXXXIV Corps and the Twenty-First Panzer on immediate top alert. Marcks then called General Max Pemsel, Dollmann's chief of staff, and told him that he believed the Allied invasion was definitely in progress. This was shortly after 2:00 a.m. on June 6.

Since his commander was absent, Pemsel immediately placed the Seventh Army (which had one panzer, two fully equipped infantry, and three static infantry divisions) on the highest state of alert and telephoned Rommel's chief of staff, General Hans Speidel, at La Roche-Guyon at 2:15 a.m. Pemsel repeatedly insisted throughout the night that a major invasion was taking place. Speidel then called Rundstedt to pass along Pemsel's conclusions. As both Rundstedt and Speidel were still convinced that the real invasion was to be at Pas-de-Calais, they believed that the paratroop landings were a diversionary attack to take attention away from the Fifteenth Army at Pas-de-Calais. To satisfy Marcks, they did take the Ninety-First Air Landing Division and mobile units of the 709th Infantry out of reserves to counterattack the American paratroopers in the western Cotentin Peninsula.[13]

As reports increased during these early-morning hours, Rundstedt's suspicions grew. He telephoned Rommel, who was at his home. Afterward Rommel spoke to Speidel and told him to ready a counterattack by the Twenty-First Panzer and concentrate all the divisional area reserves under one command. Then at 10:30 a.m. Rommel left to race back to France.

At 3:00 a.m. on June 6 Rundstedt ordered the highest state of alert for Army Group B. As a safety precaution he also requested that OKW release the Twelfth SS Panzer and Panzer Lehr Divisions to move them into Normandy. The request was rejected by General Jodl, Hitler's chief of staff, because the führer was sleeping, and no one dared disturb him to seek this permission.[14]

At 4:00 a.m. German major general Dietrich Kraiss, commanding the 352nd Division covering what would shortly become Omaha Beach, made a major blunder. He sent his reserve regiment on bicycles in pursuit of paratroopers who were in reality only Rupert dummies. This soon proved to be a costly error.

If Rommel had been in Normandy, he might have succeeded in persuading Hitler to release the panzers. Certainly he would have galvanized the senior staff officers to react more vigorously in mobilizing the local units. As Rommel had predicted in his diary, the Wehrmacht's muddled response showed the fatal cracks in this vaunted military machine. "Failing a tight command in one single hand of all the forces . . . victory will be in great doubt."[15] Without the panzers in the strategic reserve, only the coastal forces' stubborn defense stood between the Allied invaders and establishing a successful lodgment in France.

In the early-morning light of June 6, a German artillery officer behind Sword Beach gazed seaward through his binoculars. He was startled to see the horizon filling up with hundreds of ships. He later recalled, "It was an unforgettable sight. I had never seen anything so well organized and disciplined. We watched, absolutely petrified, as the armada steadily and relentlessly approached."[16]

## THE CURTAIN RISES

Spanning an unprecedented length of fifty-five miles, the Allied fleet appeared off the Normandy coast. On the far western zone was the beach at the base of the Cotentin Peninsula code-named Utah. Ten miles to the east was Omaha Beach, west of the Norman capital of Bayeux. To the east of Bayeux were the British and Canadian beaches of Gold and Juno. The British beach Sword lay due north of the key crossroad city of Caen. (See Map 5.) An infantry division was to land on each of these five beaches.

The Normandy beaches have a very gradual rise. But tides greatly vary between eighteen to twenty-four feet. This means the width of the beaches has a great range between high and low tides. To avoid Rommel's numerous beach booby traps, Montgomery made the decision to land at low tide. Navy Combat Demolition Units were to clear pathways before the second and third waves came ashore.

Due to these tidal conditions the Americans landed before the British by sixty to eighty minutes. The attack was scheduled to begin two hours after low tide (6:30 a.m.).

Timing was a significant factor for the air and naval bombardment of German defenses in Normandy. Neither the Royal Air Force (RAF) nor the US Army Air Force would commit to either the size or timing of their D-Day bombing operations until shortly before June 6. Their lack of cooperation with SHAEF only added to OVERLORD's uncertainties.

At midnight before the landing began, over one thousand aircraft from British Bomber Command shattered the Germans' sleep. This was the beginning of five thousand tons of bombs, aimed over the next five hours on ten major German gun batteries.[17] This did not alert the enemy to the invasion since the Allies had been bombing all along the coast of France for many months.

Almost the entire US bomber fleet next took to the skies. Over 1,600 B-26 Marauders and more than 1,300 B-17 Flying Fortresses and B-24 Liberators appeared in a thunderous pathway ten miles across. "We went to bed about 11:30 p.m. on June 5," recalled Glen Wiesner, a B-17 copilot. "Fifteen minutes later, the lights went on and a loud voice boomed, 'Everybody up! Everybody flies today!'" This was the big day! "Crossing the English Channel . . . we could see that fantastic sight of the many, many vessels. . . . We were timed to bomb the enemy shortly before our troops hit the beach." They dropped their bomb load just before 6:00 a.m.[18]

Casey Hasey, a B-26 squadron bombardier, attacked the long-range gun emplacement at St. Martin de Varreville minutes before the American landings. (See Map 5.) These guns had a range of up to twenty miles. Hasey remembered, "I zeroed in on those barrels sticking out of the concrete . . . the concussions I felt were strong, and heavy and scary . . . I couldn't believe it. Not a shot was fired at us. Our suicide mission turned out to be a milk run—apparently we had surprised the Germans."[19]

## UTAH BEACH—"WE'LL START THE WAR FROM RIGHT HERE"

The planning and actual beach landings were controlled by the commanders of the American and British naval task forces. Admiral Alan Kirk decided to begin lowering the assault boats about eleven miles offshore in contrast to the seven to eight miles chosen by the British admiral. This was done to keep the US landing ships out of range of German shore batteries. Admiral Ramsay had taken the position that this was an unnecessary precaution as the considerable strength of Allied counter-bombardment would smash the German guns. Kirk's decision made the run to the beach three hours instead of two. It was about 2:30 a.m. when the Americans began transferring troops to their landing craft.[20]

The Western Task Force, however, did not open naval fire until 5:50 a.m. Kirk had reduced the preliminary bombardment to only thirty to forty minutes from the two hours recommended by Ramsay and implemented by Admiral Vian for the British Eastern Task Force. Kirk thought the Americans would gain the advantage of surprise. He was gravely mistaken.

In the midst of the naval bombardment at 6:00 a.m., 269 Martin Marauder medium bombers of the US Ninth Air Force attacked under the two-thousand-foot cloud ceiling. They dropped almost five thousand bombs along the length of Utah Beach, obliterating many German positions.[21]

The naval bombardment continued once the bombers departed. Allied destroyers picked out targets of opportunity. However, ship congestion offshore and the smoke and dust raised by all the shelling and bombing reduced the bombardment's accuracy.[22]

At 4:55 a.m. the first waves of infantry landed on Utah Beach. One of their targets was a strongpoint named W-5 commanded by the veteran lieutenant Arthur Jahnke of the 709th Infantry Division. Only twenty-six days earlier Rommel had personally inspected this position. Satisfied that Jahnke was working hard to strengthen his bunkers, he presented him with an accordion, an award that Rommel frequently gave out for meritorious service.

After the air and naval bombardment had knocked out most of Jahnke's strongpoint guns, he gasped in disbelief at the countless ships of Operation NEPTUNE heading for him. But they were landing at low tide. Rommel was wrong. Now all the German beach obstacles they had labored to lay were useless. The fields of fire from the German guns that were still functioning also had been set for a high-tide landing.

Then Jahnke saw a strange specter emerge from the ocean surf—peculiar small land vessels. They were the Allies' ingenious DD tanks. These amphibian tanks had inflatable canvas flotation skirts and rear-mounted dual propellers to power them in the water. But they were fragile, safely launched only in calm waters. Lieutenant John Richer USN, commanding the DDs' sea deployment at Utah Beach, fortunately decided to move their launch from six thousand yards to a calmer two thousand offshore. Of the forty DD tanks launched, thirty-one made it to shore where Jahnke watched helplessly as these tanks eliminated the German bunkers one by one.[23]

Behind the beach, where the first wave was targeted to strike, stood a row of ten-inch guns transplanted from the French Maginot Line, now dug into a high cliff. Below them were batteries of deadly German 88mm guns. However fate now intervened on the side of the Allies.

Three of the four pilot boats for the landing were destroyed by German mines. Due to the heavy current and in an effort to make up for lost time, the sole remaining control craft headed for the wrong beach.

The first wave landed two thousand yards (1.2 miles) farther south than planned into an accidental gap in the beach defenses. The assistant division commander, Brigadier General Theodore Roosevelt Jr., the son of former president Theodore Roosevelt, came in with that first wave. Once ashore he figured out that it was the wrong place. Move the landing a mile northward or strike inland? "We'll start the war from right here!" Roosevelt said. It was the right decision.[24]

By midmorning the German resistance had ceased. The US Fourth Division's greatest challenge proved to be moving through the dunes and the twelve-mile-square area flooded behind Utah Beach. At 11:10 a.m. the Fourth Division scouts linked up with paratroopers from the 101st Airborne. By day's end they were four miles inland.

The Utah landing was one of D-Day's major accomplishments. In fifteen hours, twenty-three thousand men landed along with 1,700 vehicles. The Fourth Infantry Division suffered only 197 casualties on June 6.[25]

## OMAHA BEACH—"A HELL OF A MESS"

At 5:20 a.m. the first landing craft carrying soldiers of the Twenty-Ninth Division and First Division set off toward Omaha Beach. As they were launched ten miles offshore, it took them over one hour in heavy seas before they landed on Omaha Beach at H-Hour. "With unbelieving eyes," recalled Franz Gockel of the German 716th Infantry Division who was stationed in a bunker, "we could recognize individual landing craft. The hail of shells falling on us grew heavier, sending fountains of sand and debris into the air."[26]

The landing zone that Gockel defended was by far the toughest objective of the five OVERLORD beaches. Omaha Beach was a crescent-shaped amphitheater with high bluffs 100 to 150 feet in height nestled between cliffs at either end. Below a seven-thousand-yard beach of sand and shingle jetted upward at about a forty-five degree angle.

Above and immediately below the bluffs the Germans had placed guns of 75mm or larger caliber, thirty-five pillboxes, and dugouts equipped with 88mm or 75mm guns as well as sixty light and thirty-five small artillery pieces. In front of the fortifications were thirty-five anti-tank guns and eighty-five machine guns, six mortar pits, thirty-eight rocket pits, and four field artillery positons. Numerous booby-trapped obstacles and mines were strewn across the beach.[27]

These defenses were manned by the 716th Coastal Defense Division composed mainly of Slav and Polish "volunteers." Also present were units from the 352nd Infantry Division, a tough, skilled, and disciplined collection of veterans transferred from the eastern front to Normandy. While being driven to Germany, Rommel recalled that only one of the division's brigades had been placed at the coast. The other two were held in reserve several miles away. He resolved that upon his return he would order Kraiss to move the remaining brigades to the coast.

Behind these defenses the Germans placed artillery positions and naval batteries in huge turrets to support the beaches. However nowhere in Normandy were these batteries sufficient to repulse the Allied fleet and landings.[28]

At 5:40 a.m. thirty-two amphibious tanks (DDs) were launched. Unlike Utah Beach they started too far out at sea by ten miles. The three-to four-foot waves swamped their flotation skirts, sending twenty-seven tanks to the ocean bottom. Few of the 135 tank crewmen were rescued. Also all the amphibious trucks carrying 105mm field guns sank. Omaha's assault troops had no field artillery and little tank support after landing.[29]

The naval bombardment began at 5:50 a.m. led by the battleships *Texas* and *Arkansas*. The American battleships were supported by British and French heavy cruisers. Flying giant French tricolor flags large enough to be seen from the shore, the *Montcalm* and *Georges Leygues* had to fire on their homeland.

During the bombardment 480 B-24 Liberator bombers dropped 1,285 tons of bombs aimed at thirteen specific targets. But the thick cloud cover from the weakening storm obscured the targets. The bombardiers had to drop by radar. To avoid hitting the Allied landing craft, they delayed an extra five to twenty seconds before releasing their bombs. Some landed up to three miles into the French countryside behind Omaha Beach. More cows and chickens were killed than Germans.[30]

Rocket launching vessels (LCTs) delivered the last phase of the bombardment. Each launching rack had 1,080 sixty-pound, three-foot-long rockets. Each LCT hurled sixty-five thousand pounds of ordinance at the beach. Eight LCTs were off Omaha. Because of a navigation error, these ships sailed in the wrong direction. Most of their ordinance fell short, landing harmlessly in the sea.[31]

The Germans in back of Omaha Beach waited, protected by their bombproof fortifications. None of the air, naval, or rocket bombardments penetrated or destroyed their bunkers.

Once this bombardment ceased, the eight hundred German troops took up their defensive positions. Behind their intact installations the Germans waited for the first wave of landing craft to reach the beach before they unleashed what became a hell-like killing zone.

Each American landing craft held thirty-one men and one officer. In the long ride to the beach the men became soaked and cold. Most were seasick after a heavy breakfast of bacon and eggs. Few took seasickness pills, fearing drowsiness in combat. Swamped in heavy seas, ten or more landing craft sank.

At 6:30 a.m. the first wave of 1,450 men jumped into the water off Omaha Beach from thirty-six landing craft. "They must be crazy," said a

German infantry sergeant in a bunker overlooking Omaha Beach. "Are they going to swim ashore right in front of our muzzles?"[32]

A fully equipped infantry man carried sixty to ninety pounds of equipment and several days of extra rations. Navy coxswains reacted to the heavy flow that day by dropping the landing craft ramps too early. Troops fell into water over their heads and drowned from the weight of their gear. Others stranded on sandbars were left exposed. Many who made it to the shore found it necessary to discard their equipment and weapons or had their guns jammed by wet sand.[33]

When the Germans opened fire at 6:30 a.m. their eighty-five machine guns concentrated on each landing ramp as it hit the shore. Thirty men massed together were perfect targets. Engineers followed the first wave in, loaded with TNT to clear beach obstacles. Sixty percent of their equipment littered Omaha Beach that day. One of their craft received a direct hit. The detonation killed everyone aboard.[34]

Infantrymen who somehow made it across that beach huddled behind a small bank of shale. Badly disoriented and disorganized, they were trapped.

At 7:00 a.m. the second wave struggled to land. Their rate of survival was as low as soldiers in the first wave. Those who made it onto the beach had a suicide run to the sea wall to join the huddled mass of men. Everyone on Omaha Beach saw that this situation was a disaster.

The forward elements of the First and Twenty-Ninth Infantry Divisions were being endlessly raked by German mortar, machine-gun and artillery fire. Omaha was strewn with dead and wounded and piles of wrecked equipment. This was the scene that Rommel had envisioned—the ruinous collapse of the Allied invasion.

Ben Newman, a navy radioman, sent messages between the Omaha beachmaster and the offshore fleet members: "It was a hell of a mess. Boats didn't get where they were supposed to be . . . tanks that were supposed to float . . . weren't close enough to the beach and they sank. . . . OMAHA Beach was a tough beach."[35]

It was at 8:30 a.m. that the Omaha beachmaster radioed Admiral Hall that "they were stopping the advance of follow up waves." After only two hours Omaha Beach had shut down.[36]

## "BACK INTO THE SEA"

At 9:24 a.m. General Marcks's headquarters reported that the forward positions of the 352nd Division had been penetrated at Omaha. However the situation was not critical. This motivated Marcks to request a panzer counterattack in the more threatened invasion area protecting Caen. Later at 1:35 p.m. Marcks was mistakenly informed by the chief of staff of the 352nd Infantry Division that "the Division has thrown the invaders back into the sea."[37]

But the Germans had only two regiments that morning on Omaha Beach. As noted earlier, half of Kraiss's infantry strength had been sent off during the night to investigate the exploding dummy Rupert paratroopers that were dropped south of Carentan as part of Operation TITANIC.

Kraiss further weakened his reserves. The reports from his forward battalions on Omaha Beach told him they were successfully containing the early landings. So he only sent a single battalion to reinforce them. Kraiss dispatched the rest of his last reserves toward the eastern beaches where the British had broken through.

By noon Heinrich Severloh in strongpoint 62 had fired twelve thousand rounds from his machine gun, but at midday the German Omaha Beach defenses began falling apart as ammunition began running low. While the beach was littered with First Division dead, the Americans had not been thrown back into the sea, and they were beginning to unload tanks and machine-gun carriers on the beach. Soon a tank sent a shell right through the strongpoint's aperture, and an offshore destroyer hurled multiple shells on the dugout.

The Americans had turned the German flanks. Mortars were destroyed, German infantrymen decimated. Lieutenant Frerking ordered his men in strongpoint 62 to get out, and they withdrew by intermittent leaps under the hail of fire from American tanks and naval guns.

Kraiss's mishandling of the 352nd Infantry Division saved the Allies from a major disaster in the central OVERLORD invasion sector. Antony Beevor and other historians agree that a greater concentration of the available German infantry behind Omaha Beach would have made it very difficult, or even impossible, for the Americans to hold it.[38]

## INDIVIDUAL COURAGE

The outcome of that day on Omaha was determined by the actions of individual soldiers and sailors, not divisions. This was the combat experience of the Twenty-Ninth Infantry Division. In the initial hours on the beach many officers died, and troop losses were heavy. Confusion paralyzed the division. The battle-tested First Division also suffered the same fate but used its prior combat experience to adapt and infiltrate enemy positions. By 7:30 a.m. small groups reached the higher ground to attack the German bunkers' flanks.

Brigadier General Norman Cota, commanding the Twenty-Ninth, came in on the second wave at 7:30 a.m. Seeing the desperate situation, he asked a group of men sheltering beneath the beach shingle bank who they were. When they identified themselves as rangers, he exploded, "Then goddamnit, if you're Rangers get up and lead the way!"[39] (Rangers were trained as elite US combat troops.) In response the admonished rangers pushed four-foot lengths of Bangalore torpedoes beneath a forest of barbed wire to blow a gap and then crawled forward up one of Omaha's five valley hillsides that were wreathed in smoke. Some thirty-five soldiers reached the road at the hilltop. They were gradually joined by other soldiers and NCOs who began the laborious, very dangerous task of attacking the German positions one by one.

About the same time more soldiers slowly began moving forward toward the bluff. They decided it was better to fight their way forward off the beach than to stay and die in the German death zone. Staff Sergeant William Courtney and Private First Class William Braher of the Second Rangers worked their way up the heights from the sea wall. At 8:30 a.m. they may have been the first Americans to reach the top of the cliff.[40]

By 9:00 a.m., five thousand soldiers were crammed on Omaha. The situation seemed grim. Destroyer skippers saw the beach situation was desperate. Although not ordered to do so, individual captains sailed back to the beachfront and opened fire on the German positions on the high bluffs. Shortly past 8:30 a.m., Rear Admiral John Hall, who was in command of the Omaha Beach landings, ordered all the destroyers to join in smashing the German bunkers. More than a dozen US and British destroyers sailed to within eight hundred to one thousand yards, as close as their shallow draft allowed, to blast enemy positions to pieces. In some instances Allied tanks used their firepower to direct the destroyers to also target the same positions. Over the next ninety minutes, the Allied destroyers helped turn the tide of the battle for Omaha Beach.[41] A disaster had been averted.

As historian Stephen Ambrose recounts, "The effect on the troops on OMAHA of the destroyers' heroic and risky action was electric."[42] General Omar Bradley, who was not a great navy admirer, was forced to admit that "the Navy saved our hides."[43]

Between 9:00 and 10:00 a.m. units of the Sixteenth Infantry fought their way to the top of the bluff. In close hand-to-hand fighting, aided by the destroyer's bombardment, they moved across Omaha Beach clearing the fortifications.

Because most of the shore radios had been lost, there was little shore-to-ship communication. Thus Bradley and Admiral Kirk did not know of these breakthroughs. "Never reinforce failure" was a military principle that caused them to consider evacuating Omaha Beach. The men might have been shifted to Utah or the British beaches. However, at 10:45 a.m. they decided to land the reserve 115th Infantry. By noon there were four major breaches in the German defenses.

At Omaha's west end, Private Ray Moon of the 116th Infantry looked back toward the sea. "The view was unforgettable. . . . The scene below reminded me of the Chicago stockyard cattle pens and its slaughter house."[44]

Some German troops, now cut off on the bluffs, attempted to retreat from their positions. But most of the defenders fought on until their ammunition was exhausted.

At 1:30 p.m. General Leonard Gerow commanding the V Corps radioed to Bradley that "the troop formerly pinned down on the beaches . . . advancing up the heights behind the beach."[45] At 4:00 p.m. General Clarence Huebner, First Infantry Division commander, landed to direct beach operations. By dark the American position at Omaha Beach was a narrow strip of Normandy, ten thousand yards wide and only two thousand to three thousand yards deep. It was a foothold.

Omaha had been a near-run thing. It was the closest to outright failure of all the D-Day beaches. The Americans wanted a bridgehead sixteen miles wide and five miles deep. By the end of the day, it was barely the width of the beach. A few units made their way two miles inland, but most were still below the bluffs. Nearly forty thousand men landed. The Twenty-Ninth suffered 2,440 casualties, the First Division 1,744. Most of the 2,400 Americans who died for this strip of sand perished in the first two hours. Bradley later wrote, "OMAHA Beach was a nightmare. Even now it brings pain to recall what happened."[46]

Fig. 6.1. Buildup of Omaha Beach reinforcements. (US government)

The Germans lost 1,200 men, 20 percent of their defending forces.[47] Because they failed to organize any counterattacks, they lost their best chance to snuff out the invasion on Omaha.

## REVENGE FOR DUNKIRK

Lieutenant General Sir Miles Dempsey of the British army was a veteran of Dunkirk and the North African and Italian campaigns. He was given the command of three D-Day beaches: Gold-British, Juno-Canadian and Sword-British. (See Map 5.) Montgomery, the overall Allied ground commander, and Dempsey decided on 7:30 a.m. as the landing H-Hour in order to ensure a longer shore bombardment and a shorter assault run on the beach. One hundred thirty-seven warships laid down a devastating two-hour preliminary bombardment. The British moved their troop transports three to four miles closer to the coast for a shorter assault run-in.[48]

While the fleet bombardment was commencing, German E-boats made their one and only attack on the NEPTUNE armada. Two torpedoes missed, but a third hit and sank the Norwegian destroyer *Svenner*. Most of its crew was saved. The HMS *Warspite* fired back with its fifteen-inch and four-inch guns destroying one E-boat. The remaining German flotilla made a fast exit behind an intentional smoke screen.

The midnight attack by RAF Bomber Command also covered these three beaches. The D-Day attack was the heaviest Bomber Command had mounted to that time. The Flying Fortresses of the Eighth US Army Air Force also conducted an early-morning raid.

Along the entire twenty-four miles of the three invasion beaches, the British and Canadian soldiers faced less challenging terrain than that of Omaha and Utah. These were low beaches with a sea wall beyond. Summer resorts or villas lined a coastal road. Behind the coast was flat, open terrain.

On these three beaches the German forces deployed ten infantry companies, fifty mortar teams, five hundred machine guns, and ninety artillery pieces. Over a secondary defensive zone, four to six miles deep, were fourteen infantry companies and twenty-two artillery batteries with over one hundred guns. Beyond them were another five infantry battalions and more guns. Finally, around Caen the Twenty-First Panzer Division waited.[49]

As the three assault waves made their shorter runs into the beaches, British fleet destroyers guarded their flanks with their 4.7-inch guns engaging enemy beach batteries. Other smaller destroyers moved very close inshore for added assault fire support. The Second Tactical Air Force (RAF) rocket-firing typhoons flew low blasting the German defenses.

About forty-five minutes before the assault, sixteen landing craft gunships opened an intense close-range bombardment on beach defenses. Fifteen minutes later, twenty-two rocket launching landing craft each hurled a thousand five-inch rockets every minute and a half. Despite the virtual invulnerability of the bigger casemated German batteries, the combined impact of the longer, more intense British naval and air bombardment had the positive effect of silencing, at least for a time, nearly all of the fixed German batteries. When some batteries finally opened fire, they were engaged by the Allied fleet and again lapsed into silence.[50]

As the landing craft neared these beaches the British and Canadians had a greater personal incentive than their American counterparts. Now they were returning to northwestern Europe to avenge the stain of the retreat from Dunkirk exactly four years earlier.

## GOLD BEACH

Though the sea was very rough, the British troops rushed ashore meeting little resistance. The German defenders, mainly Russian "volunteers," rapidly surrendered. However one strongpoint, the village of Le Hamel, held out until midafternoon. (See Map 6.) Yet by midday, British troops reached Creully, five miles inland.

The Forty-Seventh Royal Marine Commandos' objective was to push inland and travel west along the coast to help take Port-en-Bessin. (See Map 5.) The marines were to link up with the Americans from Omaha Beach. Neither made it to their goal on that day.

Once the thin perimeter of German defense caved in, the Fiftieth Infantry Division advanced almost to the town of Bayeux, their principal objective. Many German infantrymen hid and did not surrender. They attacked the flanks and rear of the advancing British assault, slowing but not stopping the advance from Gold. By the end of the day the British landed twenty-five thousand men on Gold Beach, suffering only 413 casualties.[51]

Fig. 6.2. Gold Beach British Fiftieth Infantry Division going ashore. June 6, 1944. (Photo by Midgley [Sgt.] No. 5 Army Film & Photographic Unit)

## JUNO BEACH

The Third Canadian Division was eager to avenge the 1942 Dieppe raid disaster. The four hundred Germans that the 2,400 Canadians encountered on the coast put up a stiff resistance. It took them over three hours to take the town of St. Aubin-sur-Mer. (See Map 6.) Once the thin line of the German defensive zone was broken, the Canadians had a relatively easy advance inland.[52]

But this advance was slowed by the chaos on the beaches. Later in the day as the tide rose, Rommel's beach obstacles took a heavy toll when the landing craft attempted to back off the beaches after unloading. Twenty out of twenty-four of the lead boats were seriously damaged or destroyed by the day's end. This delayed the landing of follow-up second and third waves of reinforcements, thus seriously disrupting the timetable for the day's ground objectives.[53]

The Ninth Canadian Infantry Brigade had as its main goal the airfield near Carpiquet just west of Caen. (See Map 6.) "Our instructions were . . .

to stop at nothing . . . but to get to Carpiquet airport [nine miles inland] . . . and to capture and consolidate the airport," said Sergeant Stanley Dudka of the North Nova Scotia Highlanders.[54]

The enemy had been completely overcome. Chaos reigned at the airfield. The Luftwaffe was blowing up the installation in a frenzied evacuation. The road to the airport and Caen lay open. Yet the Highlanders were ordered to stop. They never even got close to taking Carpiquet. Upon reaching Villons les Buissons they were halted (see Map 6) over their commanders' misplaced fears of a German counterattack.

Montgomery and Eisenhower were delighted that Juno held a lodgment up to six miles deep. However the failure to take the airport on D-Day proved to be a very costly one over the following weeks. The Caen airfield was to witness some of the most intensive fighting of the entire Normandy campaign. Over a month elapsed before the British occupied Carpiquet after suffering major casualties.[55]

## SWORD BEACH

The Sword Beach landings were preceded by heavy battleship fire that smashed the German strongpoints. The battleships HMS *Ramillies* and *Warspite* and monitor HMS *Roberts* fired many salvos of fifteen-inch shells at the defensive shore batteries. This was strongly supported by four cruisers, including the Polish warship *Dragon* and thirteen destroyers. The British LCTs launched their DD amphibian tanks less than a mile from the beach. Thirty-four out of forty DDs made it to shore.[56]

With this excellent support the British troops knocked out the remaining German beach defenses, largely clearing Sword Beach by 8:30 a.m. Specialized British armor also did a rapid job of clearing lanes through minefields and using napalm tanks to incinerate German bunkers. The early landings went so well that a coxswain of a LCA (Landing Craft Armor) returning for a second load told others on the deck of the transport, "It's a piece of cake!"[57]

French inhabitants along the beach rushed out of their homes with bottles of wine and cider saved for liberation day. They were given to the gratefully surprised Englishmen with cries of "Vive les Anglais." The soldiers received many hugs and kisses as they advanced.[58]

The Third Infantry Division had D-Day's most important objective—to take the city of Caen. Eight miles inland, its capture would protect the invasion's left flank from the expected German counterattacks. This was a heavy commitment. In late May British army intelligence had discovered the presence of the Twenty-First Panzer Division around Caen. Its official history reported that in spite of the intelligence Montgomery did not considerate it necessary to revise or strengthen his plan to capture Caen. Also most significantly Monty decided not to even tell the commanders of the Third Infantry Divisions about the presence of the Twenty-First Panzer.[59]

The original Twenty-First had been destroyed with the Afrika Korps in February 1943. A new Twenty-First Panzer was created in May 1943 by General Edgar Feuchtinger with a complement of three thousand men. Its tanks and armored vehicles came from German scrapyards or from captured equipment. However, by June 1944, it had a total strength of 16,300 men and had also been equipped with 146 new Mark IV panzers.[60]

The Third Division had a double mission on D-Day. First, it linked up with the British airborne that had secured Pegasus Bridge. Secondly, their 185th Brigade had the assignment of taking Caen. By 11:00 a.m. its three battalions had reached Hermanville for the push to the city. (See Map 6.) They were to be supported by the King's Shropshire Light Infantry that was supposed to be mounted on the tanks of the Staffordshire Yeomanry and advance with the 185th Brigade to Caen. In the confusion of D-Day, this complex military choreography began to break down.

The supporting tanks failed to get off Sword Beach because of congestion. The exit routes were still under German fire, causing a pileup of vehicles. The infantry was told to walk to the rendezvous point. This seriously delayed the advance toward Caen and gave the Germans time to organize a counterattack. Unlike German armored divisions, whose mobile infantry (called Panzer Grenadiers), kept pace with the panzers by riding in armored half-track vehicles cross-country, the British armored divisions kept their supporting infantry in trucks confined to roads. If the British armor and support infantry had landed together with half-tracks for the infantry, the Eighteenth Brigade as a combined strike force would have immediately set off to seize and hold Caen before any counterattack was launched by the disorganized local German reserves.

Adding to this British deployment problem was the stubborn German defense of the Hillman strongpoint. This virtual fortress caused an intense firefight that slowed the 185th Brigade's advance for most of the afternoon. All of these delays gave the Germans the precious time they needed to overcome their initial disorganized response and launch a determined counterattack.[61]

## "IF YOU DON'T SUCCEED . . . WE SHALL HAVE LOST THE WAR"

The Twenty-First Panzer Division near Caen did not make a lightning response to the Allied landings. Hitler's divided command system and hesitancy among local German commanders mishandled the Twenty-First Panzer all day on June 6.

This did not mean that some German officers did not show initiative. At 1:30 a.m. Colonel Hans Von Luck of 125th Regiment of the Twenty-First Panzer Division responded immediately to the first reports of the airborne landings. He gave orders to assemble his regiment. By 2:30 a.m. his officers and men were lined up beside their tanks with their engines running waiting for orders. They waited a long time for Hitler to wake up.

Finally at 10:00 a.m. Lieutenant General Rudolf Schmundt woke Hitler up. Eisenhower had just announced to the world that the Allies had launched the Normandy invasion. Hitler ordered an immediate conference with Keitel and Jodl.[62]

As they entered Hitler shouted, "Well, is it or isn't it the invasion?"[63] Hours passed as the man who previously guessed Normandy as the landing site changed his mind again. "My opinion," he finally announced, "is that this is not the real invasion yet."[64] Finally he made the decision to release to Rundstedt's command the two panzer divisions that he had requested before dawn. Hitler gave orders for the Allied troops to be "annihilated" by the end of the day.[65] It was after 4:00 p.m. by the time these orders reached the two panzer divisions. Earlier there had been predawn darkness, and until midday the panzers' advance would have been obscured by clouds. Now without cloud cover, the Allied air forces owned the skies. Movement was delayed until darkness had fallen. Only the Twenty-First Panzer at Caen could save the day.

Blumentritt, Rundstedt's chief of staff, speculated that even if the Twelfth SS Panzer Division had been released at about 1:00 a.m., they would not have reached the Caen area before daylight at 4:00 a.m. The Allied air force would have intervened. Being nearer the battle area, the Twelfth SS might have been able to support the Twenty-First Panzer's attack by the afternoon. With luck the Panzer Lehr might have arrived during the evening of June 6 at the earliest.[66]

About 6:00 p.m. Rommel had reached Rheims on his way to Normandy. He called Speidel at La Roche-Guyon and learned all the bad news regarding the delayed panzer counterattack. He then climbed back into his car. Historian Liddell Hart theorized, "It is possible that they would have been released earlier if Rommel had not been absent from Normandy. . . . Rommel . . . often spoke to Hitler himself on the telephone."[67] Later that day, Rommel exclaimed, "My God! If the 21st Panzer can make it, we might just be able to drive them back in three days!"[68]

Because of Hitler's self-imposed delay, General Marcks did not get permission to release the Twenty-First Panzer tanks until the British and Canadians were well established on the beaches and moving inland. It was not until 7:00 p.m. that the Twenty-First Panzer Division joined forces with the 192nd Panzer Grenadier Regiment (a divisional reconnaissance unit) at the jumping-off point for their attack northward into the Canadian-British bridgehead. Their target was the British beaches. Taking a page from the Desert Fox, General Marcks traveled forty miles from St. Lo to personally oversee this crucial battle.

Marcks told the battle group leader, Colonel Hermann von Oppeln-Bronikowski, "Oppeln, if you don't succeed in throwing the British into the sea we shall have lost the war." The colonel saluted and said, "I shall attack now."[69] Victory or defeat now rode with a mere ninety-eight German panzers.

From atop a small hill, Marcks showed him the gap several miles wide between the Juno and Sword beaches. The German spearhead was to proceed north from Lebisey and drive through this gap between the towns of Langruné and Lion-sur-Mer on the coast to reinforce the German coastal bunkers. (See Map 6.) With this three-mile-wide wedge the Germans could begin to roll up the Allied beachheads in both directions.

Meanwhile the Third British Division had finally learned of the presence of the Twenty-First Panzer Division when it ran into it on Périers Ridge. The British knocked out several Mark IVs. Afterward the Germans veered off to the west, and the British pressed on southward toward Caen.

The leading company of the King's Shropshire Light Infantry, a few hundred trudging riflemen who had been left marooned on the beach, advanced to within two miles of the objective when it was hit by a wall of intense enemy fire from a wooded ridge outside of Lebisey. No reinforcements arrived to continue what had been envisioned as a bold push to Caen. Instead, the British retreated to Biéville and dug in. Weeks would pass before the British advance to take Caen resumed.

Meanwhile on the German left, one-half-dozen tanks supported by a company of infantry made it through the British lines and drove northward. At approximately 8:00 p.m. this little battle group reached the coast at Luc-sur-Mer and linked up with the German coastal defenders, remnants of the 716th Division, to await more tank reinforcements.

About fifty panzers had been dispatched to strengthen the German wedge when, by sheer coincidence of timing, about 250 British gliders appeared overhead. This was the planned reinforcement fly-in of the Orne River bridgehead, the largest on D-Day, by the British Sixth Airborne Division.[70]

The Germans mistakenly thought it was a lightning response to the Twenty-First Panzer Division's breakthrough. "No one who saw it will ever forget it," declared Panzer Grenadier Werner Kortenhaus. "Suddenly the hollow roaring of countless aeroplanes, and then we saw them, hundreds of them, towing great gliders, filling the sky."[71] The Germans lost heart, panicked, and withdrew. Their retreat was another major D-Day blunder.

That evening the British occupied six square miles of Sword Beach, twenty miles long but only three to six miles deep. The entire Third Division had landed with the Twenty-Seventh Armored Brigade, but these units were stopped three miles short of Caen. About twenty-nine thousand men were now ashore, at the cost of around one thousand casualties for that day.[72]

Compounding the failure of a German counterattack on D-Day was the lack of any serious air attack to stop the Allied landings. "Where is the Luftwaffe?" was a question repeatedly asked by desperate German soldiers scanning the sky over Normandy.

On D-Day only 319 aircraft were available to the Luftwaffe in the West. The Germans flew just 309 sorties on June 6. Most were intercepted and shot down. Only two German Focke Wulf 190 fighters broke through the Allied screen of over five thousand fighters to strafe Sword Beach and miraculously survived. Isolated German flak batteries provided all the token air protection that the Seventh Army could expect on D-Day. They accounted for most of the 127 Allied aircraft lost. From early morning to late that night the Allies had absolute air supremacy.[73]

Rommel was not in the best of moods when he finally reached his chateau headquarters at 10:00 p.m. He asked about the Twenty-First Panzer counter-attack, but no details had arrived. Rommel wanted to know where the Panzer Lehr and Twelfth SS were. They had been held up by Hitler's indecision. "Madmen," said Rommel. "Of course, now they will arrive too late."[74]

Later his aide-de-camp, Captain Helmuth Lang, approached his chief. "Sir, do you think we can drive them back?" he asked. "Lang, I hope we can," came his answer. "I've nearly always succeeded up to now."[75] Because of a weather surprise Rommel had missed the most important battle of his career and a decisive one for Germany as well.

## RESULTS "HOW CLOSE IT WAS"

When midnight came on June 6, a full moon shone over the fifty-mile Normandy front. The 156,000 British, American, and Canadian troops had penetrated no more than about ten miles inland. Omaha Beach was only just hanging on. Except for Gold and Juno, none of the other three bridge-heads had yet linked up. Few of the ambitious targets for D-Day had been achieved. (See Map 7.)

However it was still a tremendous success for the Allies. Hitler's Atlantic Wall had been breached. The complex NEPTUNE assault plan had largely worked. Allied casualties had proven remarkably light. SHAEF planners had predicted twenty-five thousand casualties, including ten thousand dead on D-Day. Instead total estimated casualties were fewer than twelve thousand (6,600 American, 3,500 British and 1,000 Canadians). Twenty-five hundred soldiers were dead. Admiral Ramsay summed up the day in his diary: "Still on the whole we have very much to thank God for this day."[76]

The Germans had contained the Great Invasion but not repulsed it. With a nearly dysfunctional system of command, it is amazing how well the Germans did on the "longest day." Rommel's strategic and tac-tical approach was vindicated. Overwhelming Allied air superiority made a mobile defense almost impossible that day and throughout the OVER-LORD campaign.

The Germans almost achieved a tactical victory in the Omaha Beach sector. If more of the 352nd Infantry had been on the beaches, the landings would have failed. At Caen, the initial counterattack of the Twenty-First Panzer Division was successful in stopping the British advance to take the city. If the division had attacked earlier in the day, they would have reached the coast and placed a strong wedge dividing Juno and Sword beaches. If Rommel had been successful in placing two additional panzer divisions behind the Allied invasion beaches, they would have created havoc on D-Day. For the Germans June 6 and 7 were the decisive days for defeating the OVERLORD operation.

By nightfall of June 6 the German front containing the invasion was in a precarious situation. All available reserves were committed. Rommel noted that reinforcements were still in transit, delayed by Allied air interdiction. Ammunition was running low, and economy was required all along the German lines. A feeling of hopelessness began to spread.[77]

For the Allies the very boldness of Montgomery's plan to take and hold Caen on D-Day ensured its failure. Max Hastings termed it "a substantial strategic misfortune."[78] The overall failure of British senior commanders to warn their assaulting forces of the presence of the Twenty-First Panzers was inexcusable. Could they have reinforced the Third Division and better orchestrated the landings by delivering a stronger armor-infantry Caen assault on D-Day? The fact that these alternatives were not even considered is evident by examining Montgomery's diary and papers from early June 1944.[79]

After June 6, Montgomery makes no mention of his initial failure to take the city. As historian Carlo D'Este states, "To have taken [Caen] according to plan . . . would have needed . . . some sort of miracle."[80]

Monty's failed plan to capture Caen on D-Day stalled the entire Normandy campaign. However on June 10 he still told General Bradley how pleased he was with its progress. Bradley smiled and admitted they were better than during the opening hours of D-Day. "Someday," Bradley explained, "I'll tell General Eisenhower just how close it was in these first hours."[81]

Even more telling was how on June 6 the vaunted Desert Fox could do nothing right. When Speidel phoned to tell him of the amphibious invasion, Rommel was devastated. "How stupid of me!" he said, thinking of his failure to persuade Hitler to place more panzers on the coast.[82]

He immediately called his aide Lang to get his car ready. "Imagine Lang," Rommel said with bitter irony, "the great day has come. The Allies are landing in Normandy and we are here!"[83]

Before he left his wife's fiftieth birthday celebration on June 6, the third stroke of bad luck befell the field marshal. He gave his wife gray suede shoes from Paris. But like most husbands, Rommel had no idea of her shoe size. They didn't fit.[84]

# CHAPTER 7
# WHO WAS IN CONTROL?

"Indomitable in retreat, invincible in advance, insufferable in victory."

—Winston S. Churchill on General Montgomery (1958, alleged)[1]

## THE MORNING AFTER

When dawn came on June 7, the Allied foothold on Normandy was tenuous. The risks of success or failure did not end on D-Day. Nowhere had any of the Allied units achieved all of their D-Day objectives.

The British had failed to dislodge German forces from the key crossroad city of Caen and its Carpiquet Airfield. Only the forces on Gold and Juno beaches had linked up. The other invasion beaches remained isolated enclaves.

The Americans' lodgment was too narrow. Omaha Beach was still under mortar fire. When Admiral Ramsay arrived at 11:45 a.m., he found a scene of great confusion with the beach so densely covered by casualties and equipment wreckage that it was blocking traffic between the beach and the shore.

Inland on the Cotentin Peninsula behind Utah Beach, dawn found the Eighty-Second Airborne Division in a precarious position. They remained isolated and almost out of ammunition. As the day progressed, the Eighty-Second was reinforced by glider infantry and finally was linked up with seaborne forces from Utah Beach. By nightfall the Americans had forced their way deeper into the Cotentin with a bridgehead eight miles deep and nine miles long. Meanwhile the Americans on Omaha succeeded in advancing their lines about four miles south of the landing beaches.

June 7 was a better day for the British. Bayeux was almost entirely evacuated by German forces, enabling the British to liberate the town with little damage. Port-en-Bessin, between Omaha and Gold beaches, also was liberated. This small harbor facility was the planned first stage site of the British Pluto oil pipeline so vital to the support of the invasion. By the night of June 8, the First US Infantry Division made contact with the British near Port-en-Bessin, finally linking up all of the five beachheads.

General Montgomery landed in Normandy on June 7, and General Bradley set up his headquarters near Pointe du Hoc on June 8. However, it was not until June 10 that Admiral Ramsay judged Omaha Beach secure enough to allow LSTs to run up on the beach and discharge their cargoes.

For the first fifty days of the Normandy invasion, German defenses remained so strong that Allied advances were limited. German reserve forces were continuously thrown into the fight, endangering the Allied beachheads. Montgomery's failure to take Caen and his change of strategic plans caused turmoil within the Allied command and altered the final outcome of the OVERLORD operation.[2]

## THE FATAL RACE

When General Rommel arrived at his headquarters on June 6 at 10:00 p.m., he realized that the period of great vulnerability for the Allied bridgehead would last only a few days. Late in the afternoon of that same day, Hitler had finally released the First SS Panzer Corps reserve. It began a slow advance toward Normandy that verged on a nightmare as Allied aircraft severely punished these and other units. Fighter-bombers cratered roads, attacked railroad marshalling yards, and destroyed trains in daylight raids. Tank deployment was hampered as they needed to be loaded on rail flatbed trucks for transport because their tracks wore out over long distances. Rommel's warnings about Allied air power proved completely correct.

On June 6, OKW ordered the Second SS Panzer Division from Toulouse, the Seventeenth SS Division from the Loire Valley, and other infantry units to reinforce the Normandy sector. The Second SS Panzer took seventeen days to make a 450-mile journey. Normally it took five.[3]

Thus German reinforcements arrived late in driblets, strung out along the roads. Infantry were exhausted from long, forced marches. Allied air interdiction kept fuel supplies from reaching the panzer divisions, leaving them chronically short of fuel.[4]

If Rommel had been able to reinforce Normandy rapidly with divisions taken from the Fifteenth Army around Pas-de-Calais, he might have driven the Allies back into the sea. However, Rommel, Hitler, and Rundstedt remained convinced that the main Allied invasion was still to come across the Straits of Dover. Normandy was only a diversionary attack before the main blow. Operation FORTITUDE continued to deceive the German leaders.

Top secret Ultra intercepts of German-coded radio messages, however, told the Allies that the Germans were set to significantly reinforce Normandy. On June 7, Hitler ordered four infantry divisions and the 116th Panzer, their strongest armored division in the West, to move from Pas-de-Calais to attack the Normandy bridgehead.

To counter this move, Eisenhower authorized one of the Allies' most successful double agents, Juan Pujol Garcia, code-named Garbo, to reinforce the deception of Operation FORTITUDE that the current Normandy attack was a diversion. Shortly after midnight Garbo radioed his German contact, "This is the fake, you have to believe me."[5]

At 7:30 a.m. on the morning of June 10, Jodl, Hitler's chief of staff, telephoned the headquarters of Rundstedt in Paris. Since he was still asleep, Rundstedt's operation officer General Bodo Zimmermann took the call. Jodl told him that Hitler had received unimpeachable information that Pas-de-Calais was about to be invaded. Therefore, Hitler fatefully had canceled the all-out reinforcement of Normandy. All units en route to Normandy from Pas-de-Calais were to immediately return to their original positions. Later Zimmermann recalled that this was "the decision that lost the war for Germany."[6]

Rommel had to counterattack with only piecemeal reinforcements. Early on June 8 he ordered the Twenty-First Panzer Lehr Division and Twelfth Panzer Division to attack side by side in order to pierce the Allied front line between Bayeux and Caen. (See Map 8.)

Unexpectedly that same day, General Marcks was given the entire Allied plan of operations from D-Day onward. They were found on a dead

American beachmaster's body in a shell-riddled landing craft on the Vire River. Marcks sent them immediately to Rommel and Rundstedt.

But what good were the enemy plans if Rommel lacked the forces to foil them? It proved easier to order the decisive counterattack than deliver it. The Twelfth Panzer Division had arrived but was so short of fuel, it could not attack. Around Caen, the Twenty-First Panzer waged a bitter battle with the Third British Division. The Panzer Lehr was still struggling in from Chartres badly decimated by Allied fighter-bombers that succeeded in wounding its commander, General Bayerlein.[7]

When the First SS Panzer Corp's attack finally began on June 9, Allied naval and concentrated artillery gunfire inflicted heavy losses. In a postwar interview with Liddell Hart, Rundstedt stated his surprise on how the battleship fire greatly hampered the German counterstroke. Allied fighter-bombers also contributed to halting the German advance with saturation bombing. The sheer volume and accuracy of the naval gunfire completely surprised the panzers. On June 10 Rommel also wrote, "The effect of the heavy naval guns is so immense that no operation of any kind is possible . . . either by infantry or tanks."[8]

The secret to the accuracy of the Allied naval shelling was the placement of forward naval observers with the frontline units. In a matter of minutes they communicated directly with warship fire-control centers to accurately pulverize German positions.[9]

The last major German counterattack was planned for dusk on June 10. Again Ultra intercepts (decoded enemy messages) helped the Allies through pinpointing the exact headquarters location of General Geyr von Schweppenburg's Panzer Group West. On the evening of June 10, rocket-firing Royal Air Force (RAF) Typhoon squadrons flying low located Geyr's headquarters, which had not been properly camouflaged. The RAF attack destroyed all the radio equipment, thus incapacitating the signal's battalion. Geyr was wounded, and seventeen other officers were killed. Panzer Group West was decimated, and the attack was canceled. Yet even if such a counterattack had occurred, it would have, as we will see, run head-on into Montgomery's belated second effort to take Caen.[10]

Where was the Luftwaffe during all of these attempted German counterattacks? The German troops' grim humor was that the Allied planes had silver paint. The Luftwaffe planes were colorless and rendered invisible. In

France they say the planes are on the Russian front. On the Russian front they say they are in France, and in Germany they say they are at the front.

Approximately one thousand fighters and bombers were transferred from Germany and Italy to attack the Allied buildup. Through June and July this number of aircraft was maintained despite the loss of one thousand planes by July 7. Yet no more than 250 fighters were sent up daily due to the vastly superior Allied air forces. The Luftwaffe incurred very high losses, and their airfields were pounded by continuous raids. Supply, repair, and pilot replacement efforts broke down.[11]

Nightly German air raids over the Allied beaches were limited to 80 to 120 bombers. Many were mine-laying sorties that deployed large quantities of a new type of pressure-sensitive oyster mine. These mines were very hard to detect, and as there were no effective countermeasures against them, they accounted for most of the Allied ships sunk during NEPTUNE.

Another important Luftwaffe weapon was the rocket-propelled Henschel HS 293 radio-guided aerial bomb. This early air-launched guided missile struck the USS *Meredith* at 1:00 a.m. on June 8. She later sank after a second German bomb attack.[12]

The Allies, however, were able to effectively counter the German naval attacks. From their bases at Cherbourg, Boulogne, and Le Havre, fast German E-boats conducted nightly sorties on Allied warships on the extreme flanks of the invasion and on cross-channel traffic. Some Allied ships were damaged but at great cost to the German E-boats. The Kriegsmarine pinprick attacks never materially altered the Allied channel operations or the buildup of forces in France.

German U-boats were rendered ineffective by the massive air-surface antisubmarine screen that enveloped all Allied shipping operating in the English Channel. On the night of June 7 a British Liberator bomber piloted by Ken Moore, a Canadian officer, sank two German U-boats within twenty-two minutes, thus making naval history. During the month of June, twenty-five U-boats were sunk, twelve in the channel and the Bay of Biscay.[13]

Based on Ultra decrypt of Enigma signals, Admiral Ramsay initiated a naval sortie by the Tenth Destroyer Flotilla that smashed the German Eighth Destroyer Flotilla west of its Cherbourg base. These were the last German destroyers able to attack NEPTUNE shipping. On June 14, 325

Lancaster bombers destroyed about forty German surface vessels in an attack on the Port of Le Havre. Thus by the end of June, both the Luftwaffe and Kriegsmarine were broken reeds.[14]

## HITLER'S POLICY STRAITJACKET

A few minutes after midnight on June 12, the Germans deployed a new offensive weapon that might have altered the course of the Normandy invasion. Launched from Holland, the first V-1 rockets struck London. Hitler believed that he could break British morale with relentless V-1 attacks on their capital. Between June and October 1944, over 9,500 V-1s hit London. Extensive areas of Central London were ultimately evacuated as the bombardment unnerved many people.

Because Hitler thought that this use of theV-1s would decide the war, he refused to direct those rockets against the British embarkation ports or the massive concentration of Allied ships off the Normandy coast. The V-1s had the potential of seriously disrupting the invasion's logistics. If this new weapon, which had been hitting London at the rate of one hundred per day, had been switched to the invasion bridgehead, it might have forced the withdrawal of Allied naval units from the French coast. Fortunately for the Allies, this did not happen. Hitler had made another fateful decision.[15]

By June 10 Rundstedt and Rommel both realized that their efforts had a scant chance of success in Normandy. They doubted the German army's ability to throw the Allies back into the sea. Thus they wanted to wage a defensive campaign with a free hand to deploy their forces. But even before the invasion, Hitler had tied their hands with a rigid no withdrawal policy. Shortly after D-Day he repeated these orders.

To their despair, Rommel and Rundstedt knew the piecemeal commitment of the panzer divisions was a fatal race to simply plug the gaps in their defensive lines, like an emergency fire brigade. This ultimately would lead to collapse. Hitler had set up a battle of attrition that Germany could not win.[16]

After the war, Rundstedt explained to Allied interviewers why this was a "great mistake." "I wanted to relieve them with infantry divisions but they were always too closely engaged and anyway were under fire from the Navy. I wanted to establish the infantry behind the Orne, get them properly dug-in, but I wasn't allowed to yield ground [by Hitler]."[17]

By June 11 Rommel told Keitel the hopelessness of their situation: "[T]he enemy has complete control of the air over the battle area up to a distance of about a hundred kilometers behind the front, and with powerful fighter-bomber and bomber formations immobilizes almost all traffic by day on roads or in the open country."[18]

Rommel understood that his soldiers could only stop the Allied breakout for a time at the cost of heavy casualties on both sides. He further realized that Germany could not win in Normandy, nor win the war. On June 14, Rommel wrote to his wife, "The situation does not improve. We must be prepared for grave events. The troops are fighting with the utmost courage, but the balance of strength tips more heavily against us every day."[19]

During the Normandy campaign Hitler's politically driven command and control policies were disastrous for the German military. His interference ranks high among the many factors leading to the ultimate defeat of Germany.

## MONTY'S BIG LIE

In the early morning of June 7 Montgomery landed in France. He was unperturbed by the British and Canadian failure to take Caen and its airfields. He reported that "all was going well and the original plan was being worked to. . . . Caen was not captured."[20]

On June 11 Montgomery made his first attempt to disguise a change in his own plan when he informed General Alan Brooke that "my general policy is to pull the enemy on to Second Army [British and Canadian] so as to make it easier for First Army [American] to expand and extend the quicker."[21]

Eisenhower thought that Monty's June 11 message was an admission that his original plan had been nullified by the Caen failure. Ike interpreted this British switch to the defensive as Montgomery's reversion to his previous battlefield behavior of overcaution and reluctance to risk heavy casualties. At that time whatever Monty's intention, it was not clear to the other Allied commanders.[22]

Montgomery's later attempts to pretend that the Normandy ground battle unfolded according to his original planning documents are ludicrous. His biographer Nigel Hamilton offers this explanation: "Like a master chess player, he knew it would be a long battle. . . . The slogging match could now begin."[23] This scenario implies that Montgomery sought to mount a siege of Caen. This was exactly the opposite of what the British wanted because of their limited manpower reserves.

Until Montgomery's June 11 invention of his new strategy, he had always made it perfectly clear that D-Day required an initial aggressive thrust that gained more ground and broke through the German defenses to take Caen. British-Canadian armored forces would rapidly move onto the Falaise plain, then toward the Seine and Paris. This was Montgomery's original planned "feint" at Caen that would draw the German panzers into a battle highly favorable to the Allies. Overwhelming British-American air superiority and the mobility of their much larger armored forces would destroy any German counteroffensive. This "feint" in turn would assist a faster American breakthrough in support of the British.

Instead Montgomery distorted his intentions in later years by pretending that the British and Canadians carried out his original plan by holding a line north of Caen into mid-July. This is one of the great myths of World War II.

It was only after D-Day that this new strategy became his plan. None of Montgomery's preinvasion planning, reports, or presentations ever suggested that the British would stop short of attacking Caen. Thus Montgomery opened the door to what became a long battle of attrition in Normandy.[24]

## CAEN-ROUND TWO: VILLERS-BOCAGE

In the first week after D-Day, Montgomery did not order an all-out attack on Caen. On June 7 to June 8 the British Third Division did renew its initial D-Day attack, but it was understrength and was easily defeated with heavy losses. Montgomery concluded that a frontal assault on Caen was doomed to failure as he wrote General Simpson, "I have decided not to have a lot of casualties by batting up against the place."[25]

Montgomery's new plan was to encircle Caen with a simultaneous attack by General Miles Dempsey's Second Army from east to west. I Corps formed the left pincer. On June 10 just as the corps began its attack, Rommel launched his own offensive to the east of Caen, thereby blunting

Montgomery's planned envelopment. The Twenty-First Panzer Division rapidly routed the I Corp's attack. The objective of the right pincer, headed by the Seventh British Armored Division, was to drive rapidly inland twenty miles from the coast and take the key area-road network around Villers-Bocage. (See Map 8.) This was bocage country with sunken lanes and ten-foot-high hedgerows. The British were totally unprepared to fight in this beautiful but treacherous terrain, but they did reach Villers-Bocage on June 13 at 8:00 a.m.

Fig. 7.1. Generals Dempsey and Montgomery. (Photo by Morris [Sgt.] No. 5 Army Film & Photographic Unit)

All that stood between these British tanks and German encirclement was a tiny First SS Panzer Reserve of five Tiger tanks and one Mark IV commanded by Captain Michael Wittmann, a famed panzer ace. After reaching the outskirts of Villers-Bocage, he observed a column of twenty-five British tanks and half-tracks leaving the village. The British column had stopped for further infantry reconnaissance. While waiting to advance, the tankers unexpectedly dismounted from their tanks. This was a fateful mistake.

Wittman sprang into action. Screened by a hedgerow, he took some of his sixty-ton Tiger tanks and ran down the parked unmanned tanks, firing broadsides at them and setting them ablaze. With the column finished, Wittman burst into Villers-Bocage and destroyed more of idled British tanks before withdrawing to rearm. He returned in the early afternoon with his entire force and crushed the outgunned British. Later in the day he was finally stopped by reinforcing British armor.

This ended one of the most amazing engagements in the history of armored warfare. At the cost of four tanks, Wittman's attack had destroyed thirty British tanks and armored vehicles. The battle of Villers-Bocage was a German victory and the second Allied failure to take Caen. Two months passed before Villers-Bocage was taken by the Allies.[26]

Both sides now dug in around Caen awaiting reinforcements. Reminiscent of World War I, the Norman countryside became lined with entrenchments and barbed wire with outbreaks of artillery and mortar fire. Montgomery's promised war of movement had stopped almost before it had started. Dempsey feared that the front had congealed. The suspicion arose that the formidable Seventh Armored Division had lost its esprit de corp. Its veterans felt that they had already seen their fair share of combat in the Mediterranean.[27]

Sensing a crisis, on June 15 Eisenhower and Air Chief Marshal Sir Arthur Tedder flew to Montgomery's headquarters to assess what was happening. From June 13 to 15, Monty wrote,

> The turning point of the battle was I think on 12 June, when the thrust line of 7 Armd DIV . . . broke through and reached VILLERS BOCAGE on morning 13 June. We were then in a position to be able to force a German withdrawal . . . [14 June.] The situation in that area is still a bit confused. . . . I have got to be certain of my position, step by step. . . . I would be stronger still if I had CAEN itself, but I am quite well posi-

> tioned as things are at present. . . . I have therefore decided to be defensive in the CAEN sector . . . but aggressively so. [June 15.] The situation in the CAUMONT-VILLERS BOCAGE area is now well in hand.[28]

Monty's account glossed over the important fact that the British were forced to retreat after gaining an important objective. Instead of an offensive to take Caen, Monty switched to the defensive. How could this still be aggressive? When his planned attack fell flat, how could everything still be "well in hand"?

Thus in his meeting with Ike, Monty declared he had everything under control. He bristled when Eisenhower suggested that he lost the initiative to Rommel by not breaking through his flank around Caen and making the promised breakthrough toward Falaise. Montgomery's mismanagement and denial proved a costly mistake and set up a pattern he would repeat over and over again.[29]

## BOCAGE HELL

From the air Normandy was a picture of bucolic splendor with green quilts of fields outlined by husky hedgerows. Crisscrossing the countryside, shaded lanes sometimes formed into leafy tunnels running between the fields. *Larousse*, the French dictionary, defines the bocage as a "pleasantly shaded woodland."[30]

These man-made barriers enclosed first the Celtic farm fields, then grazing livestock during the Roman era. Over one thousand years of growth bound the hedgerows' roots into solid, earthen embankments with steep faces. The base alone rose from three to six feet. From this impenetrable base hawthorn, brambles, and trees often grew to a height of twenty feet.

This bocage terrain, some fifty miles deep, was mainly located between the Orne and Vire Rivers. (See Map 9.) Within it were thousands of small fields one hundred to two hundred yards long, some no more than the size of a homesite. The hedgerows became a perfect defense system for the German army. Also much of this area had been flooded by Rommel as an added defensive measure.

American soldiers trapped on country lanes flanked by hedgerows saw only a few yards in any direction and were limited to moving forward or backward. Small breaks in this bocage allowed entry into enclosed fields. But hidden German machine gunners were in perfectly concealed positions to decimate American infantry as they groped their way along the roads and wagon trails or crawled to attack in these fields.

Fig. 7.2. Bocage/hedgerows of Normandy. (Archives Normandie 1939–1945)

Tanks were of little help. This was appalling tank country. The hedgerows were perfect for concealing defending German panzers, antitank guns, and mortars until an American Sherman tank was at point-blank range. Moreover, the tanks were not able to smash through these earthen dikes. They had to go over them, making their undersides easy prey for close-range antitank weapons, such as the German Panzerfaust (a bazooka-type device). Tank mobility was further limited by the numerous streams, rivers, steep hills, and valleys in this area.

The Wehrmacht called it a *schmutziger buschkrieg*, a "dirty bush war." The Germans had learned on the Russian front how to make up paucity in troops, artillery, and most importantly the Luftwaffe. Every position was meticulously camouflaged.

Fig. 7.3. A British Universal Carrier drives through a gap made in a hedgerow. (© Imperial War Museums [B 7582])

The battle of the bocage became a slow, plodding hell. It was a head-on slugfest on a microscale, fought over and over again. For almost two months the Americans were trapped in this maze with seemingly no way out.[31]

Bradley and the rest of the American command had grossly underestimated the significant difficulty of fighting in the bocage. Bradley knew there were hedgerows in Normandy. But training exercises in English hedgerows thought to be similar was like comparing Bunker Hill outside Boston to Mount Everest in the Himalayas. A 1943 First Army report had advised that special tactics for fighting "through bocage country should be given considerable study." Obviously this was not done.[32]

Even General George C. Marshall, US Army chief of staff, pleaded ignorance of the deadly hedgerow. "We had to pay in blood for our lack of knowledge."[33]

Fig. 7.4. German tank concealed in a hedgerow. (Bundesarchiv, Bild 101I-738-0275-09A / photo: Arthur Grimm)

The Allied planners of NEPTUNE were preoccupied with the difficulties of securing the beachheads and the armored advance to the Caen-Falaise plain. They never seriously considered how unpromising the bocage terrain was for an American offensive. They might have had second thoughts about their choice of invasion beaches had they realized this.

The most important reason why the Americans failed to plan sufficiently for fighting in the bocage was because in Montgomery's original campaign plan, much of the bocage was to be bypassed. The Allies were to pivot southeastward by taking Caen on D-Day. There the Falaise plain offered many more and better roads and wide-open fields for armor deployment. Of course, Montgomery did not take Caen on D-Day or soon thereafter.[34]

Despite the obstacles of the bocage, the US Ninetieth and Ninth Infantry Divisions and the Eighty-Second Airborne Division hacked and chewed their way through these hedgerows and the entrenched Germans with more Yankee grit than any tactical finesse. The most apparent weakness in the American June ground attack was the lack of sufficient training given to the infantry divisions to coordinate with separate tank battalions. Armor and infantry radios operated on different channels. To develop mutual infantry-armor confidence and awareness, the tanks in Normandy installed infantry-type radios tuned to the infantry radio net. Army signal companies also attached telephones or microphones so that infantrymen were connected with the tankers inside.

On June 18 they finally reached the west coast, having cut an eighteen-mile path across the Cotentin Peninsula. (See map 10.) The Americans now turned north toward their principal objective, the port of Cherbourg.[35]

## THE MAN WHO WOULD BE KING

After Germany's crushing defeat of France in May and June 1940, an obscure French officer, General Charles de Gaulle, fled to England and gradually assumed leadership of the Free French Forces. In 1944 de Gaulle persuaded Eisenhower that he was the only French leader capable of rallying the Resistance in France and thus ably assisting the Allied invasion and liberation of his country.

De Gaulle spent 1916 to 1918 during World War I in a German POW camp. Between the wars he became an early advocate for the offensive use of armored units in the French army. This made him unpopular with the military leadership of France who had a defensive mindset. The loss of over one million soldiers in World War I caused them to build the Maginot Line, designed to be a massive barrier for the next war.[36]

De Gaulle was only a colonel when World War II began. After the German armored breakthrough at Sudan, he was given command of an improvised Fourth Armored Division. On May 17, 1940, he slowed the German advance to the English Channel with two hundred tanks, but with no air support his success was only temporary. This brought him a promotion to brigadier general, and shortly afterward on June 5, he was appointed under secretary of war in Premier Paul Reynaud's government.

On June 16 he learned that Marshal Philippe Petain had formed a new government and planned to seek an armistice with Germany. Because de Gaulle had strongly opposed surrender and feared arrest, he boarded a small plane at Bordeaux on June 17 and fled to England. The next day he made his famous address to the French people on the BBC, urging others to continue the war against Germany. "Whatever happens, the flame of resistance must never go out and will not go out."[37]

Fig. 7.5. General Charles de Gaulle. (Office of War Information, Overseas Picture Division)

De Gaulle was arrogant, demanding, haughty, and very difficult to deal with. He was determined to be the leader who would restore France to its great power status after its humiliating defeat in 1940. Churchill was almost driven mad by de Gaulle's extreme intransigence, yet respected his determination to fight on against long odds.[38]

Very few of Free French joined him at first. Most French people believed that after the fall of France, Britain would be forced to conclude an armistice with Germany. This never deterred de Gaulle who immediately began to organize the Armée Secrete (FCNL) as a French paramilitary resistance organization. Up to 22,500 men were parachuted into France, and weapons were stockpiled. They gradually became ready to act on D-Day in support of the Allied landing in France. The FCNL also prepared for a national uprising to be launched in conjunction with the invasion.[39]

De Gaulle needed to convince the Allies that he had broad support across French society. Some of the resistance groups had come under the control of the French Communist Party. An internal conflict broke out between the Communists and the Free French resistance groups. The Communists sought to foment a national insurrection with the full participation of French and foreign resisters and then form a left-wing government. De Gaulle, on the other hand, sought to have his Free French forces pave his way to land in France, liberate Paris, and acclaim him the leader of the French government. Then de Gaulle planned to take the lead in reestablishing France's role as a great power during the closing days of the war in Europe.

While recognizing the value of de Gaulle's Free French movement, both Roosevelt and Churchill were skeptical of his contention that he represented the French government in exile. Unlike the Polish, Dutch, Norwegian, and other legitimate government leaders that had fled to London to escape the Nazi invasion, de Gaulle in 1940 was neither an elected official nor a widely recognized leader of France. Roosevelt and Churchill took the position that free elections should be held after the liberation in which the French people would decide on the form of government and its leadership.

As SHAEF's military leader, Eisenhower sought to drive the Germans out of France and avoid internal political disorder during this process. He did not exclude the possibility of creating an interim Allied Military Government in Occupied Territory (AMGOT).

However as D-Day approached it became very difficult for the Allies to cut de Gaulle's Free French out of the liberation of their own country. By 1944 de Gaulle had established his headquarters in French Algeria. Free French army forces were fighting with the Allies in Italy.

Roosevelt and Churchill reluctantly concurred that de Gaulle should be flown to England on June 4 so that Eisenhower could brief him on OVERLORD.[40]

Eisenhower and his deputy Walter Bedell Smith charmed de Gaulle into cooperating with the OVERLORD effort. But Eisenhower explained the Allied dilemma in a secret June 3 memorandum:

> All our information leads us to believe that the only authority these Resistance Groups desire to recognize is that of de Gaulle's and his Committee [FCNL]. . . . De Gaulle is apparently willing to cooperate only on the basis of our dealing with him exclusively, the whole thing falls into a rather sorry mess. De Gaulle is, of course, now controlling the only French military forces that can take part in this operation. Consequently, from a purely military viewpoint we must . . . deal with him alone.[41]

After June 6 the French underground launched a widespread campaign to attack Germans throughout the country. They also helped the Allies in their advance across France by providing vital intelligence on enemy positions and strength.

On June 14 de Gaulle, with Eisenhower's approval, embarked from Portsmouth for Normandy on the Free French destroyer *La Combattante* provided by Admiral Ramsay. It was exactly four years to the day that the Nazi army had marched into Paris.

British officers met de Gaulle's party at the beach and drove the general to meet Montgomery for lunch. Afterward they were driven to Bayeux, home of the famous Bayeux Tapestry that told the story of another invasion—William the Conqueror's 1066 landing in England. Ignoring Churchill's condition for his visit of no public meetings, de Gaulle stepped onto an improvised platform outside the Sous-Prefecture (town hall) and addressed a large crowd that broke into cheers. At the speech's conclusion he said, "The Government of France salutes Bayeux—the leading town of French liberty."[42] All then sang the "Marseillaise" After receiving pledges of support from local officials, de Gaulle departed. He repeated this assertion of authority in two nearby towns, Isigny and Grandcamp. By the time he departed that night, de Gaulle was firmly in control. Eisenhower had helped him make the difficult leap from being a minor general to becoming the acclaimed leader of France. De Gaulle's next stop would be Paris.[43]

## "FIGHT AND DIE WHERE HE STANDS"

By mid-June Hitler was still insisting that his forces would throw the Allies back into the sea. Sensing "defection" he summoned Rundstedt and Rommel to Margival near Soissons, France. They met (June 16) in a large elaborate concrete command center built to direct the German invasion of England in 1940, not the Allied landings from England in 1944.

Rommel began with a grim review describing "the seriousness of the situation . . . how impossible were the conditions under which the German soldier was being forced to fight."[44] The field marshal wanted to carry out a limited withdrawal beyond the range of the Allied fleet to launch a panzer counterattack on the British army's flank.

Hitler refused. No withdrawal, "every man shall fight and die where he stands."[45] Any other solution was defeatism. Rommel had been forced to improvise, using the Normandy landscape's bocage as the stage for small unit firefights that hinged on the fighting strength of the individual solider to hold or to take a position. At first the more seasoned German veterans had an advantage over many less-experienced Allied soldiers. But this was a battle of attrition that could end in only one way for Germany.

Seated on a high stool Hitler swept aside his field marshals' warnings and told them his plans for the next phase of the German Normandy operation. Four panzer divisions were on their way from Russia to France. They would create a Schwerpunkt (center of effort) by launching a drive at the junction of the Allied armies. Meanwhile his new V-weapons' bombardment of London would help win the war by breaking British morale. His field marshals then pleaded with him to direct this weapon against the invasion's beaches or ports in England.

Hitler summoned the commanding general of V-weapon ballistics, Lieutenant General Erich Heinemann, to their conference. He explained that the margin of error of these missiles was huge—up to nine to twelve miles from the intended targets. This would endanger German troops in the bridgehead. Heinemann's admission revealed that it was still technically impossible to accurately launch German V-weapons at the Allied armies. Viewing his commanders as mere subordinates to his military genius, Hitler thought them politically naïve and dismissed their estimates and judgments.[46]

Rommel finished the situation report by frankly urging an armistice to end the war. An enraged Hitler cut his favorite field marshal off: "Don't occupy yourself with that issue—look after your invasion front."[47]

## THE GREAT STORM—"CUT THEM OFF IN THEIR REAR"

OVERLORD's logistics were always Admiral Ramsay's top long-term worry. Supply issues were critical from the very beginning and were never completely solved during the entire campaign.

During the three days following June 6, a huge backlog of ships jammed the anchorages. Bureaucratic army/navy procedures slowed the unloading. Ramsay ordered the ships unloaded and the cargos sorted afterward. Soon the backlog cleared.

During the week immediately following D-Day, the average daily arrival of vessels carrying men, stores, and equipment for the Allied buildup in the beachhead included forty LSTs, seventy-five LCTs, twenty LCIs (L), twenty-five Liberty ships, thirty-eight Coasters, and nine Troopships.[48]

On June 18 everything in both American and British sectors was "all tickety-boo" (a phrase Montgomery used for military perfection).[49]

The weather had been basically benign. On June 18 the two artificial Mulberry harbors were unloading seven ships simultaneously. Unexpectedly in the early hours of June 19, Normandy was hit by the worst storm in nearly forty years. Few men or supplies landed for three days. Some eight hundred ships were beached or lost. The American Mulberry off Omaha Beach was destroyed. The British Mulberry at Arromanches was damaged but repairable.

In three days the "Great Storm" destroyed many more Allied ships than the Germans had damaged in sixteen days of fighting.[50] Hitler had always predicted that bad storms would overturn the Allied invasion. A period of "foul weather and storms [will] cut them off in their rear [making] everything . . . all right."[51]

At first it may have appeared that the führer was right. In the three days before this storm, daily landings averaged over 29,000 tons of supplies, 5,800 vehicles, and 34,000 troops. The daily logistics from June 19 to June 22 plummeted to 7,300 tons of supplies, 2,400 vehicles, and 9,800 troops. American ingenuity now saved the invasion.[52]

Fig. 7.6. Wrecked pontoon causeway of one of the Mulberry artificial harbors, following the storm of June 19–22, 1944. (US Navy Photograph: SHAEF-OSS, collection, Archives Branch, Naval History and Heritage Command, Washington, DC)

Before the Mulberry harbors were completed, LCSs, LCVPs, LCTs, Rhino-barge-type ferries, and DUKWs amphibious trucks were used for discharging troops and cargo from freighters and transports onto the beaches. A crucial decision was made to also allow the large LSTs to drive up right onto the beach. After discharging their cargo the lighter LSTs floated off on the next high tide. Normandy's soft, sandy beaches caused little ship damage.

After the American Mulberry was destroyed, this use of LSTs increased dramatically. It was soon discovered that each Mulberry pierhead accommodated only two LSTs at a time. However Utah and other appropriate beaches accommodated dozens of LSTs. The British Mulberrys were faster at unloading a few ships, while the beached American LSTs were slower at discharging but simultaneously unloaded many more ships at once. Ultimately both methods were employed at the same time. A logistics crisis passed as the flood of supplies for the invasion once again continued.[53]

Larry Hendrickson was a lieutenant on LST 527 sailing from Weymouth and other southern English ports to Utah, Omaha, and other Normandy beaches. He recalled, "The beaches were a flurry of activity—10 to 20 ships at a time would unload or wait to unload while jeeps and other vehicles scurried around the sand transporting men and supplies. . . . We made 45 trips from June 6, 1944 to May 8, 1945. . . . It took 10 or 12 hours to make the trip across the channel."[54]

One month after D-Day, despite the ruinous storm, 1,000,000 men, 200,000 vehicles, and 700,000 tons of supplies were delivered to the Normandy bridgehead. Once again a Hitler prediction of the path to victory was proven wrong.[55]

## CHERBOURG DELAY

Bradley had cut off the Germans on the Cotentin Peninsula by June 18. He had hoped to take the vital port of Cherbourg by June 21. On that same day Montgomery had sent Bradley the order, "First US Army will thrust toward La Haye du Puits and Coutances beginning on 21 June."[56]

Unfortunately on June 19, the Great Storm lashed Normandy and offensive operations slowed to a near halt. General Joseph Collins's VII Corps (Ninth, Seventy-Ninth, and Fourth Divisions) were delayed for two days in their advance toward Cherbourg. Nicknamed "Lightning Joe," Collins was the commanding general on Guadalcanal and was known as an aggressive hands-on leader. The storm, like the bocage, had slowed down the US Cherbourg attack. (See Map 10.)

It was not until June 21 that the Americans were deployed to assault the city. General Karl von Schlieben had withdrawn his German forces into the heavy fortifications surrounding the city. The defenses of Cherbourg were very formidable. Before the war the city was an important French naval base. The Germans further fortified these defenses to the point of impregnability. Although the Allied air forces laid down a massive aerial bombardment on June 22, they inflicted very little damage to the German defenses. American troops were reluctant to assault the strong fortifications.

Operation NEPTUNE included plans for a naval bombardment of Cherbourg to speed the city's surrender and save its harbor facilities. Ramsay, however, was not very confident that the Allied capital ships could knock out the German batteries. Rear Admiral Morton Deyo commanded a mainly American task force consisting of the US battleships *Texas*, *Arkansas*, and *Nevada* with twelve- and fourteen-inch guns; US cruisers *Tuscaloosa* and *Quincy* along with British Cruisers HMS *Glasgow* and *Enterprise*, each with six-inch guns; as well as a strong screening force of destroyers and minesweepers.

These Allied ships were up against a formidable foe. For example, the Hamburg Battery had four 280mm (eleven-inch) guns, far larger caliber than any the Allies had previously faced. Expert naval gunners from the Kriegsmarine manned these guns. The battery was encased in heavy concrete, steel-reinforced casemates. Cherbourg's batteries consisted of twenty gun-housing casemates.

On June 26, the guns of the Allied capital ships fired 376 large caliber shells for two hours and twenty minutes.[57] The fleet also offered to fill call-fire requests from Collins's ground forces then assaulting the city. At 2:51 p.m. the task group retired, but they had not suppressed the German defenses. German marksmanship, however, proved very accurate. The USS *Texas* suffered two hits; USS *O'Brien*, USS *Barton*, and USS *Laffey* were all hit, and the HMS *Glasgow* had two hits and one very near miss.

The Allies did have some successes. The USS *Texas* landed a fourteen-inch shell directly on one of the big German guns, knocking it out. The Allied bombardment also helped undermine the German garrison's fighting spirit, although some of the forts held out for one or two days after the city's surrender.

After the June 22 air assault, Collins began his attack on Cherbourg's outer defenses. Two days later it became a battle of close encounter, with house-to-house fighting. General Schlieben's main goal was to delay the fall of the city until his engineers had thoroughly wrecked the harbor, as Hitler had ordered him to leave the harbor a field of ruin unusable for receiving Allied supplies. Late in the day of June 23, fires set by the Germans raged across Cherbourg, consuming military installations, buildings, and supplies that might support the Allied invasion. During that night a tremendous explosion and fireball engulfed the harbor's Gare Maritime. A German demolition team blew up an entire freight train loaded with dynamite inside the port terminal. The concussion was felt by soldiers in their foxholes well outside the city.[58]

Schlieben did not surrender to Collins until June 27, when a ceremony was held at the Hotel de Ville (city hall). It took two more precious days for the outer forts to surrender.

The port of Cherbourg was a scene of complete devastation. "The demolition was masterful," said Colonel Alvin O. Viney, the engineer who planned to rehabilitate the port, "beyond a doubt the most complete, intensive, and best-planned demolition job in history."[59] When Ramsay came to Cherbourg on July 6, he noted in his diary, "The damage is unbelievable. . . . Dry docks and basins undamaged but blocked by numerous ships and craft. It will take anything up to 3 months to clear away these wrecks."[60] Yet by early September the port became operational, moving twelve thousand tons per day of supply, about half of its normal capacity.

There was great jubilation over the fall of Cherbourg in the Allied camp. It capped the most dramatic advance since D-Day. But the advance to Cherbourg fell short of heightening the pace of the Allied advance or improving the invasion's vulnerable logistics and anchoring the bridgehead.

The Allies were behind schedule. Taking the northern Cotentin Peninsula had taken too much time. An ammunition drought became so severe that Bradley had to tap his emergency ammo dump, and supplies had to be airlifted to the bridgehead. Between the weather and the bocage, Bradley had made little progress fulfilling Montgomery's order to drive farther south toward Coutances. When on June 27 General Everett Hughes, Eisenhower's "eyes and ears" during OVERLORD, reported that there were new movement delays of Bradley's First Army, the supreme commander had second thoughts about the current SHAEF command arrangements. Eisenhower told Hughes, "Sometimes I wish I had George Patton over there!"[61]

On the day of Cherbourg's surrender (June 27) Ramsay released all the US battleships and cruisers back to Admiral Ernest J. King, chief of US naval operations. King had demanded the return of these ships on June 19, seven days before the Cherbourg bombardment, in order to expedite the upcoming invasion of southern France (ANVIL/DRAGOON, August 13).[62]

On June 20 Ramsay officially ended Operation NEPTUNE. In the fleet of seven thousand ships, only 267 were lost. The Germans sank 108 vessels (mostly victims of mines), including twenty-five warships (only 1.5 percent). Severe weather caused the loss of 153, and six were sunk by marine hazards.[63]

Fig. 7.7. German destruction of Cherbourg Port. June 1944. (Archives Normandie 1939–1945)

In the judgment of naval historian Craig Symonds, "It was an astonishing chronicle of perseverance and productivity." A "highly professional Bertram Ramsay" led a team of dedicated people who made NEPTUNE's success possible.[64] On July 26, Ramsay wrote, "Because it all went so smoothly it may seem to some people that it was all easy and plain sailing. Nothing could be more wrong. It was excellent planning and execution."[65]

By July 5, the millionth Allied soldier landed in Normandy. An "apt and timely enough testimony to NEPTUNE's success," wrote Correlli Barnett.[66] Ramsay would continue to be in charge of the massive naval logistics for OVERLORD. But once Operation NEPTUNE ended, SHAEF ignored his warning that it was logistically vital to quickly capture a major port to support the Allied advance across Europe into Germany.

## EPSOM: THE BLITZ THAT "CRACKED"

While Bradley was advancing toward Cherbourg, Eisenhower was fuming over Montgomery's delay in taking Caen. On June 22, the Soviets launched Operation BAGRATION on the Russian front. Over the next three weeks more than 350,000 German soldiers were killed or captured, and the Russians ended up at the gates of Warsaw.[67]

This put added pressure on the Western allies to do their part. Montgomery, however, insisted first on "tidying up his administrative tail" (i.e., deploying an overwhelming abundance of soldiers and weapons before attacking).[68] Finally on June 18, he sent a directive to Bradley and Dempsey stating that his "operations against Caen will be developed by means of a pincer movement from both flanks."[69] The Great Storm then struck in the English Channel, delaying his Operation EPSOM from June 23 to June 26.[70]

Monty intended to use all three corps of his Second Army plus additional armored units: sixty thousand soldiers and over six hundred tanks. General Richard O'Connor's VIII Corps was to spearhead the attack to the west of Caen, supported by XXX Corps. They would establish a bridgehead south of the Odon River then advance to the Orne River. The key was to capture Hill 112 between the two rivers. (See Map 11.) I Corps attacking north of Caen would prepare to eliminate the German salient and clear the city.[71]

In a message to Eisenhower on June 25, Monty assured him, "[The] blitz attack of 8 Corps goes in tomorrow at 7:30 hrs and once it starts I will continue the battle on the eastern flank till one of us cracks and it will NOT be us."[72] On June 29 the British Eleventh Armored took Hill 112. Meanwhile German panzer counterattacks were countered by the Fifteenth British Infantry Division that turned the German attack into a rout. O'Connor wanted to then drive the Eleventh Armored to seize a bridgehead over the Orne River beyond the Odon.

Unfortunately, information on this important victory did not reach General Dempsey, commander of the British Second Army. He remained in the dark, still believing a major German panzer thrust was still to come. At headquarters Dempsey and Montgomery jointly decided to play it safe and pulled back the Eleventh Armored Division off Hill 112 instead of reinforcing it and continuing O'Connor's advance. This was a tragic decision. Future battles to take Hill 112 were some of the most grisly ones of

OVERLORD, degenerating into a number of murderous hand-to-hand fights recalling the trench warfare of 1914–1918.

Montgomery halted EPSOM on July 1 even though a second German counterattack by the Second Panzer Corps also was defeated. This aborted attack was a costly one for British forces as the British VIII Corps suffered 4,020 casualties in the five-day engagement and infantry losses ran well in excess of 50 percent. Once again the successful advance by British troops who were nearing their objectives was negated by the commanding officers' failure of nerve. Like the D-Day advance on Caen, and the Villers-Bocage ploy, EPSOM was a dismal failure.[73]

## STALEMATE

Eisenhower's great frustration over Monty's direction of the Normandy land battles is easy to understand. With EPSOM he had told Eisenhower, "I am prepared to have a show down with the enemy on my eastern flank for as long as he likes."[74] But after only five days of battle it was Monty who was the one who "cracked," not Rommel. As historian Antony Beevor observed, this was Montgomery's well-established command behavior in which he "had the unusual gift of persuasively combining very bold speech and very cautious action. His handling of the Normandy ground battle was an excellent example of his self-delusional leadership."[75]

Even Ramsay, one of the few principal Normandy commanders who got along with the temperamental Monty, began to suspect that the stalemate developing in the land battle was the result of Montgomery's generalship. Ramsay noted in his diary, "Our 2nd Army more or less held down and our 'blitz attack' listed for Wednesday now postponed . . . ostensibly owing delay in build up! But I have my doubts whether that is really the cause. Certainly this long pause on the 2nd Army front is most regrettable."[76]

Yet Montgomery kept assuring everyone before, during, and after EPSOM, "My general broad plan is maturing quite reasonably well." (Letter to General Alan Brooke, June 27).[77] "[I] am well satisfied with present situation." (Message to Winston Churchill, June 29).[78] "Our tactics must remain unchanged. . . . To retain the initiative. . . . To develop operations for the capture of Caen as opportunity offers—and the sooner the better." (Directive to Bradley and Dempsey, June 30).[79]

But what plan was Monty referring to? His first plan was to take Caen on D-Day and position the Allied armored divisions on the Falaise plain, with the American breakthrough on the right avoiding the bocage country. After moving southward into Brittany, the Americans and British would join up for an eastward advance toward Paris.

Or was Monty now referring to his recently hatched plan B. He formally announced this new plan on June 30 to Bradley and Dempsey after his third attempt to capture Caen failed. "My broad policy, once we had secured a firm lodgment area has always been to draw the main enemy forces into the battle on our eastern flank [British/Canadian], and to fight them there, so that our affairs on the western flank [American] could proceed the easier."[80]

Montgomery's evasions became too much for Eisenhower and the other OVERLORD commanders. He simply refused to acknowledge the failure of his original D-Day strategy. Eisenhower began to see that the implications of this new holding strategy amounted to a siege of Caen. This was no breakout toward Paris. Bradley also told Eisenhower not to expect a quick breakout, as his divisions were tied down in the bocage.

The first major failure of the OVERLORD operation started here. Because Montgomery's British and Canadian forces did not quickly seize Caen on D-Day, the Germans were given time to concentrate their panzer divisions around the city. Before the invasion Monty had warned that this must be avoided at all costs. So now he tried to turn his defeat into a victory through an unimaginative and inadequate cover-up of the collapse of his original plan. Montgomery constantly repeated this artifice, hoping that his fellow commanders and posterity might come to believe it. He was wrong.

By the end of June, the Allied invasion of Normandy had deteriorated into a stalemate. The British, Canadians, and Americans had established a solid invasion bridgehead, but Montgomery's failure to take Caen allowed the Germans to bring in reinforcements, thus making it harder for the Allies to seize this key city and launch the breakout to liberate France. Bradley's American army had consequently been forced into a confusing and costly battle of the hedgerows for which they were ill-equipped and ill-trained.[81]

## "MAKE PEACE—YOU FOOLS!"

The British attack on June 26 forced Rundstedt and Rommel to redeploy the newly arrived SS panzer corps from an attack formation into the defense of the Caen perimeter. Gunfire from Royal Navy ships off the Normandy coast was able to inflict significant damage on German forces from over eighteen miles away. The shell craters were twenty feet across and ten feet deep. Rommel and Geyr von Schweppenburg were shaken by the loss of men and equipment that they could not replace. By June 25, the Wehrmacht had lost 47,070 men, including six generals.[82] Rommel saw his tanks reduced to stiffening the weakened German infantry divisions struggling to hold the line. Although the SS panzer corps finally mounted a counterattack in the Bayeux sector on June 29, it did not achieve any major breakthrough.

This murderous battle of attrition was not confined to the panzer divisions. General Dietrich von Choltitz, new commander of the LXXXIV Corps, complained that his units were losing up to a battalion and a half of troops per day from artillery fire and air attacks. The German commanders in Normandy were united in demanding that something had to change before their steadily weakening line collapsed.

At the height of the EPSOM battle on June 29, the hopes of Rundstedt and Rommel were raised when Hitler summoned them both for a second meeting at Berchtesgaden. Before their arrival the two field marshals reached this full agreement on how to save the situation: Withdrawal from Caen. Have the infantry hold the line on the Orne River. Allow the rest and refit of the panzer divisions. Then launch a powerful counterattack on the Americans' flank in the Cherbourg Peninsula. (See Map 12).

Hitler made them wait for six hours before receiving them at 6:00 p.m. The field marshals gave their views that the army was being destroyed and needed to be redeployed. Hitler was furious and refused. Rundstedt told Liddell Hart, "There was no plan any longer. We were merely trying, without hope, to comply with Hitler's order that the line Caen—Avranches must be held at all costs."[83]

Upon their return from Berchtesgaden, they learned of the failed panzer corps strike at Bayeux. On July 1 Rundstedt, with Blumentritt, his chief of staff, listening in, called Keitel, the OKW chief of staff, and told him that the position "was impossible." The German troops could "not withstand the Allied attacks, much less push them into the sea."[84]

Keitel asked, "What should we do?"

"Make peace you fools," the field marshal snapped.

## WHO WAS IN CONTROL?

As the month of June ended the Allies were waging a series of confused battles that were largely contrary to their originally stated plans or those of the Germans. We might legitimately ask the question, "Who was in control?"

For the Allies—the ground commander Montgomery had become basically incapable of either leading or wanting to lead the called for offensive breakout. Bradley was literally bogged down in the hedgerows. In England, Eisenhower, the supreme commander, remained oddly detached in this crisis. He did not want to interfere. The direction of OVERLORD began to drift.

For the Germans—Hitler had absolute control over the Wehrmacht's deteriorating Normandy fortunes. Both Rundstedt and Rommel had become mere pawns on the führer's warped battlefield chessboard.

# CHAPTER 8
# BREAKOUT BLUES

"Neither Ike nor Brad has the right stuff. Ike is bound hand and foot by the British and does not know it. Poor fool. We actually have no Supreme Commander."
—General George S. Patton, 1944[1]

## HITLER'S AX FALLS

On July 2 Hitler, furious over Field Marshal von Rundstedt's frank criticism, relieved him of his command. Field Marshal Günther von Kluge was ordered to replace him. Hitler wanted to sack Field Marshal Rommel but relented because it would lower morale at the front and in Germany as well as leave a disastrous impression abroad.

Kluge was with Hitler on July 1 when Keitel appeared and gave him Rundstedt's message about ending the war. Hitler made a snap decision to place Kluge in command of the West. Called "clever Hans" (his family name means "clever" in German), Kluge was an energetic, quick-witted, aggressive soldier, who was not popular with his colleagues. He had distinguished himself as commander of the Fourth Army during the 1940 conquest of France. He was considered ruthless and cold. Kluge hated Hitler, but he was bound to him by honors and favors Hitler had bestowed on him. Kluge, like Rundstedt, had been given 250,000 reichsmarks as a present by his grateful führer.[2]

Kluge was with Hitler at Berchtesgaden after Kluge's six-month recovery from injuries in an air crash on the Russian front. Hitler had been considering him as the new commander of the German Central Army Group that was then melting away from the massive Russian summer offensive.

Fig. 8.1. Field Marshal Gunther von Kluge. (Bundesarchiv, Bild 183-2004-0524-500/photo: o.Ang)

Kluge arrived at La Roche-Guyon, Rommel's headquarters, on July 5. He immediately began arguing with Rommel deriding his overly pessimistic assessment of conditions in Normandy. Rommel flared up and told Kluge to take a personal tour of the Normandy front and talk to the field commanders before making any accusations.

Over the following days Kluge did just that, something he had often done throughout the war. The response from all the officers in the Seventh Army, Fifth Panzer Army, and the First and Second SS Corps was unanimous—the situation was dire.

Kluge completely changed his prior views and even apologized to Rommel. Kluge now backed the written strategic assessment that Rommel had sent to Hitler at the end of June. Within a few days Kluge's earlier cheerful and confident attitude regarding the Normandy front had become very somber and realistic. Hitler was not amused by this dramatic change in Kluge's perspective.[3]

## ALLIED STALEMATE CONTINUES

A month into the invasion the Allied bridgehead remained only a beachhead. The concentration of troops and vehicles grew to such an extent that the combat zone looked more like a crowded parking lot at a major sports event than a modern battlefield. The bridgehead was too small for maneuver. It was so thin that ground personnel standing at the Isigny airstrip (see Map 13) could watch a flight of P-51 aircraft take off, bomb the enemy, return to land, and never lose sight of the Allied planes.

At D+30 the Nazi swastika still flew over Caen, which made Montgomery look foolish. Bradley's First Army was wedged into a devilish terrain between hedgerow and swamp. Forward movement was painstaking for both infantry and armor.[4]

Allied casualties began to resemble trench warfare losses from World War I. Young Allied soldiers had to be stacked up like cordwood in long rows awaiting burial. Normandy became one of the most murderous operations of the war with more of the casualties happening after D-Day. The British had limited manpower to replace these casualties.

The Allied offensive had broken down. David I. Hall says it was "[l]acking an effective tactical doctrine and short of new ideas."[5] Fearful of

German panzer counterattacks, the Allies at first landed too much armor, leading to inappropriate ratios of armor to infantry units. In the hedgerows Allied tanks without enough infantry support became easy targets for the Germans. Most of the British, American, and Canadian soldiers in Normandy had very little knowledge or experience with infiltration tactics that many in the German infantry had learned at the Russian front. The Wehrmacht was still a formidable foe whose combat quality turned out to be far higher than the Allies had first predicted.

Bradley and Montgomery mounted limited offensive operations in early July. Little ground was gained, and casualties were high. OVERLORD's ground operations were deadlocked.

## BRADLEY'S OFFENSIVE FIZZLE

In early July, Bradley's First Army had reorganized from the Cherbourg operation in preparation for the great breakout offensive toward Coutances. (See Map 13.) When Bradley held a press conference on July 3, reporters pressed him for the date of the new offensive to take St. Lo. This was the biggest city in that part of the Cotentin Peninsula that controlled the roads for the intended breakout to Coutances. "This is off the record," Bradley told them before giving an answer. "I'd guess six days." It would take about twice as long to advance those seven miles.[6]

On July 4 at high noon, a 1,600-piece American artillery barrage opened the offensive, blanketing the whole front with a tremendous explosion. Yet from its green light onward the great offensive breakout fell apart, as Jonathan Jordan says, "like a wet biscuit."[7] Heavy rains often scrubbed ground-air support. The Americans struggled through rivers of mud made by the Germans flooding operations into the thick hedgerows of the bocage country.

In the center, Lieutenant General Charles "Cowboy Pete" Corlett's XIX Corps attacked across severe hedgerow terrain straight toward St. Lo. Major General Troy Middleton's VIII Corps and Major General Joseph "Lightning Joe" Collins's VII Corps struck on the right in an all-out drive down the peninsula's west coast toward Avranches. On the left, Major General Leonard Gerow's V Corps protected Montgomery's flank near Caumont. (See Map 13.)

Progress became a measure of yards rather than miles. Middleton's troops averaged only a thousand yards a day during the next two weeks while suffering ten thousand casualties. On July 14 an unnerved Bradley ordered Middleton and Collins to halt their drive. Corlett continued toward St. Lo, originally a June 11 objective. Corlett took St. Lo on July 18 but at a cost of another five thousand men.[8]

Bradley's breakout only moved the Allied line about seven miles at a cost of forty thousand battle casualties. The crack Panzer Lehr Division was particularly key in adding to the staggering US casualties. Moreover, the combat effectiveness of another ten thousand men was impaired by battle fatigue. Bradley's great July offensive had fizzled out as an unstainable slaughter at a cost of seven thousand GIs per mile.[9]

The high casualties triggered a feeling of despair among the troops who participated. Hedgerow warfare was physically very confining. It seemed to isolate the small combat teams from each other, thus leaving them with the feeling that they were on their own. Some of the divisions fighting here were largely newly arrived inexperienced troops. They had not been given any special training to fight in a hedgerow maze and were experiencing the difficult transition from training to combat.

Morgan's original COSSAC plan had the Normandy breakout targeted from Caen southward because tanks could better maneuver on the flat Falaise plain. This would have given the Allies the upper hand in a war of maneuver. Instead the offensives in the St. Lo area, where the bocage was at its worst, forced the unprepared Americans into brutal combat that resembled jungle warfare.

Charles Bonesteel, a US topographical staff officer, repeatedly warned Montgomery that the Americans could not achieve a breakout without huge casualties. Bonesteel proved correct regarding the casualties, and the breakout did not come quickly. Meanwhile Montgomery ignored the bloodletting and stuck to his "plan," launching only a series of diversionary attacks around Caen.[10]

## MONTGOMERY'S OPERATION CHARNWOOD: TOO LITTLE, TOO LATE

On July 7 Montgomery mounted another effort to capture Caen—Operation CHARNWOOD. It began with a major air strike by 460 British heavy bombers dropping over 2,600 tons of bombs.[11] Using the strategic bomber force that previously had concentrated only on the enemy's war-supporting infrastructure (railroads, refineries, factories, etc.) was an unorthodox technique. The air force barons, Air Chief Marshal Arthur Harris of British Bomber Command and Lieutenant General Carl A. Spaatz of the US Strategic Air Force, strenuously resisted this shift to a tactical target. As previously mentioned, bad relations between Montgomery and Eisenhower and the air chiefs persisted throughout the entire OVERLORD operation. Both Eisenhower and Churchill finally had to personally intervene and insist that the temporary use of these bombers was absolutely necessary for this renewed offensive.

The massive air bombardment of Caen was followed by two days of bitter fighting by 115,000 men of the British Third, Highland Fifty-First, and Canadian Third Divisions. But Operation CHARNWOOD was only a partial success. It took only the northern half of Caen reaching the banks of the Orne River where it divides the city at a cost of eighty tanks and over 3,500 casualties.[12] (See Map 14.)

The capture of the northern half of the city was more symbolic than useful. Caen itself was dominated by the heights of the Bourguébus Ridge, located about four miles to the southeast. In Caen's eastern suburb of Cormelles, German observers perched in the tall towers of an immense steelworks could still spot all British movements below.

The British did take the Carpiquet airfield and reached the banks of the Orne and Odon, but it was too little, too late. The key to the OVERLORD plan was the rapid capture of the city of Caen or its bypass by an Allied offensive. CHARNWOOD gained little territory. Montgomery failed to provide even enough ground to deploy the bulk of the First Canadian Army still waiting across the channel in England.[13]

## MONTY'S MIND GAMES

By early July a din of criticism rose from other commanders, the press, and politicians over the lack of progress on the ground in Normandy. Disbelief mounted because of the disparity between what the map showed and what Montgomery claimed. The critical question remained, what Allied strategy would regain the ground initiative and propel their armies across France into Germany?

While this storm gathered around Montgomery, he sat in splendid isolation inside his camouflaged mobile caravan, Tactical Headquarters (Tac), surrounded by his pet dogs and birds. His three caravans served as his office, sleeping quarters, and map room. His personal wood-paneled caravan had once belonged to an Italian general and was captured from Rommel during the campaign in Libya. The largest single component of this mobile headquarters was the Signals Service, capable of receiving top secret Ultra and other coded messages. The Tac staff consisted of his chief of staff, Major General Francis de Guingand, and a team of young liaison officers acting as Monty's eyes and ears. Senior officers rarely visited, and VIPs and other visitors were only grudgingly accepted by Monty.

Thus isolated from typical headquarter politics, personalities, and leadership pressure, Montgomery was totally absorbed in battlefield tactics, and all else fell by the wayside. He believed, "A commander must have time to think."[14]

Montgomery was not a team player, and his self-imposed aloofness in command also inflated his ego to the point of tragic overconfidence in his "plan." It accentuated his unwillingness to confide in anyone, including Brooke, Dempsey, de Guingand, Eisenhower, or Bradley, about how to move the Allied forces forward.[15]

What was behind Montgomery's thinking that might help explain his slowness in taking Caen? Why had he suddenly shifted the "plan" from a British-Canadian-led offensive breakout strategy to one of limited attacks?

Britain had been at war since 1939. Churchill made it very clear to Montgomery that the United Kingdom was saddled with huge war debts, a declining industrial base, and a manpower pool weakened by 500,000 empire casualties after almost five years of war. Although Britain had mobilized the highest percentage of its population of all the combatant nations (over four million), it was reaching the end of its manpower reserves. Churchill feared that the manpower situation would diminish his influence with Roosevelt and his status in the "Big Three Conferences" with Roosevelt and Stalin in deciding the postwar future of Europe.

By July 17 British and Canadian losses were 37,563. Though actual D-Day casualties had been fewer than expected, the situation went rapidly downhill afterward. British infantry casualties were 80 percent higher than estimated, with fewer and fewer available replacements.[16]

In mid-July Adjutant General Sir Ronald Adam was sent by the War Office to warn Montgomery and Dempsey that replacements would run out during the next few weeks. They would have to "cannibalize" (i.e., break up) some divisions to maintain the rest.[17]

Montgomery had to live with the fact that the Second Army was shrinking with each passing week. As he wrote to Alan Brooke, "The Second Army is now very strong; it has in fact reached its peak and can get no stronger; it will in fact get weaker as the manpower situation begins to hit us."[18]

Only after the war did Montgomery publicly acknowledge that the serious British manpower shortage caused him to change his "plan" on taking Caen. In an unpublished interview he admitted,

> We were short of ammunition, we were short of troops. . . . If we had failed [to take Caen], we would have been forced on the defensive. We might have had such losses that we could not even hold the ground we had. . . . You must remember that the British Army was a wasting asset. We had not the manpower to replace heavy casualties. The War Office told me before D-Day that it could guarantee replacements only for the first month. . . . It would have been very easy for me to yield to the public criticism and the American pressure and to have made greater efforts to gain ground on this flank. It might have helped my immediate reputation but it would have crippled the British Army.[19]

Montgomery believed that a major sustained British offensive to take Caen would lead to heavy casualties. Instead throughout June, July, and early August he mounted a whole series of limited attacks. In the long run, Monty's attrition strategy failed. The failure to take Caen quickly stalled the entire Allied offensive and resulted in heavy British infantry casualties.

Montgomery became an "attrition general" who paradoxically could not afford to fight attrition battles. In Normandy he re-tailored his battle plans that supposedly would compensate for these British-Canadian manpower limitations.

The set-piece battle was the forte of Montgomery and many other British commanders. As at El Alamein, this strategy allowed him to concentrate his forces—"tidy up," then cautiously and methodically "grip" the battle according to his set "plan."

At Caen and afterward to the end of the war, Monty's limitation was his lack of quick exploitation to follow up rapidly on battlefield success. As Bradley and Patton later pointed out, Monty's insistence on a "tidy" front slowed down his advance and allowed the enemy to reestablish a new defensive line that in the long run cost him more casualties and greater delay.[20]

On D-Day his "plan" to take Caen by assault failed miserably. Monty then modified his original scheme from offense to attrition, but he never admitted it. Colonel Christopher Daronay, a member of his tactical staff headquarters, wrote that Montgomery tried to "make himself bigger by saying he planned it all beforehand. He didn't."[21] Montgomery gloried in being the great general, the hero of El Alamein. "He did not feel able," says his biographer Alun Chalfont, "to admit to any weakness at all. Everything must be seen as run on oiled wheels along carefully laid tracks."[22]

Montgomery's operational approach was a holdover from his World War I experience on the western front—use a "colossal crack" to hit the enemy with devastating modern firepower. In the opinion of historian Antony Beevor, "The idea that high explosives saved British lives became almost addictive."[23]

Montgomery's "colossal crack" battlefield strategy proved to be very misleading for his Allied partners. Time and time again Montgomery seemed to promise the desired breakthrough but only delivered massed Allied firepower and a half-hearted infantry/armor general assault.

## SACK MONTGOMERY

Thus the stage was set for a major effort to remove Montgomery from his command of the Allied ground forces. The small size of the Normandy bridgehead was only 20 percent of what had been expected by the first half of July. The Allies needed more room to mount a successful breakout.

In early July 1944, Churchill was very angry as he believed that the World War I stalemate was being repeated. His government would not survive another holocaust, such as the Somme battles of World War I (over 400,000 British casualties). These fears were not groundless. According to historian Max Hastings, the infantry rates of loss in Normandy before the breakout were comparable with those of 1916.[24] Churchill feared it might be a year before a breakout. A protracted war might end his government and see Britain's decline. The specter of earlier failures at Gallipoli in World

War I that had been wrongly blamed on him, and Norway and Greece in the current conflict, closed in upon him.

On the evening of July 6 Churchill met with Brooke and viciously excoriated Montgomery's generalship. Brooke recorded in his diary that at 10:00 p.m. he had a "frightful meeting" with Winston that lasted until 2:00 a.m. "He began to abuse Monty because operations were not going faster . . . that he was over cautious. I flared up and asked him if he could not trust his generals for five minutes instead of continuously abusing them and belittling them. . . . He was furious with me, but I hope it may do some good in the future."[25]

Brooke's policy as chief of staff was to offer advice and criticism but leave the commander on the spot free to make his operational decisions. Throughout the war Brooke was generally successful in fending off Churchill's impulses to intervene in military decisions, although this made for a stormy relationship between these two leaders.

In this instance Brooke was successful with Churchill, who backed down on replacing Montgomery. Brooke had complete faith in Montgomery's operational judgment. "I don't interfere with him. He is an incomparable tactician."[26] Brooke's blank-check faith in Montgomery's command decisions would often be misplaced during OVERLORD and afterward.

Montgomery's lack of success in achieving a breakout in Normandy and his overarching, self-aggrandizing personality also made him a target of resentment at SHAEF, now led by Tedder, Eisenhower's deputy. The British officers began seeking to have Monty sacked. The American officers at SHAEF also joined in and pushed hard for Eisenhower to replace Montgomery as Allied ground force commander.

But Ike remained very reluctant to do this even though Churchill had intimated that he would back him if he decided that a British commander needed to be replaced. This occurred a few days after the Normandy landings when he met with Churchill and Brooke. After the war Eisenhower recalled that Churchill was particularly disappointed over Montgomery's failure to capture Caen on D-Day. Churchill told Ike that as the supreme commander he could sack any British officer "no matter what his rank," by telling him and General Brooke, "and the individual would be promptly removed!"[27] Since Montgomery was the target of Churchill's immediate anger, it appeared to Eisenhower that even Monty was not exempt from removal if the ground campaign stalled.

But Eisenhower's only response at this juncture was to attempt to push Montgomery forward by writing him a long pleading letter on July 7: "We have not yet attempted a major full-dress attack on the left flank [the British position] supported by everything we could bring to bear." Ike told Monty that they must all make "a determined effort to prevent a stalemate."[28]

The next day Monty assured Ike that the campaign was under control and moving forward: "I am, myself, quite happy about the situation. I have been working throughout on a very definite plan. . . . I think the battle is going very well. . . . [This was while CHARNWOOD was grinding to a premature halt.] There will be no stalemate."[29]

Another means that Eisenhower could have used to end the Normandy stalemate was to take command of the land battle as had been originally intended after the Allied bridgehead was established. Various weak excuses have been offered as to why Eisenhower hesitated to take the reins of command, including that he lacked a command post in Normandy, that he needed Churchill's approval, or such action would destabilize the Anglo-American alliance.

These were contributing issues, but it is now apparent that Eisenhower always preferred only having executive control over a military operation and allowing the other Allied commanders to direct the day-to-day ground battle. This was the established pattern of his earlier command experiences in North Africa, Sicily, and Italy. Both Brooke and Montgomery saw Eisenhower's command style as continuing evidence that he was only a political general and had neither the experience nor ability to lead the ground campaign.

Alas for the Allied command, OVERLORD badly needed Ike's direct intervention at decisive moments to cap the victory. As we will see, this command failure would compound the shortcomings of his subordinates.[30]

## CAEN CONUNDRUM CONTINUED

Montgomery revealed the "very definite plan" previously mentioned to Eisenhower at a July 10 conference with Bradley and Dempsey in his command caravan near Bayeux. He outlined a two-pronged envelopment campaign involving both the British/Canadian and American forces.

Dempsey had proposed a major attack with three armored divisions to overrun Caen and break out into the Falaise plain. Although Montgomery balked at first, after three days he agreed to the Dempsey plan, now code-named GOODWOOD (the second operation named after a British race-course, EPSOM being the first). Bradley was to plan the American campaign, which was subsequently given the code name COBRA.

COBRA and GOODWOOD were both born out of past failures. Both would use massive air power to obliterate German defenses. Major armored units were to surge over enemy fortifications. Their aim was to initiate a breakout across France. However, their massive air power requirements meant they could not occur simultaneously. GOODWOOD was to launch on July 18 and COBRA on July 21, offering a potential double envelopment of the German defensive front.[31]

Dempsey's initial GOODWOOD plan, Monty proclaimed, would "deliver a killing blow" and permanently "crush the German hold on Caen."[32] There were five phases to GOODWOOD: (1) use saturation air and naval bombardment to obliterate enemy defenses; (2) deploy 750 tanks for a wide penetration of the German front; (3) outflank both sides of the Germans in Caen's south suburbs; (4) take the Bourguébus Ridge, backbone of the German front; and (5) strike out toward Falaise. (See Map 15.)

Monty immediately began a propaganda effort to build up this offensive. On July 12, Montgomery wrote to Eisenhower that as a result of the initial air strikes, "My whole eastern flank will burst into flames on Saturday and the operation on Monday may have far reaching results."[33] The next day he recorded in his diary, "I decided that the time had now come to strike really heavy blows designed to knock loose the present enemy shackles that are now hemming us in."[34] On July 14 he wrote to Tedder at SHAEF, "Plan if successful promises to be decisive."[35] The same day he told Brooke, "I have decided that the time has come to have a real 'show down' on the eastern flank and to loose a Corps of three armored divisions into the open country about the Caen-Falaise road. . . . The possibilities are immense."[36] Montgomery's communications so widely raised hopes at SHAEF that Eisenhower was moved to write, "I would not be at all surprised to see you gaining a victory that will make some of the 'old classics' look like a skirmish between patrols."[37]

Montgomery's instructions to his ground commanders, however, were far different from his public proclamations. His July 10 directive states that an Orne River bridgehead was to be established "if this can be done without undue losses."[38] On July 15 he covertly clipped GOODWOOD's wings with a written directive to Dempsey that contained much more modest goals. The British advance was to stop only a third of the way to reaching Falaise. Montgomery wrote that the objective of the operation was "[t]o gain a good bridgehead over the ORNE through CAEN, and thus to improve our positions on the eastern flank . . . [and] generally to destroy German equipment and personnel."[39] Monty would decide how far to push the attack. He withheld this information from SHAEF and Brooke.

Montgomery's change from a "breakout" plan to a "tie-down" better fit his preference for attrition warfare. Strangely this major change was never transmitted below the level of corps commanders nor beyond the personnel of the Second Army staff. Montgomery never even fully briefed all the senior staff of the Twenty-First Army Group. This revised GOODWOOD plan was supposedly sent to SHAEF on July 17. However it was never received!

After the war Brigadier David Belchem, chief of operations at the Twenty-First Army Group, stated that Montgomery deliberately withheld the change to more limited objectives for GOODWOOD in order to keep SHAEF support, especially that of the air forces. "The reason for the secrecy was to avoid disclosure above all to Tedder . . . and Eisenhower that Goodwood was intended to pin down the enemy armor in the British sector. Goodwood was to have very limited objectives in terms of distance."[40]

GOODWOOD had been oversold to OVERLORD's senior commanders as an overwhelming surprise attack. Is it astonishing that after Monty's great breakout had failed, they felt misled, even lied to, and wanted Monty's head in a sack?

The problem was Montgomery's peculiar command perspective. He always wanted to be seen as the victor. His final GOODWOOD orders gave him enough leeway so no matter what the final outcome he could claim that everything had proceeded according to his "plan."[41]

## GOODWOOD'S BREAKOUT CHARADE

Early on July 18 over seven hundred heavy artillery guns opened fire on the German lines joined by naval vessels in the bay of the Seine. Overhead the first wave of a giant air offensive of two thousand heavy and six hundred medium bombers of the RAF and USAAF began dropping about eight thousand tons of bombs. For four hours the Allied air fleet carpet-bombed German positions while British and Canadian troops watched the massive destruction with rising excitement.[42]

In theory the enemy defenses were smashed. Tanks were flipped over. Machine-gun posts demolished. Infantry trenches and their occupants buried. Anti-tank guns smashed. Soldiers dazed and shaken surrendered to the first advancing tanks.

Yet the carpet-bombing was far from totally effective. The greatest number of bombs and shells fell into empty woods and fields. In particular, the scattered batteries of German 88mm flank batteries escaped without direct hits. German Tiger tanks unexpectedly came into action. Extensive minefields remained intact in front of the British advance units.

At 7:30 a.m. the lead armor of the Eleventh Armored Division began its advance through a few narrow lanes cleared of minefields. Soon huge traffic jams developed while the Guards and Seventh Armored Divisions waited for the Eleventh to clear and cross the bridges over the Orne. (See Map 15.)

After the bombardment the Germans' zonal defense in depth on the Caen-Falaise plain was still largely intact. Their several fortified lines were covered by interlocking firing positions. Panzer Group West's reserve units stood nearby to launch furious counterattacks. This was possibly the best German defense system that Rommel had devised during the entire Normandy campaign.

The British armor now poured through a bombed gap two miles wide and three miles deep. But the infantry remained on its flanks or held up in minefield traffic jams. This meant that the armor rolled forward alone without mutual armor-infantry support, the most effective tactical formation.[43]

Part of this failure was due to the acute infantry shortage plaguing the British army. As Dempsey noted, "I was prepared to lose a couple of hundred tanks. So long as I didn't lose men."[44]

On the right wing the Eleventh, Seventh, and Guards Armored Divisions advanced. Facing them was the Twenty-First Panzer Division, other elements of the First SS Panzer Corps, and artillery and flank Luftwaffe units that had been evacuated from Caen. Here the Allied bombardment was not as devastating as at GOODWOOD's offensive center. (See Map 15.)

Once the British forces advanced past Cagny, they planned to redeploy in a vast "V" armored wave to smash toward the Falaise plain. Part of the German defense included Battle Group Luck commanded by Major Hans von Luck. Scouting on the forward edge of the German defensive line, he was startled at the magnitude of this British armored advance.

Luck dashed into Cagny where he saw an 88mm Luftwaffe antiaircraft artillery battery. He ordered the battery's captain to redeploy and attack the British armor. The captain refused. "Major, my concern is enemy planes, fighting tanks is your job. I'm Luftwaffe." Luck drew his pistol and replied, "Either you're a dead man or you can earn yourself a medal."[45]

The captain moved his guns into an apple orchard to stop the British until German reserves could be moved into position. The first advancing tanks were hit at almost point-blank range. A reinforced line of seventy-eight 88s poured devastating rounds of fire on the British armored advance.[46]

What was not destroyed by the 88s was subsequently wiped out by the Tiger tanks of the First SS Panzer Corps and its deeply echeloned defenses. The remainder of this day turned into the biggest tank battle of the OVERLORD campaign. Masses of British Sherman and Cromwell tanks were attacked by the outnumbered but superior German Tiger and Panther tanks. German panzer grenadiers equipped with Panzerfaust (an anti-tank weapon) and sticky bombs also confronted the British armored advance. The GOODWOOD tank wave began to lose its momentum. At nightfall the German First SS Panzer Division renewed the counterattack, inflicting terrible losses.[47]

As O. H. Marstan, a wireless operator with the Grenadier Guards, recalled, "The whole area was ablaze, tanks on fire and abandoned, carriers, half-tracks, motor vehicles, all knocked out."[48]

During the night of July 18, Canadian forces captured most of the city of Caen. Though this was important, the principal objective of GOODWOOD was to drive a British armored wedge deep into the German defenses in order to break through to the Caen-Falaise plain and thus be in position for the follow-up breakout.[49] This was not going to happen.

By the afternoon of July 19 the Germans had reformed their entire front line. On July 20, amid several German counterattacks, Montgomery canceled GOODWOOD. His breakout charade was over.[50]

Monty's greatest mistake was launching a massive armored frontal assault against Germany's strongest defensive positions. Montgomery could have sent his forces to push through around Caen. He thus might have avoided the over five thousand casualties and loss of over four hundred tanks incurred in this failed offensive. Dempsey and de Guingand both agreed that a greater GOODWOOD advance had been possible, including the capture of all the Orne bridges from Caen to Argentan. But Monty lost his nerve.[51]

Instead the Germans had turned the battlefield into what historian Carlo D'Este called "a massive scrapyard of broken and burnt-out British armor."[52] Another observer described GOODWOOD as "the death ride of the armored divisions."[53]

Montgomery mistakenly shelved the bold GOODWOOD plan to keep his infantry losses low. Yet it was thc infantry that suffered high casualties. The Allies had a vast pool of equipment to rapidly replace all the British tank losses.

In the final analysis GOODWOOD was one of the most poorly planned and delivered Allied offenses of the war in Europe. It was Montgomery's greatest failure up to that time.[54]

## "A MONSTROUS BLOOD BATH"

A large part of GOODWOOD's failure can be credited to Erwin Rommel. As previously mentioned, he prepared the German dispositions as a layered in-depth defense on the Falaise plain. Its success and Montgomery's caution scuttled the British breakthrough. GOODWOOD was to be Rommel's last victory.

By mid-July Rommel knew that a major Allied offensive was coming soon. By then German intelligence suspected that divisions subordinated to Patton's First US Army Group for the supposed "real" invasion at Pas-de-Calais were reinforcing the OVERLORD bridgehead. They also reported to Rommel the effectiveness of the Allied attacks that resulted in "systematic and mathematically exact destruction of the defenders through artillery barrages and carpet bombing."[55] A German corps commander described these defensive battles around Caen and in the Cotentin Peninsula as nothing less than "a monstrous blood-bath."[56]

Rommel already believed that the battle in Normandy and the war was already lost for Germany. Since D-Day, the Seventh Army had sustained casualties of over 94,000 soldiers and 2,300 officers, while receiving only 6,000 replacements. By July 25, the Germans were outnumbered 3.8 to 1. Four hundred eighty-one tanks and assault guns had been destroyed by July 31. A further 470 were in repair workshops. This comprised over 50 percent of the Wehrmacht's armored forces in Normandy. Rommel estimated that at this attrition rate the entire front would implode within thirty days.[57]

Yet despite this extremely high casualty rate, the German soldiers fought on in Normandy with great skill, bravery, and unremitting tenacity. Their tactical ability and, for some, ideological fervor, played a role. But since the war historians have discovered that personal desperation and fear also explained some of their behavior in combat.

During the entire First World War, only forty-eight German soldiers were executed for military infractions. However between 1939 and March 1943, over 1,500 combatants had been shot for desertion and so-called acts of "subverting the will of the people to fight." By June 1944, over seven thousand soldiers had been put to death. As the Wehrmacht collapsed in France by the late summer of 1944, many of the German soldiers captured by the Allies were suffering from extreme battle fatigue.[58]

Writing after the war, General Fritz Bayerlein, commander of the Panzer Lehr Division, voiced the opinion that by the summer of 1944 Rommel believed that it might become necessary to negotiate a reasonable peace even if it meant opposing Hitler. However, Rommel felt that any coup d'état would be a mistake if it took place before the Allied invasion. He thought that if he could repel the Allied invasion, the Western Allies might be willing to sign an armistice to fight side by side with a new Germany against the Russians.

After the July 20 attempt on Hitler's life he told his son, "The attempt on Hitler was stupid. What we had to fear with this man was not his deeds, but the aura which surrounded him in the eyes of the German people."[59]

Rommel and Speidel, his chief of staff, came to realize that the collapse of the Normandy front was imminent. However on July 15 before taking any action, Rommel sent Hitler what was to be his last blunt assessment of the deteriorating situation. His purpose was to state his case clearly and prevent anyone in the future from accusing him of stabbing Hitler in the back to end the war:

> The situation on the Normandy front is growing worse every day and is now approaching a grave crisis. . . . Our casualties are so high that the fighting power of our divisions is rapidly diminishing. Replacements from home are few in number. . . . Material losses are also huge and have so far been replaced on a very small scale. . . . The newly arrived infantry divisions are raw . . . even the bravest army will be smashed piece by piece, losing men, arms and territory. . . . Supply conditions are so bad that only the barest essentials can be brought to the front. . . . In the foreseeable future the enemy will succeed in breaking through our thin front . . . and thrusting deep into France. . . . The troops everywhere fighting heroically, but the unequal struggle is approaching its end. . . . I feel myself in duty bound to speak plainly on this point.[60]

At the time that Rommel sent this report, he was prepared to open negotiations with the Allies. He had won over Kluge as well as many other German officers and prominent civilians. However before he acted, fate intervened.[61]

On July 17, the day before GOODWOOD began, Rommel had spent many hours inspecting the front. At 4:00 p.m. he left Sepp Dietrich's First SS Panzer Corps headquarters to drive back to his own La Roche-Guyon command post. Rommel's staff car was on a secondary road near the hamlet of St. Foy de Montgommery when he was ambushed by two Allied fighter-bombers (was Monty getting his revenge?). Captain Helmuth Lang, Rommel's aide, described the results of the attack:

> The enemy aircraft, flying at great speed, came up to within 500 yards of us and the first one opened fire. . . . Rommel was wounded in the face by broken glass and received a blow on the left temple and cheekbone which caused a triple fracture of the skull and made him lose consciousness immediately. . . . The driver lost control of the car. . . . Marshal Rommel . . . was thrown out, unconscious, when the car turned over and lay stretched out on the road.[62]

Treated locally at first and later transferred to a Luftwaffe hospital, Rommel was given little chance of recovery. Three days later he was still close to death, when on July 20, Colonel Claus von Stauffenberg tried to blow up the führer.[63]

At 12:50 p.m. a huge explosion from a bomb planted by Stauffenberg destroyed the conference room at Hitler's Wolf's Lair headquarters in East Prussia. Though other officers died or were severely injured, the führer escaped with only superficial injuries. Operation Valkyrie was another of the many failed attempts to rid Germany of Hitler. It had been led by General Beck, Stauffenberg, Kluge, and others who decided to act before the Normandy front imploded and the Russians occupied Poland and East Prussia. They planned to use Rommel as a well-known figurehead and Kluge to negotiate an armistice with the Western Allies.

Hitler's vengeance afterward knew no limits. Valkyrie's failure resulted in another bloodbath with over seven thousand so-called conspirators rounded up by the Gestapo. More than 4,900 of them were executed.[64]

One of the conspirators, Colonel von Hofacker, broke down under hideous torture in the Gestapo dungeon at the Prinz Albrechtstrasse in Berlin. He blurted out that Rommel told him, "Tell the people in Berlin they can count on me." This forced confession triggered Hitler's decision that Rommel must die.[65]

By that time Rommel had made a miraculous recovery. An ordinary fifty-two-year-old male would have succumbed to Rommel's many grievous wounds. However his years of physical exercise and rugged constitution helped him to recover enough to be moved to a sophisticated hospital in Germany and on August 8 to his home at Herrlingen near Ulm.

As Keitel later explained to interrogators at the Nuremberg trials, Hitler realized "that it would be a terrible scandal in Germany if this well-known Field Marshal, the most popular general we had, were to be arrested and haled before the People's Court."[66] Rommel's son Manfred added that if people found out that "even Field Marshal Rommel regarded the war as lost and was advising a separate peace [it] would have been tantamount to a declaration of military bankruptcy."[67]

On October 14, SS troops surrounded Rommel's home and two generals arrived to deliver Hitler's ultimatum to either take poison or stand trial. If he selected the first option, Rommel would be given a major state funeral with full military honors and his family would be left untouched. The Desert Fox died that day. Official sources stated that he succumbed to a cerebral embolism due to skull fractures from the July 17 accident.

On October 18 Field Marshal von Rundstedt looked broken and bewildered as he delivered the funeral oration: "His heart belonged to the

Fuhrer."[68] The words could not have been more ironic. "Perhaps the most despicable part of the whole story," wrote Manfred Rommel, "was the expressions of sympathy from members of the German Government."[69]

Kluge was already reeling from the loss of Rommel and the repercussions of the failed Stauffenberg plot. After taking over Rommel's Seventh army group as well as retaining overall theater command, Kluge wrote to Hitler that the fighting potential of his meager forces had been drained to the point of desperation. Kluge wondered if Hitler understood "the tremendous consumption of forces on big battle days."[70] The Twelfth SS Panzer Division now only fielded fifteen operational tanks. The Sixteenth Luftwaffe Field Division had ceased to exist as a combat unit.

Rommel had not been allowed to construct any new defensive lines before GOODWOOD. In mid-July the panzer divisions had the strength to undertake a fighting withdrawal to newly prepared front lines. Now at the end of the month, the vital question for Kluge was how long they could hold out. He told Hitler, "The moment is fast approaching when this overtaxed front line is bound to break up."[71]

The German field commanders in Normandy knew they could not absorb further punishment of this magnitude. By the last week of July, while Kluge was at the point of desperation, he called his position an "ungeheures Kladderadatsch—an awful mess."[72]

## WHY MONTY SURVIVED

After GOODWOOD, a mounting cry now arose on both sides of the Atlantic—"Sack Montgomery!" For once Monty privately became visibly worried, though he publically still maintained the fiction that all was proceeding according to his "plan."

Let us consider his record in Normandy:

First, on D-Day Montgomery had planned to take Caen and perhaps even get his tanks to Falaise. He missed by a good three miles to even enter Caen's outskirts.

Second, he planned a double envelopment through Villers-Bocage that was driven back in defeat.

Third, EPSOM was a planned "right hook" to sweep around Caen that was brought to a standstill by the German armored reserve.

Fourth, CHARNWOOD, his head-on assault plan to bomb Caen into rubble, came to an abrupt halt at the river dividing the city, leaving the dominating heights south of the city and the open Falaise plain still in German hands.

Fifth, GOODWOOD was billed as Monty's ultimate breakthrough plan. Before it started, he secretly scaled back this objective, as a result achieving little at a great cost in men and material. He did, however, make what proved to be outrageous claims and misleading statements to Eisenhower, Churchill, other commanders, and the British press on his intentions and the battle's progress.

At the start of GOODWOOD's July 18 attack, Montgomery wrote to Brooke, "Operation this morning a complete success."[73] Later that evening he sent Eisenhower a message that virtually claimed he had broken through the German line: "Am very well satisfied with today's fighting on eastern flank . . . three armored divisions now operating in the open country to the south and S.E. of CAEN."[74] This was not true.

On the next day, July 19, Montgomery issued an incredibly optimistic bulletin to the press corps stating that the British and Canadians had broken through the German positions. That day the London *Times* headline blared, "Second Army Breaks Through," and the next day's headline was "Wide Corridor through German Front."[75]

Actually none of this was true. By July 20 the British tanks were stuck in the mud from a rainstorm, and the German line was once again intact. The panzers even launched several counterattacks. Later Monty tried to do damage control when the actual battlefield results became public.[76]

Montgomery might have been forgiven if he had clearly stated all along that his intentions were only to hold the German panzers to Caen. But if his true objective had been a major breakout, as his PR campaign before the battle repeatedly claimed, then GOODWOOD was a failure and Monty was only trying to save face. In the end the press thought so, as did the RAF, Eisenhower, Churchill, Bradley, Marshall, Tedder, and the SHAEF staff.

Eisenhower was incensed over GOODWOOD's results. Captain Harry C. Butcher, Eisenhower's aide, wrote in his diary, "Ike said yesterday that with 7,000 tons of bombs dropped in the most elaborate bombing of enemy front line positions ever accomplished, only seven miles were gained—can we afford a thousand tons of bombs per mile?"[77]

The SHAEF staff had felt misled even before the operation began and by Montgomery's press briefing on its progress. Bill Williams, Monty's senior intelligence officer, called his press statements "bloody stupid."[78]

Confidence in Montgomery and the British Second Army now reached an all-time low. The deputy supreme commander, Air Chief Marshal Tedder, led a campaign to ax Monty. He complained that Montgomery was either failing as a leader or deliberately deceiving his superiors about his intentions and expectations. Tedder wrote Montgomery on July 20, "It is clear that there was no intention of making this operation the decisive one which you so clearly indicated [it would be]."[79] An enraged Tedder seriously thought of sacking Montgomery himself if Eisenhower demurred.[80] He virtually begged Ike to take over the ground war, telling him, "All the evidence available to me indicated a serious lack of fighting leadership in the higher direction of the British Armies in Normandy."[81]

Tedder had stirred the controversy up to such a level that the British War Cabinet was alarmed enough to dispatch its own liaison officer to Montgomery's headquarters to obtain a report on GOODWOOD. Montgomery refused to see this emissary whom he viewed as an intruder. He had earlier requested Eisenhower to keep all visitors away since GOODWOOD "will require all our attention."[82]

Aware of Tedder's efforts, Brooke flew to Monty's headquarters on July 19 and ordered him to cancel his no-visitor policy and to write a letter to Churchill inviting him to visit at any time. Both Churchill and Eisenhower were insisting on a personal meeting with him to vent their ire over GOODWOOD. Brooke believed Montgomery would awe them both with his mastery of the battlefield.[83]

Ultimately Brooke was proven correct. When Eisenhower and Montgomery met on July 20, Montgomery somehow managed to dampen Ike's outrage and sidestep the issues he raised. The next day Monty received a follow-up letter from Ike:

> Since returning from your Headquarters yesterday, I have been going over the major considerations that, in my mind, must guide our future actions. . . . There are also serious political questions involved. . . . You stated [on July 10] . . . "We are now so strong . . . that we can attack the Germans hard and continuously. . . ." [Eisenhower could have asked, *so why are you not doing this?*] Time is vital. . . . I was extremely hopeful and optimistic

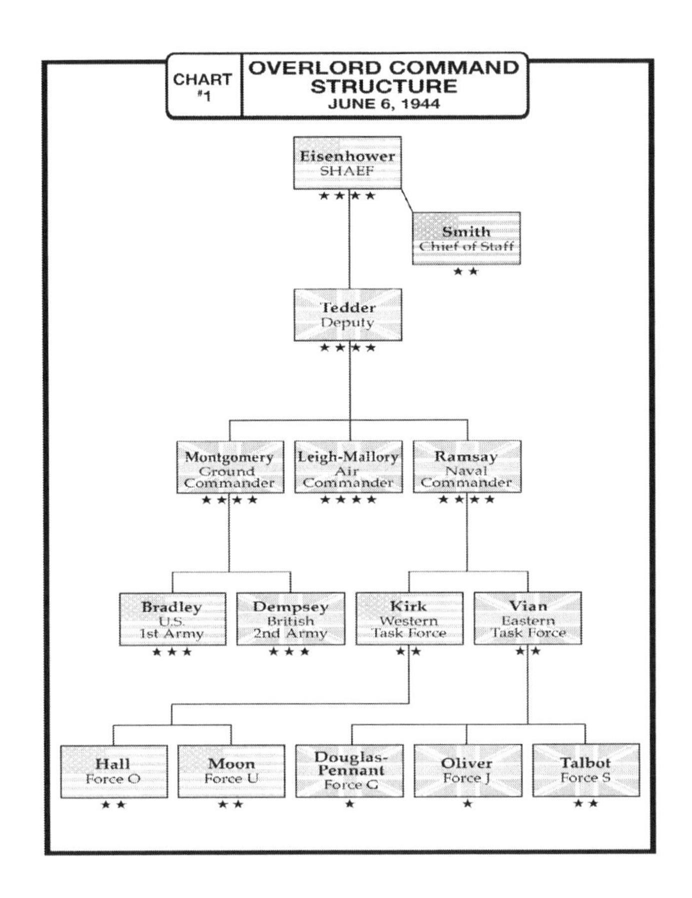
CHART #1
OVERLORD COMMAND STRUCTURE
JUNE 6, 1944
Eisenhower
SHAEF
Smith
Chief of Staff
Tedder
Deputy
Montgomery
Ground Commander
Leigh-Mallory
Air Commander
Ramsay
Naval Commander
Bradley
U.S. 1st Army
Dempsey
British 2nd Army
Kirk
Western Task Force
Vian
Eastern Task Force
Hall
Force O
Moon
Force U
Douglas-Pennant
Force G
Oliver
Force J
Talbot
Force S

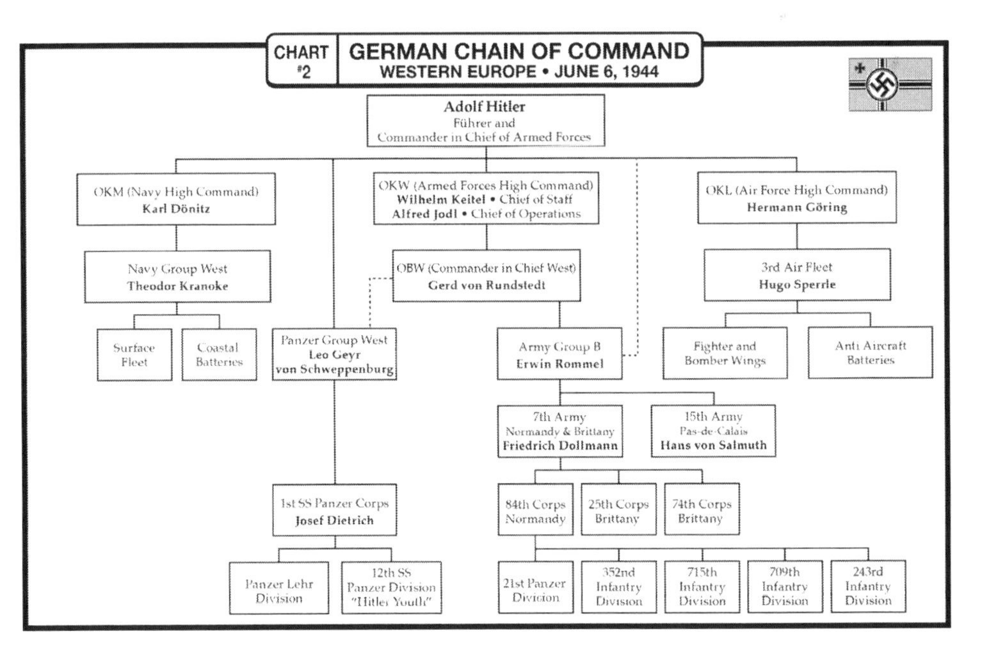
CHART #2
GERMAN CHAIN OF COMMAND
WESTERN EUROPE • JUNE 6, 1944
Adolf Hitler
Führer and
Commander in Chief of Armed Forces
OKM (Navy High Command)
Karl Dönitz
OKW (Armed Forces High Command)
Wilhelm Keitel • Chief of Staff
Alfred Jodl • Chief of Operations
OKL (Air Force High Command)
Hermann Göring
Navy Group West
Theodor Kranoke
OBW (Commander in Chief West)
Gerd von Rundstedt
3rd Air Fleet
Hugo Sperrle
Surface Fleet
Coastal Batteries
Panzer Group West
Leo Geyr
von Schweppenburg
Army Group B
Erwin Rommel
Fighter and Bomber Wings
Anti Aircraft Batteries
7th Army
Normandy & Brittany
Friedrich Dollmann
15th Army
Pas-de-Calais
Hans von Salmuth
1st SS Panzer Corps
Josef Dietrich
84th Corps
Normandy
25th Corps
Brittany
74th Corps
Brittany
Panzer Lehr Division
12th SS Panzer Division "Hitler Youth"
21st Panzer Division
352nd Infantry Division
715th Infantry Division
709th Infantry Division
243rd Infantry Division

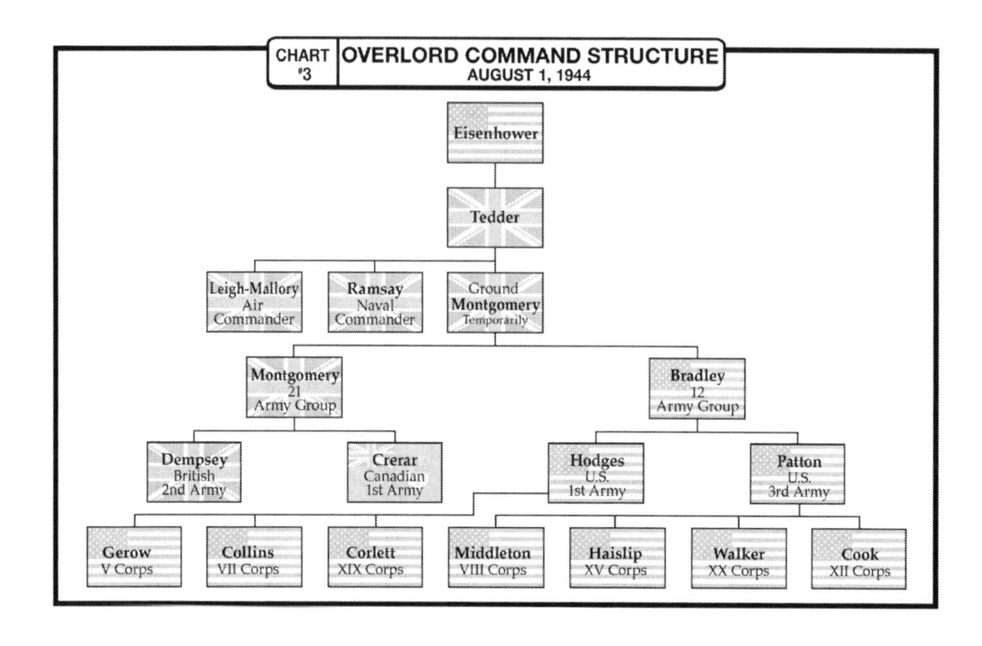
CHART #3
OVERLORD COMMAND STRUCTURE
AUGUST 1, 1944
Eisenhower
Tedder
Leigh-Mallory
Air
Commander
Ramsay
Naval
Commander
Ground
Montgomery
Temporarily
Montgomery
21
Army Group
Bradley
12
Army Group
Dempsey
British
2nd Army
Crerar
Canadian
1st Army
Hodges
U.S.
1st Army
Patton
U.S.
3rd Army
Gerow
V Corps
Collins
VII Corps
Corlett
XIX Corps
Middleton
VIII Corps
Haislip
XV Corps
Walker
XX Corps
Cook
XII Corps

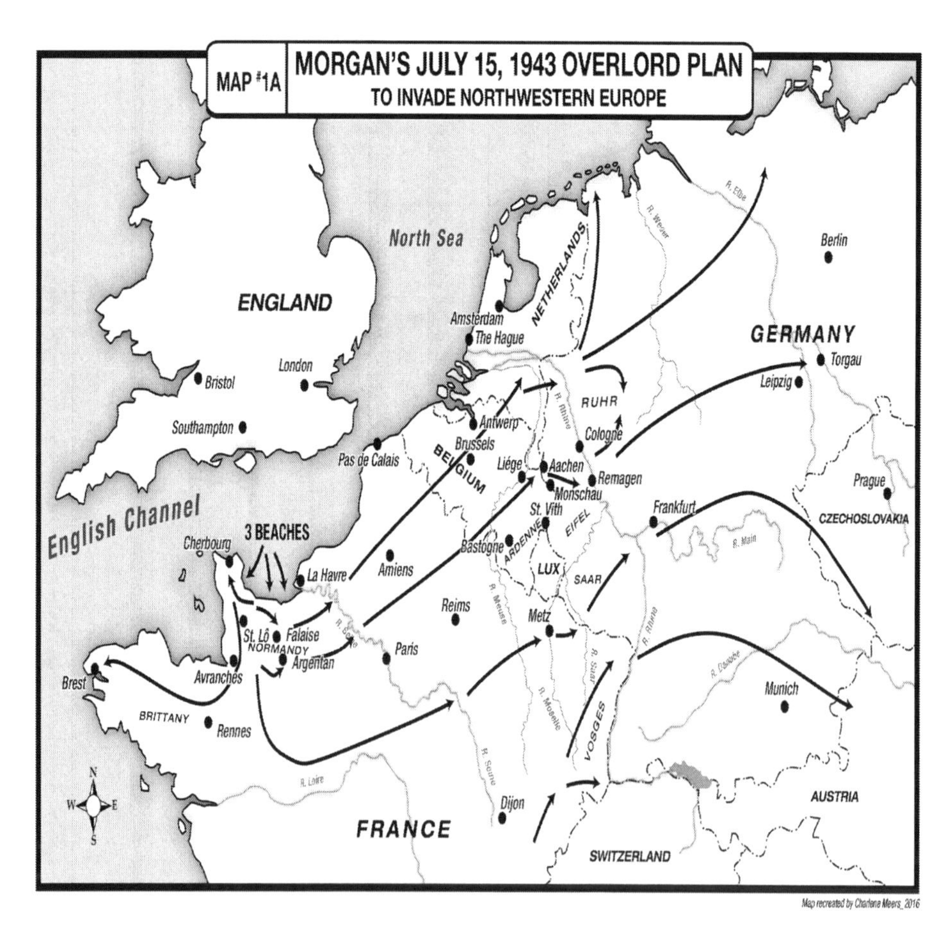
MAP #1A
MORGAN'S JULY 15, 1943 OVERLORD PLAN
TO INVADE NORTHWESTERN EUROPE
North Sea
ENGLAND
English Channel
Bristol
London
Southampton
Amsterdam
The Hague
NETHERLANDS
GERMANY
Berlin
Torgau
Leipzig
RUHR
Cologne
Antwerp
Brussels
BELGIUM
Pas de Calais
Liége
Aachen
Remagen
Monschau
St. Vith
EIFEL
ARDENNE
Bastogne
LUX
SAAR
Frankfurt
Prague
CZECHOSLOVAKIA
3 BEACHES
Cherbourg
La Havre
Amiens
Reims
Metz
St. Lô
Falaise
NORMANDY
Argentan
Paris
Avranches
Brest
BRITTANY
Rennes
Munich
VOSGES
Dijon
FRANCE
SWITZERLAND
AUSTRIA
R. Elbe
R. Weser
R. Rhine
R. Main
R. Meuse
R. Moselle
R. Saar
R. Seine
R. Loire
R. Danube
N
S
E
W
Map recreated by Charlene Meers_2016

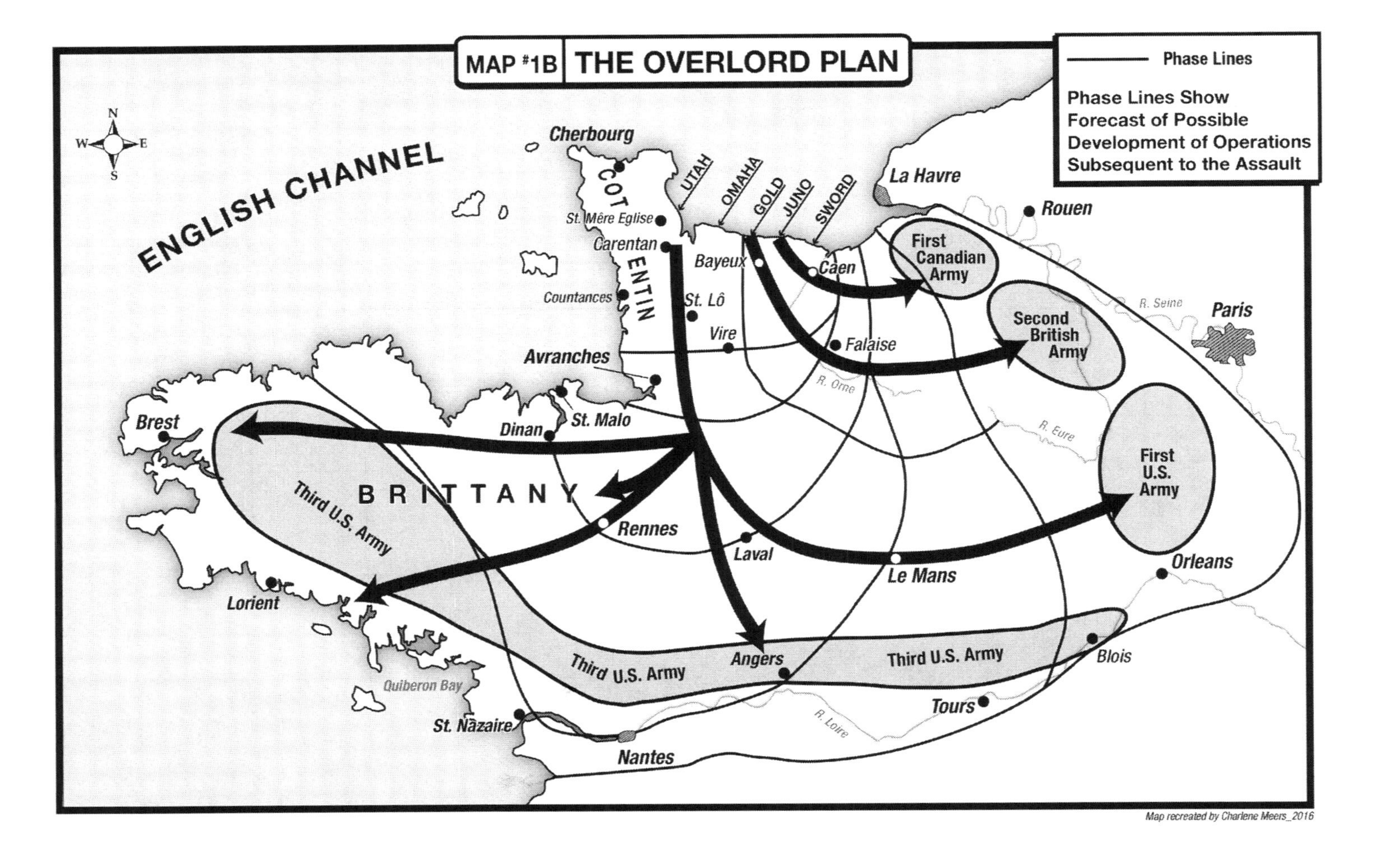
MAP #1B THE OVERLORD PLAN
Phase Lines
Phase Lines Show Forecast of Possible Development of Operations Subsequent to the Assault
ENGLISH CHANNEL
N
E
S
W
Cherbourg
COTENTIN
St. Mêre Eglise
Carentan
UTAH
OMAHA
GOLD
JUNO
SWORD
La Havre
Rouen
Bayeux
Caen
First Canadian Army
Countances
St. Lô
Vire
Falaise
Second British Army
R. Seine
Paris
Avranches
R. Orne
St. Malo
Dinan
Brest
R. Eure
First U.S. Army
BRITTANY
Third U.S. Army
Rennes
Laval
Le Mans
Orleans
Lorient
Angers
Third U.S. Army
Third U.S. Army
Blois
Quiberon Bay
Tours
R. Loire
St. Nazaire
Nantes
Map recreated by Charlene Meers_2016

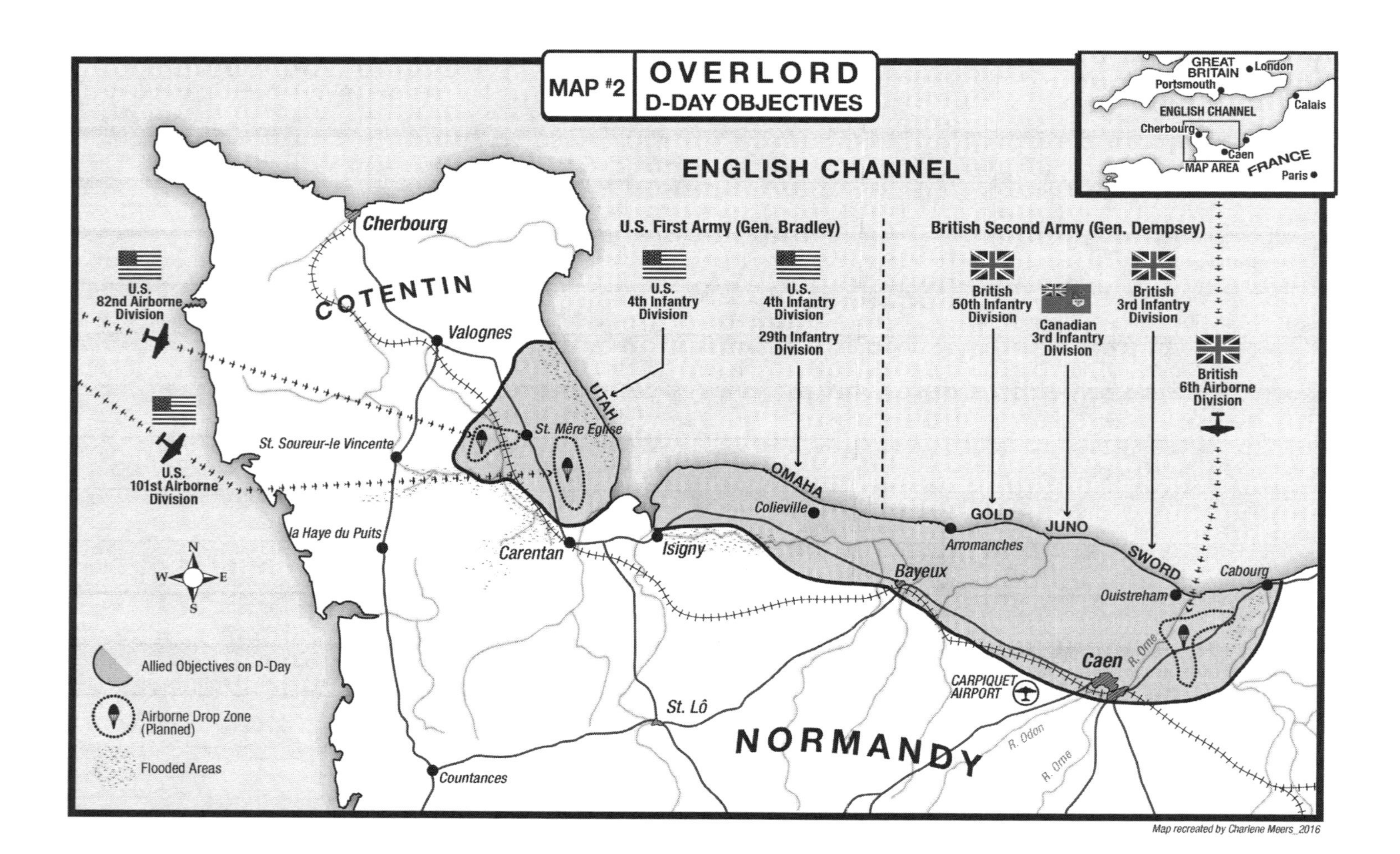
MAP #2
OVERLORD
D-DAY OBJECTIVES
ENGLISH CHANNEL
U.S. First Army (Gen. Bradley)
British Second Army (Gen. Dempsey)
U.S. 82nd Airborne Division
U.S. 101st Airborne Division
U.S. 4th Infantry Division
U.S. 4th Infantry Division
29th Infantry Division
British 50th Infantry Division
Canadian 3rd Infantry Division
British 3rd Infantry Division
British 6th Airborne Division
GREAT BRITAIN
London
Portsmouth
Calais
ENGLISH CHANNEL
Cherbourg
Caen
MAP AREA
FRANCE
Paris
COTENTIN
Cherbourg
Valognes
St. Mêre Eglise
St. Soureur-le Vincente
la Haye du Puits
Carentan
Isigny
UTAH
OMAHA
Colieville
GOLD
Arromanches
JUNO
SWORD
Ouistreham
Cabourg
Bayeux
Caen
R. Orne
CARPIQUET AIRPORT
St. Lô
NORMANDY
R. Odon
R. Orne
Countances
N
W
E
S
Allied Objectives on D-Day
Airborne Drop Zone (Planned)
Flooded Areas
Map recreated by Charlene Meers_2016

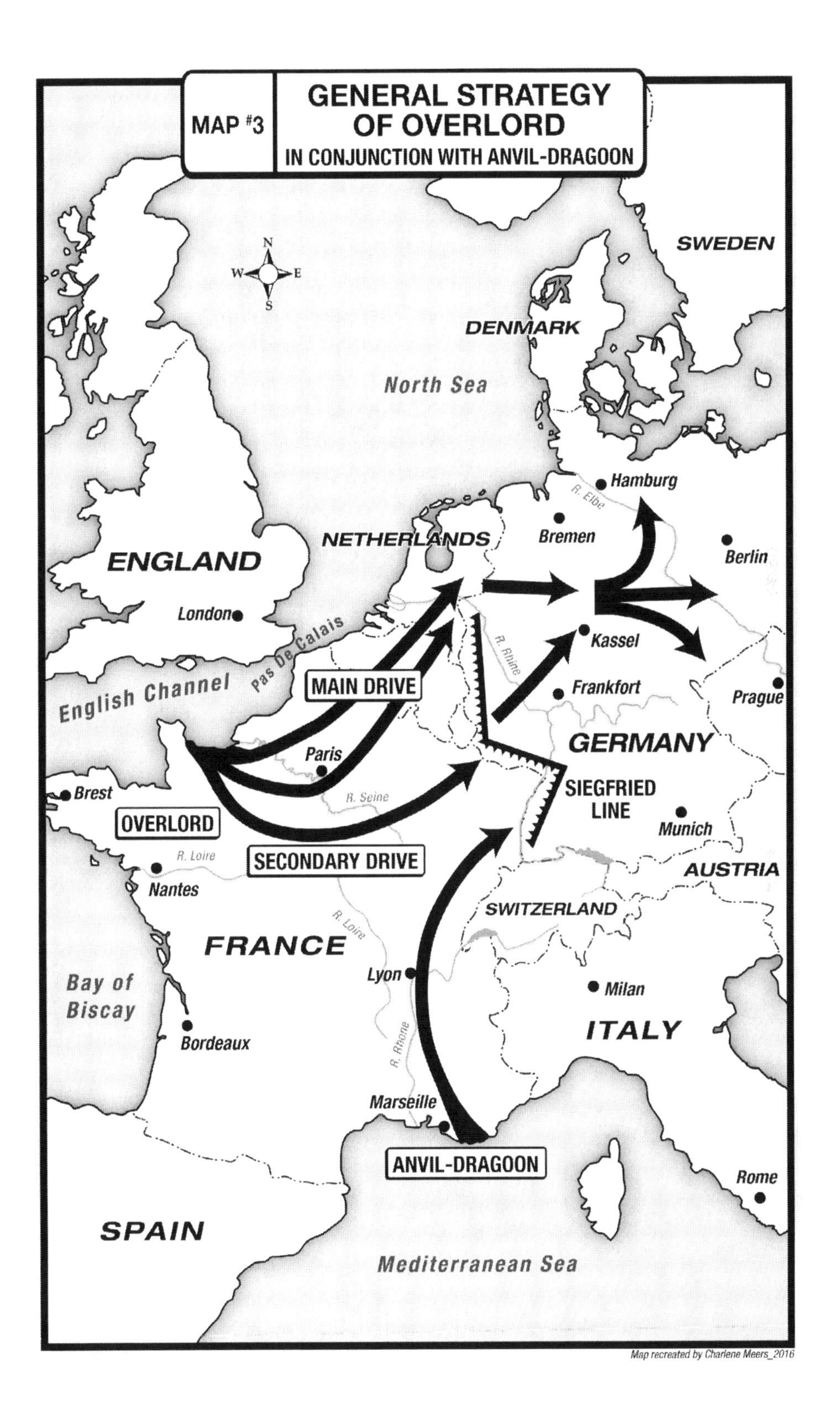
MAP #3
GENERAL STRATEGY OF OVERLORD
IN CONJUNCTION WITH ANVIL-DRAGOON
SWEDEN
DENMARK
North Sea
Hamburg
R. Elbe
NETHERLANDS
Bremen
Berlin
ENGLAND
London
Pas De Calais
Kassel
R. Rhine
English Channel
MAIN DRIVE
Frankfort
Prague
GERMANY
Paris
Brest
R. Seine
SIEGFRIED
LINE
OVERLORD
Munich
R. Loire
SECONDARY DRIVE
AUSTRIA
Nantes
SWITZERLAND
R. Loire
FRANCE
Lyon
Bay of
Biscay
Milan
ITALY
Bordeaux
R. Rhone
Marseille
ANVIL-DRAGOON
Rome
SPAIN
Mediterranean Sea
Map recreated by Charlene Meers_2016

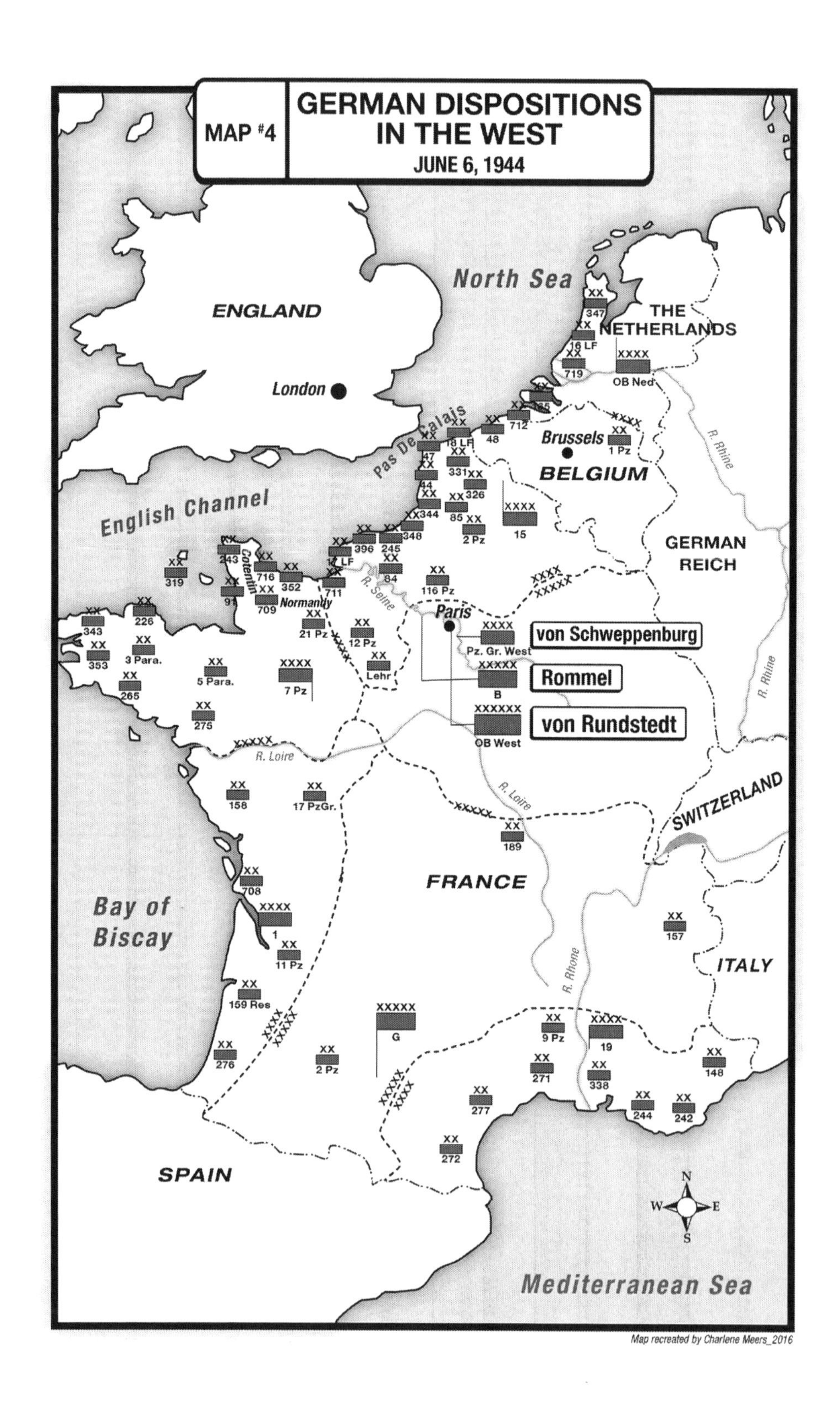
MAP #4
GERMAN DISPOSITIONS IN THE WEST
JUNE 6, 1944
North Sea
ENGLAND
London
THE NETHERLANDS
OB Ned
Pas De Calais
Brussels
BELGIUM
English Channel
GERMAN REICH
Cotentin
Normandy
Paris
R. Seine
R. Rhine
von Schweppenburg
Pz. Gr. West
Rommel
B
von Rundstedt
OB West
R. Loire
SWITZERLAND
FRANCE
Bay of Biscay
R. Rhone
ITALY
SPAIN
Mediterranean Sea
Map recreated by Charlene Meers_2016

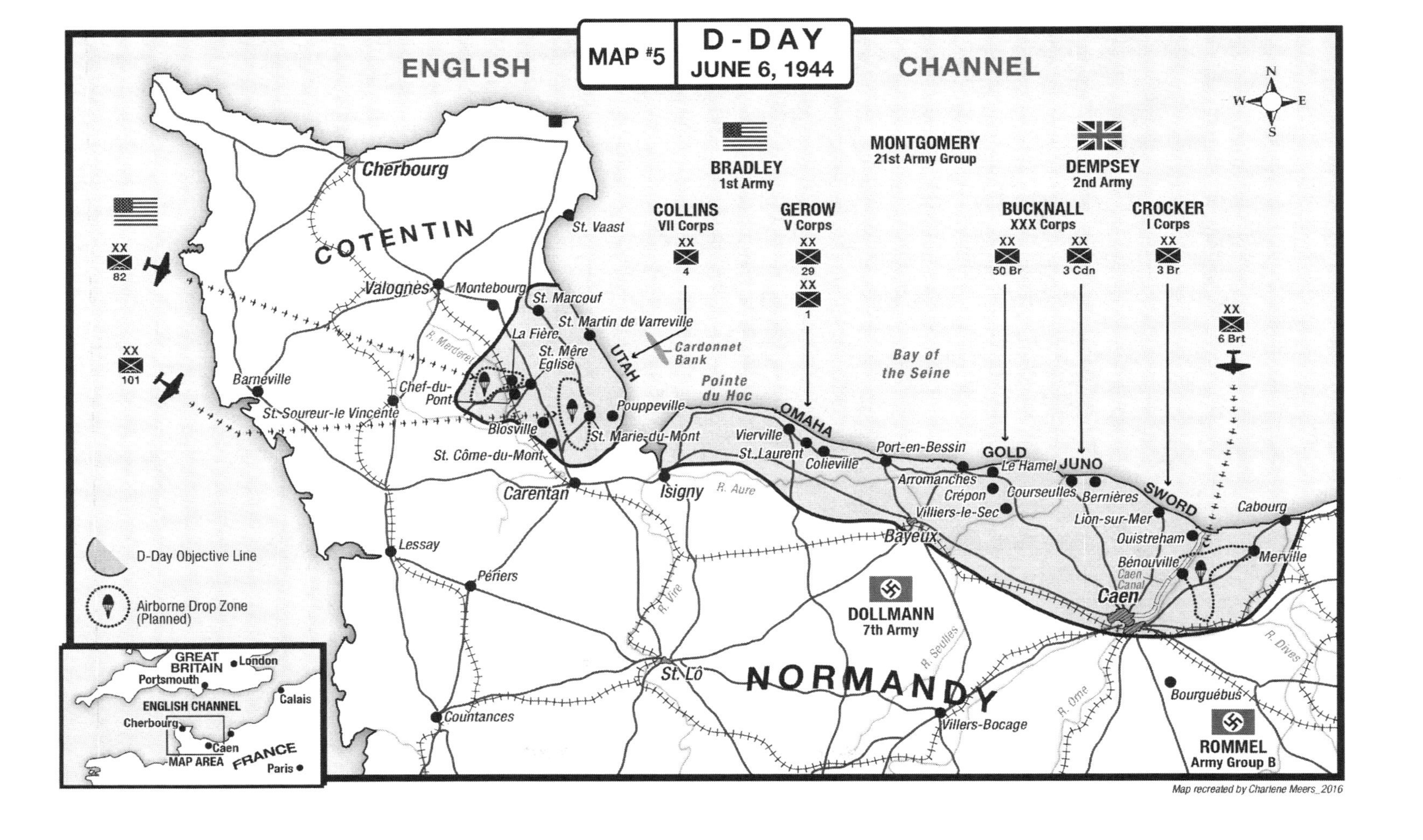
MAP #5
D-DAY
JUNE 6, 1944
ENGLISH
CHANNEL
MONTGOMERY
21st Army Group
BRADLEY
1st Army
DEMPSEY
2nd Army
COLLINS
VII Corps
XX
4
GEROW
V Corps
XX
29
XX
1
BUCKNALL
XXX Corps
XX
50 Br
XX
3 Cdn
CROCKER
I Corps
XX
3 Br
XX
6 Brt
XX
82
XX
101
COTENTIN
Cherbourg
St. Vaast
Valognes
Montebourg
St. Marcouf
St. Martin de Varreville
La Fière
St. Mère Eglise
UTAH
Cardonnet Bank
R. Merderet
Barneville
Chef-du-Pont
St. Soureur-le Vincente
Blosville
Pouppeville
St. Marie-du-Mont
St. Côme-du-Mont
Carentan
Isigny
R. Aure
Pointe du Hoc
Bay of the Seine
OMAHA
Vierville
St. Laurent
Colieville
Port-en-Bessin
GOLD
Le Hamel
Arromanches
Crépon
Courseulles
Villiers-le-Sec
JUNO
Bernières
SWORD
Lion-sur-Mer
Ouistreham
Bénouville
Caen Canal
Caen
Cabourg
Merville
Bayeux
Lessay
Périers
R. Vire
St. Lô
NORMANDY
DOLLMANN
7th Army
R. Seulles
R. Orne
R. Dives
Bourguébus
ROMMEL
Army Group B
Villers-Bocage
Countances
D-Day Objective Line
Airborne Drop Zone (Planned)
GREAT BRITAIN
London
Portsmouth
Calais
ENGLISH CHANNEL
Cherbourg
Caen
MAP AREA
FRANCE
Paris
Map recreated by Charlene Meers_2016

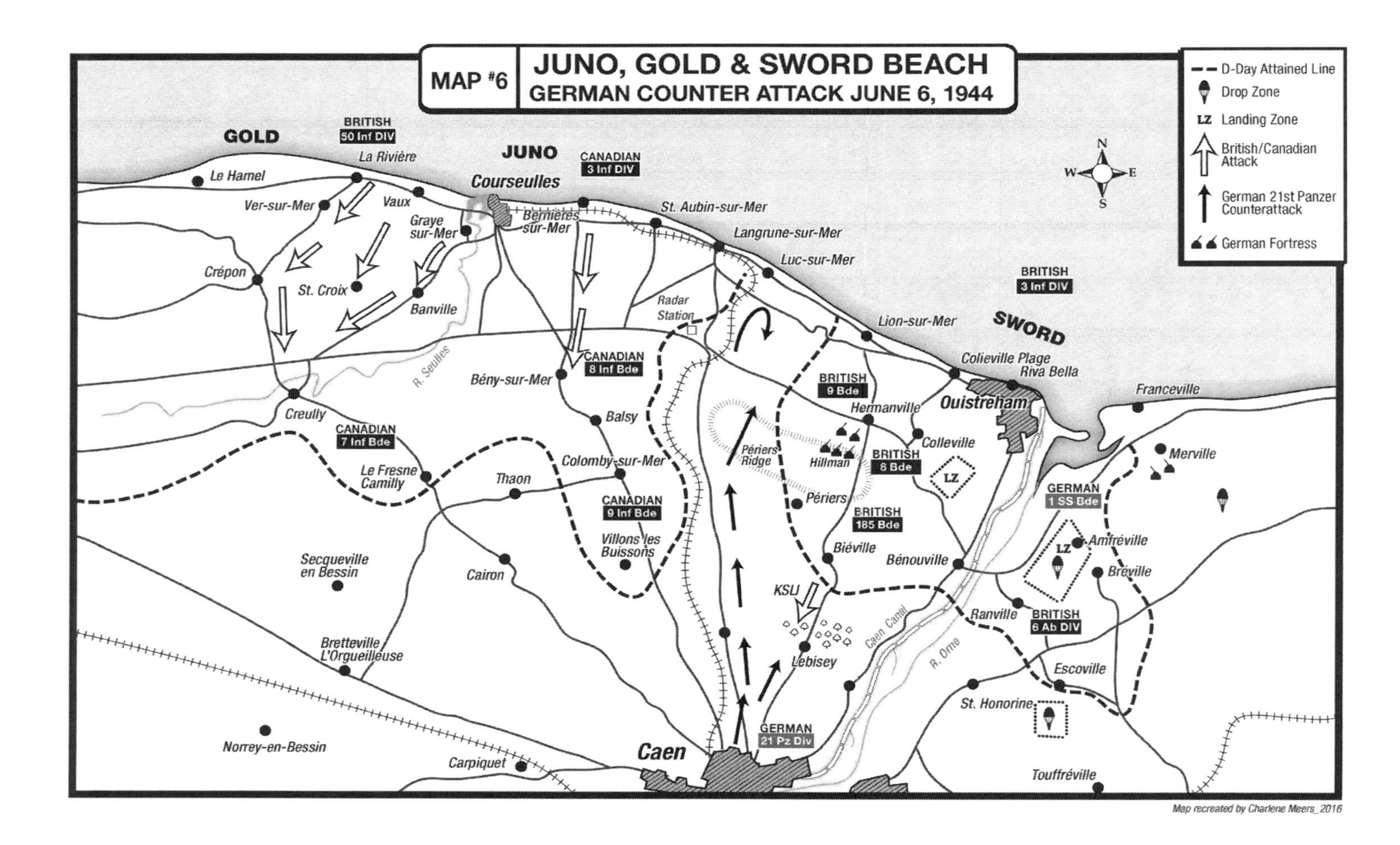
MAP #6
JUNO, GOLD & SWORD BEACH
GERMAN COUNTER ATTACK JUNE 6, 1944
D-Day Attained Line
Drop Zone
LZ Landing Zone
British/Canadian Attack
German 21st Panzer Counterattack
German Fortress
N
W
E
S
GOLD
BRITISH 50 Inf DIV
JUNO
CANADIAN 3 Inf DIV
SWORD
BRITISH 3 Inf DIV
Le Hamel
La Rivière
Ver-sur-Mer
Vaux
Graye sur-Mer
Courseulles
Bernières sur-Mer
St. Aubin-sur-Mer
Langrune-sur-Mer
Luc-sur-Mer
Lion-sur-Mer
Colleville Plage
Riva Bella
Ouistreham
Franceville
Merville
Crépon
St. Croix
Banville
Radar Station
R. Seulles
CANADIAN 8 Inf Bde
Bény-sur-Mer
Creully
CANADIAN 7 Inf Bde
Balsy
BRITISH 9 Bde
Hermanville
Colleville
Périers Ridge
Hillman
BRITISH 8 Bde
LZ
GERMAN 1 SS Bde
Le Fresne Camilly
Thaon
Colomby-sur-Mer
CANADIAN 9 Inf Bde
Périers
BRITISH 185 Bde
Amfréville
Bréville
Villons les Buissons
Biéville
Bénouville
Secqueville en Bessin
Cairon
KSLI
Ranville
BRITISH 6 Ab DIV
Caen Canal
R. Orne
Lebisey
Escoville
Bretteville L'Orgueilleuse
St. Honorine
GERMAN 21 Pz Div
Norrey-en-Bessin
Caen
Carpiquet
Touffréville
Map recreated by Charlene Meers_2016

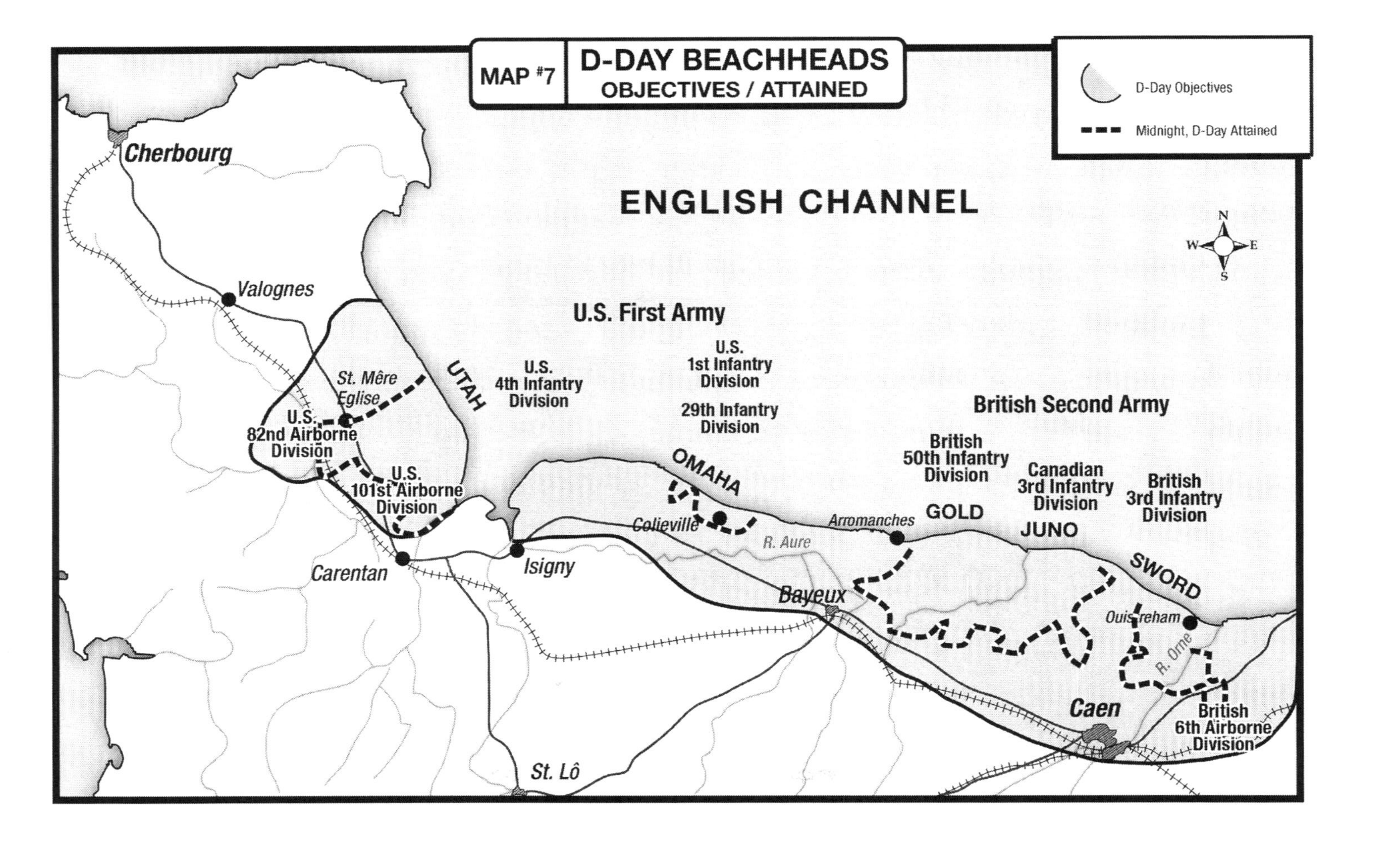
MAP #7
D-DAY BEACHHEADS
OBJECTIVES / ATTAINED
D-Day Objectives
Midnight, D-Day Attained
ENGLISH CHANNEL
N
W
E
S
Cherbourg
Valognes
U.S. First Army
U.S.
1st Infantry
Division
29th Infantry
Division
British Second Army
St. Mêre
Eglise
UTAH
U.S.
4th Infantry
Division
U.S.
82nd Airborne
Division
U.S.
101st Airborne
Division
OMAHA
British
50th Infantry
Division
Canadian
3rd Infantry
Division
British
3rd Infantry
Division
Colleville
Arromanches
GOLD
JUNO
SWORD
R. Aure
Carentan
Isigny
Bayeux
Ouistreham
R. Orne
Caen
British
6th Airborne
Division
St. Lô

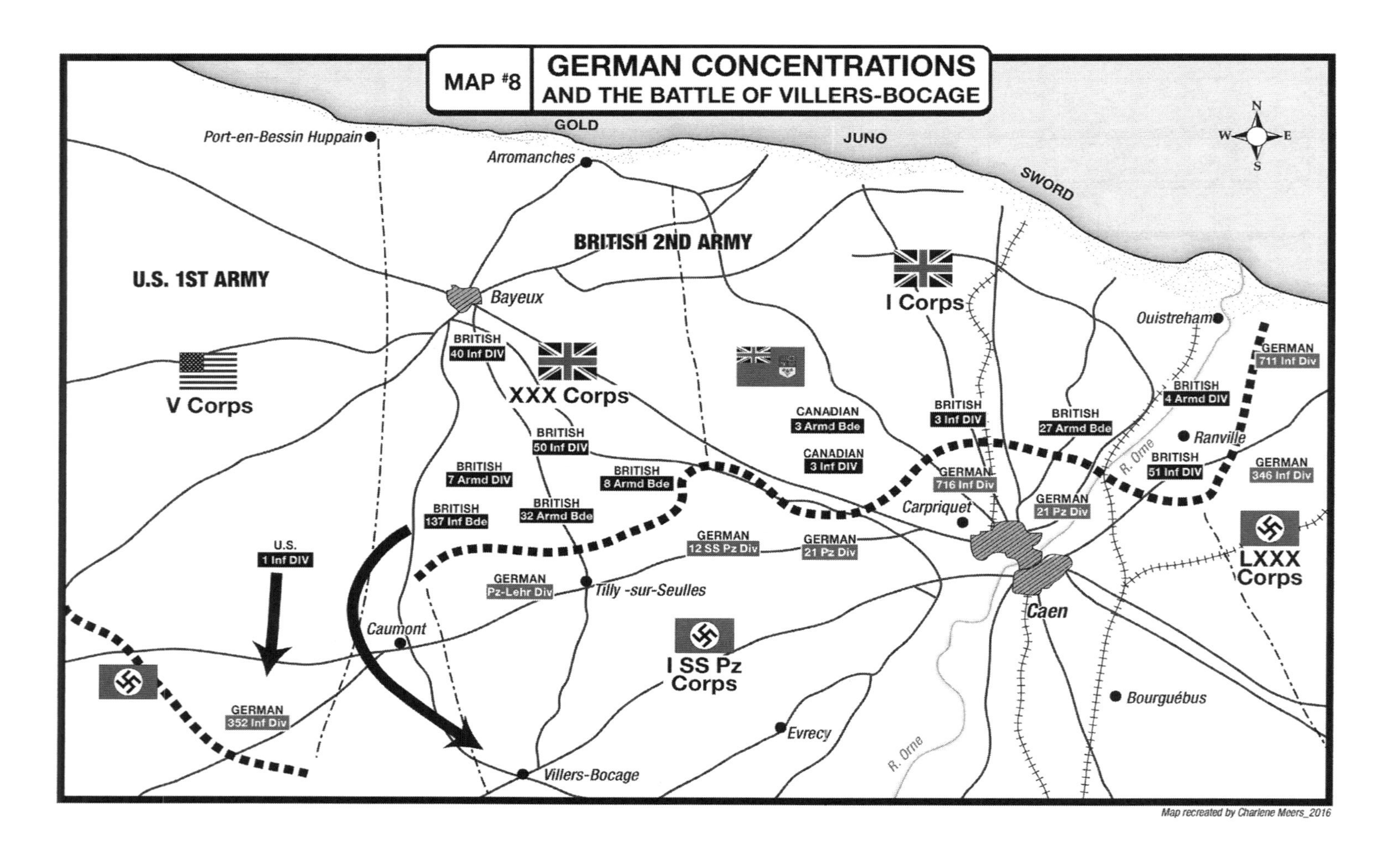
MAP #8
GERMAN CONCENTRATIONS
AND THE BATTLE OF VILLERS-BOCAGE
GOLD
JUNO
SWORD
N
W
E
S
Port-en-Bessin Huppain
Arromanches
Bayeux
Ouistreham
Ranville
Carpriquet
Caen
Tilly -sur-Seulles
Caumont
Evrecy
Villers-Bocage
Bourguébus
R. Orne
R. Orne
U.S. 1ST ARMY
BRITISH 2ND ARMY
V Corps
XXX Corps
I Corps
I SS Pz Corps
LXXX Corps
BRITISH 40 Inf DIV
BRITISH 50 Inf DIV
BRITISH 7 Armd DIV
BRITISH 8 Armd Bde
BRITISH 137 Inf Bde
BRITISH 32 Armd Bde
CANADIAN 3 Armd Bde
CANADIAN 3 Inf DIV
BRITISH 3 Inf DIV
BRITISH 27 Armd Bde
BRITISH 4 Armd DIV
BRITISH 51 Inf DIV
U.S. 1 Inf DIV
GERMAN 711 Inf Div
GERMAN 346 Inf Div
GERMAN 716 Inf Div
GERMAN 21 Pz Div
GERMAN 12 SS Pz Div
GERMAN 21 Pz Div
GERMAN Pz-Lehr Div
GERMAN 352 Inf Div
Map recreated by Charlene Meers_2016

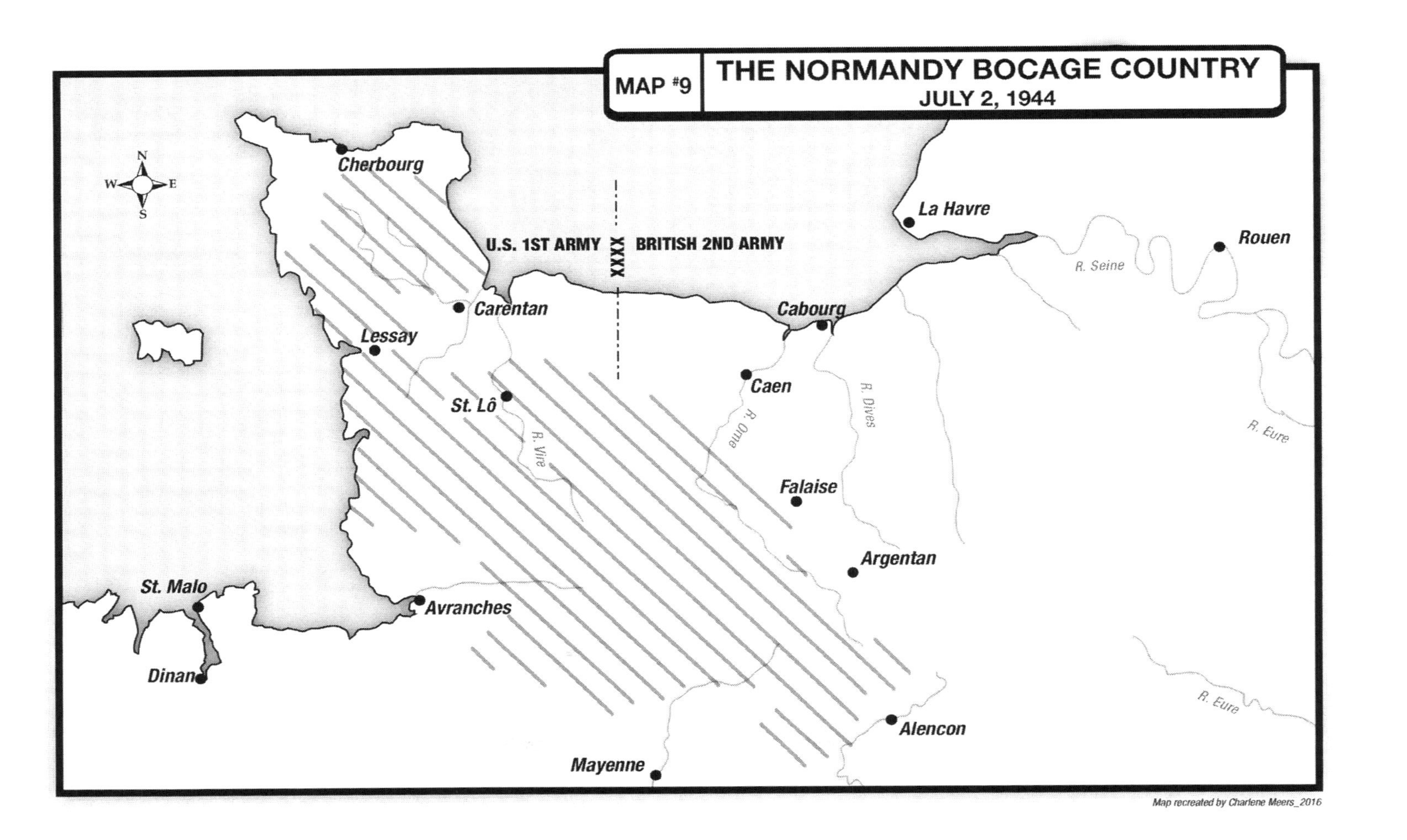
MAP #9
THE NORMANDY BOCAGE COUNTRY
JULY 2, 1944
N
W
E
S
Cherbourg
La Havre
Rouen
U.S. 1ST ARMY
XXXX
BRITISH 2ND ARMY
R. Seine
Carentan
Cabourg
Lessay
Caen
St. Lô
R. Orne
R. Dives
R. Eure
R. Vire
Falaise
Argentan
St. Malo
Avranches
Dinan
Alencon
R. Eure
Mayenne
Map recreated by Charlene Meers_2016

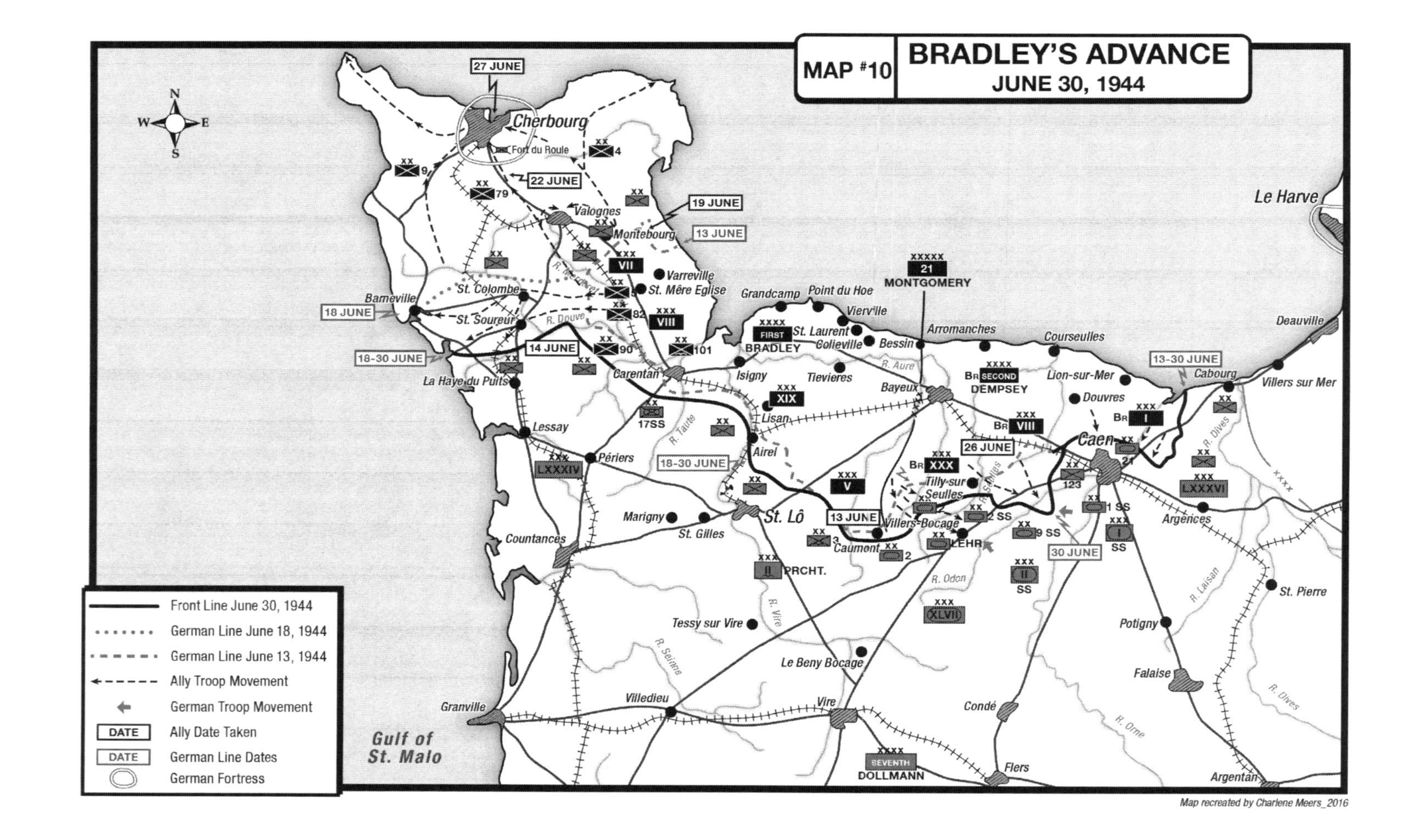
MAP #10
BRADLEY'S ADVANCE
JUNE 30, 1944
Cherbourg
Fort du Roule
27 JUNE
22 JUNE
19 JUNE
13 JUNE
18 JUNE
18-30 JUNE
14 JUNE
13-30 JUNE
26 JUNE
13 JUNE
30 JUNE
Valognes
Montebourg
Varreville
St. Mère Eglise
St. Colombe
St. Soureur
Barneville
La Haye du Puits
Lessay
Périers
Countances
Granville
Villedieu
Vire
Carentan
Isigny
Grandcamp
Point du Hoe
Vierville
St. Laurent
Colleville
Bessin
Tievieres
Arromanches
Courseulles
Lion-sur-Mer
Douvres
Bayeux
Lisan
Airel
St. Lô
Marigny
St. Gilles
Tessy sur Vire
Le Beny Bocage
Caumont
Villers-Bocage
Tilly-sur-Seulles
Caen
Cabourg
Villers sur Mer
Deauville
Le Harve
Argences
St. Pierre
Potigny
Falaise
Condé
Flers
Argentan
R. Douve
R. Taute
R. Vire
R. Aure
R. Odon
R. Orne
R. Dives
R. Laisan
R. Seinne
Gulf of St. Malo
MONTGOMERY
FIRST BRADLEY
BR SECOND DEMPSEY
SEVENTH DOLLMANN
VII
VIII
XIX
V
BR XXX
BR VIII
BR I
LXXXIV
LXXXVI
XLVII
II PRCHT.
I SS
II SS
LEHR
17SS
Front Line June 30, 1944
German Line June 18, 1944
German Line June 13, 1944
Ally Troop Movement
German Troop Movement
DATE Ally Date Taken
DATE German Line Dates
German Fortress
Map recreated by Charlene Meers_2016

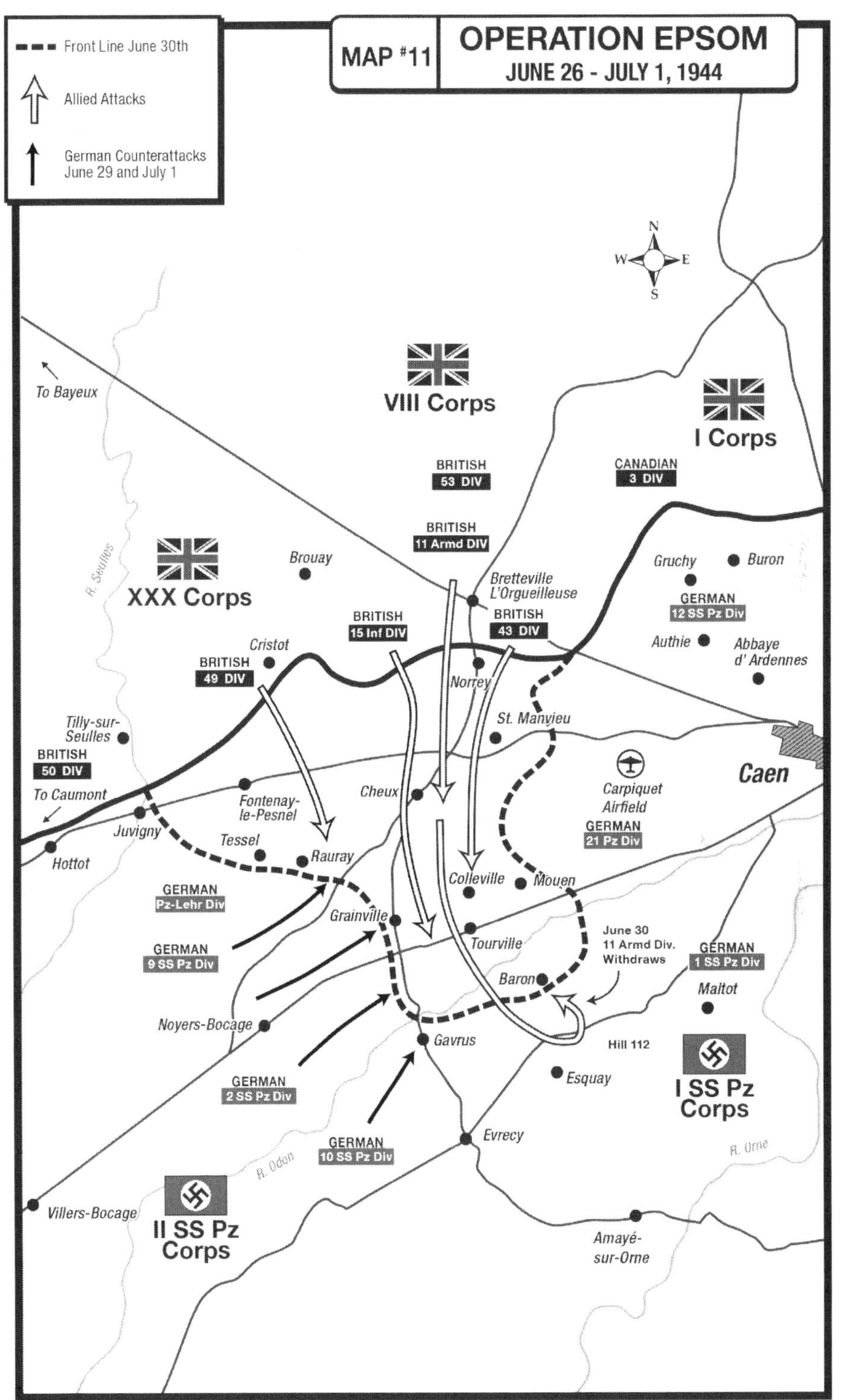
Front Line June 30th
Allied Attacks
German Counterattacks
June 29 and July 1
MAP #11
OPERATION EPSOM
JUNE 26 - JULY 1, 1944
N
W
E
S
To Bayeux
VIII Corps
I Corps
BRITISH
53 DIV
CANADIAN
3 DIV
BRITISH
11 Armd DIV
R. Seulles
XXX Corps
Brouay
Gruchy
Buron
Bretteville
L'Orgueilleuse
GERMAN
12 SS Pz Div
BRITISH
15 Inf DIV
BRITISH
43 DIV
Authie
Abbaye
d' Ardennes
Cristot
BRITISH
49 DIV
Norrey
Tilly-sur-
Seulles
St. Manvieu
BRITISH
50 DIV
Caen
Carpiquet
Airfield
To Caumont
Cheux
Fontenay-
le-Pesnel
Juvigny
GERMAN
21 Pz Div
Tessel
Hottot
Rauray
Colleville
Mouen
GERMAN
Pz-Lehr Div
Grainville
June 30
11 Armd Div.
Withdraws
GERMAN
9 SS Pz Div
Tourville
GERMAN
1 SS Pz Div
Baron
Maltot
Noyers-Bocage
Gavrus
Hill 112
Esquay
GERMAN
2 SS Pz Div
I SS Pz
Corps
Evrecy
GERMAN
10 SS Pz Div
R. Odon
R. Orne
Villers-Bocage
II SS Pz
Corps
Amayé-
sur-Orne
Map recreated by Charlene Meers_2016

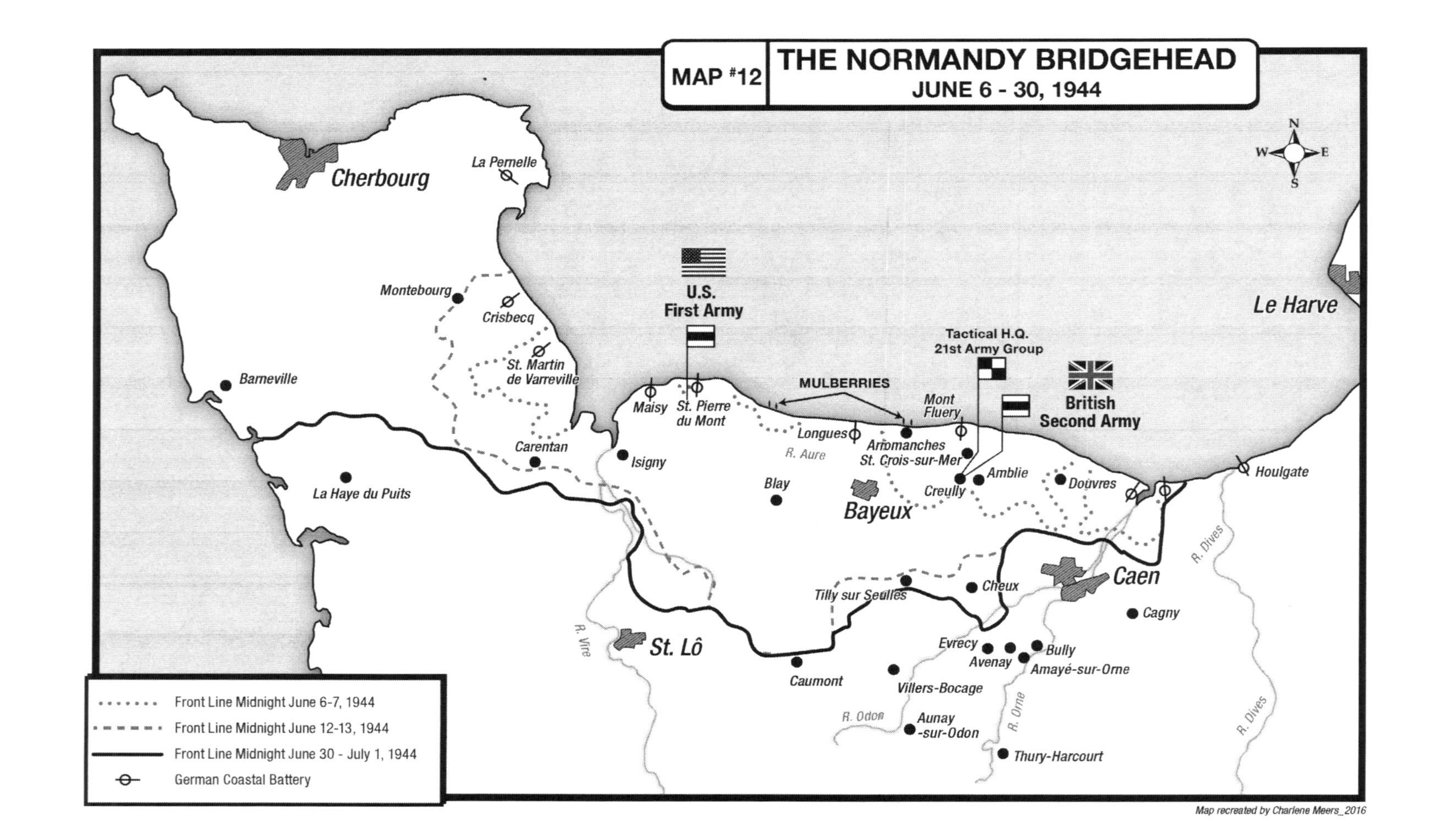
MAP #12
THE NORMANDY BRIDGEHEAD
JUNE 6 - 30, 1944
N
W
E
S
Cherbourg
La Pernelle
Montebourg
Crisbecq
St. Martin de Varreville
Barneville
Carentan
La Haye du Puits
U.S. First Army
Maisy
St. Pierre du Mont
Isigny
MULBERRIES
Longues
R. Aure
Arromanches
St. Crois-sur-Mer
Mont Fluery
Tactical H.Q. 21st Army Group
British Second Army
Le Harve
Blay
Bayeux
Creully
Amblie
Douvres
Houlgate
R. Dives
Caen
Cagny
Cheux
Tilly sur Seulles
R. Vire
St. Lô
Caumont
Evrecy
Avenay
Bully
Amayé-sur-Orne
Villers-Bocage
R. Odon
Aunay -sur-Odon
R. Orne
Thury-Harcourt
Front Line Midnight June 6-7, 1944
Front Line Midnight June 12-13, 1944
Front Line Midnight June 30 - July 1, 1944
German Coastal Battery
Map recreated by Charlene Meers_2016

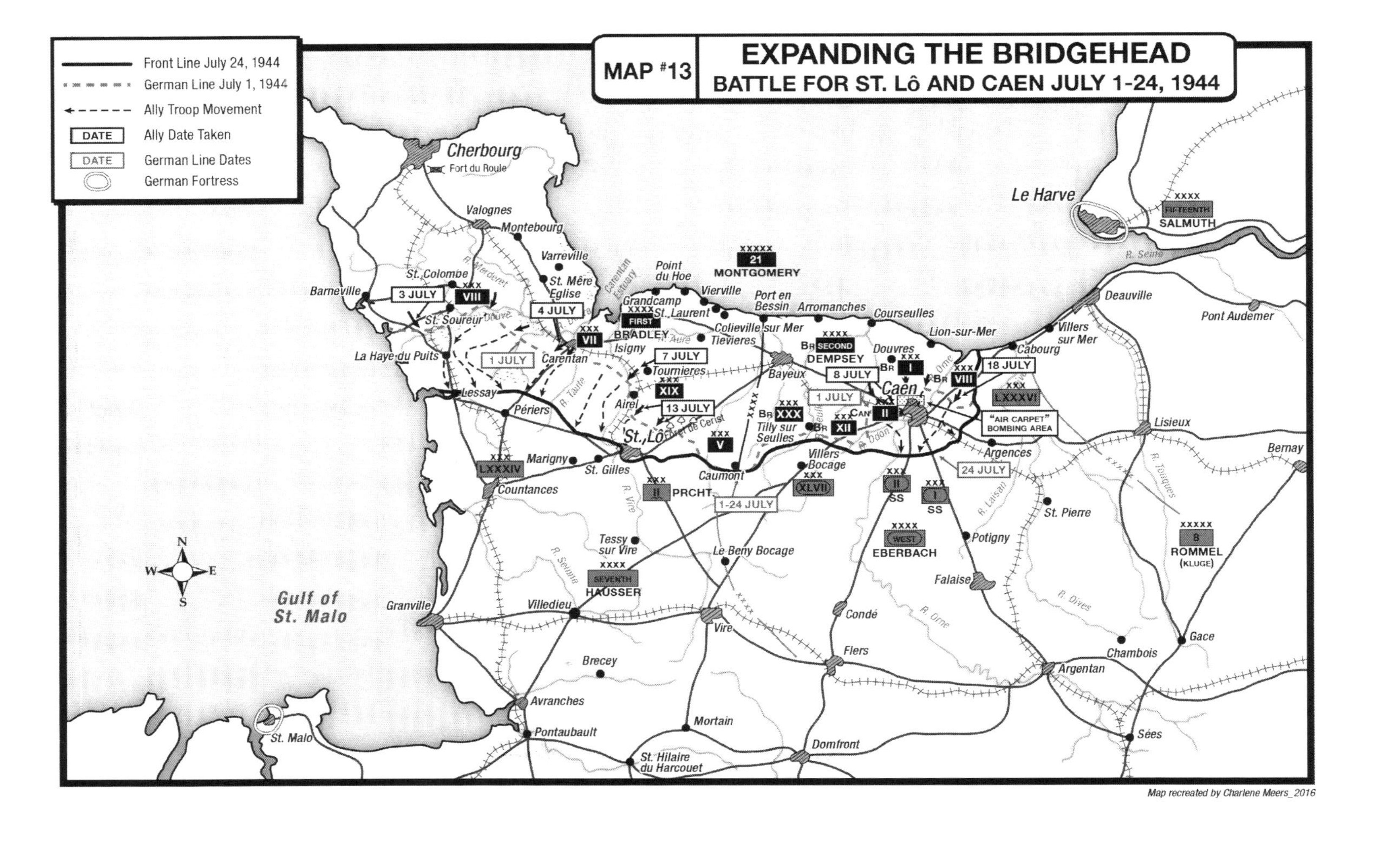
MAP #13
EXPANDING THE BRIDGEHEAD
BATTLE FOR ST. Lô AND CAEN JULY 1-24, 1944
Front Line July 24, 1944
German Line July 1, 1944
Ally Troop Movement
DATE
Ally Date Taken
DATE
German Line Dates
German Fortress
Cherbourg
Fort du Roule
Valognes
Montebourg
Varreville
St. Mère Eglise
St. Colombe
Barneville
3 JULY
VIII
4 JULY
St. Soureur
La Haye du Puits
1 JULY
Carentan
Carentan Estuary
VII
FIRST
BRADLEY
Isigny
Grandcamp
St. Laurent
Point du Hoe
Vierville
21
MONTGOMERY
Port en Bessin
Arromanches
Courseulles
Colieville sur Mer
Tievieres
SECOND
DEMPSEY
Douvres
Lion-sur-Mer
Cabourg
Villers sur Mer
Deauville
Le Harve
FIFTEENTH
SALMUTH
R. Seine
Pont Audemer
7 JULY
Tournieres
XIX
Lessay
Périers
Airel
13 JULY
St. Lô
Foret de Cerisi
V
Bayeux
8 JULY
1 JULY
Caen
I
II
VIII
18 JULY
LXXXVI
"AIR CARPET" BOMBING AREA
XXX
Tilly sur Seulles
XII
CAN
Lisieux
Bernay
R. Touques
Argences
24 JULY
Marigny
St. Gilles
LXXXIV
Countances
Caumont
Villers Bocage
XLVII
II
PRCHT
1-24 JULY
SS
SS
St. Pierre
WEST
EBERBACH
Potigny
8
ROMMEL
(KLUGE)
Tessy sur Vire
Le Beny Bocage
SEVENTH
HAUSSER
Falaise
R. Dives
Gulf of St. Malo
Granville
Villedieu
Vire
Condé
R. Orne
Gace
Chambois
Flers
Argentan
Brecey
Avranches
Mortain
Pontaubault
St. Malo
Domfront
Sées
St. Hilaire du Harcouet
N
W
E
S
Map recreated by Charlene Meers_2016

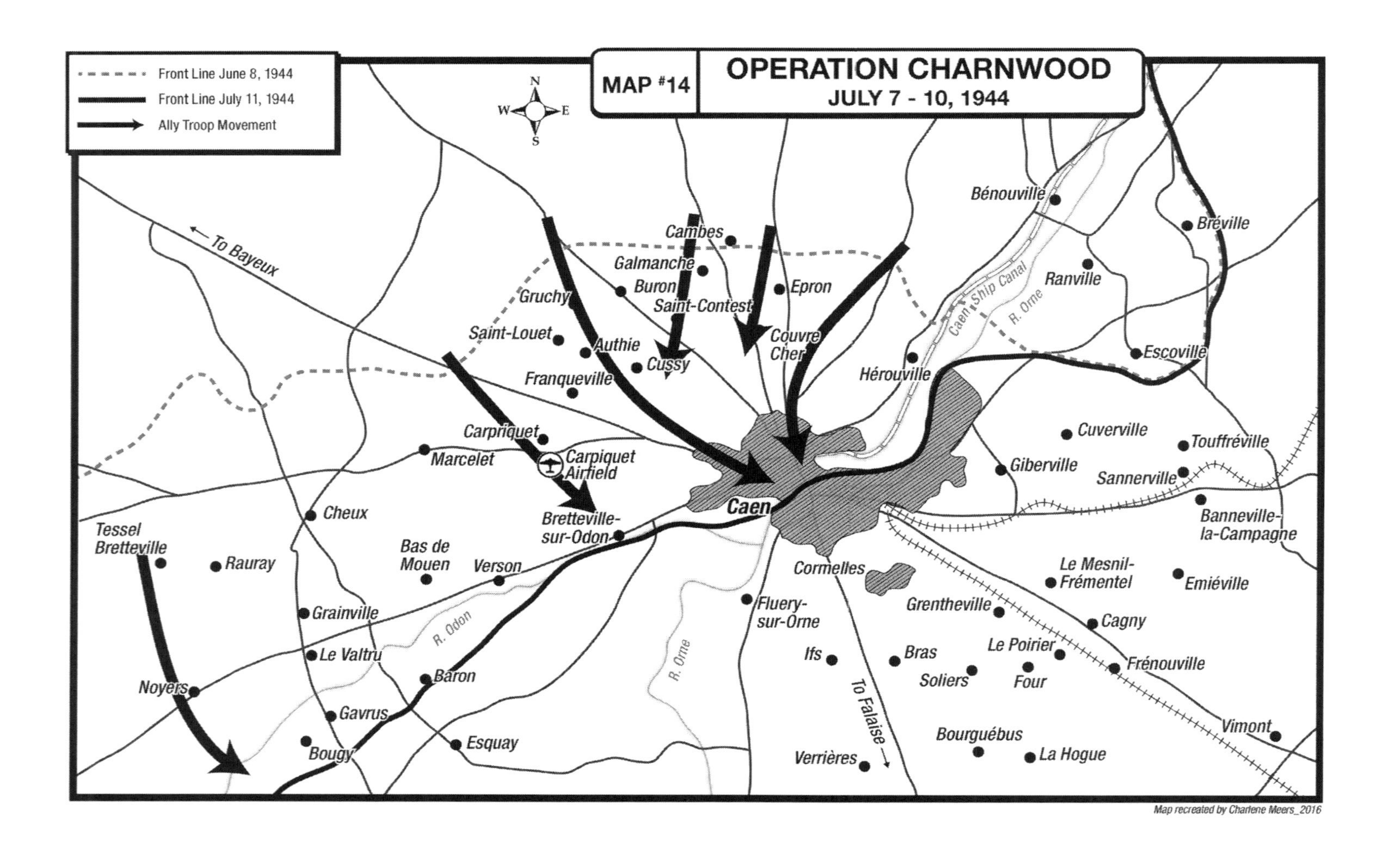
MAP #14
OPERATION CHARNWOOD
JULY 7 - 10, 1944
Front Line June 8, 1944
Front Line July 11, 1944
Ally Troop Movement
N
E
S
W
To Bayeux
Cambes
Galmanche
Buron
Saint-Contest
Epron
Gruchy
Saint-Louet
Authie
Cussy
Couvre
Cher
Franqueville
Carpiquet
Carpiquet
Airfield
Marcelet
Bénouville
Bréville
Ranville
Caen Ship Canal
R. Orne
Escoville
Hérouville
Cuverville
Touffréville
Giberville
Sannerville
Banneville-
la-Campagne
Caen
Cheux
Tessel
Bretteville
Rauray
Bas de
Mouen
Verson
Bretteville-
sur-Odon
Cormelles
Le Mesnil-
Frémentel
Emiéville
Grainville
R. Odon
Fluery-
sur-Orne
Grentheville
Cagny
Le Valtru
Ifs
Bras
Le Poirier
Frénouville
Soliers
Four
Noyers
Baron
R. Orne
To Falaise
Gavrus
Esquay
Bourguébus
Vimont
Bougy
Verrières
La Hogue
Map recreated by Charlene Meers_2016

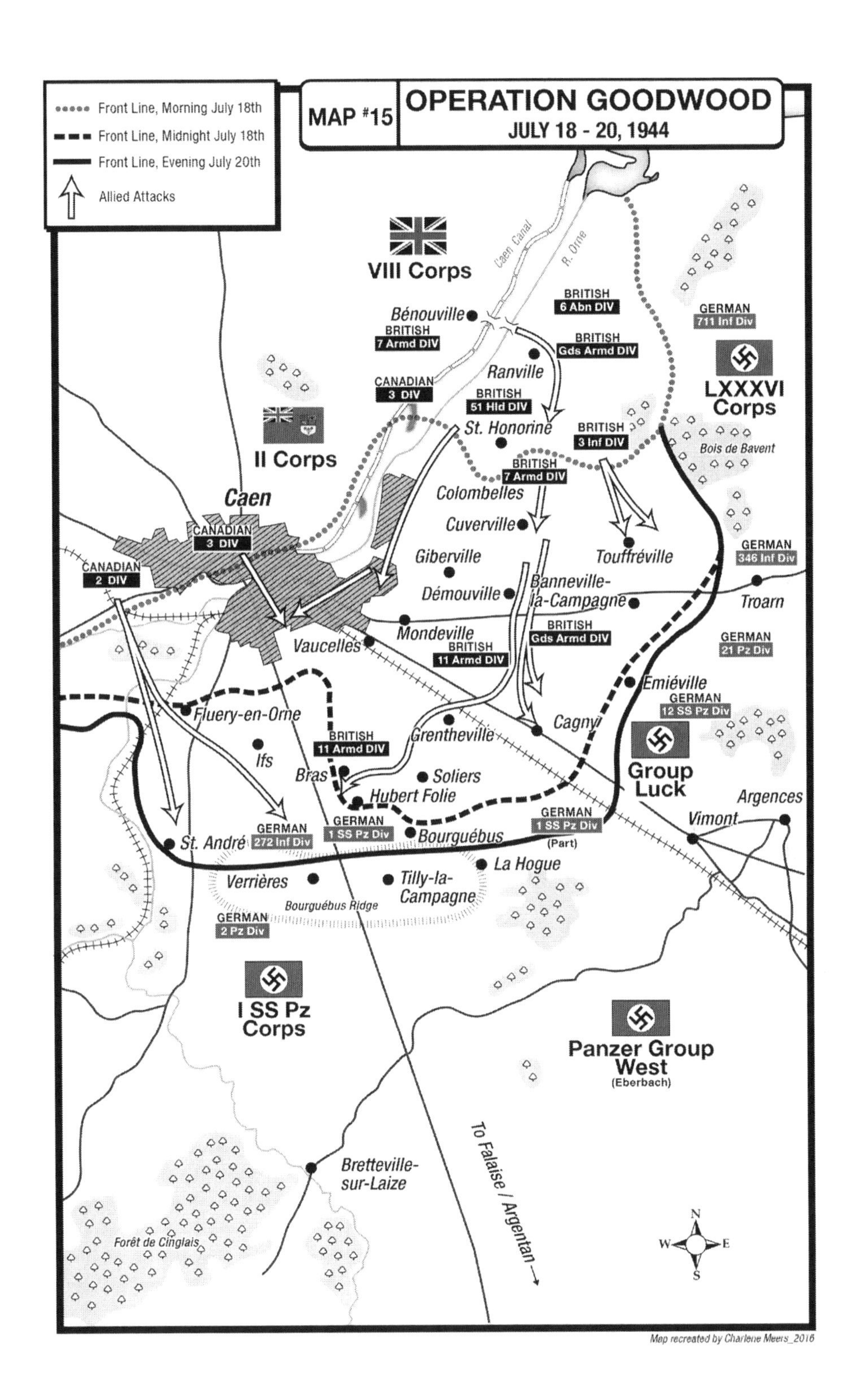

MAP #15
OPERATION GOODWOOD
JULY 18 - 20, 1944
Front Line, Morning July 18th
Front Line, Midnight July 18th
Front Line, Evening July 20th
Allied Attacks
VIII Corps
Caen Canal
R. Orne
Bénouville
BRITISH 7 Armd DIV
BRITISH 6 Abn DIV
BRITISH Gds Armd DIV
Ranville
CANADIAN 3 DIV
BRITISH 51 Hld DIV
St. Honorine
BRITISH 3 Inf DIV
II Corps
BRITISH 7 Armd DIV
Colombelles
Caen
Cuverville
CANADIAN 3 DIV
CANADIAN 2 DIV
Giberville
Touffréville
Démouville
Banneville-la-Campagne
Mondeville
Vaucelles
BRITISH 11 Armd DIV
BRITISH Gds Armd DIV
GERMAN 711 Inf Div
LXXXVI Corps
Bois de Bavent
GERMAN 346 Inf Div
Troarn
GERMAN 21 Pz Div
Emiéville
GERMAN 12 SS Pz Div
Group Luck
Fluery-en-Orne
Ifs
BRITISH 11 Armd DIV
Grentheville
Cagny
Bras
Soliers
Hubert Folie
GERMAN 1 SS Pz Div
Bourguébus
GERMAN 1 SS Pz Div (Part)
Argences
Vimont
St. André
GERMAN 272 Inf Div
La Hogue
Verrières
Tilly-la-Campagne
Bourguébus Ridge
GERMAN 2 Pz Div
I SS Pz Corps
Panzer Group West (Eberbach)
To Falaise / Argentan
Bretteville-sur-Laize
Forêt de Cinglais
N
W
E
S
Map recreated by Charlene Meers_2016

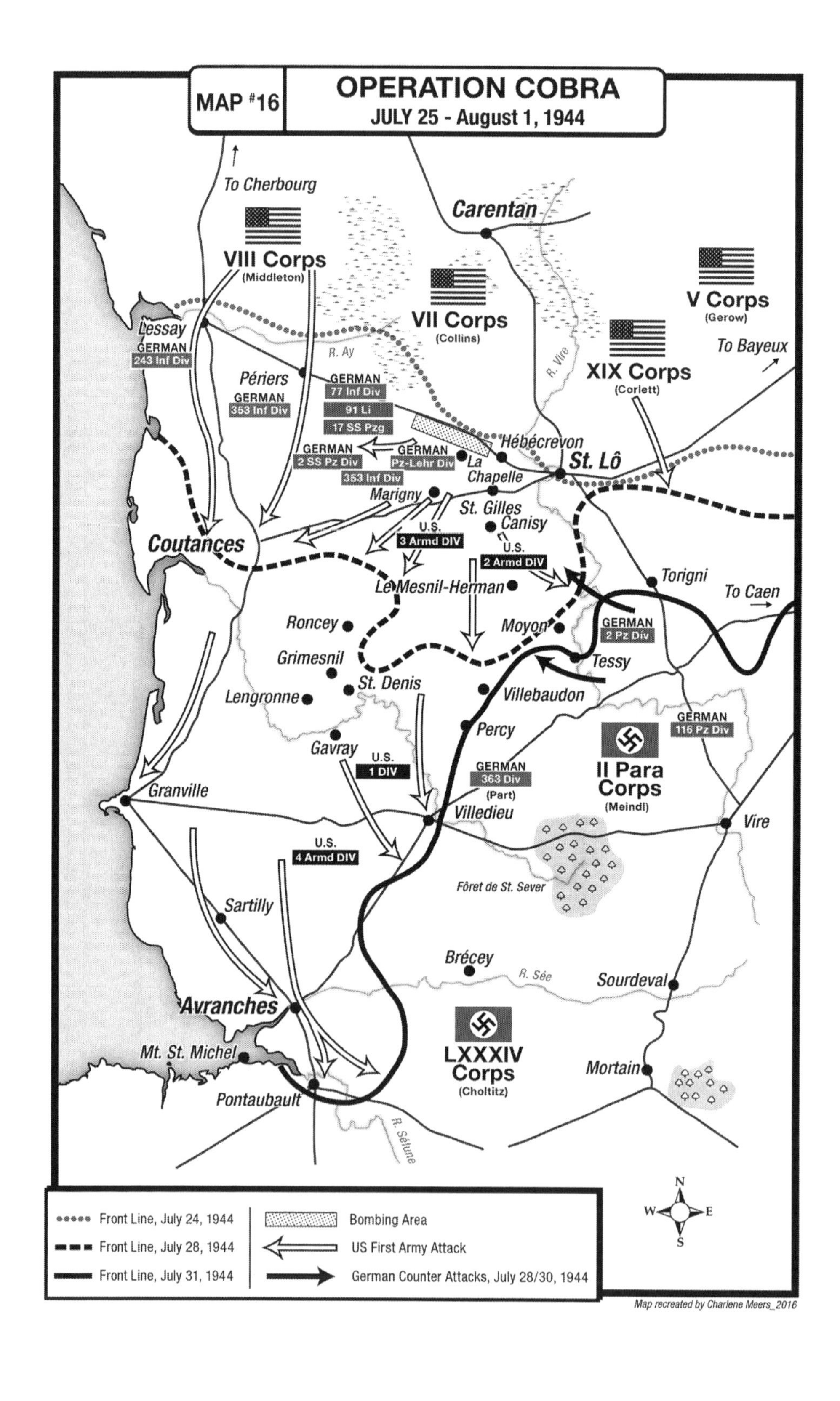
MAP #16
OPERATION COBRA
JULY 25 - August 1, 1944
To Cherbourg
Carentan
VIII Corps
(Middleton)
VII Corps
(Collins)
V Corps
(Gerow)
XIX Corps
(Corlett)
To Bayeux
R. Vire
Lessay
GERMAN
243 Inf Div
R. Ay
Périers
GERMAN
353 Inf Div
GERMAN
77 Inf Div
91 Li
17 SS Pzg
GERMAN
2 SS Pz Div
GERMAN
Pz-Lehr Div
353 Inf Div
Hébécrevon
La Chapelle
St. Lô
Marigny
St. Gilles
Canisy
U.S.
3 Armd DIV
U.S.
2 Armd DIV
Coutances
Le Mesnil-Herman
Torigni
To Caen
Roncey
Moyon
GERMAN
2 Pz Div
Tessy
Grimesnil
St. Denis
Lengronne
Villebaudon
Percy
GERMAN
116 Pz Div
Gavray
U.S.
1 DIV
GERMAN
363 Div
(Part)
II Para Corps
(Meindl)
Granville
Villedieu
Vire
U.S.
4 Armd DIV
Fôret de St. Sever
Sartilly
Brécey
R. Sée
Sourdeval
Avranches
LXXXIV Corps
(Choltitz)
Mt. St. Michel
Mortain
Pontaubault
R. Sélune
Front Line, July 24, 1944
Front Line, July 28, 1944
Front Line, July 31, 1944
Bombing Area
US First Army Attack
German Counter Attacks, July 28/30, 1944
N
W
E
S
Map recreated by Charlene Meers_2016

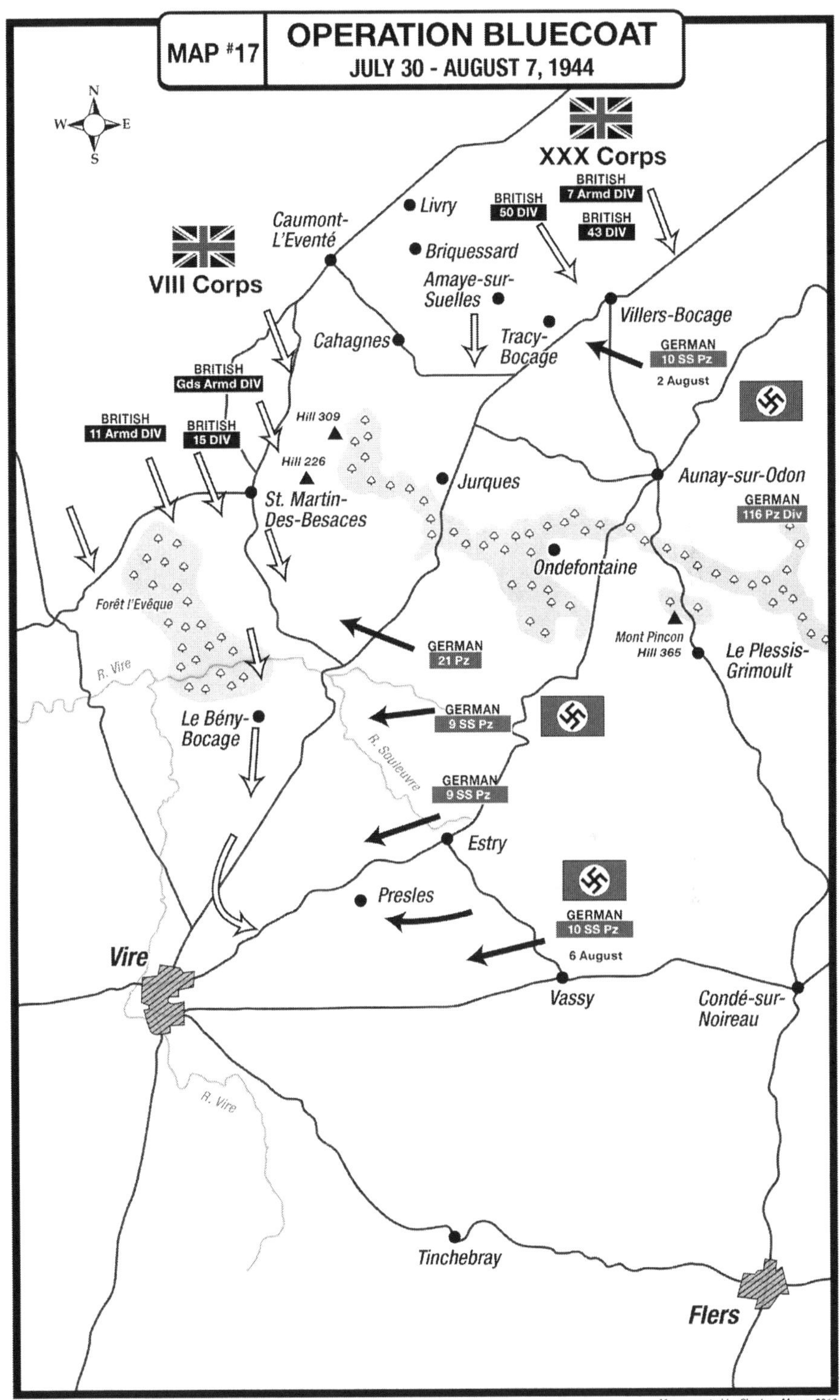


Map recreated by Charlene Meers_2016

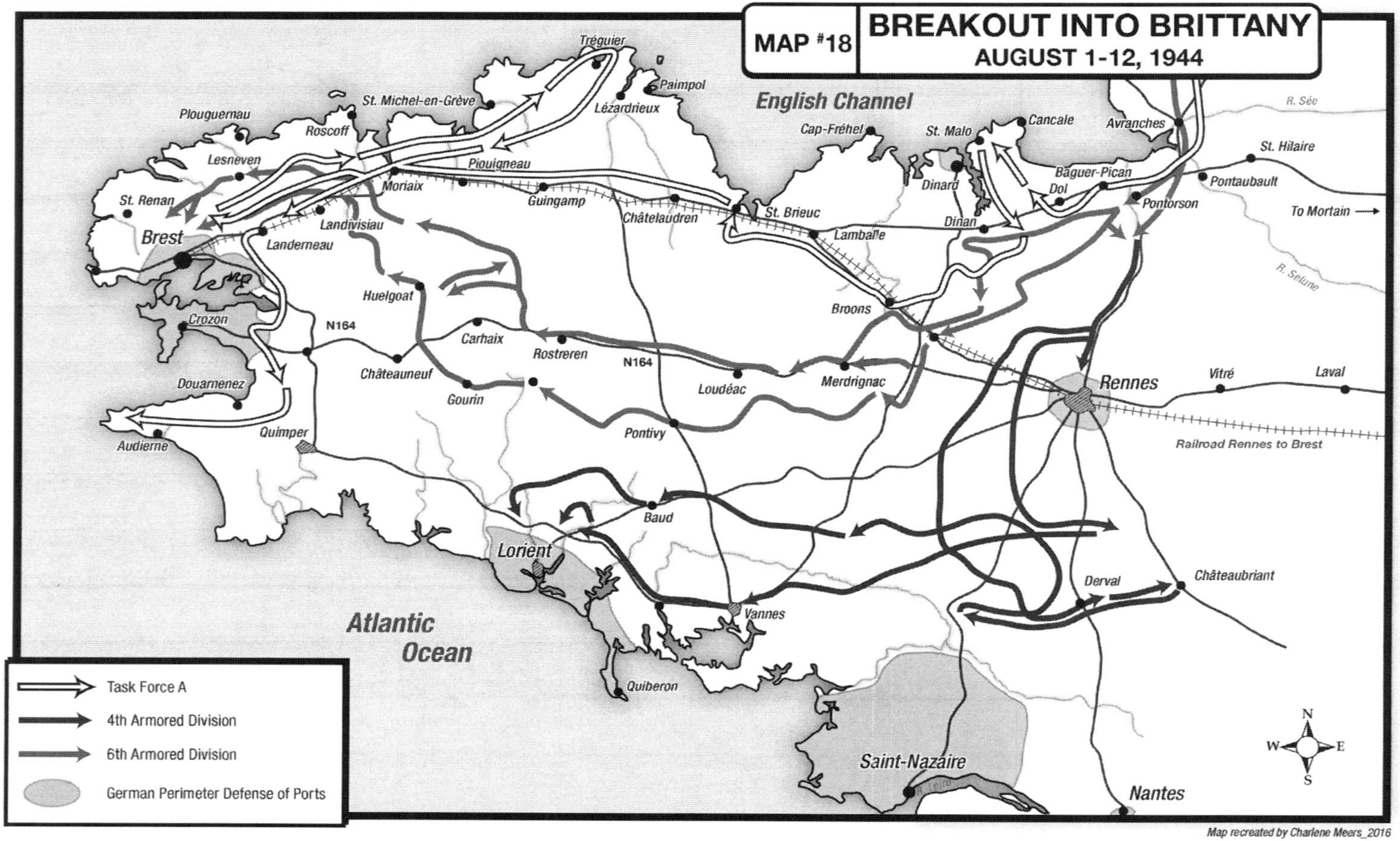

# MAP #18 BREAKOUT INTO BRITTANY
## AUGUST 1-12, 1944

English Channel
Tréguier
Paimpol
Lézardrieux
St. Michel-en-Grève
Plouguernau
Roscoff
Lesneven
Plouigneau
Morlaix
St. Renan
Brest
Guingamp
Châtelaudren
St. Brieuc
Cap-Fréhel
St. Malo
Dinard
Cancale
Avranches
R. Sée
St. Hilaire
Baguer-Pican
Dol
Pontaubault
Pontorson
To Mortain →
Dinan
Lamballe
R. Selune
Landivisiau
Landerneau
Huelgoat
Crozon
N164
Carhaix
Rostreren
N164
Loudéac
Merdrignac
Broons
Châteauneuf
Gourin
Rennes
Vitré
Laval
Douarnenez
Quimper
Audierne
Pontivy
Railroad Rennes to Brest
Baud
Lorient
Derval
Châteaubriant
Vannes
Atlantic Ocean
Quiberon
Saint-Nazaire
Nantes
N
W
E
S

Task Force A
4th Armored Division
6th Armored Division
German Perimeter Defense of Ports

Map recreated by Charlene Meers_2016

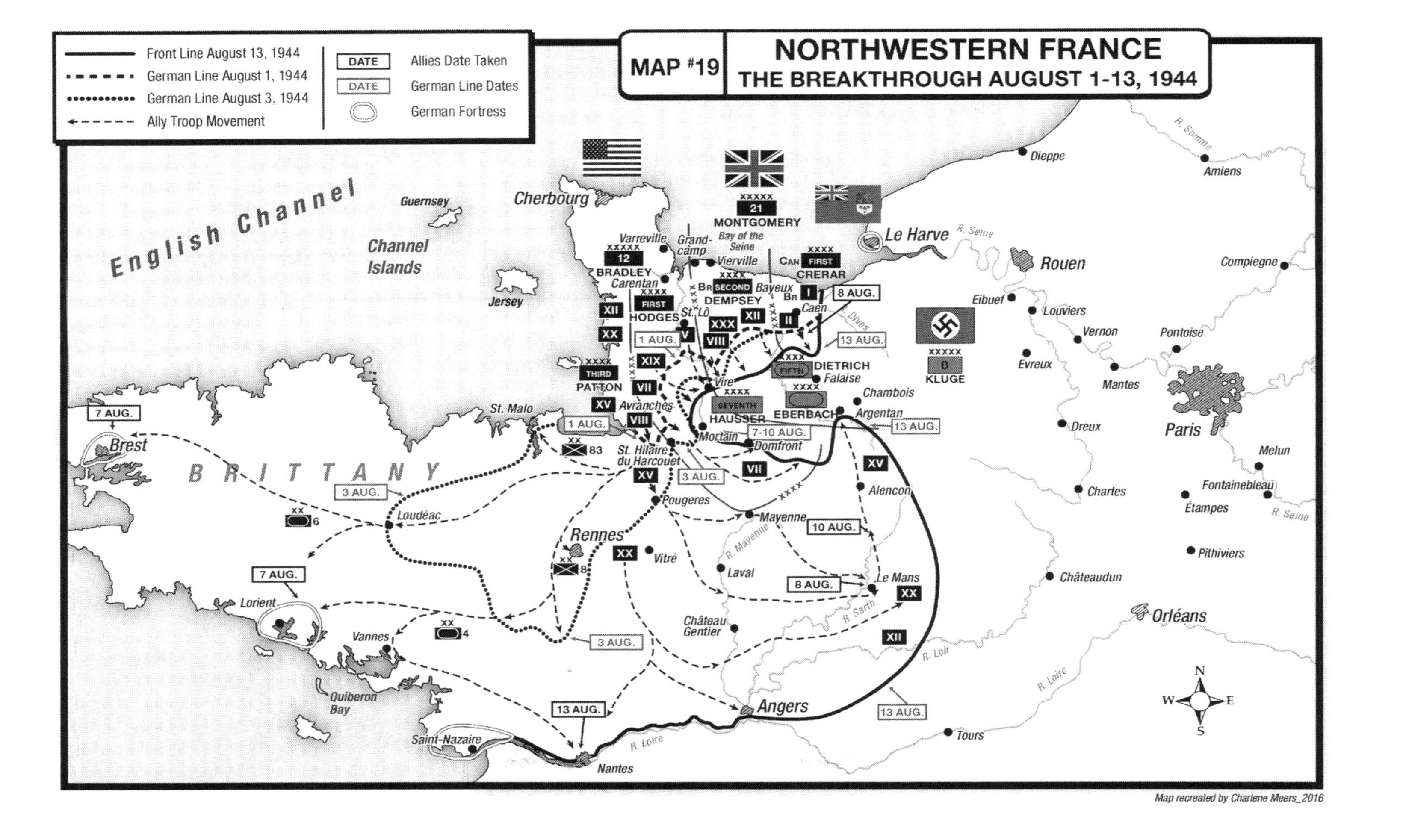

MAP #19
NORTHWESTERN FRANCE
THE BREAKTHROUGH AUGUST 1-13, 1944
Front Line August 13, 1944
German Line August 1, 1944
German Line August 3, 1944
Ally Troop Movement
DATE
Allies Date Taken
DATE
German Line Dates
German Fortress
English Channel
Channel Islands
Guernsey
Jersey
Cherbourg
Varreville
Grand-camp
Vierville
Bay of the Seine
Carentan
St. Lô
Bayeux
Caen
Le Harve
R. Seine
Dieppe
R. Somme
Amiens
Rouen
Compiegne
Eibuef
Louviers
Vernon
Pontoise
Evreux
Mantes
Paris
Dreux
Melun
Chartes
Fontainebleau
Étampes
R. Seine
Pithiviers
Châteaudun
Orléans
R. Loir
R. Loire
Tours
Angers
Nantes
R. Loire
Saint-Nazaire
Quiberon Bay
Vannes
Lorient
Brest
BRITTANY
Loudéac
Rennes
Vitré
St. Malo
Avranches
St. Hilaire du Harcouet
Pougeres
Mortain
Domfront
Vire
Mayenne
R. Mayenne
Laval
Château Gentier
Le Mans
R. Sarth
Alencon
Argentan
Chambois
Falaise
L. Dives
XXXXX 21 MONTGOMERY
XXXXX 12 BRADLEY
XXXX FIRST HODGES
XXXX THIRD PATTON
XXXX SECOND DEMPSEY
XXXX CAN FIRST CREAR
XXXX FIFTH DIETRICH
XXXX SEVENTH HAUSSER
XXXX EBERBACH
XXXXX B KLUGE
XII
XX
XIX
VII
XV
VIII
V
XXX
XII
II
I
XV
VII
XX
XV
XX
XII
BR
BR
XX 83
XX 8
XX 6
XX 4
XXXX
7 AUG.
7 AUG.
3 AUG.
3 AUG.
3 AUG.
1 AUG.
1 AUG.
7-10 AUG.
8 AUG.
8 AUG.
10 AUG.
13 AUG.
13 AUG.
13 AUG.
13 AUG.
13 AUG.
N
E
S
W
Map recreated by Charlene Meers_2016

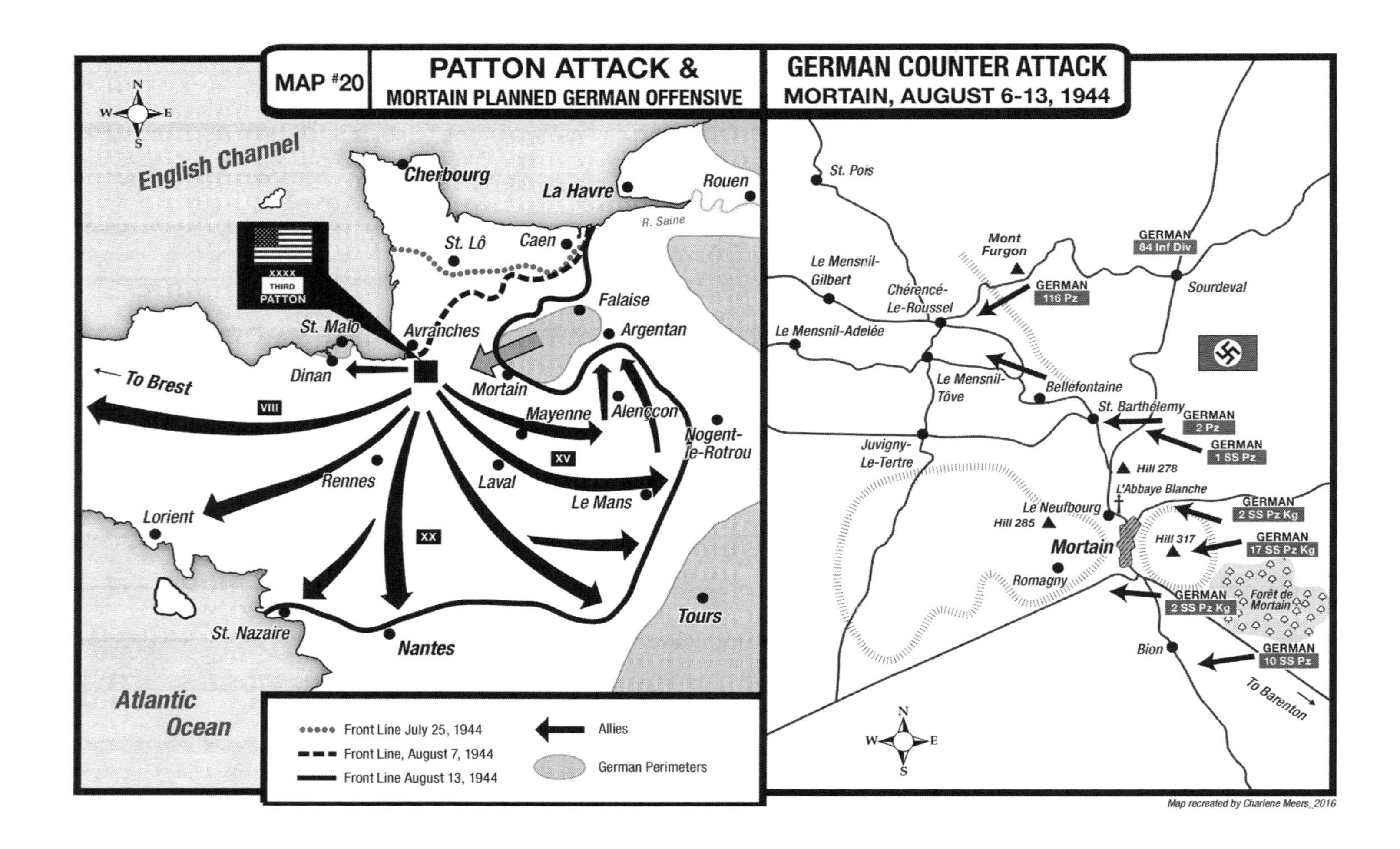
MAP #20
PATTON ATTACK &
MORTAIN PLANNED GERMAN OFFENSIVE
English Channel
Cherbourg
La Havre
Rouen
R. Seine
St. Lô
Caen
XXXX
THIRD
PATTON
St. Malo
Avranches
Falaise
Argentan
Dinan
To Brest
Mortain
VIII
Mayenne
Alençcon
Nogent-le-Rotrou
XV
Rennes
Laval
Le Mans
Lorient
XX
Tours
St. Nazaire
Nantes
Atlantic Ocean
Front Line July 25, 1944
Front Line, August 7, 1944
Front Line August 13, 1944
Allies
German Perimeters
GERMAN COUNTER ATTACK
MORTAIN, AUGUST 6-13, 1944
St. Pois
Mont Furgon
GERMAN 84 Inf Div
Le Mensnil-Gilbert
Chérencé-Le-Roussel
GERMAN 116 Pz
Sourdeval
Le Mensnil-Adelée
Le Mensnil-Tôve
Bellefontaine
St. Barthélemy
GERMAN 2 Pz
GERMAN 1 SS Pz
Juvigny-Le-Tertre
Hill 278
L'Abbaye Blanche
GERMAN 2 SS Pz Kg
Le Neufbourg
Hill 285
Mortain
Hill 317
GERMAN 17 SS Pz Kg
Romagny
GERMAN 2 SS Pz Kg
Forêt de Mortain
Bion
GERMAN 10 SS Pz
To Barenton
Map recreated by Charlene Meers_2016

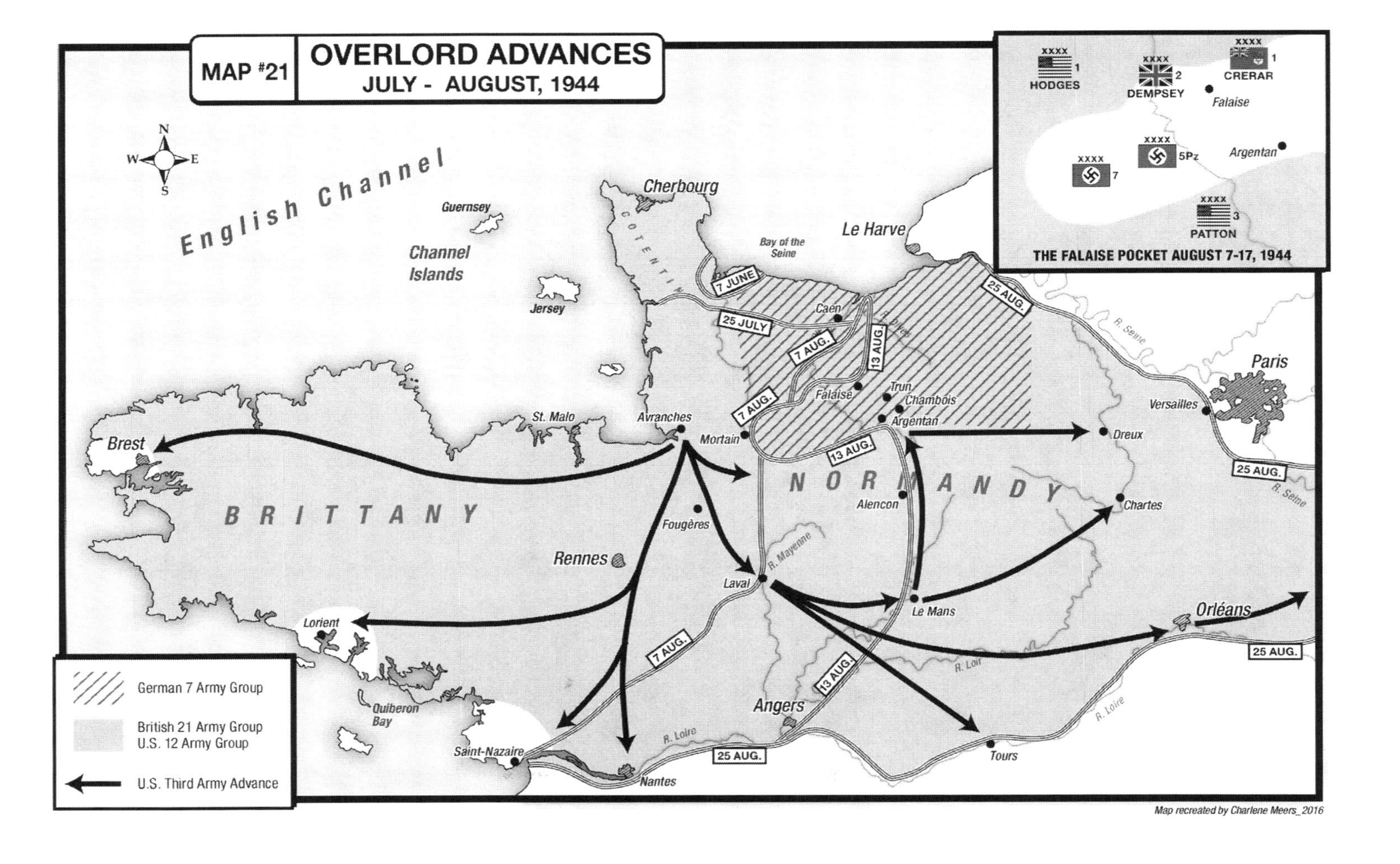
MAP #21
OVERLORD ADVANCES
JULY - AUGUST, 1944
English Channel
Guernsey
Channel Islands
Jersey
Cherbourg
COTENTIN
Bay of the Seine
Le Harve
7 JUNE
25 JULY
7 AUG.
13 AUG.
25 AUG.
Caen
Falaise
Trun
Chambois
Argentan
Mortain
Avranches
St. Malo
Brest
BRITTANY
NORMANDY
Alencon
Fougères
Rennes
Laval
R. Mayenne
Le Mans
Dreux
Chartes
Versailles
Paris
R. Seine
Orléans
R. Loir
R. Loire
Tours
Angers
Lorient
Quiberon Bay
Saint-Nazaire
Nantes
German 7 Army Group
British 21 Army Group
U.S. 12 Army Group
U.S. Third Army Advance
HODGES
DEMPSEY
CRERAR
5Pz
PATTON
THE FALAISE POCKET AUGUST 7-17, 1944
Map recreated by Charlene Meers_2016

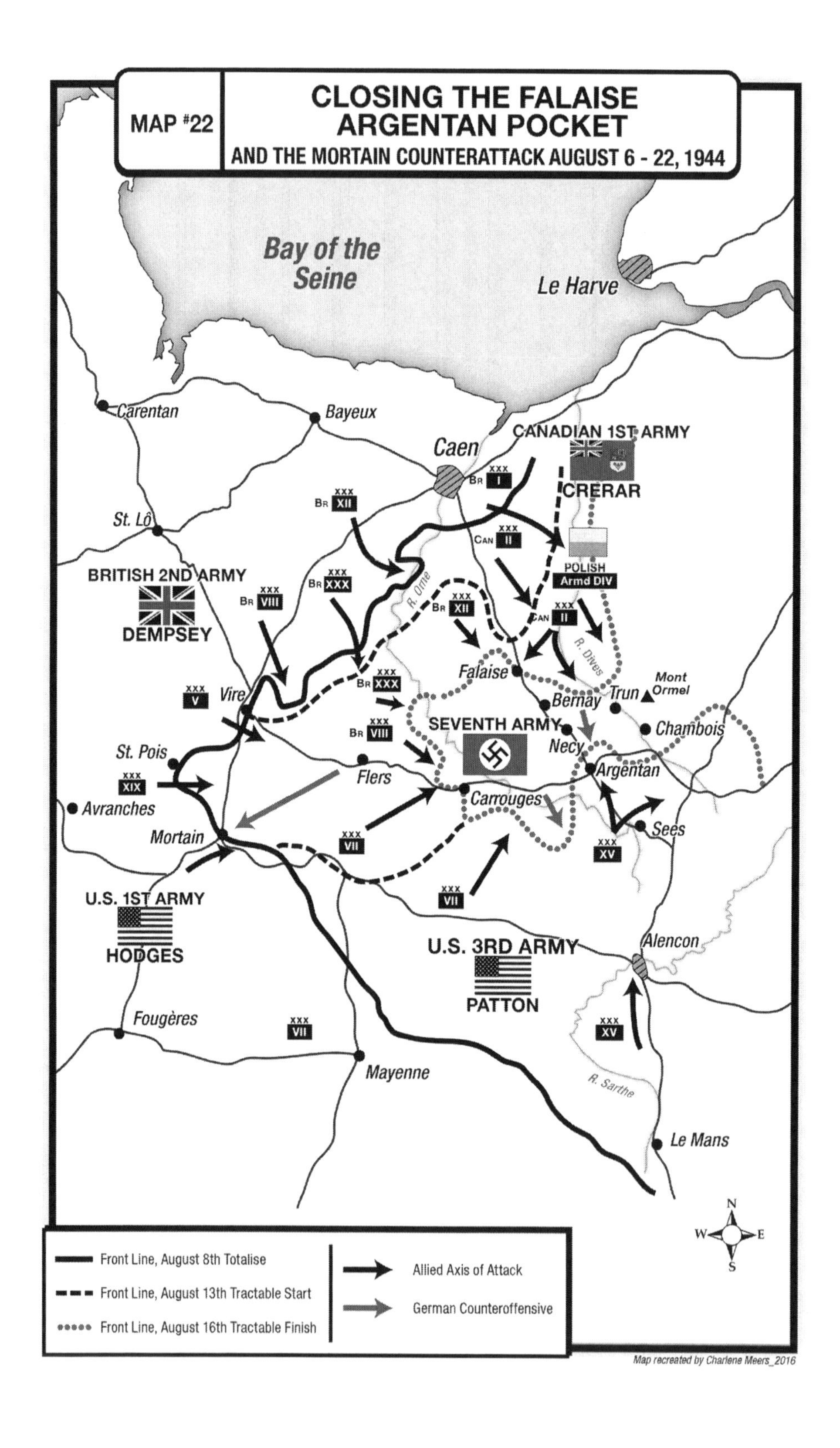
MAP #22
CLOSING THE FALAISE ARGENTAN POCKET
AND THE MORTAIN COUNTERATTACK AUGUST 6 - 22, 1944
Bay of the Seine
Le Harve
Carentan
Bayeux
Caen
CANADIAN 1ST ARMY
CRERAR
St. Lô
BRITISH 2ND ARMY
DEMPSEY
POLISH
Armd DIV
R. Orne
R. Dives
Falaise
Mont Ormel
Trun
Bernay
Chambois
Vire
SEVENTH ARMY
Necy
St. Pois
Flers
Argentan
Carrouges
Avranches
Mortain
Sees
U.S. 1ST ARMY
HODGES
U.S. 3RD ARMY
PATTON
Alencon
Fougères
Mayenne
R. Sarthe
Le Mans
Front Line, August 8th Totalise
Front Line, August 13th Tractable Start
Front Line, August 16th Tractable Finish
Allied Axis of Attack
German Counteroffensive
Map recreated by Charlene Meers_2016

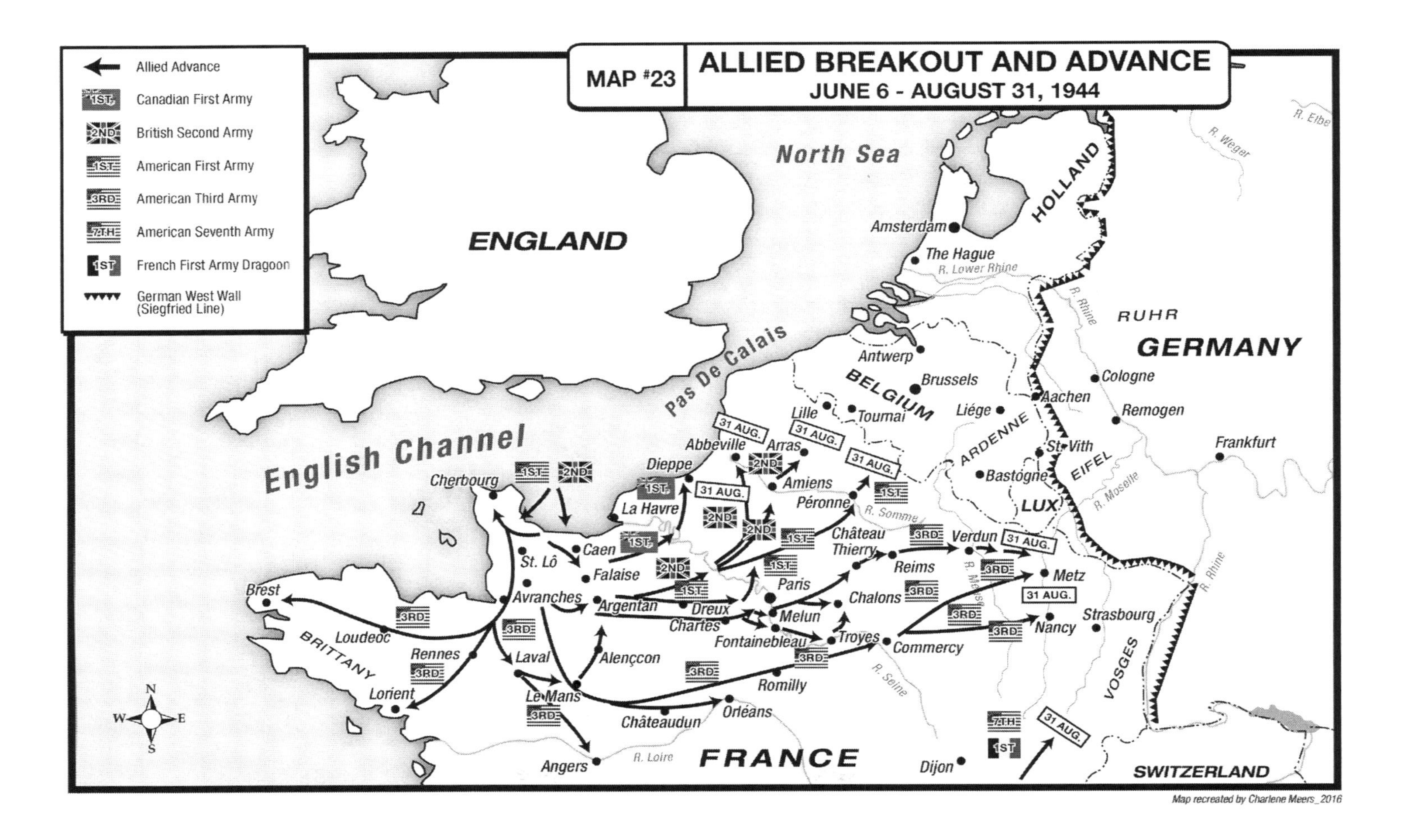
MAP #23
ALLIED BREAKOUT AND ADVANCE
JUNE 6 - AUGUST 31, 1944
Allied Advance
Canadian First Army
British Second Army
American First Army
American Third Army
American Seventh Army
French First Army Dragoon
German West Wall (Siegfried Line)
ENGLAND
North Sea
English Channel
Pas De Calais
HOLLAND
BELGIUM
LUX
GERMANY
RUHR
FRANCE
SWITZERLAND
BRITTANY
ARDENNE
EIFEL
VOSGES
Amsterdam
The Hague
Antwerp
Brussels
Lille
Tournai
Liége
Aachen
Cologne
Remogen
Frankfurt
St. Vith
Bastogne
Abbeville
Arras
Amiens
Péronne
Dieppe
La Havre
Cherbourg
Caen
St. Lô
Falaise
Avranches
Argentan
Dreux
Chartes
Paris
Melun
Fontainebleau
Château Thierry
Reims
Chalons
Verdun
Metz
Nancy
Strasbourg
Troyes
Commercy
Romilly
Orléans
Châteaudun
Alençcon
Le Mans
Laval
Rennes
Loudeoc
Lorient
Brest
Angers
Dijon
R. Elbe
R. Weger
R. Lower Rhine
R. Rhine
R. Moselle
R. Somme
R. Meuse
R. Seine
R. Loire
31 AUG.
Map recreated by Charlene Meers_2016

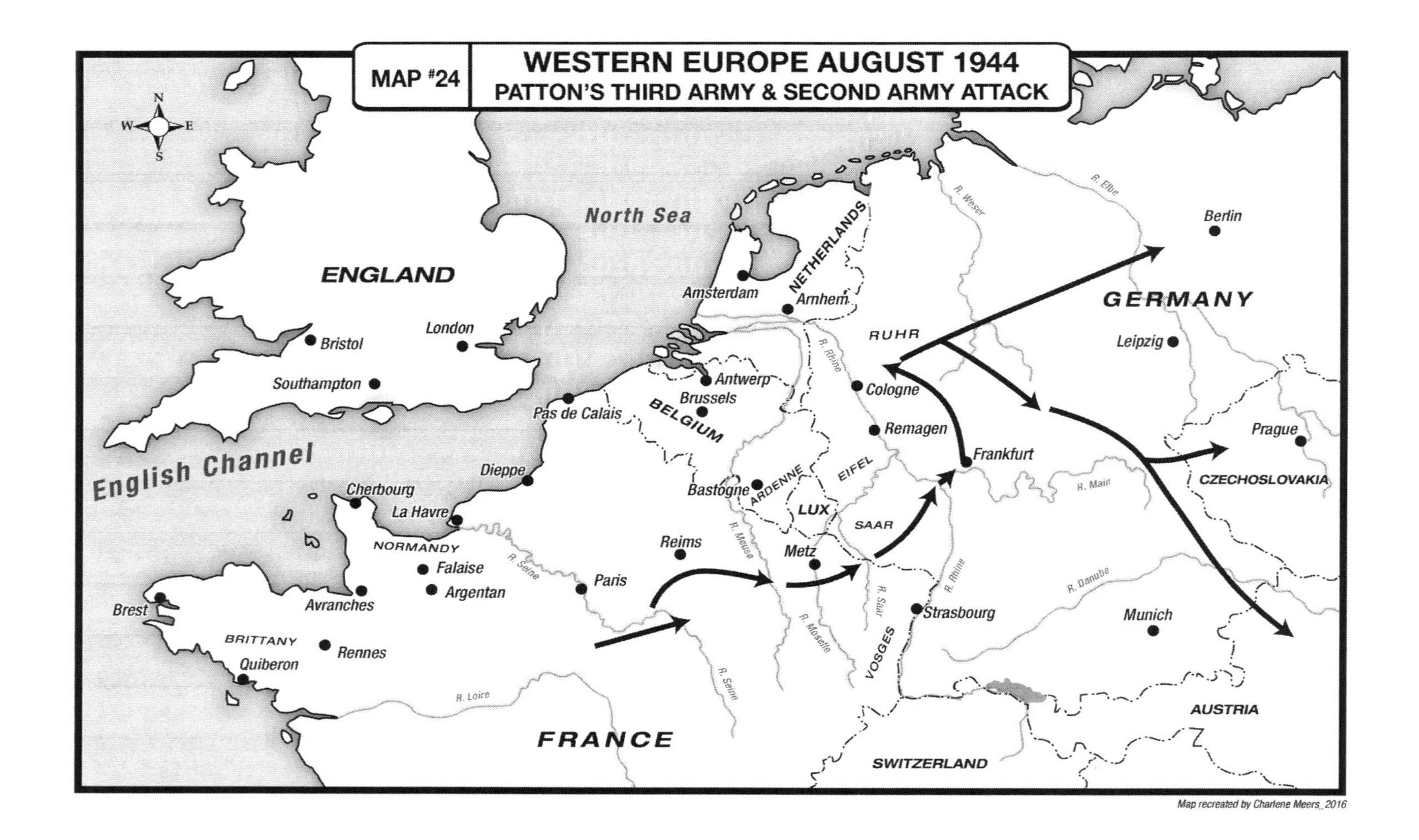
MAP #24
WESTERN EUROPE AUGUST 1944
PATTON'S THIRD ARMY & SECOND ARMY ATTACK
N
W
E
S
North Sea
ENGLAND
Bristol
London
Southampton
English Channel
Amsterdam
NETHERLANDS
Arnhem
R. Weser
R. Elbe
Berlin
GERMANY
RUHR
Leipzig
R. Rhine
Antwerp
Cologne
Brussels
BELGIUM
Pas de Calais
Remagen
Frankfurt
Prague
CZECHOSLOVAKIA
R. Main
Dieppe
Cherbourg
La Havre
Bastogne
ARDENNE
EIFEL
LUX
SAAR
NORMANDY
Falaise
Argentan
R. Seine
Paris
Reims
R. Meuse
Metz
R. Saar
R. Mosette
R. Danuba
Strasbourg
Munich
Brest
Avranches
BRITTANY
Rennes
Quiberon
VOSGES
R. Loire
AUSTRIA
FRANCE
SWITZERLAND
Map recreated by Charlene Meers_2016

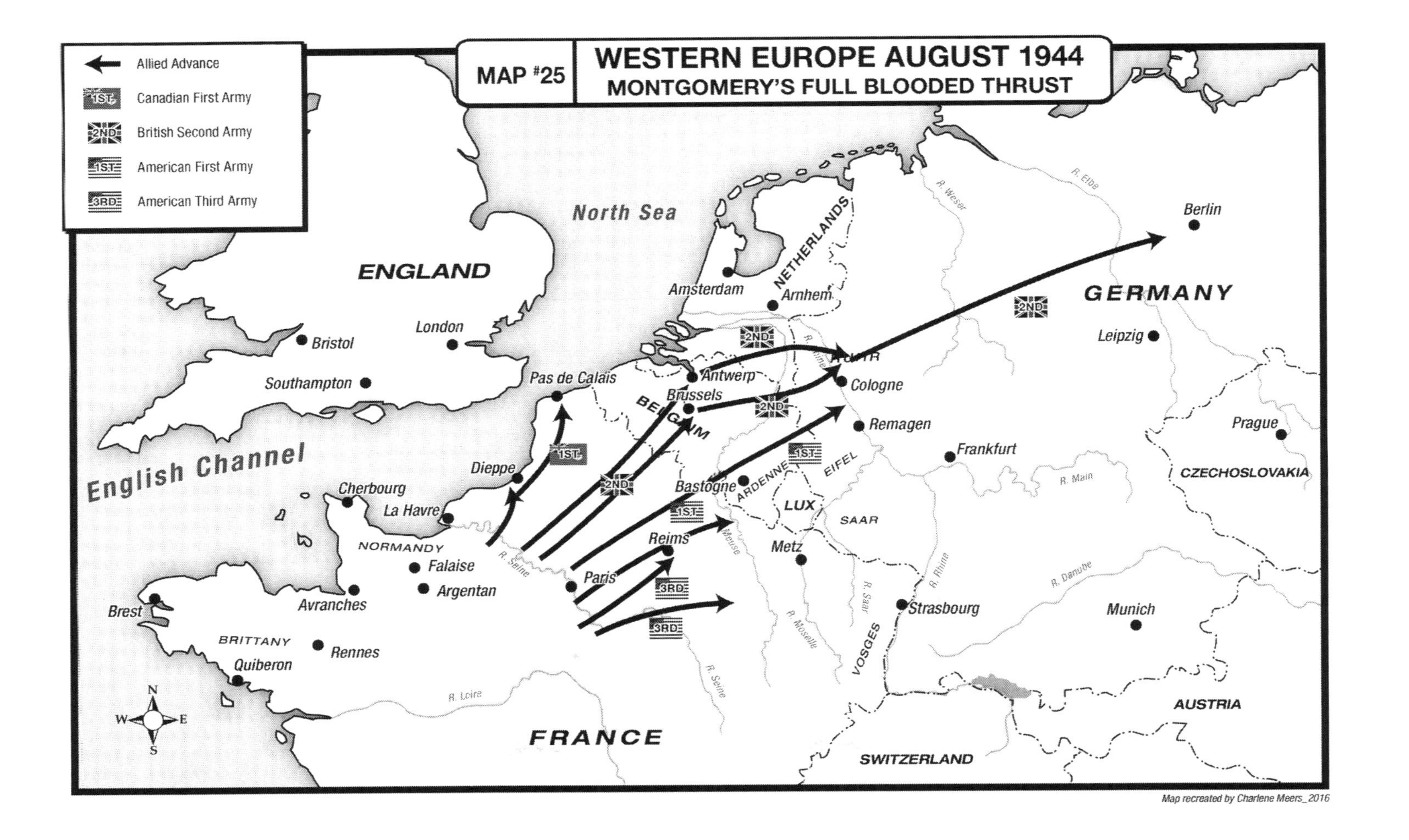
MAP #25
WESTERN EUROPE AUGUST 1944
MONTGOMERY'S FULL BLOODED THRUST
Allied Advance
Canadian First Army
British Second Army
American First Army
American Third Army
North Sea
ENGLAND
English Channel
NETHERLANDS
GERMANY
Berlin
Amsterdam
Arnhem
Leipzig
Bristol
London
Southampton
Pas de Calais
Antwerp
Cologne
Brussels
BELGIUM
Remagen
Prague
Frankfurt
CZECHOSLOVAKIA
Dieppe
Cherbourg
La Havre
Bastogne
ARDENNE
EIFEL
LUX
SAAR
NORMANDY
Reims
Metz
Falaise
Argentan
Paris
Brest
Avranches
Strasbourg
Munich
BRITTANY
Rennes
Quiberon
VOSGES
AUSTRIA
FRANCE
SWITZERLAND
R. Elbe
R. Weser
R. Main
R. Seine
R. Meuse
R. Saar
R. Rhine
R. Danube
R. Moselle
R. Loire
1ST.
2ND
3RD
N
W
E
S
Map recreated by Charlene Meers_2016

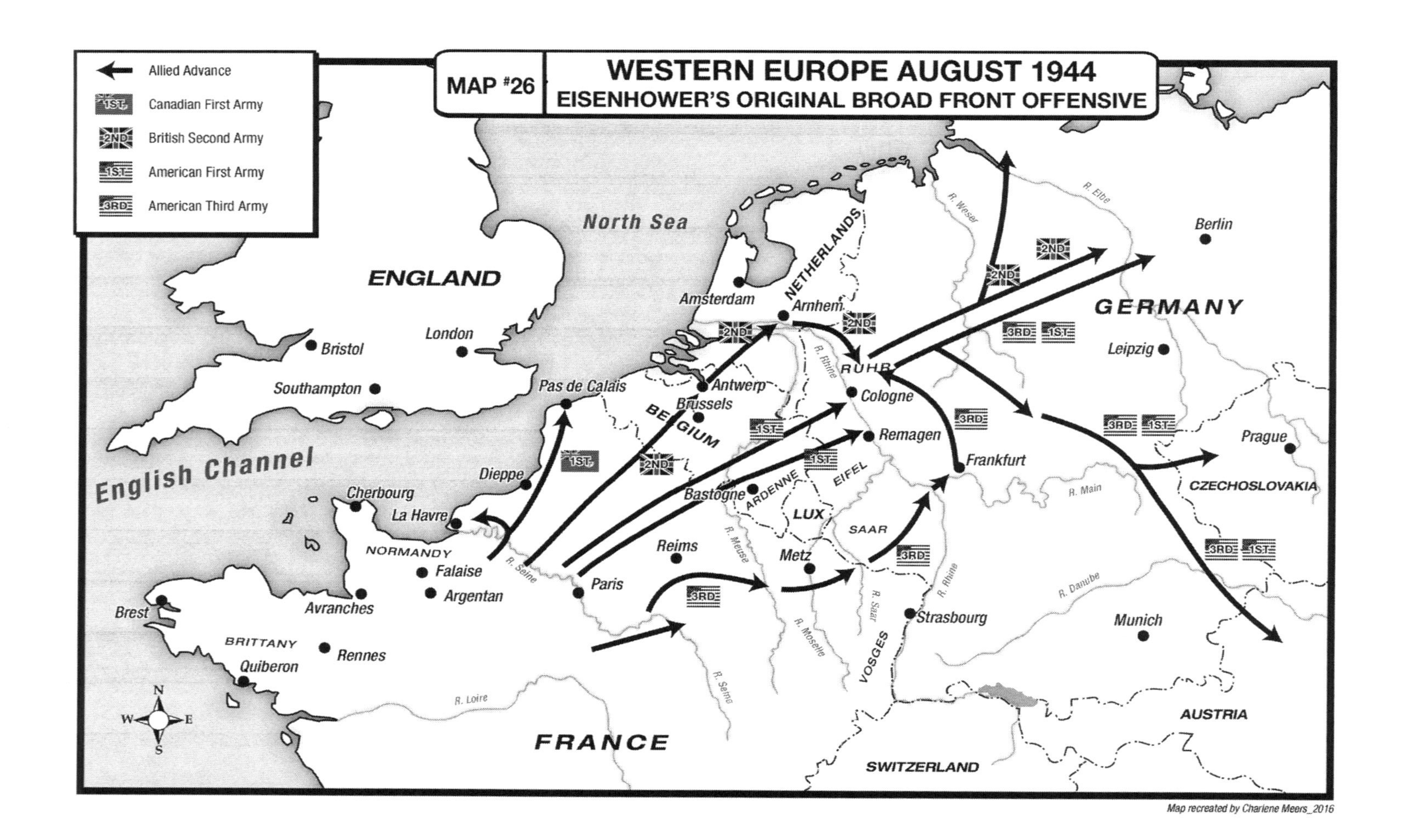

MAP #26
WESTERN EUROPE AUGUST 1944
EISENHOWER'S ORIGINAL BROAD FRONT OFFENSIVE
Allied Advance
1ST. Canadian First Army
2ND British Second Army
1ST. American First Army
3RD American Third Army
North Sea
ENGLAND
English Channel
Bristol
London
Southampton
NETHERLANDS
Amsterdam
Arnhem
GERMANY
Berlin
Leipzig
Prague
CZECHOSLOVAKIA
RUHR
Cologne
Remagen
Frankfurt
Pas de Calais
Antwerp
Brussels
BELGIUM
Dieppe
Cherbourg
La Havre
NORMANDY
Falaise
Argentan
Avranches
Brest
BRITTANY
Rennes
Quiberon
Bastogne
ARDENNE
EIFEL
LUX
SAAR
Reims
Metz
Paris
Strasbourg
VOSGES
Munich
AUSTRIA
SWITZERLAND
FRANCE
R. Weser
R. Elbe
R. Rhine
R. Main
R. Danube
R. Meuse
R. Moselle
R. Saar
R. Seine
R. Loire
N
W
E
S
Map recreated by Charlene Meers_2016

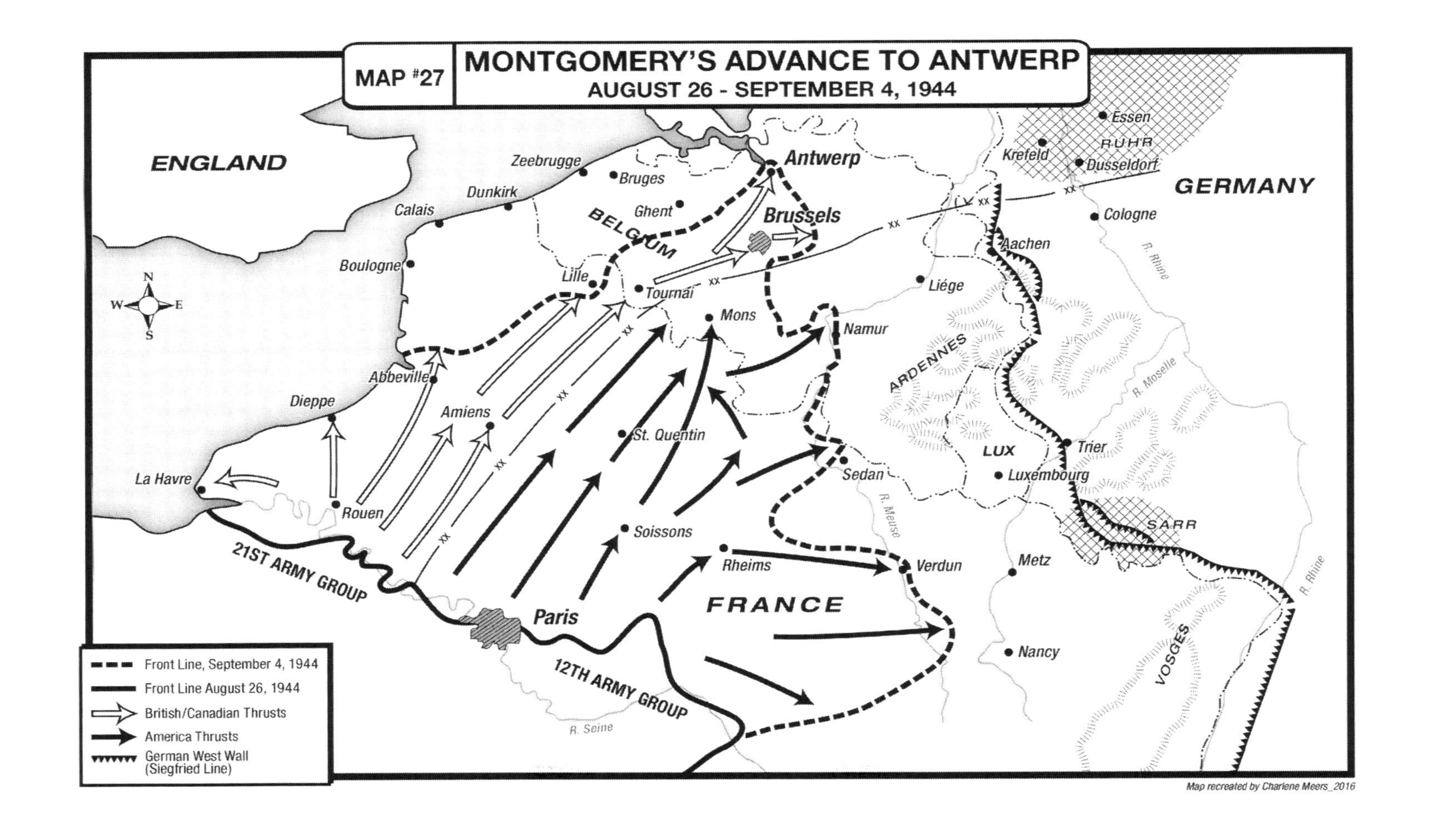
MAP #27
MONTGOMERY'S ADVANCE TO ANTWERP
AUGUST 26 - SEPTEMBER 4, 1944
ENGLAND
GERMANY
BELGIUM
FRANCE
LUX
ARDENNES
RUHR
SARR
VOSGES
Zeebrugge
Bruges
Antwerp
Dunkirk
Calais
Ghent
Brussels
Boulogne
Lille
Tournai
Mons
Namur
Liége
Aachen
Krefeld
Essen
Dusseldorf
Cologne
Abbeville
Dieppe
Amiens
St. Quentin
La Havre
Rouen
Soissons
Rheims
Verdun
Sedan
Paris
Trier
Luxembourg
Metz
Nancy
R. Rhine
R. Moselle
R. Meuse
R. Seine
21ST ARMY GROUP
12TH ARMY GROUP
N
S
E
W
Front Line, September 4, 1944
Front Line August 26, 1944
British/Canadian Thrusts
America Thrusts
German West Wall
(Siegfried Line)
Map recreated by Charlene Meers_2016

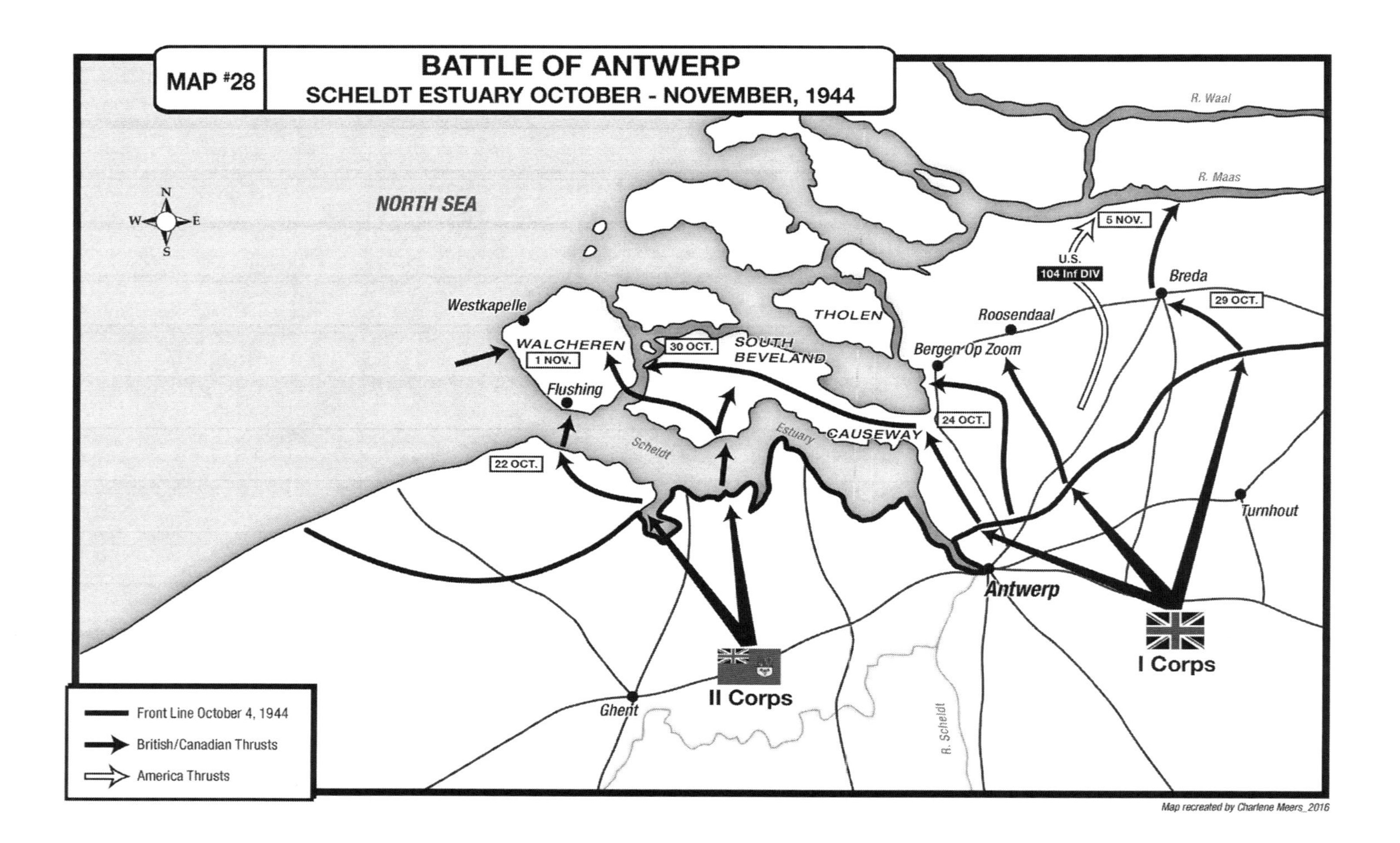
MAP #28
BATTLE OF ANTWERP
SCHELDT ESTUARY OCTOBER - NOVEMBER, 1944
R. Waal
R. Maas
NORTH SEA
N
W
E
S
5 NOV.
U.S.
104 Inf DIV
Breda
29 OCT.
Westkapelle
THOLEN
Roosendaal
WALCHEREN
1 NOV.
30 OCT.
SOUTH BEVELAND
Bergen Op Zoom
Flushing
24 OCT.
Estuary
CAUSEWAY
Scheldt
22 OCT.
Turnhout
Antwerp
I Corps
II Corps
Ghent
R. Scheldt
Front Line October 4, 1944
British/Canadian Thrusts
America Thrusts
Map recreated by Charlene Meers_2016

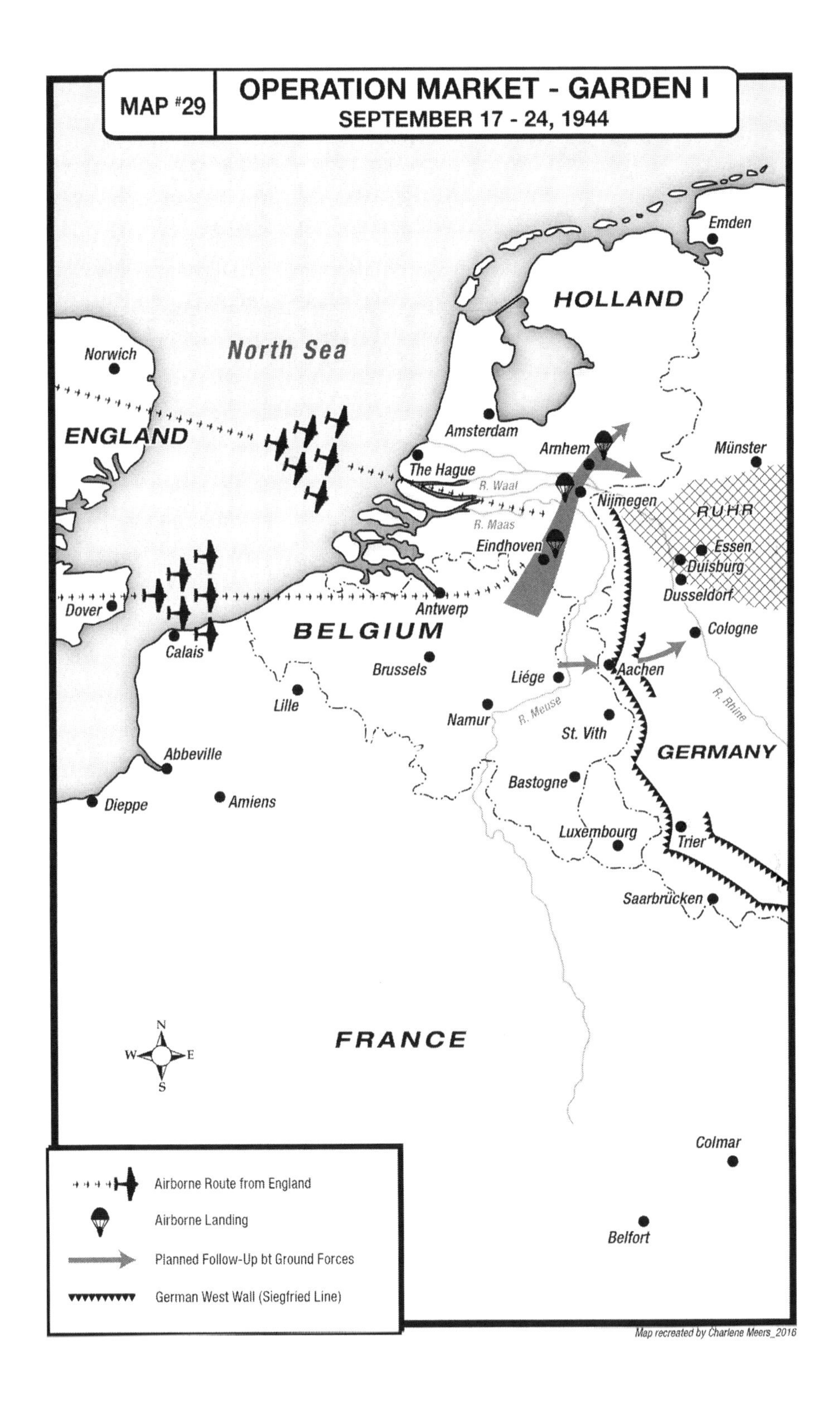

MAP #29
OPERATION MARKET - GARDEN I
SEPTEMBER 17 - 24, 1944
Emden
HOLLAND
North Sea
Norwich
ENGLAND
Amsterdam
Arnhem
Münster
The Hague
R. Waal
Nijmegen
RUHR
R. Maas
Eindhoven
Essen
Duisburg
Dusseldorf
Dover
Antwerp
BELGIUM
Calais
Cologne
Brussels
Liége
Aachen
Lille
Namur
R. Meuse
R. Rhine
St. Vith
GERMANY
Abbeville
Bastogne
Dieppe
Amiens
Luxembourg
Trier
Saarbrücken
N
W
E
S
FRANCE
Colmar
Belfort
Airborne Route from England
Airborne Landing
Planned Follow-Up bt Ground Forces
German West Wall (Siegfried Line)
Map recreated by Charlene Meers_2016

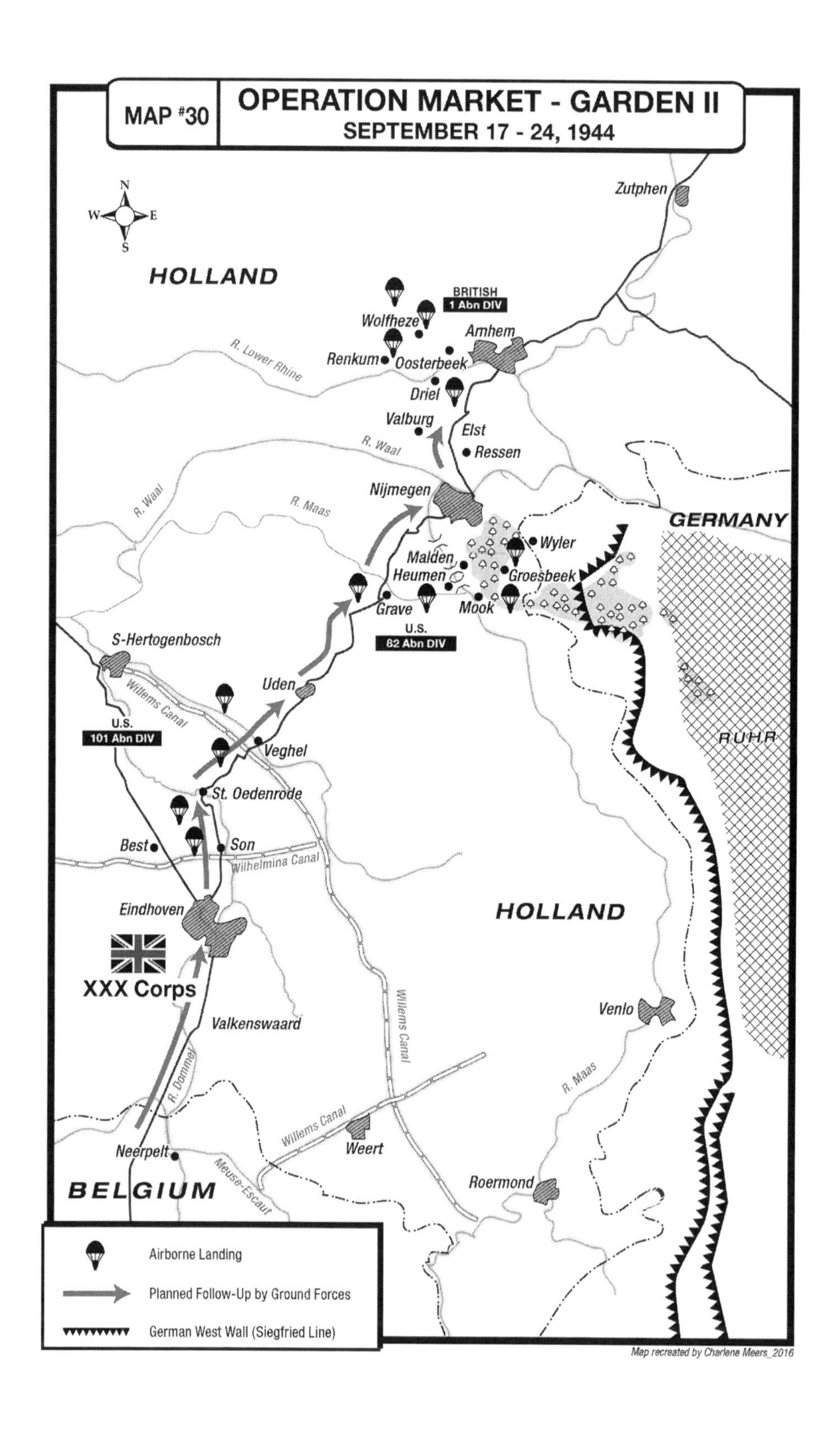
MAP #30
OPERATION MARKET - GARDEN II
SEPTEMBER 17 - 24, 1944
N
W
E
S
HOLLAND
Zutphen
BRITISH
1 Abn DIV
Wolfheze
Arnhem
R. Lower Rhine
Renkum
Oosterbeek
Driel
Valburg
Elst
R. Waal
Ressen
R. Waal
Nijmegen
R. Maas
GERMANY
Wyler
Malden
Heumen
Groesbeek
Grave
Mook
U.S.
82 Abn DIV
S-Hertogenbosch
Uden
Willems Canal
U.S.
101 Abn DIV
Veghel
St. Oedenrode
Best
Son
Wilhelmina Canal
RUHR
Eindhoven
HOLLAND
XXX Corps
Valkenswaard
Willems Canal
Venlo
R. Dommel
R. Maas
Willems Canal
Weert
Neerpelt
Meuse-Escaut
BELGIUM
Roermond
Airborne Landing
Planned Follow-Up by Ground Forces
German West Wall (Siegfried Line)
Map recreated by Charlene Meers_2016

> [over the beginning of GOODWOOD]. I thought that at least we had him [the enemy] and were going to roll him up. That did not come about. . . . I feel that you should insist that Dempsey keep up the strength of his attack.[84]

This was Ike's harshest rebuke of Montgomery during the OVERLORD campaign.

After reading this letter, Tedder thought it was "not strong enough. Monty can evade it. It contains no order."[85] Yet Ike's letter did seem to shake Montgomery up, as he wrote on July 22, "There is not and never has been any intention of stopping offensive operations on the eastern flank. For that reason I have regrouped. [Why not renew the attack?] Does above assure you that we see eye to eye on the main military problem. If NOT do please let me know."[86]

It was not until July 30 that Montgomery would renew his offensive with Operation BLUECOAT. As we will see, this attack was also a disaster.[87]

During this leadership crisis Montgomery prevailed upon Brooke to tell everyone in England that OVERLORD was succeeding according to his plan. Brooke remained his firm supporter. He still believed Monty was the only commander capable of leading the Twenty-First Army Group.[88] As Brooke confided in his diary, "With that Supreme Command set up it is no wonder that Monty's real high ability is not always realized."[89]

Churchill traveled to Montgomery's headquarters on July 21. Churchill had been seething over Monty's lack of aggressiveness since shortly after D-Day. We do not know what they discussed. One of Montgomery's Tac staff officers said it was common knowledge that Churchill had come with the relief order in his pocket.[90] It was not used.

In many ways Montgomery and Churchill's fate were inexorably intertwined. The British leadership had built up Montgomery as the great commander—the "Hero of El Alamein." After many battlefield setbacks, this was the first major British victory of World War II and served as an important morale booster for the British people. Churchill's credibility as Britain's great wartime leader now largely rested on the success of both OVERLORD and Montgomery. Removing Montgomery might have caused a crisis that would bring down Churchill's government as well. As historian William Weidner indicated, "It was apparent that Churchill needed Montgomery nearly as much as Montgomery needed him."[91]

While Montgomery retained his position as commander of the ground forces, the patchwork conditions of OVERLORD's leadership remained unchanged. In his diary a frustrated Brooke posed this critical question: "Will we ever learn to 'love our allies as ourselves'??!! I doubt it!" He then explained why: "There is no doubt that Ike is all out to do all he can to maintain the best of relations between British and Americans, but it is equally clear that Ike knows nothing about strategy and is *quite* unsuited to the post of Supreme Commander as far as running the strategy of the war is concerned!"[92]

Brooke recognized Eisenhower's greatest strength. But he failed to give any credit to the skills Eisenhower and other American commanders were developing as they gained battlefield experience. In fact it was on the American sector that plans for a successful Normandy breakout were being worked out.

## CONFRONTING THE BOCAGE HELL

Bradley was very depressed as he sat in his command post after the fall of St. Lo. His seventeen-day offensive had suffered the highest proportional American losses of the entire European war. And he had not broken out. But how could he do it? Seeking to discover a solution, he erected a huge map of Normandy in his headquarters. The bocage seemed an endless maze.[93]

There were just too many hedgerows that had to be cleaned up one at a time. The infantry became dulled by fatigue as this endless combat process seemed to have no end in sight.

Sherman tanks littered the countryside. They tried to enter these fields by the few obvious bocage openings or exposed their vulnerable undersides by going over the hedgerow's top. Engineers developed a device nicknamed the "salad fork." A pair of stout timber prongs were affixed to a tank and were then rammed into a hedgerow. Two small tunnels were created into which high explosives were packed. When detonated, a gap was blasted that allowed the passage of a tank. However these procedures took too much time, were too hazardous, and consumed huge amounts of explosives.[94]

Yankee innovation came into play. Captain Jimmy de Pero of the Second Armored, 102nd Cavalry Reconnaissance had a bull session with his men to chew on the hedgerow problem. One of his men, a Tennessee hillbilly named Robert, asked him, "Why don't we get some saw-teeth and put them on the front of the tank and cut through these hedges?"[95]

In the crowd was Sergeant Curtis G. Culin, known as a shrewd soldier and chess player.

He thought it was a good idea. Strewn across the Normandy beaches were an array of steel teeth-like obstacles the Germans had deployed to rip apart landing-craft hulls. Some had been taken from the German West Wall (Siegfried Line); others were pieces of the "Czech hedgehog" defenses. Culin welded a steel scrap of several tusklike prongs, teeth that held down the tank belly while the tank burst though the hedgerow by force.[96]

Fig. 8.2. Rhino tank. (© Imperial War Museums [B 9336])

Culin's company commander got General Gerow to contact Bradley's staff. On July 14 Bradley personally attended a demonstration. With Culin's cutter you just aimed the tank and the hedgerow exploded as the Sherman burst through covered with dirt and shrubbery. Desperate for a solution, Bradley ordered the cutters installed using the scavenged beach obstacles. By July 25 three out of every five tanks were equipped with what was dubbed the "Rhino." In order to maintain tactical surprise, Bradley banned the deployment of the Rhinos until the launch of COBRA.[97]

By themselves the Rhinos did not completely overcome the bocage terrain. However in the coming Normandy breakout, they became an important tool combined with other innovative tactics. They gave Bradley's tanks the ability to maneuver across the Normandy terrain. The German panzers had to remain on the roads, but the American Shermans now could cut cross-country and outflank the enemy.[98]

## PATTON'S "DOGHOUSE" STATUS

On July 6, exactly one month after D-Day, Patton, his aides, and his bull terrier Willy boarded a C-47 transport at 10:25 a.m. at an airfield near Salisbury, England. With two other C-47s and four P-47 escorts they flew for one hour to an airstrip just behind Omaha Beach. For the previous two days the Third Army's men and equipment had begun embarking on LSTs for France.

Though Patton was in Normandy he was not allowed to make any contributions in ending the stalemate on the ground. The entire seven weeks, between D-Day and the activation of his Third Army (August 1), were for Patton the most frustrating days of World War II.

Partially this occurred to preserve the Operation FORTITUDE deceit that Patton was still in England commanding the First US Army Group's final preparations for launching the main Allied invasion against the Pas-de-Calais. This deception tied down the large forces of the German Fifteenth Army that were kept stationed across the Straits of Dover, thereby depriving Rommel of significant reinforcements for Normandy.

The major reason for Patton's exile from command had occurred much earlier. The two outrageous slapping incidents of shell-shocked soldiers in a field hospital had cost Patton the command of the Seventh Army during its invasion and occupation of Sicily. These incidents nearly cost him any role in OVERLORD.[99]

Fig. 8.3. Generals Patton, Bradley, and Montgomery. (Photo by Morris [Sgt.], No. 5 Army Film & Photographic Unit)

Then at the end of April 1944, Patton's impromptu speech to a ladies' club in Knutsford, England, was a second bombshell that nearly got Patton sent back to the United States for the rest of the war. Patton made the off-the-cuff comment, "It is the evident destiny of the British and Americans, and of course the Russians, to rule the world."[100] A hidden newsman reported on his overweening statement. Afterward the public relations blowup in the United States was so bad that Marshall wanted to send Patton home. He left the final decision up to Eisenhower.

Patton reported to Eisenhower on May 2. Life-long friends, and Ike's best fighting general, he gave Patton another chance. According to his deputy Beetle Smith, Ike told Patton, "I expect from now on that you will please keep your goddamned mouth shut. When it is time for you to speak, I WILL TELL YOU!"[101]

After this Patton was deathly afraid of doing or saying anything that would put him back in the doghouse. As Eisenhower explained to Bradley, "All he wants is the chance to get back into the war. For a time he thought he was through."[102] Eisenhower was right in believing he would now set aside his ego and loyally serve under Bradley, as Patton was acutely aware that any further negative incidents would deprive him of participating in OVERLORD.

By July, however, Patton was very concerned about the failure of the Allies to achieve a breakout. He confided in his diary that Eisenhower was "bound hand and foot by the British."[103] Patton wrote, as a result, "We actually have no Supreme Commander—no one who can take hold and say that this shall be done and that shall not be done. It is a very unfortunate situation to which I see no solution."[104]

## COBRA—WHOSE IDEA?

Since D-Day George S. Patton, always innately restive, was chafing at the bit, fearing the war might end without him. Though on June 8 he wrote in his diary, "Apparently things are not going too well and one gets the impression that people are satisfied to be holding on, rather than advancing."[105] On July 2, he observed that Bradley should have attacked on a narrow front to achieve a breakthrough.[106]

The terrain where Bradley's First Army was to achieve a breakout was intimately known to Patton. In 1913, in what his wife called their second honeymoon, Patton had personally reconnoitered almost every square foot of Normandy's bocage country. Then in 1917 he had trained his World War I tank corps in the region. Patton believed he had a plan to get through the tortuous bocage:

> I could break through [the enemy defenses] in three days if I commanded. They try to push all along the front and have no power anywhere. All that is necessary now is to take charge by leading with armored divisions and covering their advance with air bursts [ground-air tactical bombing]. Such an attack would have to be made on a narrow sector, whereas at present we are trying to attack all along the line.[107]

Before he had left England, Patton spent the whole night of June 30 to July 1 drafting an offensive plan for a Normandy breakout that his biographer Farago calls his "Opus No. 1."[108] He proposed that one or two armored divisions followed by two infantry divisions converge in a rapid dash aimed at Avranches. (See Map 16.) Patton's thrust straight down the coastal highway might be costly in tanks, but on this narrow front, it would achieve a breakthrough to Avranches in forty-eight hours.

Farago relates that Patton had told Bradley about his plan as early as June 26 and sent him a written version on July 2. Bradley, however, did not seem very interested in any suggestions coming from Patton. He had not been his first choice as an army commander but was imposed upon him by Eisenhower. Bradley still feared Patton's "impetuous habits."[109]

Bradley wrote of his struggles in early July to come up with a plan using "a giant eight-foot map of the beachhead."[110] After coming up with an outline of a plan, Bradley asked for a critique from a number of his aides. By July 11 COBRA was officially born.

Farago states, after Patton studied the COBRA plan, "He had no doubt that somehow he had inspired it and Bradley—deliberately or unwittingly—had copied his ideas."[111] Patton was positive that COBRA was actually a modified version of his own Opus No. 1. Still being "in the doghouse" Patton never raised any claims to the plan's origins. "I don't care," Patton told his secretary, "if I don't get any credit for the idea as long as they allow me to carry it out."[112]

However, Patton's giant ego is much in evidence in his diary comments of July 12: "Brad says he will put me in as soon as he can. He could do it now with much benefit to himself, if he had any backbone. Of course Monty does not want me as he fears I will steal the show, which I will."[113]

In spite of these hidden rivalries and resentments among the Allied commanders, COBRA proved the plan that finally propelled the Allies out of the Normandy beachhead. With Bradley as its father, COBRA would be one of the most decisive battles of the OVERLORD campaign.

Operation COBRA, the other half of Monty's two-pronged German envelopment plan, became the battlefield "safety valve" that helped save Monty's role as general ground commander. If COBRA had also failed, the public pressure to remove Montgomery, and perhaps other commanders, might have been too great to ignore.

# CHAPTER 9
# PATTON UNLEASHED

"Rush them off their feet."

—General George S. Patton[1]

As of July 23 the Allied gains were still quite unimpressive. After seven weeks, OVERLORD was still well behind schedule. Its farthest advance was between only twenty-five to thirty miles inland along an eighty-mile front. Casualties had been heavy: British-Canadian—forty-nine thousand; American—seventy-three thousand. These losses, however, were completely replaced by July 25 as sixteen new British-Canadian divisions (591,000 troops) and seventeen US divisions (770,000 troops) had landed inside the Normandy bridgehead. But the Allies now badly needed a new tactical boost for a breakout.[2]

## COBRA'S VENOM

Bradley's COBRA breakout attack plan differed greatly from Montgomery's GOODWOOD assault. As previous broad-front attacks had failed, Bradley's assault concentrated on a narrow six-thousand-yard front, five miles west of St. Lo. It too would use intensive bombing, but unlike GOODWOOD, the US Ninth and Thirtieth Infantry Divisions would lead the assault to hold its shoulders, backed up by the US First Division and the Second Armored Division. A corps of three armored divisions and mechanized infantry would then push (see Map 16) up the coast of the Cotentin Peninsula to the crossroads at Coutances. Then the motorized infantry and armor would drive on to Avranches at the base of the Brittany peninsula.

From that key road junction Bradley would launch Patton's new Third Army for the advance into Brittany and the seizure of its strategic ports. Bradley's goal for COBRA was to conquer the Brittany ports and advance beyond the entangling bocage country. The lightning advance of Patton's Third Army, however, turned COBRA from a breakthrough advance into a major breakout.[3]

The spot that Bradley chose for the COBRA breakthrough was the strategic St. Lo–Périers-Lessay road. At several points this key artery intersected the only coastal road for the advance to Coutances and Avranches. It was in terrain that was favorable for attacking German positions from the air.

On June 19 Bradley flew to the Allied air force headquarters at Stanmore, north of London. He wanted to ensure that there was a "safety zone" to protect his ground forces from airborne friendly fire. Bradley personally explained COBRA's requirements to Trafford Leigh-Mallory, Major General Elwood R. "Pete" Quesada, who headed the IX Tactical Air Command with its P-47 Thunderbolt fighter-bombers, and the other heavy-bomber air barons. Their consensus was that they needed a 3,000- to 1,500-yard safety zone to avoid hitting American ground forces. Bradley finally settled for a 1,250-yard border to the bomb zone to prevent the Germans from recovering before the American advance reached them.[4]

Miserable rainy weather delayed the opening air bombardment and COBRA's ground attack from July 21 to July 24. Despite the reservations of weather forecasters, Leigh-Mallory set the carpet-bombing for noon on July 24. After personally flying to France for a last-minute check, he canceled the air attack. But it was too late. The Eighth US Army Air Force bombers were already airborne. Three hundred fifty bombers released their bomb loads. Some fell near American ground troops, which had only dug a few foxholes for protection. Twenty-five Americans were killed and 131 wounded by so-called "friendly fire."[5]

On July 25 the skies gradually cleared. On that day British forces were still in combat with six German panzer divisions that fielded 645 tanks. Bradley's offensive was facing only two panzer divisions, the Panzer Lehr and the Second SS Panzer, with a total of 190 tanks. Nine other badly battered German infantry divisions also opposed the American attack.[6]

At 9:38 a.m. Allied Ninth Air Force fighter-bombers began a twenty-minute assault on the German front. The entire 1,800 B-17s and Liberator heavy bombers of the Eighth Air Force created a corridor of death four miles wide and two miles deep. They dropped over 2,000 tons of high explosives and more than 2,500 tons of fragmentation bombs mixed with white phosphorous and napalm. But they too were sometimes short of the targeted front. US ground troops made desperate efforts to identify their positions using yellow panels and smoke markers but to no avail. In this enormous conflagration, 111 American ground troopers died, 490 were wounded, and 200 were disabled by shell shock. The entire command headquarters of the Ninth Division's Third/Forty-Seventh Infantry Regiments was decimated. Despite being warned, Lieutenant General Lesley J. McNair, commander of army ground forces, went up to the front to witness this unprecedented bombing attack. He was the highest-ranking officer to be killed in northwestern Europe.[7]

The Panzer Lehr Division was in the center of this inferno. General Fritz Bayerlein, Panzer Lehr commander, said in a postwar interrogation, "It was hell. The planes kept coming like a conveyor belt. . . . My front line looked like a landscape on the moon. . . . All my front line tanks were knocked out."[8]

After the bombing, American artillery smashed the Germans with fifty thousand rounds. The total devastation was unbelievable. "I looked out of the bunker. The world had changed," said Major Joachim Barth, commander of the German 130th Anti-Tank Battalion, "our tanks were stuck in holes; in others, the big guns had tipped over."[9]

Thousands of German soldiers died from the COBRA bombing attack. Tanks were obliterated, command posts decimated, and an entire Wehrmacht parachute regiment disappeared. Advancing into the target area, an American infantry officer observed that "all kinds of trucks, guns and machines of every type were in twisted disorder over the deeply-scarred soil."[10]

The bombing and artillery assaults, however, did not succeed in wiping out all the German forces. A notation in the First US Army diary stated that the massive bombing had only a "negligible" effect. The first response was that "breakthrough for which we had all hoped had failed to materialize."[11]

At 11:00 a.m. General Joseph Collins's VII Corps of armor and infantry attacked under and behind the previously mentioned heavy artillery barrage. They met ferocious resistance from German soldiers who had taken shelter in tunnels, trenches, foxholes, or dug-in armored vehicles. Intense fighting over heavily cratered ground hindered the American advance. In fact the Americans barely got across the St. Lo–Périers highway. On the first two days the US advance only went forward five miles.

After the first seven hundred yards, the Fourth Infantry Division encountered German tanks concealed in sunken lanes behind hedgerows. However, the Rhino tanks enabled the Americans to bypass these German positions and continue their advance. The accompanying infantry and engineers then dealt with these German outposts. But on the first day, the Fourth Infantry became bogged down on its way to La Chapelle, advancing only about a mile and a half.[12] (See Map 16.)

For Eisenhower and Bradley COBRA's first day seemed something of a bust. They didn't know how brittle the German defensive forces had become. But Collins had discovered that the Germans no longer formed a continuous belt of defense. Because of their tremendous losses, the German forces now only formed a crust that could be outflanked.[13]

At that moment Bayerlein's Panzer Lehr lay decimated on the front line. Desperate to stop the American advance Kluge sent a staff officer with the order to hold the St. Lo–Périers line—"not a single man was to leave his position!"[14] Bayerlein sent back this bitter message:

> Out in front every one is holding out. . . . Every one. My grenadier and my engineers and my tank crews—they're all holding their ground. Not a single man is leaving his post. Not one! . . . They're lying in their foxholes mute and silent, for they are dead. Dead. . . . The Panzer Lehr Division is annihilated.[15]

Collins sensed that the Germans' communications and command structure had been seriously compromised. He saw the physical evidence from their severed telephone wires and broken radio antennas. Collins also deduced this from the Germans' lack of coordination and their failure to launch prompt counterattacks.

He then took a big risk by ordering two of his three mobile divisions to attack on the morning of July 26. Collins's decision proved decisive, for except around Marigny, the German opposition began to melt away that day.[16]

The First Infantry Division and the Third Armored Division broke through on the right. Brigadier General Maurice Rose's Second Armored

Division and the Thirtieth Infantry Division then struck on the left, advancing south toward Saint-Gilles. (See Map 16.) Rose had trained them to "marry up" infantry to armor, with eight men of the Thirtieth riding on a Second Armor's Sherman tank or four infantrymen on a light tank. They moved off the roads and maneuvered across the fields where the Rhino tanks spent an average of only two and half minutes cutting through a hedgerow.

By midafternoon the Second Armored Division (nicknamed "Hell on Wheels") drove through Saint-Gilles heading south. At the end of July 26, it was nearly ten miles behind the former German lines.

This was an astounding day for the American army. As Collins's VII Corps advanced, General Troy Middleton's VIII Corps attacked across the Lessay-Périers road (see Map 16) with his Eighth, Ninetieth, and Eighty-Third Infantry Divisions. They established a bridgehead over the Ay River in order to move south toward Coutances. This was a significant accomplishment. The Allies had at long last broken clear through the German positions. This was no time to stop. All units were ordered forward.

On July 27 the Seventy-Ninth Division captured Lessay and the Eighth moved south, while the Ninetieth occupied Périers. By that evening Coutances had been captured.[17]

On July 28 the advance accelerated down the coastal road. German counterattacks were rapidly broken up by air attacks. With the sea to their right, the Sixth Armored Division leaped ahead almost thirty miles. If the Germans tried to block the road, an air liaison officer traveling in an advance tank quickly called in a squadron of P-47 Thunderbolts and usually within fifteen minutes, the German position was obliterated. This was the key contribution of General Quesada, who is credited with inventing the methodology of "close air support" by integrating tactical air power with infantry, artillery, and armor as part of a total coordinated attack.

Quesada also placed some of his airmen with lead tank columns in the Second and Third Armored Divisions. They communicated directly with each other over VHF radio. As the Thunderbolts screamed into the attack, they fired at point-blank range with machine guns and dropped five-hundred-pound bombs and napalm. The rugged P-47 Thunderbolt fighters had never before done this on a large scale. The P-47s also flew reconnaissance and attacked targets assigned prior to takeoff as well as others that developed during a battle and were approved by a central ground command center. The P-47s provided an invaluable constant air umbrella over the armored advance.

During the first six days of COBRA, in only the VII Corps operations zone, the IX Tactical Air Force destroyed 362 panzers and assault guns as well as damaging another 216. An additional 1,337 vehicles were destroyed and 280 damaged. The roads were clogged with destroyed and burning German equipment. Quesada's concept of "close air support" was a critical part of the COBRA breakout. It became a key component of Patton's "American-style blitzkrieg" in the breakout across France.[18]

The Wehrmacht literally began to fall apart. Since the Americans cut all cable and telephone lines, most commanders lost track of their troops' location. In many areas, German troops did not even realize the Americans already had broken through. With almost no information reaching his headquarters, Kluge had few battle details. But by July 27, one condition became very clear. He told Hitler's headquarters that the Americans were "running wild."[19]

The Germans were often shocked to find Americans were now far behind what had previously been the front line. On several occasions, German motorcycle troops discovered too late that they had driven up to American vehicles. What resistance that was left came from small groups of soldiers who were surrounded or fighting to make their escape. General Paul Hausser of the Seventh Army, a formidable SS commander, stated that ten of his divisions had disintegrated. They had become only scattered bands of demoralized men without equipment or leadership. Chaos on the roads meant that ammunition, food, and fuel did not get through, and panzers and vehicles were abandoned. Combat action became so confused that in one episode an American medic found himself sharing a slit trench with a German medic. They both nervously pointed to their Red Cross armbands. Then they frisked each other for weapons before returning to treat the wounded. Another American medic noted that the rapid advance of the Second Armored Division resulted in fewer fatalities from booby traps or land mines. The hasty German retreat left them little time to sow these seeds of death.[20]

German morale now began to crack. On the night of July 26, a corporal, who had received a German Iron Cross in Gold for extreme bravery on the eastern front, told a senior medical officer at an aid station that "this is no longer a war here in Normandy. . . . Our Highest Command [Hitler] doesn't do anything to help us. . . . Well, for me the war is over." Another wounded infantryman joined in: "This piece of iron which hit me, should have hit the Fuhrer's head on 20 July, and the war would be over already!"[21]

By July 30 the spearhead of the VIII Corps, the Fourth Armored Division, had reached Avranches. (See Map 16.) Finding the two bridges over the Sée River undamaged, they entered the city without encountering any German resistance. The tanks then raced four miles farther south to the key crossroad town of Pontaubault and captured it unopposed. Here the road network led south, east, and west. The prized gateway for the Allied advance into Brittany and the pursuit of a shattered Wehrmacht lay open before them.

That day Kluge spoke to Speidel, the chief of staff for Army Group B. Speidel told Kluge his left flank had ceased to exist. Other officers put it much more bluntly. It was a *Weltuntergangsstimmung*—the collapse of their whole world.

Later that day a stunned Kluge told General Gunther Blumentritt, OB West chief of staff, "It's a madhouse here. . . . Someone has to tell the Fuhrer that if the Americans get through at Avranches they will be out of the woods and they'll be able to do what they want. . . . It's a crazy situation."[22]

## BLUECOAT "DISASTER"

While the Americans' rapid advance continued, Montgomery still had British and Canadian forces mount small, largely ineffective attacks. However, pressure was building from London to renew the British offensive. Churchill sent a message to Montgomery on July 26, stating he was glad for the Americans' "good success today. It would be fine if this were matched by a similar British victory."[23]

In a second message the next day, Churchill wanted to know about the "serious set-back"—a Canadian offensive to take the Verières Ridge, a strip of high ground on the route from Caen to Falaise, had been unsuccessful resulting in heavy casualties—announced by SHAEF and told Monty, "It certainly seems very important for the British Army to strike hard and win through."[24]

Montgomery immediately replied, "I know of no 'serious set-back'. Enemy has massed great strength in the area south of CAEN to oppose our advance in that quarter."[25] On July 27 he also sent a directive to Bradley, Dempsey, Patton, and Crerar asserting it would be virtually impossible to advance against the German positions southward toward Falaise: "He is so strong there now that any large scale operations by us in that area are definitely unlikely to succeed."[26]

Monty would only reverse course when a letter from Brooke arrived on July 28 in which he warned that Eisenhower and Churchill were growing increasingly restive over Montgomery's failure to mount a major offensive. His mentor bluntly told Monty, "I feel personally quite certain that Dempsey must attack at the earliest possible moment on a large scale."[27]

When Brooke lit his fuse, Montgomery replied that same day, "It will be on the largest scale and everything will be thrown in . . . pressed with the utmost vigor and all caution thrown to the winds. . . . He [Dempsey] must step on the gas."[28] Of course this was all part of Monty's original "plan."

Montgomery's promised offensive, Operation BLUECOAT, kicked off on July 30. BLUECOAT began near Caumont (west of Caen) with the objectives of seizing the important road junction at Vire and Mont-Pincon, thus securing the highest ground south of the Bourguébus Ridge. (See Map 17.)

Though O'Connor's VIII Corps advanced well on the right flank, Lieutenant General Gerard Bucknall's XXX Corps became bogged down. British infantry-armor cooperation had improved somewhat, but their lighter-armored Churchill and Cromwell tanks melted before the German Tiger Panzers and huge assault guns.

Though the British enjoyed ground superiority of three-to-one and had total control of the air, the initial attack went nowhere. The XXX Corps was driven back to its line of departure. It had been attempting to smash through some of Normandy's heaviest bocage terrain. The performance of the XXX Corps and division commanders was also very weak.

Over the next two days Dempsey sacked Bucknall and two division commanders. Some British officers thought that this should have occurred after the earlier Villers-Bocage fiasco. Alun Chalfont termed the initial BLUECOAT attack a "disaster." It was not until August that the cautious British offensives slowly began to make headway and finally reached their original D-Day goal of Falaise by mid-August.[29]

On August 2 Montgomery incredibly alleged in a letter to Sir James

Grigg, secretary of war, "The broad basic plan . . . is now unfolding in the exact way in which it was intended. This is very gratifying."[30]

## "LET'S TAKE A CHANCE NOW THAT WE HAVE THE BALL"

On the American front, COBRA was shaping up to be Bradley's greatest victory. Once General John Wood's Fourth Armored Division took Coutances on July 27, Bradley decided to recast COBRA from a breakthrough into a breakout. The operation's sudden success forced him to make the decision that he now needed Patton to fully exploit the German collapse.

Patton had been literally chaffing at the bit to get involved with COBRA. Even Eisenhower, who usually remained detached from field operations, had earlier urged Bradley to make the Third Army operational and use Patton's skills in offense to guarantee a breakthrough. But Bradley remained afraid of Patton. Keeping Patton at arm's length was made even more awkward by the fact that major components of his Third Army—including its entire VIII Corps—were already part of the COBRA offensive.

After the war Bradley admitted,

> My own feelings on George were mixed. . . . I was apprehensive in having George join my command for I feared that too much of my time would probably be spent in curbing his impetuous habits. . . . But at the same time I knew that with Patton there would be no need for my whipping Third Army to keep it on the move. We had only to keep him pointed in the direction we wanted to go. George soon caused me to repent these uncharitable reservations, for he not only bore me no ill will but he trooped for Twelfth Army Group with unbounded loyalty and eagerness.[31]

On July 27 Bradley called Brigadier General Hugh Gaffey, Patton's aide, and told him to have his boss contact him immediately. Patton was out inspecting the 101st Evacuation Hospital, a gasoline dump, and several other sites near his headquarters. At 4:45 p.m. he called Bradley. "George," Bradley announced, "this is it. . . . You'll supervise operations in VIII Corps zone as Deputy Army Commander." To keep the deception of Operation FORTITUDE working Patton would remain the mystery man of OVER-

LORD "to keep the Germans guessing." Bradley wanted Patton to remain in the background assisting General Troy Middleton, VIII Corps designated commander, in speeding up the advance on Avranches. Bradley did offer Patton this inducement: "The quicker Patton got the VIII Corps to the threshold of Brittany, the sooner he would be able to enter battle at the head of his army [Third Army]."[32]

Patton moved quickly and quietly took over VIII Corps headquarters. He immediately moved Wood's Fourth and Gerow's Sixth Armored Divisions through the infantry to the front of the advance. The Fourth and Sixth now took the lead forward. On the evening of July 28, Wood occupied Coutances. Patton then moved his own headquarters on up to the Coutances-Saint-Lô road. (See Map 16.)

On July 29 Patton drove through Coutances to check on the progress of Major General Robert Gerow's Sixth Division's advance to Avranches. He found it halted at the Sée River by German fire and a wrecked bridge. Patton wrote in his diary, "I asked him [Gerow] whether he had been down to look at the river, and he said 'No'. So I told him that unless he did do something, he would be out of a job!"[33]

Patton then went down to the river, was not shot at, and found that the river was not over a foot deep. He then directed the division to cross the river.

On the evening of July 30 the first units of the Fourth Armored Division entered Avranches. They were quickly reinforced the next day. Patton knew the town well. Over thirty years earlier he and his wife, Beatrice, had looked across the bay on a bluff two hundred feet above Avranches to the famous Benedictine Abby, Mont St. Michel, perched on a rock eight miles away. From this strategic location, he ordered the Sixth Armored Division to cross the Sélune River at Pontaubault and with the rest of Middleton's VIII Corps proceed into Brittany.

This advance unlocked the door to the west coast of the Cherbourg Peninsula and outflanked the entire German position in Normandy. Patton's tanks would clear the enemy from Brittany. Then they would begin a grand sweep eastward toward Le Mans and Chartres.

This was a great victory, yet an ironic one for Patton because he was not its bona fide commander. Bradley sent him word that the Third Army would be born officially at high noon on August 1.

Patton's diary contains his poem, "Absolute War," that beyond doubt asserted what he now intended to do: "Let's take a chance now that we have the ball. . . . Let's shoot the works and win! Yes win it all."[34]

## "WE ARE HAVING ONE OF THE LOVELIEST BATTLES YOU EVER SAW"

OVERLORD's moment of greatest opportunity had arrived. The situation kept rapidly changing to the Allies' advantage. The British and American armies needed a plan to capitalize on the opportunities that the Normandy battlefield now afforded them. Eisenhower, Montgomery, and Bradley were slow to cope with this fast-moving situation and at first fell back on the original OVERLORD assumption that it was necessary to take Brittany's ports to support American logistical needs.

However by August 4, Eisenhower realized that this plan was now outdated. Bradley had planned to send all of Patton's Third Army into Brittany. The original plan was now canceled. Minimum forces could do the job, while the rest of his army advanced southward to the Loire and eastward to envelop the entire German Seventh Army.

Those plans coincided with those of Patton. He was eager to take advantage of the great opportunities offered by the enemy's rapid disintegration. With the activation of Patton's Third Army, the Twelfth US Army Group came into being. Bradley was promoted to assume this enlarged command; the First Army was turned over to General Courtney Hodges.[35]

With the expansion of the American ground forces, Eisenhower moved to France on August 7 and set up his headquarters near Tournières. (See Map 13). He met with Bradley the next day and urged him to "destroy the enemy now."[36]

On July 31, Patton addressed his last staff conference before the Third Army was activated:

> I want to thank you all for your long endurance and faithful service while we were waiting for this great opportunity. . . . Now, gentlemen. . . . The harder we push, the more Germans we'll kill. . . . Pushing means fewer casualties. I want you to remember that. [Patton's method was to move constantly and fast so that the Germans had no time to organize a counterattack.]

> There's another thing I want you to remember. Forget this Goddamn business of worrying about our flanks. We must guard our flanks, but not to the extent we don't do anything else. . . . Flanks are something for the enemy to worry about, not us. . . . We are advancing constantly and we are not interested in holding anything, except the enemy. . . .
>
> Gentlemen, you've done outstanding work. And I want to thank you for it. I am proud of you.[37]

Patton's genius in aggressive command was based on his ability to see the big battlefield picture. He discerned the primary objective miles ahead of the actual front. Patton's basic plan was to warp drive forward and capitalize on the mobility and punch of his tank divisions while maximizing German disorder. He poured over small-scale Michelin road maps that gave him the details he wanted most: road networks, rivers, railroads, and details about the terrain in general. He memorized an area's geography long before he set foot on the battlefield. Thus while keeping in mind the general objective of a battle, he could best judge how to deal with each specific geographic obstacle.

Few people realized that while Patton was in the doghouse, he spent part of his time in England studying the actual routes used nine centuries earlier by William the Conqueror for his campaigns in Normandy and Brittany. He reasoned correctly that the same routes, now modern roads, had to be useable terrain for his army. Patton also invested a great deal of his time studying the road maps of Western Europe, particularly in the places where he expected to fight.

When Patton was in the field during Third Army campaign operations, he carried a special operations map, ten by twenty inches in size, that was covered and waterproofed. Significant towns, crossroads, rivers, etc. were all marked with secret code identification numbers. When he radioed his headquarters, he referred to the code number of the location where he wanted something done. His chief of staff, the signal officer, and Colonel Oscar W. Koch, head of Third Army intelligence, had identical copies. Koch was the most brilliant and original member of Patton's command team. Some believed that Koch had the most penetrating brain in the field of intelligence in the US Army.

Patton at heart was a cavalryman. His plans emphasized fast decisions, rapid execution, and balanced risk. Patton's general plan for the coming

Third Army campaign was to employ a leapfrog tactic: when the advance guard of a column encountered resistance, the enemy was to be surrounded and contained on the spot. Immediately another advanced guard unit would continue onward until it struck opposition. This leapfrog tactic would be repeated over and over again. In this way, the enemy was kept in a perpetual state of shock and confusion, and given no time to organize or deliver a counterattack.

Patton employed that same type of tactics that had brought the Wehrmacht its greatest victories in Poland, France, and North Africa. But now Patton was applying his own "blitzkrieg in reverse" on the Germans.

Patton's additional intelligence source was popularly called "Patton's Household Cavalry." Under Patton's personal direction, Colonel M. Fitchett's Sixth Cavalry Group, equipped with radio sets, conducted continuous patrols that ranged far and wide across the entire front and the Third Army's flank. The group was composed of squadrons, and they were divided into troops. Each was made up of about twenty soldiers equipped with jeeps, tanks, armored cars, half-tracks, and guns. Their mission was to move fast, surprise the enemy, outflank, confuse, ambush the Germans, and withdraw. They sent a steady stream of reports directly to Patton's command post.[38] Thus, Patton often knew more about specific unit actions along the front than did the corps or division on the spot. The knowledge that Patton knew what was happening provided the motivation for improved frontline unit performance.[39]

Patton's advanced organizational methods and command skills won the respect of the Third Army's staff and fired their imaginations. After attending a staff briefing by Patton, a young officer wrote to his father, "I will go with him to the ends of the earth."[40]

When Patton and his Third Army strode upon the Normandy stage on August 1, they were fully prepared for the battle ahead. After almost two months of attritional warfare, the Allies had reduced the German army to tatters. Allied air power controlled the skies. It had broken the German logistics chain, made daylight troop movement virtually impossible, and denied aerial reconnaissance intelligence to the German commanders. Patton gloried at how quickly his forces were advancing. As he wrote to a cavalry officer under whom he had served, "We are having one of the loveliest battles you ever saw. It is a typical cavalry action."[41]

Perhaps of greatest importance, since the July 20 assassination attempt, the führer had been micromanaging all the fronts. Now by launching an abortive counterattack on Patton's advance into Brittany he would make a blunder that almost ended the war in Europe.[42]

August 1944 was one of the most remarkable months of World War II. Though the war in Western Europe continued for nine more months, the Third Reich's doom was sealed in August. The variety and complexity of operations during these thirty-one days makes this phase of the OVERLORD campaign one of the most monumental events in the history of modern warfare. Historian Nigel Hamilton contends that "Patton was to give perhaps the finest performance of 'headlong' mobile operations ever seen in military history."[43]

## THE BRITTANY SWEEPSTAKES

It was high noon on August 1 in Brittany when the Third Army became fully operational. Patton's Fourth and Sixth Armored Divisions thrust to the west. The main prizes for the "Brittany Sweepstakes" were the seaports of Saint-Malo, Brest, Lorient, and Saint Nazaire. (See Map 18.) In OVERLORD's original plan these ports would support the growing logistical demands of the invasion. It was a race to see if the Americans could secure these ports before the Germans destroyed them. The crossroad city of Rennes was also noted as an important jumping-off place for Patton's eastward thrust. (See Map 18.)

At the opening gun the Sixth Armored and Seventy-Ninth Infantry Divisions raced first to Saint-Malo and then onward to Brest. The Fourth Armored and Eighth Infantry Divisions moved rapidly on Rennes. The XV Corps with the Fifth Armored, Eighty-Third, and Ninetieth Infantry Divisions were deployed between the Sée and Sélune Rivers. (See Maps 17 and 18.)

Very few German troops were left to oppose the American Third Army in Brittany. The Wehrmacht could only muster ten understrength battalions of infantry and four Ost (east) battalions of anti-Bolshevik Russians. These units and an additional fifty thousand naval, air, and support troops were clustered in or around the seaports.[44]

From all over the jam-packed OVERLORD beachhead, soldiers and equipment converged on a narrow corridor between Avranches and Saint

Hilaire, through which the entire Third Army had to pass. This created one of the worst traffic jams ever, about ten miles south of Pontaubault. In one of the OVERLORD campaign's best instances of staff work, the Third Army sent clusters of senior officers out onto the roads feeding into the key intact bridge at Pontaubault. Their orders were to keep all the vehicles moving, disregarding any strict sequence of units. One divisional commander said he had spent most of his time that day acting as a traffic cop.

When Patton was personally held up in Avranches by a hopeless tangle of trucks, he jumped from his jeep into an umbrella-type police box at the center of a square, and for an hour and a half he directed traffic, exhibiting his characteristic mixture of profanity and élan. The effect on the drivers was said to have been electric.

Fig. 9.1. General George S. Patton in France. (US Army)

In an attempt to stop this flood of American forces, the Germans sent in the entire bomber force of Luftfotte 3 (i.e., air fleet) to take out the key Pontaubault bridge. They were unsuccessful due to the accuracy of American antiaircraft gunners and numerous Allied fighters.

After crossing the bridge, the bunched-up columns were unscrambled by having each road clearly marked with the destination point of each division. Due to this deployment innovation, all of the Third Army's seven divisions raced into the new theater of operations in just seventy-two hours. As the rear guard crossed this bridge, Patton's forward columns had driven eighty miles farther. Within three days a hundred thousand men and their equipment had fanned out to participate in the Brittany Sweepstakes.[45]

Now Hitler attempted to make this race harder for the Third Army to win. The führer ordered all the Brittany ports to be held as fortresses. There was some justification for this move as these coastal troops lacked mobility and had been depleted in strength. Many of the original Wehrmacht divisions defending Brittany already had been pulled into the Normandy battle. Herbert Essame estimated that approximately 200,000 German soldiers, sailors, and airmen were isolated in these fortresses. Some did not surrender until the end of the war.[46]

By the early evening on August 1, Wood's Fourth Armored Division was approaching Rennes. This provincial capital was sixty miles south of Avranches. Rennes was a hub from which ten main roads radiated and was vital for Patton's eastward thrust. Here Wood struck strong German resistance. During the night the Ninety-First Infantry began arriving and was teamed up with the Thirteenth Infantry to take Rennes. Meanwhile the Fourth flanked the city and cut seven of the ten highways converging on Rennes, virtually isolating it. (See Map 18.)

A contest of wills and an extremely daring offensive also began on August 1. Middleton ordered Gerow, the commander of the Sixth Armored Division, to take Dinan. Soon afterward Patton arrived and told Gerow to instead head for Brest and bypass all resistance. Patton had bet Montgomery that Gerow could take Brest by Saturday night. To accomplish this feat, the Sixth would have to travel two hundred miles in five days and then take the town. On August 2, they arrived on the outskirts of Dinan, which they found to be a German stronghold that they accordingly bypassed. By the evening of August 3, Gerow's leading units were at Loudéac, one hundred miles from Brest. (See Map 18.) Then Middleton intervened and ordered Gerow to backtrack and first take Dinan as a first step for seizing the port of Saint-Malo. The next morning Patton arrived as Gerow was planning the Dinan attack. Patton asked Gerow, "What the hell are you doing here?" Gerow handed Patton Middleton's order. "I'll see Middleton. You go ahead where I told you to go."[47] Middleton had caused a day to be wasted. The Sixth Armored lightning advance continued, reaching Brest on the evening of August 6. However by then the city had been strongly reinforced by the Germans. Remarkably Gerow had advanced over two hundred miles in less than seven days with casualties of only 120 killed and four hundred wounded. It was an astounding military feat. If it had arrived a day earlier, the Fourth might have been able to take Brest.

Although the bulk of the American forces were shifted eastward in early August, a long and basically useless campaign to capture Brittany's ports continued. Saint-Malo fell after two more weeks of siege warfare by twenty thousand US infantry troops, but the port was wrecked. After being reduced to rubble, Brest was captured on September 18 at a cost of ten thousand US casualties. Lorient and Saint-Nazaire remained under siege by American troops to the end of the war in 1945. These ports were never rehabilitated.[48]

As August began, Eisenhower and other members of the Allied high command recognized that the original OVERLORD plan to capture the Brittany ports was outdated, as they were too far from the emerging theater of operations to be of logistical value. In a diary entry on August 4, Patton recorded that he was directed to swing most of the Third Army eastward toward the Seine River.

The XV Corps was to attack in the direction of Le Mans across the Mayenne River between Mayenne and Laval. (See Map 19.) They plunged into an eighty-mile-wide gap devoid of German troops. By midnight on August 6, Major General Ira T. Wyche's Seventy-Ninth Division was almost in Laval. Major General Wade Haislip's XV Corps had raced forty-five miles eastward close to Le Mans. The stage was set for the potential envelopment of the German Seventh Army west of the Loire. This was a rare opportunity for the total destruction of the enemy.[49]

The German generals saw this catastrophic situation. When American tanks had reached Rennes, General Bayerlein wrote that it "had shattering effect, like a bomb-burst upon us."[50]

## HITLER'S FOLLY

As Patton's Third Army began its drive eastward, Major General Courtney Hodges of the First Army pushed the Germans out of Vire. (See Map 19.) The First Infantry Division meanwhile took Mortain on August 4 and the important Hill 314 that dominated the area. The town thus far had been undamaged by the fighting. Its occupation helped to forge a link with Patton's units to the south.

At 2:00 a.m. on August 7, intelligence alerted Patton of an imminent, large-scale German attack against the First Army. There was a twelve-mile gap between the First and Third armies south of Avranches, with the Third's supply line running through it. (See Map 20.) At that moment, Patton had his Thirty-Fifth Infantry Division moving through this gap. He ordered it to be committed in support of the First Army. Few American commanders believed that the Germans would attack. Instead they anticipated a German withdrawal across the Seine to regroup and hold a new defensive position. Hitler had other ideas.[51]

The führer thought he could take advantage of the exposed Allied position at Avranches. He watched Patton's bold attack with amazement. "Just look at that crazy cowboy general driving down to the south and into Brittany along a single road and over a single bridge with an entire army!"[52] Surely Hitler exclaimed some strong panzer division could cut off this bottleneck with a thrust of only sixteen to nineteen miles? They then could cut off the Third Army before turning north to also crush the Normandy beachhead. (See Map 20.)

Hitler believed that Operation Lüttich or, as the Allies named it, the Mortain counterattack was "a unique, never recurring opportunity for a complete reversal of the situation!"[53] It was code-named Lüttich (German for "Liège") after the city in Belgium, the site of a key battle at the beginning of World War I exactly thirty years earlier that opened the way for the German attack on France.[54]

Early on August 3 Kluge received Hitler's orders to close up the gap at Avranches by withdrawing panzers from other parts of the Normandy front. Kluge had already considered such an operation but rejected it as impossible to accomplish without major reinforcements. According to OB West operations officer General Bodo Zimmerman, Kluge cabled this warning to Hitler: "Tanks are the backbone of our defense, where they are withdrawn, our front will give way. . . . If, as I foresee, this plan does not succeed, catastrophe is inevitable."[55] This counterattack was mounted with four understrength panzer divisions—just 145 panzers in all (the average strength of one Allied armored division).

Fig. 9.2. Hitler and Admiral Erich Raeder in discussion at a map table. Also present are (left to right) Field Marshal Walther von Brauchitsch, General Alfred Jodl, Field Marshal Wilhelm Keitel, and an unidentified Kriegsmarine staff officer.

Operation Lüttich was launched soon after midnight on August 7. The panzer divisions were short of tanks, men, and oil. They were poorly briefed and worn out. The counterattack was doomed before it even began. The 116th Panzer Division never left its jump-off position. The First SS and Second SS Panzer Divisions did overrun Mortain and Saint-Barthelemy. But on the key Hill 314, seven hundred men from the US 120th Infantry Regiment refused to give ground to the German attackers. Surrounded for five days and supplied only by air drops, the 120th fought valiantly, suffering three hundred casualties. (See Map 20.)

An attack by the Second Panzer Division managed to advance within two miles of Avranches before being halted by the Third Armored Division and the Thirty-Fifth Infantry Division. The Allied air forces had been grounded by fog, but at midday on August 7 the skies cleared. Rocket-firing Typhoons of the RAF Eighty-Third Group remorselessly destroyed columns of German tanks, guns, and vehicles strung out along the roads and byways. Overhead, American Mustangs ruled the skies and shot down or drove off the feeble Luftwaffe air support. Many German fighters were destroyed as they took off from their bases. This was the largest fighter-bomber attack of the Normandy campaign. Paul Carrell states, "[F]or the first time in military history a . . . land offensive was eventually halted from the air."[56]

By August 8 Kluge's attack was literally dying in its own tracks as continuous air attacks caused panzer personnel to begin abandoning their tanks and equipment. Hitler refused to acknowledge the ground-air situation and instead ordered a renewal of the offensive for two more days. Hitler's final ice-cold, lunatic judgment on Operation Lüttich was, "Success only failed to come because Kluge did not want to be successful!"[57]

The overwhelming defeat of the German counterattack left what remained of the Wehrmacht's panzers and mobile infantry in a completely exposed pocket of Hitler's own making. Now Patton raced east and hooked northward to cut off the Germans. The British needed to complete the pincer movement by thrusting southward to ensnare the entire German Seventh Army and potentially end the war.[58]

# CHAPTER 10
# FALAISE FOLLIES

"I believe that . . . the XV Corps . . . could have gone on to Falaise . . . and definitely and positively closed the escape gap."

—General George S. Patton[1]

"Some questions being asked in London as to why Patton could not try to close the gap from the south."

—Group Captain F. K. Winterbotham,
chief of Air Department,
Secret Intelligence Service (Ultra)[2]

## IKE'S FRONT ROW SEAT

The Falaise operation of August 1944 remains one of the most controversial of World War II. Could the pocket have been closed earlier, entrapping most of the German forces in northwestern France? This chapter will explore how rivalries and faulty communications among the Allied commanders shaped the outcome of this pivotal campaign.

On August 7 to keep pace with the breakout and rapid advance of the Allied armies, Eisenhower established an advanced command post (codenamed SHELLBURST) in Tournières, Normandy. (See Map 13.) His proximity to the commanders would enable Ike to actively participate in decision making as the Falaise operation developed, and as OVERLORD's supreme commander he would have direct responsibility for the decisions that were made during the next ten crucial days.[3]

As stated previously, Allied ground forces regrouped on July 25 to accommodate the activation of Patton's Third Army. His command and that of General Courtney Hodges of the First Army became part of the US Twelfth Army Group under General Bradley. At the same time, Montgomery's Twenty-First Army Group was expanded to now include the First Canadian Army commanded by Lieutenant General Henry Crerar and Dempsey's Second British Army. (See Chart 3.) At this time Marshall pressed Eisenhower to finally assume command of OVERLORD's ground forces. He resisted by telling Marshall that a "woeful insufficiency in Signal troops made it impossible to discharge all the [SHAEF] . . . responsibilities and at the same time take over the broad operational coordination necessary between Army Groups."[4] This left Montgomery in charge for another fateful month. Eisenhower would soon regret his hasty decision not to assume command of the ground forces as the crucial events at Falaise unfolded.

## THE BIG PICTURE ON THE FORMING OF THE FALAISE POCKET

By early August the disposition of Hitler's armies in France and northwestern Europe had radically changed. Only three divisions of the Fifteenth Army remained east of the Seine, where there had been fifteen in mid-July. The German panzer divisions clustered around Caen had moved westward for the abortive Operation Lüttich around Mortain. Along the coast north of the Seine, only five divisions remained to repel the illusionary second invasion. In the interior of Normandy ten infantry divisions faced the Canadian and British forces. Another five were scattered to oppose Patton's eastward drive from Le Mans to Paris.

The majority of the Wehrmacht force's nineteen divisions had been severely ravaged. The present field of operation had become so confined that the panzers were incapable of waging a war of maneuver. The Falaise Pocket was thus born and offered the Allies an opportunity to deliver a potential knockout blow through the strategic envelopment of the German forces. (See Map 21.)

While the German forces were shrinking, the Allied armies steadily increased. This included the addition of Free French and Polish Armored Divisions and the Canadian Fourth Armored Division, which with their two infantry divisions now formed the First Canadian Army. In the two months since the beginning of Normandy operations, the size of the US Army forces had grown ten times larger. The Twelfth Army Group now deployed fourteen infantry and six armored divisions.[5]

The first evidence for a potential Allied envelopment of the German Seventh Army and the Panzer Reserve emerged on August 4. Both Patton and Eisenhower recognized this opportunity and redeployed the majority of American troops toward the east. Patton sent Walker's XX Corps southeast to the Loire River and Haislip's XV Corps from Laval to drive eastward in the direction of Le Mans. (See Map 21.) Patton also notified Haislip to get ready for bigger things.

On August 8, Bradley confided in his aide, Chester Hansen, "The German is either crazy or he doesn't know what's going on. I think he is too smart to do what he is doing. He can't know what's going on in our sector. Surely the professional generals must know the jig is up."[6]

Hansen said, "Hitler is your greatest ally, sir?"

Bradley replied, "Yes, perhaps he is."

That same day, the Third Army was advancing at almost all points of the compass from its central geographic position on the Normandy battlefield: west into Brittany, south toward the Loire, and most importantly east to Le Mans. Patton wrote to his wife, "This army had a big day."[7]

On August 7, twenty-four hours after the Germans began their counterattacks at Mortain, Montgomery launched Operation TOTALIZE, a Canadian Army assault toward Falaise. This operation had been planned prior to any discussion of the possibility of enveloping German forces in conjunction with the Americans.

Eisenhower and Bradley met to discuss the potential of encircling the German army on August 8. First reports indicated that the Canadians had broken through on the Falaise road. If Patton's Third Army sprang northward from Le Mans through Argentan to Falaise, this short hook would trap the Germans inside a tight pocket. (See Map 21.) Eisenhower assured Bradley that the Allied Air Transport Service (ATS) could deliver up to two thousand tons of supplies each day to the American forces. A US armored division needed at least sixty thousand gallons of fuel a day, and its twenty-one thousand men required thirty-five tons of rations per day.[8] Bradley thought this opportunity came "once in a century. . . . We're about to destroy an entire hostile army."[9]

That same day Bradley called Montgomery to explain the new plan. After Bradley told Monty that Eisenhower agreed with this, Monty with a degree of reluctance accepted the change to a shorter envelopment. He originally wanted a longer hook reaching to the Seine. Monty warned Bradley that full responsibility for the plan's success rested with him. Since the US objective was Argentan, twelve miles inside the British operational boundary, Bradley also received Monty's permission for this incursion in order to close the Falaise Pocket. This concession implied acceptance for doing whatever it took to entrap the Germans, boundary lines be damned.

Montgomery immediately ordered Dempsey to conform to the new plan for a short hook. That afternoon Eisenhower drove over to Montgomery's headquarters to reinforce his understanding of the operation and make sure that Monty ordered the Canadian army to make a maximum effort to close their side of the pincer and meet Patton's XV Corps.

Bradley ordered Patton's XV Corps north from Le Mans to the Army Group boundary at Argentan, where they were to hold this position. He told Patton that he didn't want American troops running into the Canadian or British forces coming down from Falaise. Though, like Montgomery, Patton considered a longer hook to envelop more Germans a better strategy, he was elated to get an envelopment started. In a letter to his wife on August 8 Patton wrote, "I am the only one who realizes how little the enemy can do—he is finished." He also speculated, "We may end this in ten days."[10]

Bradley also released to the XV Corps three divisions: the Thirty-Fifth and Eightieth Infantry and the French Second Armored Division that he had held back to meet the German Mortain counteroffensive. They would join Patton's one armored and two infantry divisions at Le Mans. Patton's spearhead would then attack from Le Mans to Alencon and finally Argentan and then meet up with the Canadians driving down from the north to close the entrapment.

Ike pushed Bradley and Montgomery to "pull a Clausewitz," i.e., to focus on destroying the enemy rather than just gaining more territory. On August 9, Eisenhower sent an enthusiastic letter to his boss General George C. Marshall: "Patton will march toward Alencon and Falaise . . . we have a good chance to encircle and destroy a lot of his [German] forces."[11] (See Map 21.)

Patton now had the way and the means to carry out the historic order he had been waiting for since arriving in Normandy. In a memo to General Hugh Gaffey, his chief of staff, he wrote, "The purpose of the operation is to surround and destroy the German army west of the Seine."[12] In Patton's order to Haislip he stated that the mission was "to destroy Germans in your front [i.e., encirclement]."[13] While the southern pincer of the Falaise encirclement was set to close, the northern pincer lacked a similar drive and focus.

## THE NORTHERN PINCER: CONFUSION REIGNS

Montgomery had promised Eisenhower that he would mount a rush down the Falaise road to meet Patton at Argentan. Unlike Montgomery's earlier "colossal cracks," Operation TOTALIZE was designed as a genuine breakthrough offensive with a frontal assault on the German lines. The greatly admired General Guy Simonds of II Canadian Corps planned and commanded TOTALIZE.

TOTALIZE began (August 7) with a night attack by Crerar's First Canadian Army, the Polish First Armored Division, and the Fifty-First Highland Division. Seven mobile columns of tanks and infantry carriers attacked, proceeded by four tanks abreast. They advanced about six miles by the dawn of August 8. (See Map 21.)

That morning a massed formation of over five hundred B-17 bombers attacked six defensive targets. Due to an appalling lack of communication between ground and air forces, some bombs fell short and killed or wounded 315 Poles and Canadians. The resulting confusion among the troops had the fatal effect of slowing down Simonds's day offensive. By the afternoon of August 8, TOTALIZE had ground to a halt ten miles short of Falaise, having reached only twelve miles south of Caen.[14] (See Map 22.)

However Montgomery had taken no steps to further reinforce the Canadian and Polish offensive toward Falaise. He seemed to have little sense of urgency. On August 9 he wrote to Brooke, "FALAISE itself is in reach of our guns . . . there are great possibilities in the present situation . . . we have a good chance of closing the ring."[15]

By midnight on August 11, their advance moved another three miles after costly fighting. Simonds then relieved the armor with infantry divisions. With another seven miles to reach Falaise, and another twelve miles to Argentan, the offensive ended. The troops believed they could not advance to Falaise without another heavy-bomber assault. Chester Wilmot believes that there is little doubt that if Montgomery had used his more experienced and available Seventh Armored Division to reinforce the Fourth and First Armored that TOTALIZE would have been completely successful in helping the Americans close the gap. Instead TOTALIZE failed to push aside two depleted German divisions that had but sixty tanks that had been reduced to thirty-five panzers by day's end.[16]

Montgomery seems to have continued to vacillate about using a short hook versus a long hook. On August 10 he still ordered the taking of Falaise but also ordered the Canadian armored forces to close the pocket by moving toward Trun/Argentan, later again changed to Trun/Chambois on August 16.[17]

Montgomery's inconsistency paralleled his lack of basic resolve in closing the Falaise gap itself. In an August 11 directive he told the Allied army commanders, "Obviously, if we close the gap completely we shall put the enemy in the most awkward predicament. . . . As the gap narrows the enemy is certain to re-act."[18] Why was Monty stating the obvious?

He also changed his orders no less than five times on who would take Falaise: August 4 assigned to Crerar, August 6 to Dempsey, August 11 to both Crerar and Dempsey, August 13 to Dempsey, and finally August 14 back to Crerar.[19] This parallels his previous actions during multiple battles around Caen when he repeatedly halted successful advances because of his fears over what was on the other side of the hill.

Brooke did not help the situation as he did not encourage Montgomery to launch an immediate drive and close the gap. Instead he wrote to Monty on August 13, "I have been watching your battle with enormous interest. There are wonderful possibilities."[20]

From August 12 to August 13, the Canadian Second Infantry Division made a limited attack, but the six days after TOTALIZE Montgomery largely spent "tidying up" in preparation for Operation TRACTABLE, a set-piece assault on Falaise.

## THE SOUTHERN PINCER: GAINING FORCES AND SURGING FORWARD

Patton's advance toward Falaise began on August 10 as the four divisions of Haislip's XV Corps attacked toward Argentan led by the Second French Armored and the Fifth US Armored Divisions. They borrowed trucks to mechanize Haislip's Seventy-Ninth and Ninetieth Infantry Divisions. The Ninetieth Infantry supported the Second French Armored, while the Seventy-Ninth Infantry supported Fifth Armored in their drive toward the town of Sées. (See Map 22.)

Haislip's advance met only scattered German resistance. Kluge found it impossible to inject more German units from northwestern France to confront the Third Army. A series of brief, intense skirmishes reduced the Ninth Panzer Division to less than twelve tanks and decimated the 708th Infantry Division.

As Patton's Third Army advanced north toward Alencon, scratch German combat units were thrown together from personnel at this major supply and maintenance base for the Seventh Army. Men from the supply depot, maintenance platoons, and panzer repair shops were mixed in with the remains of the Panzer Lehr Division. Cooks and mechanics were trained to use the Panzerfaust anti-tank weapons. Alencon's doom was sealed. The Wehrmacht in France was collapsing.

On the morning of August 12, the French Second Armored seized a basically undefended Alencon. At the same time the Fifth Armored crashed into Sées, defended only by a bakery company. Both the Second and Fifth then immediately moved north toward Argentan. A mix-up of units traveling on the main access road into the town delayed their arrival until that afternoon. By the time a French patrol entered Argentan on August 13, the Germans had rushed in reinforcements. This precluded the town's capture for more than a week. However, Patton's advanced units reached a position that put them within twelve miles from closing the Falaise Pocket. (See Map 22.)

That same day Patton ordered Collins's VII Corps, the First Infantry, and Third Armored Divisions to close the gap between their positions at Mayenne and the XV Corps. This they did by driving over twenty miles that day northeastward until they reached the outskirts of Carrouges where they attacked the First SS Panzer Division. With their rapid advance VII

Corps linked up with the left flank of the XV Corps, creating a solid wall between the US First and Third armies.

The Allies had formed a solid Falaise Pocket about thirty-five miles long and fifteen miles wide, encircling the enemy with the British Twenty-First Army Group on the northern and northwestern portion and the American Twelfth Army Group along the southwestern and southern portions. (See Map 22.) Trapped inside were over 100,000 to 250,000 troops of the German Seventh Army and their surviving panzer forces. Patton was positioned to act as the proverbial cork in the bottle.[21]

That day Patton wrote in his diary, "The XV Corps . . . has taken Alencon and the Sées-Argentan line and is in battle to the north. This corps could easily advance to Falaise and completely close the gap."[22]

At 9:30 p.m. on August 12, Haislip signaled Patton that the Fifth Armored was about to secure Argentan. Patton had previously told Haislip to ignore the constantly changing army boundaries and to go slowly beyond Argentan toward Falaise until he made contact with the Canadians. Patton had no intention of halting Haislip's advance. He had already been working hard at reinforcing Haislip's XV Corps. Patton deduced that if the Germans attacked, they lacked the organized strength, to break through before additional Third Army reinforcements arrived. The goal of this operation was to eliminate the German army west of the Seine. It was now within sight. In Patton's judgment, continuing Haislip's advance was worth the risk.[23]

At 10:17 p.m. Patton gave the order for Haislip to continue his advance in the direction of Falaise until he made contact with the Canadians. A containing force was left behind to cover the three weakened panzer divisions at Argentan, and the Fifth Armored began a slow drive toward Falaise. During the early-morning hours of August 13, a reconnaissance unit already had advanced eight miles. Only six miles separated them from Falaise and closing the pocket.

After authorizing the continued advance, Patton called Bradley that same evening to appraise him that he was about to close the pocket. Bradley was furious. In a sharp telephone exchange he told Patton, "Nothing doing. You're not to go beyond Argentan. Just stop where you are and build up on that shoulder."[24]

After learning on the morning of August 13 that Haislip's reconnaissance had still pushed on to within a few miles of Falaise, Major General

Leven Cooper Allen, Bradley's chief of staff, called Gaffey, Patton's chief of staff, and ordered all of the XV Corps forces back to the Argentan line.

Patton could not believe that Bradley would halt the successful operation so close to victory. He called back to the Twelfth Army Group headquarters and asked for Bradley. Allen answered his call and told him that Bradley was with Eisenhower at the SHAEF advance headquarters. Failing to reach Bradley at SHAEF, Patton called Allen back to again plead his case. Allen then contacted Bradley and conveyed Patton's request to allow the Third Army to renew its push to close the Falaise Pocket.

Bradley was with Eisenhower, so they both discussed Patton's urgent request. As previously mentioned, on August 9 Eisenhower had written to Marshall declaring that Patton's Third Army would march from Le Mans toward Alencon and Falaise to close the gap and destroy the German forces in the pocket. But now Eisenhower hesitated when Bradley cast doubt on the viability of Patton's drive.

At 12:15 p.m. Patton called Allen again. Patton wrote in his diary, "I told him . . . it was perfectly feasible to continue the operation. Allen repeated the order [from Bradley] to halt on the line and consolidate."[25]

After he hung up, Patton told Gaffey, "The question why XV Corps halted on the east-west line through Argentan is certain to become of historical importance. I want a stenographic record of this conversation with General Allen included in the history of the Third Army."[26]

That day Patton wrote in his diary, "I am sure that this halt is a great mistake, as I am certain that the British will not close on Falaise."[27] Patton was proven correct on both counts.

## STOP ORDER CONTROVERSY

Four major controversies surround Bradley's stop order:

1. What command decisions were made on boundary line issues.
2. Whether the Third Army had sufficient forces to stop the onrush of retreating Germans.
3. Would US and Canadian forces collide resulting in friendly-fire casualties?
4. Whether a short hook or long hook would capture more Germans.

## 1. Command Decisions and Boundary Lines

The XV Corps had already crossed the army boundary lines that separated the operations of the Twenty-First and Twelfth Army Groups. Partly due to coalition courtesy and also under the mistaken impression that the Canadians could more easily close the pocket from the north, Bradley waited for Montgomery to continue the advance. Bradley wrote, "If Montgomery wants help in closing the gap . . . then let him ask us for it."[28] He never did.

According to historian Niall Barr, the critical decision on army boundaries had earlier taken place. As mentioned before, on August 8 Bradley telephoned Montgomery in Eisenhower's presence to receive permission for Patton to cross the then British boundary in his attack northward from Le Mans toward Argentan. Barr reports that "Montgomery acceded and also agreed that the existing boundaries could be ignored."[29] No meeting place was ever selected for the closing of the pocket by the American and Canadian forces.[30] The increased fluidity of the battlefield situation made formal army boundaries a meaningless issue. As D'Este concludes, "The boundary line controversy is a tempest in a teapot."[31]

During the evening of August 12, Montgomery learned of Haislip's advance beyond Argentan. He told his chief of staff, Major General Francis de Guingand, to "[t]ell Bradley they ought to get back." De Guingand and the other member of Monty's staff were appalled. Later when they were notified of Bradley's stop order, they pressed Montgomery to give Bradley permission to proceed with the advance. He refused. In his memoirs, *Operation Victory*, written after the war, de Guingand states his belief that the Americans' advance beyond Argentan would have closed the pocket. De Guingand blamed both Montgomery and Bradley for blocking the American advance as Monty wanted the victory to be a British/Canadian one.[32]

Bradley has always denied he contacted Montgomery for permission to continue the attack northward. Yet evidence exists that on Sunday morning, August 13, Bradley ordered his operations officer, General Kibler, to call Montgomery's headquarters. Kibler spoke with de Guingand and was denied permission.[33]

Later that day Bradley flew to Montgomery's headquarters and met with Dempsey and Monty. Dempsey later stated in his diary, "So long as the Northward move of Third Army meets little opposition, the . . . leading

Corps [of Patton's army] will disregard inter-army boundaries." Montgomery also seemed to have no objections to the XV Corps advance to Falaise.[34] If Dempsey's version is correct, then it appears that it was Bradley's choice, not Montgomery's prohibition, that stopped Patton's advance.

Fig. 10.1. Major General Francis de Guingand, chief of staff, Twenty-First Army Group. (© Imperial War Museums [H 39144])

The viewpoint of Bradley's aide was quite different. On the evening of August 14, as Patton's forces began moving eastward toward the Seine, Major Chester B. Hansen wrote about the "Falaise follies" in his diary, "It is clear now that our chance to close the German army between Falaise and Argentan has vanished for reasons both clear and difficult to conceive. It is possible that Montgomery has succumbed to his vice of exaggerated precautions. However, it would be folly to criticize Montgomery due to his prestige position among the British. . . . He occupies an almost papal immunity."[35]

A 1946 Chester Wilmot interview of Montgomery adds additional confusion over the phantom commander who had the responsibility for stopping Patton from closing the gap. Monty told Wilmot that the Third

Army was never ordered to stop at Argentan: "It was ordered to strike north on the axis Alencon-Argentan and to close the gap. If Patton stopped, he must have been stopped by opposition."[36] As historian John Keegan comments, controversy over who made the fatal command decision "was the outcome of a curious passage of inter-Allied discord."[37]

## 2. The Third Army vs. the Germans

Bradley told Patton, "You're not to go beyond Argentan. Just stop where you are and build up on that shoulder. Siebert tells me the Germans are beginning to pull out. You'd better button up and get ready for him."[38] This command was based on what Bradley later acknowledged was faulty Allied intelligence.

The assumption was that Haislip's XV Corps of four divisions might be sufficient to hold the southern jaw of the pocket but was too weak to also plug its mouth. Bradley feared that the nineteen German divisions trapped inside would stampede and overrun Patton.[39]

However on August 12 the Germans were not bolting eastward in desperate retreat. They were waiting immobilized inside their führer's self-made trap. Hitler took four more days before he gave Kluge the order to disengage (August 16).

To what degree was Patton's claim that his XV Corps was strong enough to reach Falaise and close the escape route? On the evening of August 12 Patton's reconnaissance forces told him that the only German units between the Third Army and Falaise were a regiment of antiaircraft guns that was short of ammunition, and the surviving remnants of the Ninth and 116th Panzer Divisions. There also was the First SS and Second Panzer Divisions of General Hans Eberbach's panzer group that were scattered northwest of Alencon. At best Eberbach had between seventy and eighty-two tanks. Patton's XV Corps was advancing with over three hundred Sherman tanks, twenty-two battalions of artillery, two infantry divisions, and complete command of the air.[40]

In addition to Haislip's XV Corps, Collins's VII Corps was on or near Carrouges. Walkers's XX Corps was near Le Mans. The Fourth Armored Division would arrive on August 13 from Brittany to form the XII Corps. Between August 10 and August 14 there were five US armored divisions and eight US infantry divisions in the American First and Third armies numbering over 200,000 soldiers sitting on the German southern flank. Most were capable of moving rapidly into place and permanently shutting the Falaise Pocket.[41]

Major General Richard Rohmer at that time was a reconnaissance pilot flying a Mustang in 430 Squadron of the Royal Canadian Air Force. Based on his observations and his fellow reconnaissance pilots, he reached this conclusion:

> The opportunity to complete the encirclement was at hand. . . . But there was no way the Canadians, Poles and the British Army could break through north of Falaise to "rush" south past Falaise to Argentan; they were pinned down where they were. No, if the ring was to be closed with the two German Armies inside the pocket, it would have to be done by Patton and it would have to be done at forthwith.[42]

## 3. Avoiding Friendly Fire

Another Bradley argument for stopping the XV Corps' advance was the possibility they would collide with the Canadians at Falaise in a "disastrous error in recognition."[43] Friendly fire was a weak argument. Even Bradley later suggested that landmarks or geographical features could have been used to identify a potential meeting point. Both British and American army units had generous supplies of signal rockets. There would have been little difficulty in each army using coded-light signal identification. On radio, the accents of Scots, British, and American personnel would be very apparent as they neared each other. Both armies also deployed scout aircraft. The Allied white star was conspicuously displayed on each side's tanks, jeeps, and trucks.

The American forces and British-Canadian army would have eventually met. Where they plugged the pocket was irrelevant. The goal was to do it quickly and destroy the bulk of the German army in France.[44]

## 4. Short Hook vs. Long Hook

On August 14 Bradley moved to redeploy Patton from a short hook at Falaise to a long hook at the Seine River. He believed that the majority of the Germans had already escaped and now wanted Patton to close the pocket at the Seine. Neither Ultra nor air reconnaissance confirmed this assessment.

Bradley split Haislip's command and kept two divisions at Argentan and sent the two others eastward. Montgomery immediately agreed to this change, saying he had never supported the short hook. Both commanders sought to enlarge the pocket and bring the Allied armies together at Chambois. (See Map 21.)

Whether this could be done in a timely manner to entrap the Germans remained to be seen. Shifting Patton's army away from a certain closure at Falaise to a potential closure farther eastward remains one of the worst decisions made by the Allied commanders during the OVERLORD operation.[45]

## EISENHOWER BACKS DOWN

On August 13 Eisenhower and Bradley were together when Bradley's operations officer received the news from Montgomery's chief of staff that the army boundaries were still to be enforced. Both men backed down before Monty's refusal to cooperate, though both later denied ever initiating that call. Ike later wrote that he supported "Bradley's decision to avoid friendly fire between the armies."[46]

At the critical hour for the Falaise Pocket, Eisenhower refused to potentially cause friction to the alliance and as supreme commander countermand Montgomery's refusal to cooperate. This was a pattern that Ike repeated many times with Montgomery during the campaign in France. As a result, Monty treated Ike as only a political figurehead who should not interfere with his control of the OVERLORD ground campaign.[47] Montgomery would now try half-heartedly to close the pocket from the north.

## TRACTABLE OFFTRACK

On August 14 Montgomery launched Operation TRACTABLE, a set-piece assault on Falaise. At noon two tank columns were making good progress when more than eight hundred Canadian and British heavy bombers dropped about 3,700 tons of bombs along the route of advance. Once again, bombing short inflicted more than five hundred casualties on Canadian and Polish troops. The resulting confusion meant by day's end TRACTABLE was offtrack, having advanced less than four miles. Moreover, the Germans found a copy of the attack plan in the pocket of a dead Canadian reconnaissance driver. They redeployed based on this intelligence of where to meet the Allied advance. On August 15 a breakdown in communications further confused inexperienced Canadian and Polish troops. They ended the day still short of Falaise.[48] Yet at this time Monty wrote to Brooke, "Things really do seem to be going very well."[49]

As part of TRACTABLE Montgomery abandoned the head-on thrust to close the pocket at Argentan, and on August 16 he ordered the Canadians and Poles to make a flanking move toward Trun, while the Americans attacked from the west and south toward Chambois as part of a long hook to close the Falaise Pocket. (See Map 22.) The Canadians and Poles were too weak by themselves to do the job. Unfortunately, Montgomery failed to reinforce them using his Seventh Armored Division. Also, a large part of Patton's army (Haislip's corps) had already left the area in an advance toward the Seine.

On August 16, the Canadians finally reached Falaise, the birthplace of William the Conqueror, although it took two more days to clean out resistance forces. It had been reduced to brick dust.

On the evening of August 18, the Canadian Fourth Armored and a Polish battle group occupied Trun. They had been slowed by both a commander's incompetence and by Montgomery's indecision on whether its armored brigade should continue the advance or break off for a wider envelopment at the Seine. Also the Poles lost their way heading for Chambois and ended up six miles north of the city. The encirclement remained incomplete.

Finally on August 19, the Poles and elements of the Fourth Armored reached Chambois. They met with the US Ninetieth and shook hands over their link up. Reinforced by the French Second Armored Division, the Allied forces were finally astride the escape route of the German Seventh Army inside the pocket. Though the enemy may have been in the bag, the bag was still full of holes. Allied strength between Trun and Chambois was still very spotty. Elements of the Second Panzer enlarged the holes by driving the Canadians back at Chambois to keep an escape route open until nightfall. Many German soldiers escaped. The Canadians called for reinforcements. But Montgomery's indecision on whether to seal the gap on the Dives river or to go for a longer envelopment on the Seine again delayed proper reinforcements to help seal the breach.

That same day, two Polish battle groups moved to the Mount Ormel ridge and dug in at Hill 262 during the night. (See Map 22.) The Poles were able to direct their artillery fire from Hill 262 directly at the retreating Germans. On August 20, Field Marshal Walter Model ordered units both inside and outside the pocket to attack the Polish positions. At midday units of several panzer divisions overran part of the Polish lines, allowing around ten thousand soldiers to escape. Additionally, heavy rain limited Allied air attacks, thereby helping thousands of Germans to flee out of the pocket.[50]

The next morning, August 21, though German attacks resumed, the Poles retained a blocking position on the ridge. Only small, isolated German groups were able to escape in the early-morning hours. With the noon arrival of Canadian reinforcements at Hill 262 and near Chambois, the Falaise Pocket was finally sealed.[51]

## A STALINGRAD IN NORMANDY?

As the Allies dithered over closing the Falaise gap, what was the German response inside the pocket? Hitler's repeated orders to attack at Mortain had yielded no gains except to drive more units deeper into the encirclement.

By August 14, the Germans were failing to supply their troops with day-to-day necessities. That evening Field Marshal Kluge began a frontline inspection of a rapidly shrinking battlefield. Operational prospects were grim, "roads clogged with traffic and dispirited troops."[52] The Germans had only received thirty thousand replacements with ten thousand more in transit.[53]

When Kluge arrived at Sepp Dietrich's Fifth Panzer Army Headquarters, he learned that the Canadian army's march toward Falaise had barely been stopped. If General Hans Eberbach's panzers did not successfully counterattack at Argentan, collapse was imminent. The Germans risked the loss of all the forces in the pocket.[54] (See Map 22.)

Early on August 15 Kluge set out from Bernay to travel forty miles to meet with Eberbach and General Paul Hausser, commander of the Seventh Army. Their meeting was set for 10:00 a.m. at the village of Necy. It proved to be the ride of Kluge's lifetime. The field marshal's convoy of a staff car, radio truck, and motorcycle escort was an outstanding target for Allied fighter-bombers. Kluge spent his day repeatedly driving into ditches, having his radio truck destroyed, and signal men killed. Given this unpleasant taste of a heavy artillery bombardment, a frazzled Kluge arrived at Eberbach's headquarters west of Argentan after midnight. Only then could he contact the Supreme Headquarters West to inform them of his location.

Eberbach's panzer divisions were under a remorseless attack by both the American First and Third armies. Total Allied air superiority and intense artillery fire meant that logistical supplies to his divisions had practically ceased. Hausser's Seventh Army located to the west of Argentan was retreating slowly to prevent the total collapse of the front. His Tenth SS Panzer Division was trapped, and their fuel tanks were empty. Both men urged Kluge to order an immediate retreat from the pocket.[55]

Hitler declared August 15 to be "the worst day of my life."[56] After the attempted July assassination, the führer suspected most of his senior commanders of treason. Kluge's sudden disappearance for almost twenty-four hours convinced Hitler that the field marshal was engaging in secret negotiations with the Allies.

Earlier that day Hitler received news of the Allied landings in southern France (Operation ANVIL, later renamed DRAGOON). For once the führer did not hesitate. He had earlier reached the decision that this invasion demanded that he order all German forces to immediately retreat from the south of France.

Before Kluge's reappearance, his chief of staff, Blumentritt, had insisted that the situation west of Argentan required an immediate withdrawal. Jodl's orders from Hitler were that such a decision should be made only if there was no option. He wanted Eberbach to launch an attack toward Sées to widen the corridor.

When Kluge finally reappeared, he called Jodl at 2:00 a.m. on August 16. He gave him a frank assessment of the rapidly deteriorating situation. Later at 12:45 p.m. Kluge again telephoned Jodl and forcefully reiterated his views of the impending disaster. Kluge asserted that the signs of the army's disintegration were steadily increasing. An Army Group B staff officer compared the Wehrmacht's situation on the roads of Normandy to Napoleon's retreat from Moscow in 1812.

The region's roads were basically impassable. Units intermingled with long lines of stragglers. Divisions were reduced to a miserable handful of men. The panzers sat beside the roads immobilized by lack of fuel. The troops were hungry and dispirited since rations and even ammunition only arrived erratically. Command and control was almost nonexistent except for limited radio communication.[57]

Kluge was blunt and insisted that Jodl tell Hitler, "No matter how many orders are issued . . . no power in this world [will see it carried out simply] through an order. . . . That is the situation."[58] The Germans were on the brink of a total disaster. As Alexander McKee suggests, "the qucstion was—would it be decisive, a 'Stalingrad' in Normandy?"[59]

The problems Kluge faced to achieve a successful withdrawal would not be easily solved. By August 16, the Falaise Pocket was tightening, but it was far from closed. General Rudolf Gersdorff, Seventh Army chief of staff, was still able to drive a staff car in both directions between Trun and Chambois. (See Map 21.) Another German general commented that the pocket had shrunk to about twenty-two miles long and eleven miles wide, and thus it had a disturbing resemblance to the battered German Sixth Army lozenge that had been destroyed at Stalingrad in 1943.

Allied air dominance over the pocket was absolute. The entire enclave was within range of Allied artillery. The limited east-west road network was in disastrous condition, littered with dead and wounded soldiers and destroyed equipment. All the Allied armies were tightening the perimeter thus decreasing the size of the pocket hour by hour.

By 2:30 p.m. Kluge felt he could wait no longer and told Speidel to issue the withdrawal order.[60] By then Hitler had already written off Kluge as a traitor, though no such evidence was ever produced. When Hitler finally issued his new orders they only called for the Seventh Army to withdraw across the Orne.

Hitler then ordered Field Marshal Walter Model, his "fireman," to France. (He had often rescued German forces from dire situations on the Russian front.) Kluge was ordered to immediately leave the pocket for his La Roche-Guyon headquarters. Model arrived there on August 17. The two field marshals conferred for the next twenty-four hours in order to give Model the big picture.[61]

Fig. 10.2. Field Marshal Walter Model. (© Imperial War Museums [MH 12850])

Before his departure, Kluge wrote Hitler a final letter:

> My Fuhrer . . . I did everything within my power to equal the situation. . . . Both Rommel and I . . . foresaw the present development. We were not listened to. Our appreciations were NOT dictated by pessimism but from the sober knowledge of the facts. I do not know whether Field Marshal Model . . . will still master the situation. . . . Should it not be so . . . make up your mind to end the war. The German people have borne such untold suffering that it is time to put an end to this frightfulness.[62]

Kluge left for home on August 19. He knew that the Gestapo was waiting for him in Germany. Near Metz, he swallowed a poison capsule. Many German generals on the eastern front had carried these capsules, fearing capture by the Russians, although most captured officers did not use them. Serving Hitler in Normandy could be a deadly experience for his field marshals.[63]

The German withdrawal that began on August 16 started quietly, and the movement was orderly. The Allies offered little interference. This comparative calm changed rapidly on August 17, hastened by the rapid deterioration within the Wehrmacht units. The British/Canadian and American forces both made major thrusts from the north and south that day, threatening to close the pocket. By the evening of August 17, the Germans had successfully retreated across the Orne. However, many of their divisions had disintegrated into weak units unable to defend a front line.

The survivors of fifteen shattered divisions, in all more than 250,000 men, were herded together into this compressing pocket. Sick with despair the troops were unceasingly pounded as they wandered eastward toward the remaining narrow gap between Trun and Chambois. Filled with dread, these German soldiers wondered how many would still be able to escape.[64]

On August 18, Model held his first staff conference at the La Roche-Guyon headquarters. The shrinking pocket was now only six miles deep and seven miles wide. Halfway through the meeting a dispatch arrived with the news that the Canadians had taken Trun. (See Map 22.) By this date, Model's troops were a totally spent force. On that day alone, the US Ninth Air Force destroyed four hundred vehicles. The RAF claimed another 1,159 and damaged 1,700 more. Also 124 panzers were eliminated, and one hundred others damaged.[65]

During the next two days however, a significant number of German troops were able to escape in the gap between Trun and Chambois. But on August 21, the Falaise Pocket was finally sealed. OVERLORD was officially concluded with the end of the Falaise operations.

## THE BALANCE SHEET

The Normandy region itself had been devastated, some places as severely damaged as those on the western front during World War I. Two hundred thousand buildings had been demolished. Caen was a mountain of rubble with nine thousand of its fifteen thousand buildings flattened. Falaise, Argentan, St. Lo, Coutances, and other cities and small towns were in ruins. Most of devastated Normandy was not restored until 1951.[66]

Fig. 10.3. A British soldier in Caen, after its liberation, gives a helping hand to an old lady among the scene of utter devastation. (© Imperial War Museums [B 6794])

The Falaise Pocket area had become a military wasteland. Roads were completely blocked with burnt-out vehicle wreckage and the swollen bodies of both men and horses. Severely mutilated corpses lay everywhere on the roads and in the forests. The paraphernalia of the German military machine was scattered all over the terrain—radios, Engima coding machines, typewriters, the Feldpost mailbags of the German soldiers. Near Trun, 250 wounded soldiers were discovered at a German field hospital hidden deep in the Forest of Gouffern. Massive numbers of draft animals and cavalry horses were scattered across the landscape, including a whole squadron of Don Cossacks from Hitler's foreign legions lying dead beside their horses.[67]

Fig. 10.4. Falaise Pocket destruction of German army. (Press services of First Polish Armoured Division)

What were the German casualties for the Normandy campaign and the Falaise battles? Charles Stacy reports that 740,000 German soldiers were deployed in Normandy south of the Seine. Army Group B casualties from June 6 to August 12 were 158,930. He estimates that 400,000 German troops were inside the pocket.[68] Total German losses at Falaise were ten thousand dead counted across the battlefield and fifty thousand prisoners.

How many soldiers escaped remains a hotly contested issue. Estimates range widely among D-Day historians:[69]

| Historian | National Origin | Estimate |
|---|---|---|
| Keegan | UK | 300,000 |
| Blumenson | US | 240,000 |
| Weidner | US | 200,000 |
| Romer | Canadian | 210,000 |
| McKee | Canadian | 50,000 |
| Carrell | German | 50,000 |
| D'Este | US | 20-40,000 |
| Beevor | UK | 20-30,000 |
| Hastings | UK | 20,000+ |

A telling point in this debate is that all the German panzer divisions that fought in Normandy, save one, were quickly reconstituted and returned to action. These divisions included Panzer Lehr, Second Panzer, Ninth Panzer, 116th Panzer, First SS Panzer, Second SS Panzer, Ninth SS Panzer, Tenth SS Panzer, and Twelfth SS Panzer. All of these panzer divisions fought in the Battle of the Bulge. The Twenty-First Panzer was also reconstituted and fought the Americans in the Saar region between September and December 1944.

These units reformed rapidly because of the fifteen panzer/infantry divisional commanders inside the pocket, only three did not get away. Only one of the five German corps commanders did not escape. The large number of officers and NCOs who successfully broke out was a significant key to both increasing the numbers of soldiers who escaped and the rebirth of the Wehrmacht after the Falaise battle. As a result, the morale of German soldiers during this withdrawal and afterward remained higher than anyone expected. The practical and professional ability of these German officers and NCOs helped in repairing shattered units and creating order out of chaos.[70] For all of these reasons, we believe that a higher estimated number of soldiers, in the range of 200,000, escaped from the Falaise encirclement to fight another day.

It is a judgment by many historians that during the OVERLORD campaign, the Allies faced an enemy who produced the finest fighting army of the war and one of the greatest military forces in history. As Max Hastings conclusively states, "the inescapable reality of the battle for Normandy was that when Allied troops met Germans on anything like equal terms, the Germans almost always prevailed."[71] The Allies only achieved decisive penetrations when their attacking forces met the scattered remains of German units or they had been worn down by attrition or decimated by air attack.

The German defeat at Falaise was tactical and operational due to Hitler's bungling interference. The Allied victory was not strategic because the Germans were left with the capacity to continue the war into 1945. As Raymond Callahan has said, it was "as much a German success as an Anglo-American failure."[72]

The German military historian Percy Ernest Schramm considered the Falaise operation a triumph. In many ways the German withdrawal compares favorably to the British evacuation from Dunkirk in 1940.

However, the Falaise Pocket battle basically destroyed Germany's Army Group B. The Allies captured an estimated 220 tanks, 130 antiaircraft guns, 160 assault guns, and 2,000 horse-drawn trucks. An additional 1,300 tanks, 20,000 vehicles, 500 assault guns, and 1,500 heavier and lighter field artillery pieces were captured or destroyed.[73]

Of the 750,000 Germans deployed in Normandy south of the Seine, the Wehrmacht casualties during the whole campaign (June 6–August 21) were an estimated 500,000 soldiers, including 210,000 taken prisoner, 125,000 dead, and over 160,000 wounded.

Allied losses since D-Day were significant. There were 209,000 casualties—126,000 American and 83,000 British/Canadian. This is an approximate ratio of two British/Canadian losses to three Americans. Over 36,000 Allied soldiers died.[74]

## FUMBLERS AT THE FOLLIES

On August 21, Montgomery issued a ringing declaration to his Twenty-First Army Group: "The victory has been definite, complete and decisive."[75] A day earlier he even wrote in his diary, "The victory is going to be a very decisive one."[76]

Since that day, many historians and generals have debated whether the Falaise operation was a victory, as the final results were seriously flawed by the earlier failure to close the gap on August 12 to August 14. What decisions of the Allied commanders can be blamed for this debacle?[77] A whole publishing industry has arisen looking for the ultimate scapegoat. There were multiple reasons for the Allied failure to totally encircle and destroy the entire Seventh Army and the German panzer forces on the Falaise battlefield. Let us spotlight some of the most important issues.

## 1. Montgomery

As we have already shown, on August 8 Montgomery seemed to agree that Patton could cross the Allied forces' boundary line, yet from August 12 to August 14, he refused to change the boundary lines between the British/Canadian and American forces. He also seems to have been indecisive about making either a short or long envelopment.

Moreover, Chester Wilmot and others have found that Montgomery's pincer drive from the north to close the gap "was not pressed with sufficient speed and strength."[78] He did not fully commit the Seventh Armored Division to reinforce the less battle-tested Canadian and Polish tank forces in their bogged-down drive to Falaise. If Montgomery had done so, there was a high probability the combined force would have had the punch to force their way through weak and badly battered German divisions to meet the Americans and close the Falaise-Argentan gap. Horace Edward Henderson calls this "one of his most serious and controversial blunders."[79]

William Weidner states that in large part the Falaise Pocket took too long to close because Montgomery "could not decide how to complete the encirclement."[80] Richard Lamb goes even further, ultimately concluding that this was Montgomery's "biggest error of generalship."[81]

Bradley wrote that during a dinner on August 14, he and Eisenhower had reached these conclusions: "Owing to Monty's wildly misplaced confidence in the Canadians, we thought we had missed an opportunity to annihilate the Germans and that they were escaping through the gap. Monty's plan for finally closing the gap was less than satisfactory."[82]

## 2. The Canadians

Charles Perry Stacey, the official Canadian historian, is very blunt in his assessment of the First Canadian Army's participation in the Falaise follies:

> It is not difficult to put one's finger upon occasions in the Normandy campaign when Canadian formations failed to make the most of their opportunities. In particular the capture of Falaise was long delayed. . . . A German force far smaller than our own, taking advantage of strong ground and prepared positions, was able to slow our advance to the point where considerable German forces made their escape . . . an early closing of the Falaise Gap . . . might even, conceivably, have enabled us to end the war some months sooner.[83]

General Charles Foulkes, commander of the Second Canadian Infantry Division, freely admitted that his officers and men were ill-prepared to fight this battle: "When we went into battle at Falaise and Caen we found that when we bumped into battle-experienced German troops we were no match for them. We would not have been successful had it not been for our air and artillery support."[84]

Yet in the end, it was Montgomery's decision to commit the inexperienced Canadian forces to this crucial role in the Falaise campaign. After gaining experience in this battle, the Canadian forces went on to perform well in later 1944 operations. However, the Allies paid too high a price for their poor performance at Falaise.

## 3. Bradley

A number of the reasons General Bradley gave for stopping Patton's offensive have already been reviewed. Early in August Bradley seemed to have been as enthusiastic as Patton about encircling the German forces. Hitler had placed his Seventh Army in a strategic noose with the Mortain counteroffensive. Yet a week later, it appears that Bradley's optimism had been replaced by his more characteristic caution and doubt. Years later he wrote, "I have often asked myself, if I should not have done Monty's work, and if we should not have closed the gap ourselves. Montgomery was so scared that he made the push from the west; as Eisenhower said, he squeezed the tube of toothpaste and made it go out the hole instead of closing the opening."[85]

On August 15 Bradley went to visit Patton at his headquarters. Patton recorded in his diary the state of his commander: "Bradley came down to see me suffering from nerves. . . . His motto seems to be, 'In case of doubt halt.'"[86]

## 4. Eisenhower

Eisenhower, as supreme commander of OVERLORD, was far from blameless. He was at Bradley's headquarters the night the decision was made not to allow Patton to close on Falaise. There is no doubt that this decision had Eisenhower's approval.

By his very presence in France, Eisenhower had in fact assumed command of the land forces. He had planned to take actual command on August 1 but had postponed Montgomery's demotion for exactly one month to September. This delay would create even more command problems on the battlefield. Falaise was only the first.

If Eisenhower had been a more outspoken and astute supreme commander he would have insisted on the consensus reached by him, Bradley, and Montgomery on August 8 to lift the army group boundary lines. From August 12 to August 13 he would have forced Monty's hand and made him stick to this agreement.

Since D-Day, Ike had issued no direct orders to his commanders. He had reduced himself to more of a spectator and cheerleader than supreme commander. Yet Eisenhower still bore the ultimate high command responsibility for the prosecution of OVERLORD and the final victory in Europe.

On the evening of August 12 at Bradley's headquarters, he still refrained from direct intervention at a decisive moment in the OVERLORD operation. It was obvious that a golden opportunity to encircle the entire German army in Normandy was at hand. Why did Ike take no action?[87]

## 5. The Role of National Rivalries

National rivalries were a significant factor in many decisions during the Normandy campaign and certainly played a role in Eisenhower's decision making on August 12 to August 14. There was increasing British resentment over the growing American dominance in the European campaign.

On August 9, Eisenhower had been summoned by Churchill to 10 Downing Street. The British had long been opposed to DRAGOON, the invasion of southern France. The assault was to begin on August 15, only six days away. Churchill did his best to bully and intimidate Eisenhower to cancel this operation at the last minute. Churchill even threatened to go to the king or resign as prime minister. He blustered that America had become a "big strong and dominating partner."[88]

Eisenhower told him it was too late to cancel the operation. He left the prime minister still raging and weeping in frustration. Stephen Ambrose recounts that Eisenhower later described the meeting "as one of the most difficult of the entire war."[89]

Earlier on August 7, Churchill also had argued with Bradley about the invasion: "Why break down the back door when the front door has already been opened by your magnificent American army?"[90]

On August 11, Eisenhower wrote to Churchill in an attempt to appease him. Ike was worried about the possibilities of Churchill losing faith in SHAEF "because such lack of faith would quickly be reflected in discord in our field commands."[91]

Days later, Eisenhower, perhaps fearing that he might be perceived by the British as too domineering, refused to intervene and overrule Montgomery in order to close the gap at Falaise-Argentan. Montgomery, for his part, thought that he alone was qualified to be in sole command on this battle.

Montgomery's diary entry on August 19 includes the following:

> The B.B.C. 9 P.M. news on 15 August contained a statement that Eisenhower had taken over personal command in France, and that he had under him two Army Groups. . . . This gave the impression that I had been deposed from command of the land battle under Eisenhower, and a good deal of comment took place.
>
> The B.B.C. 7 A.M. news on 16 August had a statement correcting the one of the night before, and saying that I was still in overall charge of the land operations. . . .
>
> The whole affair . . . may have been done on purpose by someone at SHAEF.
>
> It will NOT do Ike any good; people will say that just as I am about to win a big victory, he tried to step in and scoop the reward.[92]

This diary entry both confirms that Montgomery feared that the Americans and Eisenhower rather than the British and himself would be viewed as the primary determinants of the recent Allied victories as well as his perception that he had just won a great victory at Falaise.

De Guingand, Montgomery's chief of staff, reflected in his memoirs, "I regret that some British soldiers never quite appreciated the extent of our Ally's [sic] contribution and it seemed to surprise them and sometimes annoy them, that she should wish to run her own affairs, and take the leadership in Allied policy."[93]

## 6. The Role of Personal Animosities

By this stage of OVERLORD, Eisenhower disliked Montgomery and thought that Monty might ignore an order directed to him. Montgomery saw Ike as only a figurehead.

In a letter to Brooke on August 14, he bitterly attacked Eisenhower:

> Ike is apt to get excited and to talk wildly at the top of his voice!!! He is now over here, which is a very great pity. His ignorance as to how to run a war is absolute and complete. . . . However, I manage to compete somehow. One thing I am very firm about; he is never allowed a meeting between me and my Army Commanders and Bradley![94]

This is an unbelievable statement that reveals Montgomery at his worst. Nigel Hamilton calls Monty's remarks "a savage indictment."[95]

Given the fact that Monty hated to attend group meetings, what if such a meeting had been held earlier in the Falaise operation? Might Eisenhower have exercised his political skills to facilitate the Allied commanders agreeing upon a faster closure of the Falaise Pocket? Could Eisenhower ever modify Montgomery's rude views on his total ignorance of warfare? Under what conditions would Monty ever change from competing to cooperating with Eisenhower as an Allied partner, rather than as an adversary? The enemy that needed to be defeated was the Germans, *not* Eisenhower. These are some of the problems that continued to compromise the effectiveness of the Allied command structure for the rest of the war in Europe.

The lack of communication between Eisenhower and Montgomery and the jealous spite shown by the British general explains how they both contributed to the results of the Falaise follies and to the continued strategic errors that prolonged the war into 1945.[96]

## FALAISE–INCONCLUSIVE VICTORY

As part of the military campaign that ended World War II in Europe, the Battle of the Falaise Pocket was a major Allied victory. Both the German Seventh and Fifth Panzer armies were effectively destroyed as operational units.

But the Falaise Pocket operation by the Allies was also a major missed strategic opportunity. It was not until a week after Patton had reached Argentan (August 12–13), positioning US forces to close the gap, that the Falaise Pocket was finally snapped shut. We believe that due primarily to the bungling of the Allied high command, the Germans maintained their escape valve long enough to allow at least 200,000 soldiers, NCOs, and forty generals to slip through. As the old adage states, "Those who run away live to fight another day." These forces were then able to contribute to the fight in Europe for an additional eight months. The battles during MARKET GARDEN and the Battle of the Bulge prolonged the war into 1945. Colonel Ralph Ingersoll, historian of Bradley's Twelfth Army Group, commented, "The failure to close the Argentan-Falaise gap was the loss of the greatest single opportunity of the war."[97] The official United States Army history of the operation concludes that "halting the XV Corps at Argentan [was] a tactical error, a failure to take full advantage of German vulnerability."[98]

The three senior Allied field commanders—Eisenhower, Montgomery, and Bradley—as Rick Atkinson put it, "had made a hash of things."[99] Personal indecision, caution and fear, lack of coordination between British, Canadian, and American armies, the clash of egos, inexperienced Canadians battling battle-hardened Germans, all contributed to a far less decisive victory. French general Philippe Leclerc, who commanded the French Second Armored Division in Patton's Third Army heading toward Falaise, seems to poignantly summarize the experience of those who saw the opportunity that was lost and its consequences: "I had the feel that it was 1940 in reverse—complete enemy confusion, surprised columns etc. The climax on the French front at Argentan-Falaise could have been splendid. The high command decided otherwise: history will condemn them."[100] Years later in retrospect, Eisenhower admitted that if he had ordered the Falaise gap closed at Argentan, it "might have won us a complete battle of annihilation."[101]

# CHAPTER 11
# THE LOST VICTORY

> "I have never given a damn what the enemy was going to do or where he was. . . . I have always gotten to the place he expected me to come about three days before he got there."
>
> —General George S. Patton[1]

During the first two weeks of August, Patton's Third Army seized most of Brittany (except for the ports of Lorient and Brest). They also had gained the Loire River to Angers. The next phase of Patton's drive was to thrust beyond Le Mans to the northeast and Alencon.

As these events unfolded across France, Bradley observed, "There was wild jubilation in the Allied Camp. . . . Nothing of consequence lay between us and Germany."[2] The Allies looked unstoppable. Could they rapidly cross eastern France into Belgium, Holland, then cross the Rhine to Berlin? Martin Blumenson observes that many of the commanders thought that the war might "be over by the end of September!"[3]

## "HAVING A HELL OF A WAR"

On August 13, Patton was still impatiently sitting at Argentan considering what to do next. The other Allied top commanders were still engaged in fighting over where and how to finally seal the Falaise Pocket. With his agitation growing, Patton decided, "Since the XX Corps was hitting nothing, we had best send it northeast, east of Le Mans."[4] Patton's drive to the German border was about to begin.

The next day Patton flew to Bradley's command post to "sell him the plan. . . . He consented . . . to move the XX Corps on Chartres, the XV Corps on Dreux, and the XII Corps on Orleans."[5] This maneuver would encircle Paris and capture more German forces.

Patton was elated, and by 8:30 p.m. that evening he had his entire corps racing toward the Seine. The Third Army's relentless advance eastward toward Paris overran the Germans' planned defensive strongpoints before they could be fully manned.[6] (See Map 21.)

By the evening of August 15, General Gilbert Cook's XI Corps had traveled ninety miles from Le Mans. They took a strongly fortified but virtually undefended large airport on the outskirts of Orleans. The next day, they entered the city after overcoming slight opposition. A separate column of the 320th Infantry marched to Chateaudun and took the town by noon on August 17.

At Chartres, elements of the Seventh Armored Division along with the Fifth Infantry Division converged in two columns on the city and overcame determined opposition. During the evening of August 16, the last Germans withdrew.

By the morning of August 16, the XV Corps advanced sixty miles from Argentan toward Dreux. The Fifth Armored Division met only light resistance. They encircled the town and occupied Dreux that afternoon.

August 16 and 17 were big days for the Allies. Patton's Third Army had entered or captured the major towns of Dreux, Chartres, Chateaudun, and Orleans. (See Map 23.) Patton wrote his wife a few days earlier about the operation: "This is better and much bigger than Sicily. . . . This is probably the fastest and biggest pursuit in history."[7]

With Patton on the Seine, Eisenhower finally took him out of the doghouse. He lifted the blackout curtain, and suddenly Patton's name captured US and British newspaper headlines. His heavily armored columns had liberated Brittany and were barreling eastward toward Paris. Almost overnight he became America's most popular general. Patton was also promoted to the rank of major general, regular army. His name would become a legend.[8]

In letters to his early mentors, General James G. Harbord and General Charles P. Summerall, Patton outlined the Third Army's innovative tactics and operational results:

> Our chief success was due to the fact that we cut the armored divisions loose and did not tie them to the infantry. However, we always kept one combat team of infantry motorized so that in the event of a serious situation, they would be available within a few hours to the armored divisions. . . . Our losses so far have been extremely small, and we have inflicted very heavy casualties on the enemy. . . . His loss of material is something unbelievable.[9]

Eisenhower decided to take full advantage of the Wehrmacht's evident collapse in France. At a meeting with Eisenhower, Bradley pushed forward a plan that allowed Patton to make a lightning drive to Metz and the German border. Both the geography and the present weak German defenses favored a rapid mobile assault through Lorraine and into Germany. The Third Army was already charging forward because of favorable conditions. If Patton continued this momentum, the Third Army would be on track to breach the German West Wall and cross the Rhine. All of Germany would lie open before Patton. Eisenhower approved this plan on August 18.[10]

At that same meeting, Eisenhower ordered a second attempt to close the Falaise gap with a long hook between Argentan and the lower Seine.[11] As related in chapter 10, this gap was finally closed on August 21.

By then the Third Army had advanced over four hundred miles in twenty-six days. It had killed, wounded, or captured over one hundred thousand Germans while eliminating more than five hundred tanks and approximately seven hundred artillery pieces. Patton's army suffered about sixteen thousand casualties, 13 percent of all US losses in Normandy. This low number was in large part owed to the initiative and daring of all ranks. They had been trained to make spectacular advances. Patton gave them the opportunity by strongly pushing against enemy opposition and using tactics that did not allow the enemy time to reorganize their defenses. Now on the lower Seine, the Third Army stood one hundred miles farther east than the rest of the Allicd armies. The British major general Hubert Essame believed that this army was in a strong strategic position, making it "a veritable thunderbolt capable, if hurled in the right direction, of inflicting a blow which would end the war in 1944."[12]

## A KING UNCROWNED

Although part of Patton's Third Army crossed the Seine on August 19, Eisenhower hoped to delay occupying Paris. Patton's rapid advance had already outrun the Allied supply lines. Ike wanted to avoid the burden of providing the three thousand to four thousand tons of food a day needed to feed the Paris population. He also wanted to avoid intervening in a volatile political situation. However his hand was forced by the Paris resistance movement and the political maneuvers of General de Gaulle.[13]

On August 18, a general strike was called in Paris. The unified Paris resistance force, which included de Gaulle's Free French, told the people to mobilize for resistance. At 7:00 a.m. the next day, two thousand striking Paris police seized the Prefecture de Police and raised the tricolor in its courtyard. The broad boulevards of Paris were blocked with trees and paving stones. An estimated fifteen thousand armed resistance fighters manned the Paris barricades.[14]

The Wehrmacht defenses to the west of Paris numbered about twenty thousand soldiers. But many were not high-quality combat troops. Inside the City of Light were about five thousand German troops, fifty light and medium artillery pieces, ten tanks, and around sixty aircraft at the Le Bourget airport.[15]

The Paris uprising had taken the new German military governor by surprise. Posted only two weeks earlier, General Dietrich von Choltitz was known for his great experience in defensive operations. Reportedly Hitler had ordered him to leave Paris a wasteland after conducting a ruthless fortress-styled defense: "[N]othing must be left standing, no church, no artistic monument."[16]

After gunfire had broken out across the city on August 20, the Swedish consul Raoul Nordling contacted Choltitz with the offer to arrange a truce. Choltitz agreed to this in principle, but he was wavering between obedience to Hitler's orders to destroy Paris, and leaving Paris intact while surrendering to the advancing Allies.[17]

On August 20 General de Gaulle arrived at Eisenhower's SHELLBURST headquarters in Normandy. Eisenhower patiently listened to de Gaulle's haughty ultimatum demanding the immediate liberation of Paris. Eisenhower reluctantly decided that the Allies must take action to head off a potential civil war between the French Communists, who were demanding a general election across France to form a rainbow popular government, and de Gaulle and his Free French forces, who sought to reassert the authority of the prewar French state. Eisenhower ordered Bradley to send Gerow's V Corps to aid Leclerc's French Second Armored Division in freeing the city.[18]

Martin Blumenson succinctly described the situation Eisenhower faced: "The only solution seemed to be that if the Germans were ready to quit the city without giving battle, the Allies ought to enter—for the prestige involved, to maintain order in the capital, to satisfy French requests, and also to secure the important Seine crossing sites there."[19]

However, before Eisenhower's orders reached Gerow, Leclerc had taken action on his own. He sent a 150-man detachment of French armor and infantry to carry out a detailed reconnaissance toward Versailles, a town near Paris. Leclerc and de Gaulle had decided that when Allied columns entered the capital, the Free French Army would be in the vanguard.[20]

When Gerow discovered this deployment he was furious and ordered its return. Leclerc ignored those instructions. On August 22, orders reached the V Corps for the Paris deployment. Leclerc was alerted as part of this operation.[21]

That evening a Citroen sedan carrying five civilians drove into the American lines. They told the local commander they had a message for General Eisenhower. This was a deputation from Paris consisting of representatives from the Swedish Consulate, a British agent, a de Gaulle representative, and a German officer in civilian clothes speaking for Choltitz. The next morning they were sent to Patton and informed him that they had come from Paris to arrange its surrender. Patton believed them but was irritated since he was under orders not to become involved in the liberation of Paris. He immediately sent this party by light aircraft to Bradley's headquarters at Laval.[22]

On August 23, Choltitz in a telephone conversation with Speidel, Model's chief of staff at Army Group B, said that he had complied with Hitler's demands to leave Paris a field of ruins by placing tons of explosives in Notre Dame Cathedral, the Invalides (where Napoleon is buried), and the Palais Bourbon (the French Chamber of Deputies). The Paris Opera and the Madeleine Church were also scheduled for destruction. He was prepared to level the Arc de Triomphe to clear a field of fire down the Champs-Élysées. Choltitz also had plans to dynamite the Eiffel Tower and use it to block the Seine, though he found it impossible to blow up the seventy-odd bridges in Paris. (Speidel later claimed that he diplomatically and indirectly urged Choltitz not to ruin the City of Light.)

Choltitz, however, ultimately decided not to destroy the French capital. He preferred to surrender and become an American POW, rather than face war crime charges as the infamous destroyer of a great European cultural center.[23]

Leclerc's division spent August 23 in a breakneck 120-mile dash toward Paris. He reached the suburbs by midafternoon, where he found de Gaulle in the suburban presidential residence awaiting his arrival.

The next morning, Leclerc opened his final assault, running a gauntlet of isolated German fire until by 9:30 a.m. his tanks came to a halt outside the Hotel de Ville (city hall). The arrival of Leclerc's tanks brought the bells of Paris to life, and his troops were mobbed by joyful crowds celebrating the end of years of occupation.

The same morning Leclerc contacted Choltitz, via the offices of the Swedish consul, and asked him to end all German fighting in the city. About 2:30 p.m. the first French soldiers reached the Meurice Hotel, the German army headquarters. They found Choltitz's office and invited him to surrender as the commander of "Gross-Paris."

A jeep took Choltitz to the Prefecture de Police. After conferring on the capitulation terms, Choltitz signed a typewritten document. An immediate ceasefire brought fighting to a halt by 7:00 p.m. Personnel was dispatched to defuse all the prepared demolitions and to relay the surrender message to outlying German defenses.[24]

On August 26 de Gaulle led the famous victory parade down the Champs-Élysées. The uncrowned king was heralded by the people of Paris who celebrated the end of German occupation in the tens of thousands. Closely following de Gaulle were Leclerc, General Marie-Pierre Koenig, a commander of the Free French Forces, and leaders of the French resistance. They proceeded from the Arc de Triomphe to Notre Dame Cathedral for a solemn Te Deum of national gratitude for deliverance from the Nazis.[25]

General de Gaulle had elevated himself to a position of the uncrowned leader of Free French. He propagated the myth that although France was indebted to the Allies and some foreign resisters for their military assistance, the French had liberated themselves and restored national honor, confidence, and unity. His speech to the crowd outside the Hotel de Ville in Paris when he first arrived in Paris on August 25, 1944, encapsulates his assertions: "Paris liberated! Liberated by its own efforts, liberated by its people with the help of the armies of France, with the help of all of France, that is France in combat. The one France, the true France, eternal France."[26]

Fig. 11.1. General Charles de Gaulle at the liberation of Paris. August 26, 1944. (Imperial War Museums, Ministry of Information, Second World War Press Agency Print Collection)

While de Gaulle was publicly asserting his preeminence as the leader of France, he privately asked Eisenhower to give him two US divisions for a show of force to guarantee his authority. As he was the self-appointed head of his Provisional Government of the Republic of France, he was still in a precarious position with the French people.

Eisenhower was quite willing to give de Gaulle his show of force. He also wanted the people of France to clearly understand that de Gaulle had reached Paris by the grace of God and the strength of the Allied OVERLORD campaign.

Eisenhower therefore had General Norman Cota's Twenty-Eighth Infantry Division moved up from Versailles and bivouacked at Bois de

Boulogne in Paris. There the men cleaned their uniforms and equipment from the thirty-six days of dirt and grime in the battle line. They got two sets of orders: one for the parade and the second for their battle as they marched first for glory and then straight into combat.

August 29 was a sunny day as the newly polished US Twenty-Eighth Division deployed into columns with loaded guns and full bandoliers. They swung down the Champs-Élysées from the Arc de Triomphe to the densely packed Place de la Concorde reviewed by Bradley, Gerow, de Gaulle, Koenig, and Leclerc.[27]

Many people remembered how only four years earlier the conquering German Wehrmacht had marched along the same route to the tears and stunned disbelief of the Parisians. US veteran Raymond Sola at age one hundred reminisced on what he saw and felt as he marched on that August day: "I saw the joy and great adulation of the people of Paris as they watched us march past to restore their freedom."[28]

Fig. 11.2. The US Twenty-Eighth Infantry marches down the Champs-Élysées. (US Army)

The division then continued through the city northward to Saint Denis. The Germans greeted their arrival with a short artillery barrage.

Eisenhower's decision to liberate Paris, taken on his own authority, was one of his most important decisions as the SHAEF supreme commander. By giving de Gaulle the opportunity to occupy the Elysee Palace (France's presidential residence), he had installed a new government in France and prevented the real threat of a civil war. He also helped to save Paris from destruction and gave de Gaulle the means to resurrect France from the disastrous defeat of 1940 to again assume a great power status in the postwar reconstruction of Europe.[29]

In liberating France since D-Day, the United States sustained over 125,000 casualties. The people of France also paid a heavy price. Almost one thousand members of the French resistance had died in the six-day Paris insurrection. Seventy thousand French civilians were killed by Allied actions (mainly bombing during the war). This number is greater than the total of British civilian deaths from the German bombing of England.[30]

While Paris was being liberated, Operation ANVIL, the second Allied invasion of France, was launched on August 15 in the south of France. One of its goals was to land French troops to support de Gaulle's new government in Paris.

## "DRAGOONED" INTO ANVIL

Since August 1943, American planners had called for an invasion of southern France in support of OVERLORD. Eisenhower wanted this operation so that the Allied armies could be supplied through the port of Marseilles as well as through Antwerp. He also wanted General Alexander Patch's American Seventh Army and General Jean de Lattre de Tassigny's First French Army deployed to take part in the future invasion of southern Germany.

The British never stopped trying to stop ANVIL, or DRAGOON as Churchill renamed it, because the Americans had "dragooned" him into it. Churchill and the British Chiefs of Staff opposed this invasion because it would take several divisions away from the Mediterranean theater, especially the Italian front. The British advocated an amphibious operation landing at Trieste that would advance through the Ljubljana Gap in the Balkans and take Budapest and Vienna. Churchill sought to prevent a postwar Soviet domination of Eastern Europe stretching down to the Adriatic.

After being delayed several times because the sealift capacity was needed for OVERLORD, DRAGOON was finally launched on August 15. As an amphibious invasion it was second only to OVERLORD, comprising 300,000 troops, one thousand ships, and several thousand aircraft.[31]

On this D-Day, a predawn nine-thousand-man airborne assault preceded the landings of sixty-six thousand soldiers. Resistance was light, resulting in fewer than four hundred casualties but over 2,300 German prisoners.[32]

The Allied invasion along the Côte d'Azur from Nice and Marseilles was virtually unopposed. The major port of Marseilles was secured almost intact. This second invasion triggered a hurried Wehrmacht retreat from central and southwestern France. Even Hitler, for once, was forced to recognize that he had to evacuate this territory.

In only one month, far ahead of projected results, the American and French armies had virtually eliminated the entire German Nineteenth Army. They bagged over 100,000 prisoners and liberated two-thirds of southern France. The American Seventh Army and French First Army marched 475 miles north of the Riviera landing beaches to converge with the OVERLORD armies for the invasion of Germany. (See Map 23.)

Of great importance was the seizure of two main objectives, the ports of Marseilles and Toulon, in less than half the time the planners had projected. In the last three months of 1944, about one-third of the supplies and troops needed by the Allies were put ashore at these ports. As we will examine in the next chapter, Montgomery failed to make the Port of Antwerp fully operable until January 1945. It was not until then that Marseilles was superseded as SHAEF's major port. Even with Antwerp, about 25 percent of the weapons and shells used to defeat Nazi Germany went through Marseilles.[33]

Eisenhower always defended his decision to launch Operation DRAGOON both because of its important logistical contribution and its rapid success in securing southern France. After the war Eisenhower wrote, "There was no development of that period which added more decisively to our advantages or aided us more in accomplishing the final and complete defeat of German forces than did this attack coming up the Rhône Valley [from the Riviera]."[34]

## "VICTORY DISEASE"–A SHORT-LIVED MALADY

With the fall of Paris and the Third Army's rapid advances to the Seine, Eisenhower, Bradley, and other commanders began thinking that the war in Europe might soon be over. This "victory disease" raised the morale at SHAEF to new heights after the earlier months of stalemate. "Militarily the war is over," said Walter Bedell Smith, Eisenhower's chief of staff.[35]

This "victory disease" would be a short-lived malady due to three major factors—logistics problems, three competing plans for launching an invasion into Germany, and command indecision. Logistics remained a key issue throughout this campaign.

SHAEF's logistical services became known as "Communications Zone" or COM Z. It faced two overwhelming obstacles: a lack of adequate port facilities and the limited ability to transport supplies to the ever-advancing front lines.

Until the seizure of Marseilles, all of the Allied army's supplies were being unloaded over the Normandy beaches. The supply problem only increased as the lines of communication rapidly advanced eastward. Also as Allied forces advanced, they were confronted with bridges and railroads destroyed by the Germans or by Allied bombing. The army engineers could not repair them quickly enough to keep up with the Third Army's lightning advance and the needs of the other Allied armies.

Admiral Ramsay had repeatedly warned Eisenhower and his generals that the logistical needs of OVERLORD required the capture of useable port facilities. His warnings were ignored, reflecting the traditional army subordination of logistics to operational imperatives.

## THE FIRST PLAN: BRADLEY-PATTON'S SOUTHERN THRUST: THE UNFORGIVING MINUTE

On August 18, Eisenhower approved Bradley's plan for a major Allied drive south of the Ardennes. (See Map 24.) Patton was given two extra divisions for a push to the Siegfried Line. The US Third and First armies were to advance through France to the Saar industrial area, cross the Rhine, take Frankfort, and advance northeast to the Ruhr.

Patton's memoirs contains his plans for this thrust:

> On the twentieth of August at Bradley's Headquarters, I saw a map study which completely confirmed the line of advance which Bradley and I had favored since the beginning, namely, to drive through with two corps abreast and the third one echeloned to the right rear on the general axis, Nancy—Château Salins—Saarguemines—Mainz or Worms, then northeast through Frankfurt. . . . I was convinced then . . . there were no Germans ahead of us except those we were actually fighting. In other words, they had no depth. It was on this day that I definitely decided not to waste capturing Metz, but to contain it with as few troops as possible and drive for the Rhine.[36]

A serious supply problem had to be addressed before launching a Third Army drive to the German border. As the railroad lines were severely damaged, motor transport had to fill the gap.

In these desperate days to keep the advance moving, the so-called "Red Ball Express" was born out of a thirty-six-hour brainstorming session of American commanders. ("Red Ball" was a railroad express-shipping term.) On August 23, COM Z organized a special truck road route from the Normandy beaches to Chartres and Dreux. During its first eight days the Red Ball Express used nearly six thousand vehicles to deliver almost ninety thousand tons of supplies to depots nearer the front.[37]

The Red Ball Express, however, was not a viable solution to fuel-supply problems. Each day the Third Army consumed about 400,000 gallons of fuel, but it was estimated that about the Red Ball trucks consumed nearly 300,000 gallons daily getting to the front. Only the capture of thirty-seven carloads of German gasoline and oil at Sens allowed the Third Army offensive to begin east of the Seine. Other captured supplies filled important voids. Over three hundred miles of captured German telephone wire replaced used Allied stocks. Twenty-five tons of medical equipment was captured at two different locations.[38]

Airlifts also transported vital supplies. On August 25, 257 planes landed at Orleans with over five hundred tons of rations and other supplies. The next day another airlift brought eighty tons of medical supplies.[39]

Between August 20 and August 22, Patton concluded from intelligence reports that it was possible to drive into Germany through the West Wall within ten days, as the Germans would not be able to place reinforcements fast enough to block the Third Army's advance.[40]

On August 25, the Third Army set out to put Patton's assessment to the test. That day the Fourth Armored Division captured the bridgehead across the Seine south of Paris at Troyes. (See Map 23.) For the next three days, Patton toured his advanced forces and found that German opposition continued to be sporadic and confused.

On the next day, the XX Corps seized Romilly, while the XII Corps was moving toward Chalons. Then on August 28, the Eightieth Infantry Division attacked from Troyes and, by noon on August 29, took Chalons in a squeeze play. Wood's Fourth Armored Division charged about fifty miles from Troyes to the east bank of the Marne and importantly captured a German fuel depot of over 100,000 gallons of gasoline.

Also on August 28 the Seventh Armored moved through Château-Thierry and captured several Marne River bridges. Reims was encircled by the Fifth Infantry Division and fell easily on August 30. By noon on August 31, the Seventh Infantry Division had driven seventy miles to Verdun where it rolled through the town and across the river. By September 1, the XX Corps and XII Corps had jumped across the Meuse in strength. Their advanced patrols were approaching the Moselle River closing on Metz and Nancy. (See Map 23.) The Rhine was just over ninety miles beyond the Moselle.

The Third Army moved relentlessly onward. The German front was disintegrating. By August 29, Model realized that the Allies had absolute tactical superiority and had the ability to completely destroy German military forces in the west. Model had barely one hundred tanks available with only 570 aircraft to support them. The Allied superiority was twenty to one in tanks and twenty-five to one in aircraft.[41] A proposed German defensive line on the Somme never materialized. An OB West diary termed the situation an "ignominious rout" and stated that soldiers without white flags surrendered by waving chickens.[42] General Gunther Blumentritt, chief of staff of OB West, later gave this blunt summary of the German collapse on this front: "There were no German Forces behind the Rhine and at the end of August our front was wide open."[43]

As described in chapter 9, Patton's Household Cavalry, his mobile intelligence force, was deployed to identify lightly held, even vacant sectors in the German lines through which his armored forces could quickly advance, thus penetrating the enemy's rear. This strategy was a modern adaptation of Napoleon Bonaparte's concept of the "indirect approach." Patton used a mechanized variation of Napoleon's flank attack that penetrated to the enemy's rear, thereby upsetting the Germans' defensive balance and triggering confusion and disorder. Patton used his armor like cavalry by splitting them up into small independent combat groups that led to the destruction of the enemy by placing the turning force across the Germans' line of retreat.

Fig. 11.3. Patton's Third Army advances across France. (US Army)

In another era General Robert E. Lee had used another variation of this strategy on a much larger scale. He sent General Stonewall Jackson's corps on a long flanking maneuver at the battle of Chancellorsville in 1863. Stonewall struck General Hooker's Army of the Potomac in its flank and rear, causing confusion, retreat, and potentially the destruction of a major part of the Northern army. Jackson's accidental death in the midst of this battle helped to prevent a Union catastrophe but still resulted in a major Union military defeat.

Patton's tactics were used on a much smaller unit basis adapted to the absence of organized German resistance. It was a motorized advance by tanks, trucks, and jeeps that sped toward distant objectives. The Third Army's accelerated movement negated the Wehrmacht's skillful ability to organize and defend natural terrain barriers. Patton had perfected this type of opportunistic, elastic pursuit warfare that swept an overpowering Third Army to the border of Germany.[44]

Patton believed that he could rupture the Siegfried Line before the Germans reinforced and reequipped it. On August 30 due to the Third Army's rapid advance to the Meuse, Patton wrote in his diary, "It is terrible to halt, even on the Meuse. We should cross the Rhine in the vicinity of Worms, and the faster we do it, the less lives and munitions it will take. No one realizes the terrible value of the 'unforgiving minute' except me. Some way I will get on yet."[45]

On that same day he had met with Bradley and Major General Harold Bull of Eisenhower's staff. Patton pointed out to them that Allied intelligence showed that the Germans facing Montgomery in the north still deployed considerable strength while in the south the "enemy is weak and disorganized." He further stated he could break through a thinly manned West Wall in a few days with light losses. "But if we permit the Hun to man those massive emplacements, it'll take weeks and thousands of casualties."[46] Patton's evaluation proved correct.

On August 31, Patton's spearheads were barely thirty miles from the Saar industrial area and less than one hundred miles from the Rhine (see Map 23). At that moment the Germans had deployed only five undermanned divisions equipped with few anti-tank guns to hold the Moselle against six strong American spearhead divisions.

But at this strategic moment in the Third Army's advance, Patton faced a formidable obstacle. Competing pressures for gasoline and the means to deliver it became a crucial battleground. The battle for Europe had become a battle over gasoline. Patton, though feeling he was on the cusp of a great victory, lamented to his wife, "Look at the map! If I could only steal some gas, I could win this war."[47] Patton told Bradley, "[J]ust give me 400,000 gallons of gasoline and I'll put you inside Germany in two days."[48] Yet Patton's pleas for the gasoline his forces needed fell on deaf ears. What were the factors behind the decision to deny Patton's request?

## THE SECOND PLAN: MONTGOMERY'S "FULL-BLOODED THRUST"

While Patton's forces advanced through France, General Montgomery was conducting a multipronged campaign to keep his position as the commander of the ground forces and win acceptance for his competing plan for a northern thrust. On August 19 Eisenhower informed both Bradley and Montgomery that he would finally take over as ground commander on September 1. He ordered Montgomery to advance and take Antwerp and from there drive on the Ruhr. Bradley was to advance from Paris toward Metz.

The change in ground command had always been planned but much delayed by Eisenhower. Montgomery, however, was furious over his "demotion." He sent de Guingand to Ike, telling him the victory to date had been won by his personal command. The Allied forces needed to continue to operate under his single control. De Guingand delivered a missive from Montgomery that stated, "This is a WHOLE TIME job for one man. . . . To change the system of command now, after having won a great victory, would prolong the war."[49] Eisenhower politely listened to de Guingand but refused to budge.

On August 17 Montgomery went to Bradley's headquarters to enlist his support for the northern thrust. His diary for that day states, "Bradley agreed entirely with my outline plan."[50]

Then on August 23, just before a scheduled meeting with Eisenhower, Monty again flew to Bradley's headquarters to make an eleventh-hour appeal for his northern thrust. Bradley relates what happened: "By that time, I had heard about Monty's outlandish demands for Ike to abdicate and I knew that Monty had been falsely stating that I agreed with his master plan. My reception was frosty. . . . I had not changed my mind. I had *never* agreed to the main features of Monty's plan."[51]

Later that day when Eisenhower arrived with his chief of staff, Walter Bedell Smith, Montgomery insisted they meet alone in his command trailer. Eisenhower acquiesced to this insulting arrangement even though de Guingand stayed with Monty. Montgomery then patronizingly lectured Ike on his plan in which the Twenty-First Army would mount a single thrust to the Ruhr with the American First Army in support.

Montgomery's viewpoint was that the Americans already had their day in the Normandy campaign and now it was Britain's turn. They had held down most of the Wehrmacht forces, while Patton's spectacular advance met little resistance. But this would not be an all-British show as Lieutenant General Courtney Hodges of the American First Army would also take part.

Eisenhower told him, "The American public would never stand for stopping Patton in full cry, and public opinion wins wars."[52]

"Nonsense," Monty rebuked him. "Victories win war. Give people victory and they won't care who won it."

Leaving Allied politics aside, throwing everything to the north ignored current battlefield conditions as in the south the Germans were clearly more vulnerable. Eisenhower refused to take such a high-risk gamble: "I knew that any pencil-like thrust into the heart of Germany would meet nothing but certain destruction. . . . I would not consider it."[53]

Unable to move Eisenhower on either the command issue or an exclusive offensive, Montgomery shifted his ground on what support he could realize for an advance toward Germany. For the time being he wanted to have Patton halted in place. He sought to take Pas-de-Calais, Antwerp, and Brussels and go beyond toward the Ruhr. (See Map 25.) To achieve this, Montgomery wanted the airborne army for paratroop operations and the First Army assigned to him, and all available supplies.

Eisenhower eventually agreed to give Montgomery operational control of the airborne divisions and the First Army. Monty would receive "top priority" in supplies, but Ike insisted on continuing to build up the strength of the Third Army for an advance toward Metz.

Most importantly Eisenhower told Montgomery he must first capture Antwerp and get it functioning as a supply port before thrusting northeast toward the Ruhr. He also gave priority to knocking out the V-weapons launching sites causing havoc in London.

Even though in principle Eisenhower and Montgomery reached agreement on these orders, Montgomery and Dempsey had already rejected the possibility of opening Antwerp and the other channel ports thereby pocketing the German Fifteenth Army that had been deployed around Calais. Even after Monty's agreement to terms at the August 23 meeting, their attention remained fastened on a rapid thrust over the Rhine. Incredibly Montgomery's own logistical planners naively told him that once the Seine and Channel ports began operating they would be able to logistically sustain the Twenty-First Army Group's eastward advance into Germany. This caused Monty to proclaim, "I don't need Antwerp." This directly contradicted what Admiral Ramsay and SHAEF logistical planners had determined was required to sustain the offensive.[54]

## THE THIRD PLAN: EISENHOWER'S BROAD FRONT

During the end of August Eisenhower began discussions on another strategy—a broad front for the next phase of the Allied operation in Europe. In the spring of 1944, SHAEF planners presented alternative plans after the Normandy breakthrough to end the war. Among them was capturing the Ruhr Valley in the industrial German heartland that kept the Nazi war machine operating. This goal became center stage in August 1944.

There were four invasion routes to the Ruhr from northern France: through Flanders; along the northern edge of the Ardennes Forest; through the Ardennes; and south of the Ardennes through Metz, the Saar, and Frankfurt.

Eisenhower envisioned a double envelopment of the Ruhr: Montgomery's Twenty-First Army Group as the northern pincer, and Bradley's Twelfth Army Group, the southern component to complete a double envelopment. With its industrial base eliminated, the combined Allied forces could advance at will on Berlin and occupy all of Germany.

An essential component of the "broad-front" plan included opening up the major ports of Antwerp and Marseilles. They would provide the necessary logistical support for the Allied drive into Germany. Eisenhower envisioned Montgomery and Bradley's drives as two pincers that would meet behind the Ruhr in a great encirclement. Above all, Eisenhower was absolutely clear that without both ports operating at full capacity, the Allies could not sustain their advance to the Rhine and Berlin.[55] (See Map 26.)

From Eisenhower's standpoint the broad-front strategy also was an avenue for keeping the Grand Alliance intact at this critical stage in the war. Triumph would be shared by both Montgomery and Bradley's armies. Eisenhower as supreme commander was determined that neither the British nor American forces alone would win the final victory in Europe.[56]

The problem Eisenhower faced in August was that he could not deploy both pincers of his broad front. He could only deliver enough fuel for one army to advance without first taking Antwerp and getting its port facilities up and running. Antwerp was clearly in Montgomery's zone of operations.

The other issue was the state of the German army. Could it successfully resist a further Allied thrust into Germany? Perhaps the most accurate picture of German defensive capabilities at that time came from Speidel, chief of staff of Army Group B, and Blumentritt, chief of staff in the West. By the last week of August, Speidel described the Allied advance as "a foaming torrent" that had swallowed up the remnants of both the Seventh Army and the Fiftieth Panzer Army. Inside Germany there were no reserve ground forces of any significance to reinforce the western front. The current battles on the eastern front with the Russian army in East Prussia and Hungary were at their climax. They had consumed all available German reserves.[57]

## DRIVEN COMMANDERS FIGHT OVER PLANS AND SUPPLIES

Many forms of opposition and counterproposals arose to these three plans. They were triggered by differing command perspectives and national rivalries. Supplies remained a key issue.

### The American Commanders Fight for Gasoline

After Eisenhower's August 23 meeting with Montgomery, Bradley was incensed over what had transpired. He spent two days with Ike arguing over giving the American First Army to Montgomery. Tedder also agreed with Bradley. They were joined in opposing Montgomery's plan by General Kenneth Strong, Eisenhower's intelligence officer (G-2), and General Harold Bull, his operation's officer (G-3).

Ike yielded to their combined pressure and changed his directives. Instead of giving Montgomery operational control of the First Army, on August 28 Eisenhower directed that Montgomery was only "authorized to effect," through Bradley, "any necessary coordination between his own forces" and the First Army.[58]

Giving Montgomery top priority in supplies resulted in stopping the Third Army's thrust into Germany dead in its armored tracks. Trucks that were bringing gasoline and other supplies to Patton's forces were diverted to Hodges's First Army. In addition when Ike transferred the Airborne Army to Montgomery, he also took away the air transport fuel supply that supplemented the deliveries of the Red Ball Express. Cargo aircraft were held in readiness for paratrooper operations.

Eisenhower had approved Montgomery's plan to use the airborne to clear a path for his northern thrust. An airborne drop was planned at Tournai on September 3 to help trap the German Fifteenth Army. (See Map 23.) Bradley pleaded with Eisenhower and Montgomery to cancel this drop so that Patton would have enough gas to get inside Germany, but Eisenhower refused to listen. Then at the last moment Monty canceled the operation.[59]

On August 30 Bradley ordered Patton to stop at the Meuse because no gasoline was available for him. Patton immediately protested to Bradley. At a September 2 meeting at Chartres with Eisenhower, Bradley, Hodges, and Hoyt Vandenberg (the new commander of the Ninth Air Force), Patton made his plea directly to Eisenhower: "We had patrols on the Moselle near Nancy. . . . If you let me retain my regular allotment of tonnage, Ike, we could push on to the German frontier and rupture that Goddamn Siegfried Line. I'm willing to stake my reputation on that."[60]

"Careful, George," Eisenhower replied, "that reputation of yours hasn't been worth very much."

"That reputation is pretty good now," Patton responded.

Patton did not give up. With Bradley's persuasive support they both argued for at least an equal share with Monty's Twenty-First Army. "We have an excellent plan, Ike," Patton pleaded, "for a drive through the Nancy-Epinal gap. The Siegfried Line isn't manned yet, and the Huns have little if anything in the area to stop us. If you let me go and give me what we need, we can be in Germany at the Rhine in 10 days."[61]

Eisenhower would not budge. All Ike offered to Bradley and Patton was that he would allow the V Corps of the First Army and the Third Army to go back on the offensive once the Calais area ports had been taken by Montgomery.

## The British Seek to Stay in Control

The British objected both to Eisenhower's assumption of the ground command and a broad-front strategy. On August 28 Alan Brooke wrote in his diary,

> Difficult C.O.S. [Combined Operating Staffs] meeting where we considered Eisenhower's new plan to take command himself in Northern France on September 1st. This plan is likely to add another three to six months on to the war. He straight away wants to split his force, sending an American contingent towards Nancy whilst the British Army Group moves along the coast. If the Germans were not as beat as they are this would be a fatal move. . . . In any case I am off to France tomorrow to see Monty and to discuss the situation with him.[62]

Fig. 11.4. General Dwight D. Eisenhower, Omar Bradley, and George S. Patton. (Everett Collection, Inc./Alamy Stock Photo)

Encouraged by Brooke's low opinion of Eisenhower's military qualities, Montgomery confided to his diary that the supreme commander "did not know Christmas from Easter."[63]

At the September 2 Chartres meeting the implementation of a broad-front strategy was also discussed. On September 4 Eisenhower authorized his headquarters to issue an order calling for the forces north of the

Ardennes "to secure Antwerp, breach the sector of the Siegfried Line covering the Ruhr and then seize the Ruhr."[64] The southern forces were to proceed to the Rhine and through the Saar and to seize Frankfort.

Montgomery immediately sent a furious response to Eisenhower stating that there were not sufficient supplies for two fronts and that such a strategy would prolong the war. Montgomery asserted that his northern thrust had "reached a stage where one really powerful and full-blooded thrust toward Berlin is likely to get there and end the German war."[65]

## CHANGED PLANS EXACT A HEAVY PRICE

On September 5 Patton accumulated enough fuel to resume his offensive, helped by the capture of 100,000 gallons in a German fuel depot. But by then the German forces had time to reorganize, and they now appeared in strength to block his offensive. By the next day, he abandoned his immediate effort to cross the Moselle. Patton was dismayed. He wrote to his wife, "All this comes from the fatal decision of the Supreme Commander . . . to halt the Third Army until the Pas-de-Calais area is cleaned up."[66]

Worse was yet to come for Patton. He lost the race to the Siegfried Line. On September 11, units of the American First US Army successfully broke through the West Wall. Patton was embarrassed, since his most forward units were still twenty-five miles from the Siegfried Line.

Once again a great opportunity to end the war in Europe had slipped through Patton's hands. His September 11 diary entry says it all: "I wish people would stop making plans and changing their minds."[67]

The delays caused by Eisenhower's attempts at compromise and his changes in strategic plans exacted a heavy price. Of the 750,000 casualties the Allies incurred in liberating Western Europe, 500,000 were after September's lost victory.[68]

## "PURSUIT WITHOUT PAUSE"

Liddell Hart agreed with Patton that the final days in August 1944 were the "unforgiving minute." The Germans were still in shock, defenses unprepared, and all the Rhine bridges were still intact. A powerful punch by Patton, a pursuit without pause, offered a good strategy to trigger the total collapse of the German army in the West. "The best chance of a quick finish," Hart concludes, "was probably lost when the 'gas' was turned off from Patton's tanks."[69]

Fig. 11.5. The Thirty-Ninth Infantry Brigade of the US Army crossing the Siegfried Line in Germany. September 1944. (US Army)

Eisenhower's compromise strategy threw away the best opportunity to quickly end the war. Yet August 1944 was a remarkable month in the history of warfare. The tide of battle in Normandy ended in the rout of the German army. "The war could have easily ended in September 1944," Hart assures us.[70] Nigel Hamilton also agrees: "Had Eisenhower accepted Patton's Plan . . . a week before the fall of Paris, World War II might have well been won that year."[71]

What would have occurred if Patton's plan had been used instead of Montgomery's? Without doubt the Third Army and elements of the First

Army would have reached German soil. Patton would have penetrated the West Wall. In fact the area chosen for his attack was one of the more run-down and vulnerable parts of the Siegfried Line. If properly supplied, the Americans could have succeeded as the southern pincer against the Ruhr.

After the war, German general Siegfried Westphal, who was chief of staff of OB West at this time, affirmed the disastrous condition of the West Wall in August 1944 and stated what his conclusions in that period were:

> Had the Allies assigned all available ground and air tonnage for the transport of fuel, and had they used airborne units to establish bridge-heads east of the Rhine, it would have been possible for them to penetrate deeply into the Reich, push the West Front up against the East Front, and win the war before the end of the year 1944.[72]

As the British major general and military historian Hubert Essame concluded, "Providence had given Eisenhower the greatest cavalry leader [Patton] and as good an army as his country had ever produced: at the decisive moment he failed to use them."[73]

# CHAPTER 12
# THE ANTWERP/MARKET GARDEN FIASCOS

"Monty's big mistake, as the war moved to its final phase, was to allow his unassailable self-belief to blind him to certain new realities. Politics would not allow him to carry on giving the orders to great armies of Americans simply because, in his view, he was better than their generals."

—Mark Urban, author of
*Generals: The British Commanders Who Shaped the World*[1]

## STARS ON THEIR SHOULDERS

On September 1, Eisenhower assumed direct operational command of the ground forces in northern Europe. Ike had little choice. Marshall insisted on this as the preponderance of armed forces in this region was now American. US public opinion demanded action over the command question. Also the muddled Falaise operation acutely demonstrated the need for more unified command decisions.

Montgomery and Brooke resisted this change until the eleventh hour. Now Monty reverted to a position of command equality with Bradley as the British/Canadian army group commander. As Churchill anticipated intense censure from the British press and people, he arranged for Monty's promotion to field marshal. Now he outranked Eisenhower, his new boss, five stars to Ike's four. Monty and the British would continue to fight a prolonged rearguard action over who was really in command to the end of the war.[2]

Not every British commander was pleased with his promotion, Admiral Ramsay noted in his diary: "Monty made a Field Marshal. Astounding thing to do and I regret it more than I can say. . . . An insult to Ike & to America."[3]

Churchill's gesture seems most quixotic in view of the fact that the prime minister was almost surely aware that the US Congress was reactivating the rank of five-star general of the army. Eisenhower would be one of the first generals so appointed.[4]

Brooke, Monty's mentor, gave him some sage counsel in a congratulatory letter: "I should like at this moment of your triumph to offer you one more word of advice. Don't let success go to your head and remember the value of humility."[5] This sound exhortation did not guide Monty's past, present, or future behavior.

## ANTWERP: A KEY OBJECTIVE

On August 29, Montgomery launched his most spectacular drive of the European campaign. Once the Allied armies had crossed the Seine, they advanced rapidly through the north of France, and by the beginning of September, the British Second Army had crossed into Belgium. This drive was spearheaded by General Brian Horrocks's XXX Corps that surged ahead at an awe-inspiring speed, crossing the Seine east of Rouen to trap remnants of the German Seventh Army. The British advanced 250 miles in six days. (See Map 27.) Horrocks reached Amiens on August 31. Lille and Brussels also were soon liberated. Meanwhile Hodges's three American corps, now attached to the British Second Army, closed on Mons, Belgium, capturing twenty-five thousand German troops, the remains of about twenty shattered divisions left from the Normandy campaign.[6]

Meanwhile Lieutenant General Henry Crerar's First Canadian Army cleared the channel ports, taking Dieppe and encircling the German Fifteenth Army at Le Havre, Calais, and Dunkirk. The Canadians also took Ostend that fell without delay. Boulogne withstood a siege by the Canadians until September 22, Calais fell on October 1, but Dunkirk was not liberated until the war's end in May 1945. All these ports were wrecked by the Germans, preventing a quick fix to the Allies' serious supply crisis.

Fig. 12.1. Lieutenant General Henry Crerar. (Library and Archives Canada)

## THE IMPORTANCE OF ANTWERP: DIFFERING PERSPECTIVES

The real solution to the Allies' logistics nightmare was Antwerp, which was a major port in Europe with thirty miles of docks and over six hundred cranes that could handle sixty thousand tons of cargo daily. It was only sixty-five miles from the Allied forward supply depots, thus offering greatly reduced rail or truck haulage for the Allied invasion of the German Reich.

On September 4, the Eleventh Armored Division, commanded by Major General G. P. B. "Pip" Roberts (at thirty-seven the youngest major general in the British army), captured Antwerp, with its port, the second largest in Western Europe. Thanks to their quick arrival, and the heroism of the Belgium underground, the giant harbor complex fell into their hands largely undamaged. The excellent Belgian railway network, electrically operated sluice gates, and cranes were ready to receive shipping that day.

Fig. 12.2. Antwerp Harbor. 1944–45. (© Imperial War Museums [A 26597])

The sudden fall of Antwerp caught the Germans completely by surprise. For once the advance of Montgomery's forces surpassed the enemy's expectations. But at this moment of great triumph, Montgomery threw away a great victory by failing to occupy the islands of the Scheldt Estuary. Rundstedt, seeing this mistake, immediately moved sixty thousand men of the German

Fifteenth Army to block the mouth of the Port of Antwerp. Monty instead chose to begin Operation MARKET GARDEN, the attempted drive to the Rhine and the Ruhr. (Discussed later in this chapter.)[7]

An eighty-mile estuary separates the Port of Antwerp from the North Sea. The Scheldt River with its two fortified islands, Walcheren on the north bank and Breken on the south bank, controlled access to the port. (See Map 28.) Monty disregarded the supreme logistical importance to the entire Allied campaign of clearing the Scheldt and thereby opening the port.

Admiral Ramsay, the author of the NEPTUNE plan, noted in his diary on September 4, "British in Brussels and Antwerp. Latter port not badly damaged but of course it is useless until the estuary and its approaches are cleared of the enemy to permit M/S [minesweeping] to be carried out."[8] From the outset of OVERLORD, Ramsay realized that Antwerp had the capacity to handle the bulk of supplies needed to carry the Allied offensive deep into Germany, thus resolving their considerable logistical problems. Therefore his NEPTUNE plan advocated giving priority to its capture and also securing other ports to the east of the beachhead. In September 1944 the Allies were still entirely dependent on the mulberry harbor at Arromanches and the supplies landing by LST on Omaha Beach. The captured ports of Marseille and Toulon in southern France were not yet functioning. With winter approaching, Ramsay was uncomfortably aware of Normandy's vulnerability to bad weather, recalling the loss of the American mulberry following the June gale. (See chapter 7.)

On September 3, the day before Antwerp was taken, Ramsay cabled SHAEF with copies to the Twenty-First Army Group, the Admiralty, and the commander in chief at the Nore (the British naval command based at Chatham) to warn them:

> It is essential that if both Antwerp and Rotterdam . . . are to be opened quickly the enemy must be prevented from: (i). Carrying out demolitions and blocking in ports. (ii). Mining and block Scheldt. . . .
>
> 2. Both Antwerp and Rotterdam are highly vulnerable to mining and blocking. If enemy succeeds in these operations the time it will take to open ports cannot be estimated.
>
> 3. It will be necessary for coastal batteries to be captured before approach channels to the river routes can be established.[9]

Yet Montgomery did not brief General Horrocks or General Philip Roberts, commander of the Eleventh Armored Division, on the vital need to immediately secure the Scheldt Estuary when they reached Antwerp. After the war Horrocks wrote, "It never entered my head that the Scheldt would be mined, and that we should not be able to use Antwerp port until the channel had been swept and the Germans cleared from the coastline on either side."[10]

Roberts also felt betrayed as he had only vague maps of the port to work from.[11] In an interview with Richard Lamb, he said, "Monty's failure at Antwerp is evidence again that he was not a good general at seizing opportunities. My thoughts, like Horrocks' and Monty's, on 4 September were east to the Rhine. We should have looked west towards Walcheren. . . . I made mistakes at Antwerp because I was not briefed that the Albert Canal was one of the most formidable obstacles in Europe. We only had small-scale maps, and I only saw it as a thin blue line on my map."[12]

But in September 1944, Monty's ruffled vanity led him to demand a "full-blooded thrust" to the Rhine, Ruhr, and Berlin. For him Antwerp was secondary, off his personal command radar. He had declared his thrust was "to keep the enemy on the run straight through to the Rhine, and 'bounce' our way across the river before the enemy succeeded in reforming a front to oppose us."[13] This sounds like a lesson from Patton's playbook.

Yet after rapidly taking Brussels and Antwerp on September 3, the British sat idle until September 7, ordered by Monty to pause for repairs and replacement. The magnitude of his error was quickly evident as Hitler rushed reinforcements to the Albert Canal (which links Antwerp to Liège). When the British armor attacked on September 7, German defenses were strong. Horrocks's XXX Corps struggled to breach the canal.[14]

In view of the increasingly serious Allied logistical problems, Ramsay had no doubt that a combined operation to remove the Wehrmacht from the Scheldt should be given top priority. He advocated giving SHAEF's cardinal military priority to seizing the Dutch islands of Walcheren and South Beveland on the north bank of the Scheldt and that part of Belgium known as the Breskens Pocket on the river's south bank, followed by clearing the mines from these waters.

On September 10, Ramsay wrote in his diary, "Had fixed up to go to Brussels with Eisenhower to see Monty but these arrangements were cancelled & he went only with Tedder. I particularly wished to be there to press for Army to clear entrances to the Scheldte [sic] to enable Antwerp to be used."[15] Ramsay's absence from this key meeting was to have disastrous consequences for the Allies. Had he been present he would have vigorously argued the case for giving priority to opening the Scheldt rather than to MARKET GARDEN. It is difficult to believe that Eisenhower would have disregarded the arguments of a trusted colleague who was still chiefly responsible for conveying supplies across the English Channel to keep the Allied armies advancing.

As Robert Love and John Major point out, "Ramsay's absence showed how marginal naval considerations were to the military high command now that the land campaign was moving onto high gear."[16] Unfortunately, once the D-Day invasion had been successfully completed and the Allied navies had secured control of the channel, Ramsay held a somewhat marginal position at SHAEF. The generals had come to believe that the naval phase of the campaign was over, and they did not need to consult him on strategic matters, which they believed were the prerogative of the army and the air force. Given his extensive experience with interservice cooperation and the growing interdependence of the services, they appear to have taken an unnecessarily narrow point of view and one that was not in the best interests of SHAEF as a whole.

## A STORMY MEETING

At the September 10 meeting in Brussels, Montgomery presented his uncharacteristically daring plan to push a bridgehead over the Rhine at Arnhem. He next began berating Eisenhower's broad-front strategic plan. He thrust a pile of Ike's SHAEF memos under his nose and then with great disdain picked apart his supreme commander's recent orders, denouncing them as "balls, sheer balls, rubbish!"[17]

In his career Eisenhower had learned how to deal with the ire of his superiors—Churchill, de Gaulle, MacArthur, and many more. But this was a seriously disrespectful tirade by a nominal subordinate. Ike responded by gently placing his hand on Monty's knee and reminded him, "Steady, Monty. You can't speak to me like that. I'm your boss."[18]

Monty's objective was to bully Eisenhower into making him and the

Twenty-First Army Group the sole, knockout Allied offensive to end the war. Incredibly after the war Eisenhower merely states that at this meeting he "authorized to defer the clearing out of the Antwerp approaches in an effort to seize the bridgehead I wanted."[19]

The next day, Ramsay saw Eisenhower who commented that Monty was "behaving badly." "Ike does not trust his loyalty and probably with good reason," Ramsay concluded.[20]

## THE TAIL WAGS THE DOG

Over the next few weeks, it is difficult to discern what Eisenhower's priorities (if he had any) were. On September 13 after conferring with Ramsay, Montgomery, and Bradley, he issued this directive:

> Our port position is such that a stretch of a week or ten days of bad weather in the Channel—a condition that is growing increasingly probable as the summer recedes—would paralyze our activities and so make the maintenance of our forces exceedingly difficult, even in defensive roles. . . . The object we must now attain, one which has been foreseen as essential from the very inception of the OVERLORD plan, is the gaining of deep water ports to support major forces in an invasion of Germany.[21]

Yet seventeen days after Monty had captured Antwerp little had been accomplished to open the Scheldt. On September 22, during a conference at SHAEF's main headquarters at Versailles attended by twenty-three admirals, generals, and air marshals (but not Monty), Eisenhower stressed the importance of opening Antwerp to Allied shipping.[22] But he did not directly order Monty to clear the estuary before his offensive, instead allotting him the limited supplies then available to advance to the Ruhr![23]

On September 30 he told his chief of staff, Walter Bedell Smith, "I am terribly anxious about Antwerp."[24] But a week later he demanded, "Both Army Groups must retain as first mission the gaining of the line of the Rhine north of Bonn as quickly as humanly possible."[25] In August Eisenhower had told Marshall that "I was always ready to defer capture of ports in favor of bolder and more rapid movement to the front."[26]

Eisenhower's command inconsistencies seemed to flow from his conciliatory management style overriding his strategic planning. The supreme commander never seemed to issue prescriptive and unequivocal orders. Although Monty's comments at the September 10 conference were extremely rude, they stemmed from the ambiguity of his broad-front directives.

Bradley viewed Eisenhower's rapid acquiescence to Monty's MARKET GARDEN plan as another example of how he far too quickly abandoned his prior directives. An angry, disgusted Bradley told General Harold Bull, Eisenhower's G-3, "I won't have the tail wagging the dog!"[27]

Patton even tried and failed to enlist Bradley in a "protest" action to stop Monty as outlined in his diary:

> Monty does what he pleases and Ike says "yes sir." Monty wants all supplies sent to him and the First U.S. Army and for me to hold. Brad thinks I can and should push on. Brad told Ike that if Monty takes control of the XIX and VII Corps of the First Army, as he wants to, he, Bradley, will ask to be relieved. . . . Ike feels that we think he is willing us out but he has to, as Monty will not take orders, so we have to. Bradley said it was time for a showdown. I offered to resign with him, but he backed out.[28]

After the war in their memoirs, Eisenhower and Smith declared that no military campaign in history came as close as OVERLORD in following its original design. These statements are as fantastic as Montgomery's claim that all of OVERLORD went according to his "plan!"[29]

## THE TIDE OF WAR SHIFTS

On September 4, the day the Allies captured the city of Antwerp, Hitler reinstated Rundstedt as commander in chief in the West. His steady hand would now compound Ramsay's worst fears as Rundstedt immediately sought to deprive the Allies of port facilities in France and Belgium, thus swinging the tide of war in Germany's favor. By securing the north and south shores of the Scheldt, while simultaneously defending the English Channel fortresses of Le Havre, Boulogne, Calais, and Dunkirk, Rundstedt would starve the Allies of the logistical support needed for the advance into Germany. This would give Rundstedt time to gather forces to reman the Siegfried Line and frustrate a rapid invasion of Germany.

Rundstedt expected Montgomery on September 4 to advance immediately and seal off Walcheren Island and the South Beveland Peninsula from the mainland. If Monty had done so, the German Fifteenth Army would have been trapped and eliminated. (See Map 28.) The Allied halt enabled Rundstedt to rescue the remains of General Hans von Zangen's encircled Fifteenth Army under the cover of darkness. A scratch fleet of two ancient Dutch freighters, Rhine river barges, small craft, and even rafts evacuated over 100,000 troops, artillery, vehicles, and even horses across the three-mile mouth of the Scheldt Estuary into the South Beveland Peninsula. The Germans were surprised that the convoy met with no Allied naval force interference. Stiffened by fresh troops, the Germans regrouped around strong positions along both sides of the river. The causeway on South Beveland connecting it to the mainland could be defended by a small number of troops. Across from Beveland, Walcheren Island was very heavily fortified with nearly thirty batteries of powerful coastal guns, from nine-inch to three-inch in caliber, as well as other strongholds.[30]

The German navy laid a variety of mines and put other deadly obstacles in place. The ship channel leading to the Port of Antwerp would have to be thoroughly cleared before freighters could use it. As the channel is seventy-three miles long and varies in width from 300 to 1,400 yards, this presented a clearance task of great magnitude and complexity. Port access between Antwerp and the sea was locked up tight.[31]

The initial Allied response to this German buildup was insufficient. It began on September 13, nine days after Antwerp's capture, and included Crerar's First Canadian Army and the First and Fourth Polish Armored Divisions. Their tanks were largely useless for canal attacks. Canadian infantry support was ineffective. This first attack met with disaster. The Canadians abandoned the initial bridgehead across the Leopold Canal due to heavy German fire. As it was decided that the Canadians needed additional forces, the Scheldt operation was abandoned in favor of clearing French ports. For three additional weeks no opposition was offered to the continued German additional fortification of the estuary.[32]

During these critical weeks the Allies' attention was focused elsewhere. It was placed on the rushed planning, execution, and recovery from Montgomery's "full-blooded thrust" to the northeast, Operation MARKET GARDEN.

## A BRIDGE TO NOWHERE

Montgomery's recent rapid advances culminating in the capture of Brussels and Antwerp had created considerable optimism in the Second Army. This lightning drive showed that British armor could match Patton's tanks. Monty was fixated on bypassing what was left of the German Fifteenth Army and dashing nonstop over the Rhine to the Ruhr and beyond. If he had continued his push on September 4 for about thirty-six hours, the British armor could have raced through almost undefended country between Antwerp and the Rhine.[33]

Montgomery's Operation MARKET GARDEN called for a quick thrust to the Reich through a sixty-mile corridor. The "MARKET" component of the operation would involve the use of the First Airborne Corps comprising the American Eighty-Second and 101st and the British First Airborne Divisions, commanded by the British lieutenant general Frederick Browning. These forces would land at three drop zones running from west to east: Eindhoven (101st US), Nijmegen (Eighty-Second US), and Arnhem (First British). (See Map 29.) This airborne operation was monumental in scope, deploying about five thousand fighters, bombers, transports, and over 2,500 gliders. This huge air army was deployed in an unprecedented daylight attack complete with their equipment and vehicles. Owing to a shortage of aircraft to carry paratroops, these landings would be conducted over a three-day period, thus giving German defenders advance warning that a major offensive was in progress. These divisions would then link up with the "GARDEN" component, the ground force, the British XXX Corps, and part of Montgomery's Second Army, led by Lieutenant General Brian Horrocks, which would advance from their present positions into Holland. (See Map 30.)

MARKET GARDEN had two major objectives. First, the British Twenty-First Army with the airborne army was to cross the two branches of the Rhine at Nijmegen and Arnhem. Second, Hodges's American First Army was to drive on Aachen and reach the Rhine at Cologne.

The aim of MARKET GARDEN was an advance beyond the Rhine to surround the Ruhr industrial region. This advance would clear the west bank of the Rhine and outflank the German forces on the Siegfried Line, rendering it useless. Finally, the British could advance from Arnhem and capture the port of Rotterdam.[34]

Due to recent Allied successes, optimism was running high. Eisenhower was both intrigued and impressed with Montgomery's bold, imaginative plan. This was the kind of innovative mass attack he had been looking for. In a September 14 letter to Marshall, Eisenhower was extremely optimistic that MARKET GARDEN would carry the Allies up to and across the Rhine.[35]

The daring nature of the MARKET GARDEN operation was strangely out of character for Montgomery. Indeed he was later to admit that MARKET GARDEN was his greatest mistake as a commander.[36] He was well-known for his detailed planning of future operations and was quite successful in staging set-piece battles. However, he had been criticized for unnecessary caution due to his failure to deploy armored divisions in situations where they had the potential to strike rapidly and effectively. Uncharacteristically Montgomery conceived and rushed through the planning of MARKET GARDEN in a matter of weeks.

Critically, Montgomery ignored vital intelligence on the feasibility of this operation. Ultra decrypts and reports from the local Dutch resistance forces indicated that two SS panzer divisions had been sent to Arnhem to refit. Also the Fifteenth Panzer Army had been moved into Holland and was well positioned to attack the left of the advancing Allied land forces. The Ninth and Tenth SS Panzer Divisions were fanned out to the north, east, and south of Arnhem. Also deployed around Eindhoven were the thirty thousand paratroops and Luftwaffe troops that formed the core of General Kurt Student's First Parachute Army.[37]

Montgomery's plan produced a shock wave at his Twenty-First Army Group headquarters. After he received the go-ahead for MARKET GARDEN from Eisenhower on September 10, he outlined the operation on a map for one of Britain's pioneer airborne experts, Lieutenant General Frederick Browning who would command the operation. The paratroops and glider-borne forces were to secure five major bridges along a sixty-four-mile invasion corridor. They would hold the corridor open until they were relieved by British armored forces. This unsettled Browning. Pointing to Arnhem, he asked Montgomery, "How long will it take the armor to reach us?" Monty answered, "Two days." Still studying the map, Browning responded, "We can hold it for four. But sir, I think we might be going a bridge too far."[38] Montgomery did not want to hear it.

Other objections followed. The Dutch underground information and Ultra intercepts so worried Major Brian Urquhart, the First Airborne Corps' intelligence officer, that he called for the information to be confirmed again by British aerial photographs. The air reconnaissance pictures clearly identified numerous German panzers in the Arnhem air drop zones or nearby. Urquhart relayed all of this damaging information to both Eisenhower and Montgomery. Ike was so alarmed that he sent Smith to discuss this with Montgomery, but Monty lightly dismissed it all.

Montgomery chose to ignore this potentially cataclysmic information and treated it as a peripheral matter rather than as a reason to cancel MARKET GARDEN. Moreover, he now took extraordinary steps to discredit Urquhart's intelligence effort. Monty sent a senior staff medical officer, Colonel Arthur Eagger, to confirm reports that Urquhart had become "hysterical." Urquhart told the medical officer that the intelligence reports made it clear that the proposed MARKET GARDEN operation was "madness." Eagger immediately diagnosed Urquhart as suffering from exhaustion and sent him on medical leave, thus removing him far from the immediate scene.[39]

But the intelligence question would not go away. A distinguished air intelligence officer, Wing Commander Asher Lee, also deeply investigated the Ultra information. His findings were conclusive regarding the presence of substantial German armored units at Arnhem. He personally conveyed his report to Montgomery's headquarters. But he only was seen by junior staff officers, thus again dismissing the importance of this vital intelligence.[40]

General Brian Horrocks, the commander of the XXX Corps in the MARKET GARDEN operation later lamented, "Why did I receive no information about the German formations which were being rushed daily to our front? For me, this has always been the sixty-four-thousand-dollar question."[41] Elizabeth Coble states, "It is unforgiveable for intelligence of this magnitude to be withheld from subordinate commanders. Without all available intelligence, subordinate commands could not plan and equip their forces properly."[42]

Even before the operation began on September 9, General Dempsey, commander of the Second Army, had grave doubts, as he wrote in his diary,

> It is clear that the enemy is bringing up all the reinforcements he can get his hands on for the defense of the ALBERT Canal, and that he appreciates the importance of the area ARNHEM-NIJMEGAN. It looks as though he is going to do all he can to hold it. This being the case, any question of a rapid advance to the North-East seems unlikely. . . . Are we right to direct Second Army to ARNHEM?[43]

We do not know if Dempsey challenged Montgomery on the intelligence issue. However, it is important to note that this was the only diary entry from the onset of the Normandy invasion in which he questioned an order.[44]

Eisenhower also was receiving further information casting doubt on the soundness of this operation. Bradley warned him that the terrain for Montgomery's drive was unsuitable for a rapid advance as the Netherlands had numerous canals and waterways that the Germans would defend.[45] Bradley later stated, "My opposition . . . was not confined to the British diversion of effort. I feared also that Monty in his eagerness to get around Model's flank might have underestimated German capabilities on the lower Rhine."[46] Eisenhower, however, did not exercise his authority to cancel MARKET GARDEN. Smith lamented, "Having authorized him [Montgomery] to proceed, Eisenhower did not feel he could now instruct him not to do so, even though the head of his intelligence staff predicted a defeat."[47]

Brooke, the one man who might have convinced Montgomery to cancel MARKET GARDEN, had left London with Churchill and the other chiefs of staff on the morning of September 5 for the Quebec Conference, five days before Eisenhower authorized Monty to proceed with MARKET GARDEN. He did not return until September 23 by which time the operation was being wound down. It is interesting to note that MARKET GARDEN is not mentioned in his war diary.[48]

MARKET GARDEN is another example of Montgomery's inflexibility in altering his plans.[49] He also failed to provide subordinate commanders with relevant intelligence. On D-Day, invasion commanders did not know that the Twenty-First Panzer Division was deployed to oppose their seizure of Caen. The failure to seize Caen seriously impeded the progress of the Normandy campaign and cost lives. This time it would take even more lives.

On September 17, MARKET GARDEN operations were launched with a massive airborne assault. German general Kurt Student, paratroop commander, and his chief of staff stood on the balcony of Student's cottage in Holland as this massive air armada went past. Student remembered they "simply stared, stunned, like fools . . . everywhere we looked, we saw chain of planes—fighters, troop carriers and cargo planes—flying over us. . . . This mighty spectacle deeply impressed me."[50]

Montgomery's plan relied on the accelerated progress of Horrocks's XXX Corps' tank and infantry forces down one main highway to link up the invasion corridor and relieve the paratroop divisions. The progress of the Allied armies was slower than expected, as they encountered a fierce and well-conducted German resistance. As a result, it took longer than expected to capture their first objective, Eindhoven. The Germans fought stoutly for Nijmegen and its vitally important bridge, which eventually fell to a determined attack by infantry units of the Guards Armored Division. The road to MARKET GARDEN's final objective, Arnhem, was theoretically open.

A defect in the planning was the task given to the land forces to advance over the polders (fields lying close to or below sea level) that were too marshy to support the weight of tanks. Once the Nijmegen bridge was secured the tanks and infantry of the Guards Armored Division were forced to advance in single file on the road to Arnhem, meeting determined German resistance along the way.

This check of the XXX Corps' advance doomed the First Airborne Division at Arnhem. They valiantly defended their isolated position for ten days rather than the two that Montgomery had planned. On September 25, they were forced to surrender. About six thousand Allied soldiers were captured, half of them wounded; 1,174 died. At night 1,900 paratroopers were evacuated across the lower Rhine. The British First Airborne and Polish First Parachute Brigade were effectively destroyed as fighting units. Total Allied MARKET GARDEN killed, wounded, and missing exceeded seven thousand, five thousand more than on D-Day.[51]

Afterward, Montgomery insisted that the operation had been a justifiable risk. Although Montgomery described himself as "bitterly disappointed" by Arnhem and admitting mistakes were made for which he bore responsibility, he proclaimed in his memoirs, "I remain MARKET GARDEN's unrepentant advocate," noting, "In my—prejudiced—view, if the operation had been properly backed from its inception . . . it would have succeeded in spite of my mistakes."[52]

Military historians, however, have roundly criticized many facets of the MARKET GARDEN operation. Nigel Hamilton, Montgomery's chief biographer, stated that in every military dimension, "strategic, tactical, intelligence, logistical, personal . . . it was . . . a complete disaster . . . [a road] that led nowhere."[53] Arnhem was a completely avoidable disaster. Norman Davies concludes that "it was not an act of responsible generalship."[54] Alun Chalfont agrees that "Arnhem . . . showed a serious error of judgement on Montgomery's part."[55] The lightly armed airborne troops were no match for the heavily equipped SS panzer corps. Funneling the British supporting armor down narrow roads through marshland was a disaster waiting to happen.

David Bennett offers this summary judgment of MARKET GARDEN: "The truth was that the operation was too ambitious. In launching it with a tenuous supply line, no reserve build-up of supplies, a shortage of ground transport, and both VIII and XII Corps [support units to XXX Corps] unready at the start, Montgomery's professionalism had deserted him."[56]

At this juncture in the campaign, everyone on the Allied side was frustrated, angry, and depressed. The MARKET GARDEN debacle had cured the earlier "victory disease." "There was a change of mood after Arnhem," a British captain remembers. "One just didn't feel the same. We were getting rather tired."[57] Prince Bernhard of the Netherlands lamented, "My country can never again afford the luxury of another Montgomery success."[58]

Clearly Eisenhower had backed the wrong offensive. He had not backed Patton's southern thrust to the Ruhr while forcing Montgomery to seize both banks of the Scheldt Estuary to open up the Port of Antwerp. Long after the war Eisenhower admitted, "I not only approved MARKET GARDEN, I insisted upon it. What we needed was a *bridgehead* over the Rhine. If that could be accomplished, I was quite willing to wait on all other operations. What this action proved was that the idea of 'one full-blooded thrust' to Berlin was silly."[59]

For both Eisenhower and Montgomery, Arnhem was a major mistake that served to diminish them. For Eisenhower, it was a vain attempt to masterfully end the war in 1944 as the successful supreme commander of a difficult Allied coalition. As for Montgomery, it ended his dream of being the commander of a victorious British-led drive to Berlin, securing the restoration of British prestige, and marking the capstone of his military reputation. Only Montgomery's unrestrained ego remained, which continued to plague Eisenhower to the war's last act and even afterward.[60]

Alan Moorehead summed up the situation well when he wrote, "For the Allied army now no hopeful alternatives remained. There was only one way—the hard way. The immediate essential for all this was the opening up of Antwerp."[61]

## THE "BATTLES" OF PORT ANTWERP

Planning for the clearing of the Scheldt Estuary (code-named Operation INFATUATE) was begun by mid-September with Admiral Ramsay working closely with the designated land commander, the highly respected lieutenant general Guy Simonds, head of the II Canadian Corps (Crerar had been placed on sick leave). Ramsay appointed Captain Anthony Pugsley as the commander of Force T. In this role, he would plan and then lead the naval assault on Walcheren, the strategically important Dutch island on the northern side of the Scheldt Estuary.[62]

As September drew to a close, the Allied supply was in an exceedingly precarious position. On October 5 a high-level meeting was held at SHAEF in Versailles. Those attending included Eisenhower, Bradley, Brooke, Montgomery, Ramsay, Tedder, and Leigh-Mallory. Ramsay recorded in his diary,

> Very interesting exposition of situation on Army Group fronts. Monty made the startling announcement that we could take the Ruhr without Antwerp. This afforded me the cue I needed to lambast him for not having made the capture of Antwerp the immediate objective at highest priority & I let fly with all my guns at the faulty strategy which we had allowed. . . . I got approving looks from Tedder and Bedell Smith, and both of them together with C.I.G.S. [Brooke] told me after the meeting that I'd spoken their thoughts and that it was high time someone expressed them.[63]

Brooke's diary confirms that he was not pleased with what he had heard at Versailles. He noted that one fact stood out clearly: "Antwerp should be captured with the least possible delay. I feel that Monty's strategy for once is at fault. Instead of carrying out the advance on Arnhem he ought to have made certain of Antwerp in the first place. Ramsay brought this out well in discussion and criticized Monty freely."[64] We can only speculate that if Brooke had not been at the Quebec Conference, he might have strongly pushed Montgomery over opening Antwerp while preparing later for MARKET GARDEN offensive.

On October 8 an obviously pleased Ramsay noted, "I understand that the 21st Army Group plan of campaign has now been modified to give greater priority to the 1st Canadian Army at expense of 2nd Army so as to concentrate on capture of entrances to Antwerp."[65] He was to be disappointed. Montgomery did issue fresh orders on October 9, but he placed clearing the Scheldt as only the third priority for his army group.

On October 8, a major English Channel storm had struck again at the Mulberry harbor and even damaged the harbor at Cherbourg.[66] Eisenhower enraged at Montgomery's stubborn denial of logistical realities and sent a clear message, but it was still not quite a direct order on October 10 regarding opening the port:

> I must repeat that we are now squared up against the situation which has been anticipated for months and our intake into the Continent will not repeat not support our battle. Unless we have Antwerp producing by the middle of November our entire operations will come to a standstill. I must emphasize that, of all our operations on our entire front from Switzerland to the Channel, I consider Antwerp of first importance.[67]

General Frederick Morgan (the former head of COSSAC, who was then on the SHAEF staff) reflected how "it became increasingly difficult to explain to our American Commander what, on the face of it, was little short of refusal to comply with orders on the part of his British subordinate."[68]

However remember the advice Montgomery gave to Patton in 1943 during the Sicily campaign on how to handle a disagreeable order from their supreme commander: "Let me give you some advice. If you get an order from Army Group that you don't like, just ignore it. That's what I do."[69]

Eisenhower told Smith to pursue Montgomery and get to the bottom of his intransigence. Smith telephoned Montgomery and demanded a firm date when the Scheldt would be opened. Montgomery would not be bullied. He stuck to his one-man script. The Ruhr, not Antwerp, remained the principal objective. The Americans needed Antwerp, not his Twenty-First Army Group.

Apoplectic with rage, Smith called Morgan to his office and handed the receiver to Morgan. Morgan then listened as Montgomery repeated the same arguments. Finally, during a brief pause, Morgan told Monty that unless he immediately began the Antwerp operation that the Twenty-First Army Group would receive no more supplies.[70]

This further incensed Montgomery who sent an imperious memo to Smith demanding a complete overhaul of the SHAEF command structure. Monty was in the midst of an effort to gain control of the European campaign. This memo asserted, "All our troubles can be traced to the fact that there is no one commander in charge of the land battle. . . . SHAEF is not an operational headquarters and never can be. . . . The present organization for command . . . is not satisfactory."[71]

On October 8, Montgomery met with General George C. Marshall who was then in France. Montgomery arrogantly voiced his opinion that since Eisenhower had taken command of the land battle, Allied operations had become "ragged and disjointed . . . we had got ourselves into a real mess."[72] Marshall recorded that in reaction he nearly lost his temper: "[I]t was very hard for me to restrain myself because I didn't think there was any logic in what he said, but overwhelming egotism."[73]

In response to these two outbursts, on October 13 a letter was sent to Montgomery by Eisenhower on which Ike, Marshall, and Smith had collaborated. It contains two key statements: "I have been informed, both by the Chief of the Imperial General Staff and by the Chief of Staff of the United States Army that they seriously considered giving me a flat order that until the capture of Antwerp and its approaches was fully assured, this operation should take precedence over all others." It continues, "If you . . . feel that my conceptions and directives are such as to endanger the success of operations, it is our duty to refer the matter to higher authority for any action they may choose to take, however drastic."[74]

As Montgomery then realized that the top authorities were not in his court, he replied on October 16 that he was giving top priority to the Scheldt campaign.[75] After Montgomery belatedly issued his unequivocal orders for Operation INFATUATE, positive results soon followed.

On October 24 a brigade of the British Fifty-Second Division under the command of Captain Pugsley arrived by landing craft on the southern shore of South Beveland, the most easterly of the two German occupied islands on the north bank of the Scheldt. After five days of fierce fighting, the German commander on the island surrendered. (See Map 28.)

The stage was now set for a campaign on the island of Walcheren, which was connected by a causeway with South Beveland. As a large part of the island lies below sea level, the Dutch had built dikes to keep the sea out. RAF Lancaster bombers were called in to bomb the dike near the town of Westkapelle, on the western side of the island. By mid-October the dike had been breached in no less than four places, which would allow the Royal Marine Commandos to propel their landing craft into the breaches and attack the Germans from the rear.

On October 30 Ramsay set up his headquarters in Ghent next to those of Canadian general Simonds. Together they coordinated their forces for the invasion of Walcheren, which began on October 31. On that day Canadian troops began fighting along the causeway from South Beveland to Walcheren. On November 1 after a heavy shelling by the veteran battleship *Warspite* and two smaller monitor ships, all with 15mm guns, commando units landed in the Westkapelle area. At the same time following intense air and artillery attacks, the British Fifty-Second Division and Canadian troops landed at the island's main town, Flushing. It took these forces four days to drive out the Germans from the town and docks.[76] On November 3 two British infantry brigades landed on Walcheren's eastern shore to outflank German defenders that had confined the Canadians into a bridgehead on the causeway from South Beveland. Five days later, two thousand Germans from the Seventieth Division surrendered.[77] The fighting to open the port had been bitter. The Canadians sustained thirteen thousand casualties clearing the Scheldt.

On November 4, Ramsay was able to order more than ten squadrons of Royal Navy minesweepers (more than 150 vessels) to clear the Scheldt of the mines that the Germans had laid in September. Sadly one vessel struck a mine and was lost with all hands. They completed their task, removing no fewer than 267 mines, by November 26, one week earlier than had been forecasted.[78]

On November 28, Ramsay returned to Antwerp to witness the success of Operation INFATUATE. He took part in a ceremony welcoming the first ship of the first convoy to arrive at Antwerp in four and a half years.[79]

By mid-December Antwerp was unloading twenty-three thousand tons per day. It only reached full capacity in early 1945.[80]

Antwerp was at last open but no fewer than sixty days after the British first captured its dock facilities. This unnecessary delay, caused by Eisenhower's acquiescence in Montgomery's decision to stage Operation MARKET GARDEN and Montgomery's failure until mid-October to give INFATUATE the priority it needed, destroyed any remaining chance that the war in Western Europe could have been won in 1944.[81]

## SPECTACULAR FAILURES

In Raymond Callahan's judgment, Operation MARKET GARDEN "failed spectacularly."[82] The same can be said of Montgomery's astounding misjudgment in failing to immediately open up the Scheldt Estuary after the capture of Antwerp. (Though Ramsay's Operation INFATUATE succeeded once Eisenhower forced Montgomery to commit adequate forces to this effort.) Unusually for him, Montgomery later did admit that this was an error: "I must admit a bad mistake on my part. I underestimated the difficulties of opening up the approaches to Antwerp so that we could get free use of the port. I reckoned that the Canadian Army could do it *while* we were going for the Ruhr. I was wrong."[83] These two failures added to an already long list of OVERLORD's strategic blunders, missed opportunities, and tactical errors.

Eisenhower backed the wrong offensive. His failure to support the Bradley/Patton plan gave the Germans an opportunity to regroup their shattered forces in Western Europe. The Allied armies starved of supplies were stalled at the German border because of the unnecessary delay in opening the Port of Antwerp.

The extension of the war produced the abortive US Hurtgen Forest offensive and gave Hitler the opportunity to launch his doomed Ardennes offensive (Battle of the Bulge). Both resulted in major Allied casualties.

OVERLORD failed to achieve its ultimate goals: invading Germany, capturing Berlin, and ending the war in Europe. In our final chapter we will review how national rivalries tested the command structure of the Allied alliance and how the divergent leadership qualities of the principal commanders and personality clashes among them jeopardized the success of the Normandy campaign.

# CHAPTER 13
# CRISIS IN COMMAND

"We are in for an all out struggle with our American colleagues and I am frankly doubtful as to the outcome of it all."

—Sir Alan Brooke, June 1944[1]

"It is astonishing how petty and small men can be in connection with questions of command."

—Sir Alan Brooke, June 1945[2]

## A SPECIAL RELATIONSHIP BECOMES STRAINED

The special relationship between Great Britain and the United States was key to the development and execution of the Normandy campaign. It began with the close collaboration of Prime Minister Winston Churchill and President Franklin D. Roosevelt even before America's entrance into the war. During 1940 and 1941 the two countries developed very close ties as German victories threatened all of Europe. Their joint military and logistical planning foreshadowed their ultimate alliance.

This influence from the top had a powerful effect on the beginnings of Allied military planning. General Frederick Morgan who had headed COSSAC, the early planning group for the Normandy invasion, and who subsequently was a member of the SHAEF staff gave this firsthand perspective on Anglo-American cooperation: "It is regarded as a delicate hothouse growth that must be carefully tended lest it wither away. . . . At COSSAC we came to know each other pretty well, and the thought of any significant cleavage between the two nations is to any one of us, I believe, ludicrous."[3]

Yet it soon became apparent that the two allies had divergent political aims and strategic objectives. Due to American political exigencies, Roosevelt and the US chiefs of staffs sought to avoid a protracted war in Europe and to pursue a swift victory over Japan. US political and military leaders demanded the quickest and least costly road to victory.[4] General George C. Marshall summarized this scenario when he said that "a democracy cannot fight a Seven Years War."[5]

By 1943 American troops and equipment began to play a dominant role in European operations. US military and political leaders began to be increasingly insistent on launching a cross-channel invasion. As British power declined, Churchill and Brooke struggled to retain their strategic objectives by keeping operations focused on the Mediterranean theater. The British leaders never seemed able to adjust their perspective to the political reality of these new conditions. Brooke wrote in his diary,

> I despair of ever getting our American friends to have any sort of strategic vision. Their drag on us has seriously affected our Mediterranean strategy and the whole conduct of the war. . . . Instead, to satisfy American shortsightedness we have been led into agreeing to the withdrawal of forces from the Mediterranean for a nebulous 2nd Front [OVERLORD] and have emasculated our offensive strategy.[6]

General Morgan wrote in his memoirs, "I am left with a clear impression that, with command in the hands of a British leader, the whole affair [i.e., OVERLORD] might have gone very much otherwise. I go so far even to say that it might not have gone at all."[7]

The Americans were not naïve. They understood the political reasoning behind Churchill's war policies. But if these did not accomplish America's military interests, the US chiefs of staff would not support them.

Churchill, on the other hand, sought to maintain Britain's dominant position in Europe, preserve its colonial empire, and contain the menace posed by Soviet expansionism in Eastern Europe. American leaders did not foresee the postwar power struggle in Europe created by the rapid resurgence of the Soviet Union from horrendous war losses and the weakened ability of Britain and its allies to cope with this Communist threat.

The Normandy campaign was conducted during a time when the strategic aims and postwar visions of Britain and the United States increasingly diverged. This helped to further exacerbate the personal rivalries and personality conflicts of the principal Normandy commanders. We now turn to a summary of each commander's personal role in advancing or slowing the progress of the Normandy campaign and the end of the war in Europe.

## EISENHOWER: COMMANDER AS ARBITRATOR

"Dwight David Eisenhower was not born great, nor did he achieve greatness. But when greatness was thrust upon him, he met the challenge," concluded correspondent Don Cook in his summary of the supreme commander.[8]

Eisenhower was catapulted from an obscure position in a small peacetime army to playing a major role in the gradual shaping of the victorious US citizen army during the campaigns in North Africa, Sicily, and northwestern Europe. Field Marshal Erwin Rommel wrote, "What was astonishing was the speed with which the Americans adapted themselves to modern warfare. In this they were assisted by their extraordinary sense of the practical and material and their complete lack of regard for tradition and worthless theories.... Starting from scratch an army has been created in the very minimum of time, which, in equipment, armaments and organization of all arms, surpasses anything the world has yet seen."[9]

Moreover starting with the Mediterranean campaigns, Eisenhower carefully developed his command abilities of tact and diplomacy, and promoted the development of Allied unity. During OVERLORD he mastered the joint operations of land, sea, and air forces on a scale greater than what had ever before been attempted. His integrated Allied army although composed largely of British, Canadian, and US troops also contained contingents from nations overrun by the Germans, including France, Norway, Poland, Belgium, Luxembourg, the Netherlands, and Czechoslovakia. By April 1945 Eisenhower's SHAEF headquarters was huge, with a total staff of 12,028. This included 1,495 American and 1,077 British officers. Here was successful coalition warfare writ large.[10]

Eisenhower acted more as an arbitrator across the alliance rather than as a soldier. He held the Allies together through moments of great crisis by showing an amazing degree of self-effacement to at times insulting and intimidating leaders, including Churchill, Roosevelt, Marshall, Brooke, and de Gaulle as well as military subordinates. He handled this unwieldy cast of ego-driven leaders using intricate compromises that led to a victorious conclusion in Europe. Ike spent countless hours responding to difficult and emotional arguments using an accommodating manner yet not comprising his own authority.[11]

Ralph Ingersoll, historian for Bradley's Twelfth Army Group, judged that Eisenhower's leadership hinged on his ability "to conciliate, to see both points of view, to be above national interests—and to be neither bold nor decisive."[12] The truth of this judgment is borne out by Brooke's complaint that the British staff officers at SHAEF were under Eisenhower's domination, while at the same time, Bradley and Patton were openly complaining that Eisenhower was dominated by the British.[13]

Eisenhower's greatest limitation was his reluctance to exercise his prerogatives as supreme commander in battlefield decisions. Ike's conscientious tolerance at times became a liability. When the battlefield called for a leader with an action plan, he failed to intervene time after time as commander in chief.[14] He shunned giving direct orders to Montgomery, Bradley, Patton, and others. Instead he issued vague and verbose instructions that gave them great tactical leeway in picking their own objectives. As we have demonstrated, this resulted in some of the greatest tactical mistakes of the Normandy campaign.[15]

The obscurity of Eisenhower's "commands" clearly exasperated two of his American commanders. Patton lamented in his diary, "We actually have no Supreme Commander—no one who can take hold and say that this shall be done and that shall not be done. It is a very unfortunate situation to which I see no solution."[16] Walter Bedell Smith, Eisenhower's chief of staff, grew weary over his refusal to assert command and issue direct orders based on strategic objectives rather than issuing conciliatory directives. "The trouble with Ike," Smith observed, is that "instead of giving direct and clear orders, [he] dresses them up in polite language."[17] Ike continued to use this leadership style to almost the end of the war. Max Hastings succinctly labels the result: Eisenhower's failures during the northern European campaign were more "of omission than commission."[18]

General Sir Arnold Alexander well summed up the scope of the challenges that Eisenhower successfully faced as supreme commander:

> In warfare today a Supreme Allied Commander has much more responsibility on his shoulders than the straight fighting of battles. He finds himself entangled with strategic and political problems, with international relations, and with many other complicated issues far divorced from the front-line. Judging General Eisenhower against this background I think that his was an excellent appointment and that he carried out his assignment with great distinction.[19]

## MONTGOMERY: THE ROGUE COMMANDER

Before the beginning of World War II General Bernard Law Montgomery was considered an expert planner and strategist who was acknowledged as a master of the set-piece operation. He devoted extraordinary attention to the training and inspiration of his troops. He had a remarkable ability to inspire the trust and confidence of his soldiers. He was superb in selecting subordinate staff and in developing a battlefield organization. Those under his command respected him for his willingness to consult them and his concern for their well-being.

Montgomery's first claim to fame was his victory at El Alamein. This renown largely flowed from self-contrived propaganda picked up and embellished (beret and all) by the British press. At this juncture in the war, British morale was very low as their armed forces had recently suffered a string of defeats. The Battle of El Alamein and the creation of the Monty myth were means to boost public optimism in a war-weary Britain. This victory also helped to solidify the Brooke-Monty grip on the British army until the end of the war.

In his book, *The Desert Generals* (1960), Correlli Barnett was the first "to puncture the inflated Montgomery myth." He rated Montgomery an average general, able but not brilliant.[20] Barnett found that the Battle of El Alamein that was so one-sided in men and material that Monty or any other general would have had difficulty losing it. The battlefield's location and defenses had all been planned and installed for him by his predecessor Sir Claude Auchinleck, whose removal was for political not military reasons.

Montgomery knew he possessed overwhelming military resources from the day he arrived in North Africa. He was "well aware" from Ultra decrypts that Rommel's forces had been reduced "to a mere handful of tanks . . . shackled by dearth of fuel."[21] It was one of the most one-sided logistical buildup of military advantages ever seen. Even so the battle actually hung in the balance for some time, although the Afrika Korps' commander Rommel was absent until almost its very end. Monty then failed to effectively pursue and destroy Rommel's defeated forces.

After the battle Rommel wrote,

> The impression was gained of the British Commander, General Montgomery, was that of a very cautious man, who was not prepared to take any sort of risk. . . . I was quite satisfied that Montgomery would never take the risk of following up boldly and overrunning us [as the Germans retreated to Tunisia]. . . . Indeed, such a course would have cost him far fewer losses in the long run than his methodical insistence on overwhelming superiority in each tactical action, which he could only obtain at the cost of speed.[22]

When Barnett's book was published in 1960, some British historians and readers were angered by it. However, attitudes had changed by 1983 when a second edition appeared. By then Barnett found that Montgomery's reputation had been reduced to life-size. Now through the perspective of time he was viewed as an eccentric rather than as a genius.[23]

Montgomery's caution and failure to pursue the enemy persisted throughout the Normandy campaign. He hesitated in taking the initiative, pressing an advantage, and finishing off an enemy with a knockout blow. He preferred balance over boldness and was uncomfortable in fluid battlefield situations when an action did not follow his carefully laid out plans.[24] Perhaps Patton came closest to defining that imaginative quality that Montgomery lacked on the battlefield when he wrote, "One does not plan and then try to make circumstances fit those plans. One tries to make plans fit the circumstances. I think the difference between success and failure depends on the ability, or lack of it, to do just that."[25]

Montgomery infrequently went to the front and observed his battles through the eyes of his young liaison officers who reported what they knew Monty wanted to be told. He tended to see only what he wanted to see, hear only what he wanted to hear, and he lived in splendid isolation at his headquarters, blocking out most other things from his mind.

Rommel observed, "Montgomery was undoubtedly more of a strategist than a tactician. Command of a force in mobile battle was not his strong point. . . . As a result [he] made the error of planning operations according to what was strategically desirable, rather than what was tactically attainable."[26] German staff reports on British tactics during OVERLORD remarked, "A successful break in by the enemy is almost never exploited to pursuit. . . . Whenever the enemy infantry is energetically engaged they mostly retreat or surrender."[27]

Some of this reluctance to press home attacks came from instructions given by the government to conserve Britain's rapidly dwindling supply of manpower. Montgomery thus developed the "colossal cracks" operational approach that used massive firepower to capture enemy positions. He resisted all-out attacks after D-Day and reverted to the attritional siege-warfare tactics of World War I.

In the final analysis, his "colossal cracks" strategy was self-defeating. His series of restrained attacks and unaggressive leadership at Caen, Falaise, and elsewhere failed to win battles or save lives. On the other hand, Patton's strategy of "an all-out effort" actually resulted in fewer casualties compared to those experienced by other Allied armies.[28]

Montgomery's inflexibility also was apparent in his relations with fellow commanders. In his infrequent conversations with other senior officers, he relentlessly asserted his own ideas and failed to consider the arguments of his own military equals or superiors. He failed to undertake any kind of real dialogue. His mentor Alan Brooke noted in his memoirs that he had to haul him over the coals for his usual lack of tact and egotistical outlook, which prevented him from appreciating other peoples' feelings.

In point of fact, Montgomery was extremely self-centered. Alun Chalfont stated, "His vanity was monumental. . . . Montgomery was guilty of hubris squared, he was cocky when things were going well, badly or hardly at all. In fact he was cocky all the time." A reporter asked him to name "the three greatest commanders in history." Monty replied, "The other two were Alexander and Napoleon."[29] This was not intended as a joke. Major General de Guingand, Montgomery's chief of staff, offered this assessment: "Montgomery is a showman. He likes to be the principal figure on the stage. . . . He preferred to be the only speaker."[30] William Weidner found that Montgomery's obsession with control, punctuality, neatness, and excessive planning was apparent in both his military and private life.[31]

In view of his personality, it is not surprising he did well in Egypt, Libya, Tunisia, Sicily, and even Italy. There he commanded British and Commonwealth forces under his firm control. In Italy his Eighth Army was virtually an independent command. But Martin Blumenson reminds us, "Coalition warfare was never Montgomery's strong suit." He never was able to reconcile himself to Eisenhower's decision to assume the ground command on September 1, 1944, as he viewed this as a demotion. His insulting behavior toward Eisenhower as depicted in the previous chapter continued. "He became overwrought," states Carlo D'Este. "Montgomery could not find it in himself to accept Eisenhower's way of warfare on his authority." Eisenhower was "too inexperienced" and "ill-prepared."[32]

Brooke and Montgomery also seemed unable to reconcile themselves to the fact that American dominance in troops bolstered Eisenhower's command position. By early 1945 the United States fielded seventy-one divisions in northern Europe, while the British now deployed only thirteen.[33] In a November 24, 1944, letter, Brooke reinforced Monty's insubordinate behavior by saying, "Ike was no commander, that he had no strategic vision, was incapable of making a plan or of running operations when started."[34] Montgomery added to this by saying on a trip to London, "Eisenhower is quite useless. . . . He is completely and utterly useless."[35]

After the extreme stress of the Battle of the Bulge, Monty had the supreme effrontery to inform Eisenhower that his broad-front strategy had failed and sent him a suggested SHAEF directive that read,

> FROM NOW ONWARDS, FULL OPERATIONAL DIRECTION, CONTROL, AND COORDINATION OF THESE OPERATIONS IS VESTED IN THE C-IN-C 21 ARMY GROUP, SUBJECT TO SUCH INSTRUCTIONS AS MAY BE RECEIVED FROM THE SUPREME COMMANDER FROM TIME TO TIME.[36]

Eisenhower was infuriated by this communication and decided to tell the US/UK Combined Chiefs of Staff that either he or Montgomery would have to go. At this point de Guingand once again entered the fray, pleading with the supreme commander for time. After flying back to the Twenty-First Army Group headquarters, de Guingand told Montgomery that Eisenhower wanted to replace him. He reported that Monty "looked nonplussed—I don't think I had ever seen him look so deflated."[37] Montgomery then agreed to sign de Guingand's draft retraction, which stated, "Very distressed that my letter may have upset you and I would ask you to tear it up," and was signed, "Your very devoted subordinate, Monty."[38]

Montgomery created a great amount of inter-Allied friction throughout the war. Even the ego-driven Patton reached the point with Monty that he felt that "Allies must fight in separate theaters or they hate each other more than the enemy."[39] Tedder, Eisenhower's deputy, amplified almost everyone's general skepticism about Montgomery: "He is a little fellow (5′7″) who has had such a build-up that he thinks of himself as Napoleon—he is not."[40]

In June 1945 Montgomery and Eisenhower exchanged notes at the war's end. They seemed to try and reconcile (at least on paper) all their prior differences. Monty stated, "I as British general had been proud to serve under American command." Ike replied with a "very charming letter." He described Monty's note as "one of the finest things I have ever received." He then made a surprising statement: "Whenever decision was made, regardless of your personal opinion, your loyalty and efficiency in execution were to be counted upon with certainty."[41]

During the war the two famous generals had discussed the Battle of Gettysburg. Eisenhower promised to invite him to his Gettysburg farm after the war for a personal tour of the battlefield. By then Ike had been elected president.

Invitations to the First Family's Gettysburg farm were rare, usually only given to the closest personal friends. In 1957 Monty solved that problem by inviting himself. By that time he had already finished writing his memoirs, which were to be published in late 1958.

Montgomery sent Eisenhower a galley proof of the book. In it he said many uncomplimentary things about Eisenhower's command competence, including the assertion that the war could have ended in December 1944 if Ike had agreed to his pencil-like thrust across the Rhine to Berlin. Eisenhower was further startled to read that "I let him have his own way and he really planned the war."[42] The president was furious. He wrote to a friend, "My opinion [of Montgomery's book] is probably so much lower than yours that I would not like to express it even in a letter."[43]

Tensions were high when Montgomery arrived at the farm for his battlefield tour. During the tour that day Monty played up to the press as they scrambled around the historic sights. At one point Monty called over the heads of the crowd, "Both Lee and Meade should have been sacked." Then he shouted over to Eisenhower, "Don't you agree, Ike?" Resenting Monty's grandstanding and lack of good taste, Eisenhower told him, "Listen Monty, I live here. I have nothing to say about the matter. You have to make your own comments."[44]

After Montgomery's memoir was published, the president severed all ties to him. In Ike's judgment Montgomery was "just a little man, he's just as little inside as he is outside."[45]

Over the next decade Eisenhower's opinion of Montgomery continued to sharpen. In a 1963 interview with Cornelius Ryan at Eisenhower's home in Gettysburg in which they were discussing command structures and decision making from 1944 to 1945, Ike strongly expressed his ultimate frustration over his relations with the British general:[46]

> First of all he's a psychopath. Don't forget that. He is such an ego-centric that everything he has ever done is perfect—he has never made a mistake in his life. He even says that all of the Operations after we landed on D-Day went absolutely according to plan. Montgomery got so damn personal to make sure the Americans and me, in particular, had no credit, had nothing to do with the war, that I eventually just stopped communicating with him. I was just not interested in keeping up communications with a man who just can't tell the truth.[47]

After the war Montgomery served as the commander of British occupation forces in Germany, and from 1946 to 1948 he was the chief of the imperial general staff. He continued attracting controversy until his death in 1976 at eighty-eight.

## RAMSAY: THE AFFABLE COMMANDER

During our review of OVERLORD and subsequent Allied campaigns in northwestern Europe, we have seen both the great accomplishments of the Grand Alliance but also the antagonisms that clouded the relationships among the major commanders. Admiral Sir Bertram Ramsay, however, was highly professional and generally maintained cordial relations with the heads of the other British armed forces and with the Allied army, navy, and air force commanders.

His experience with combined operations long preceded his Normandy command. After his success in evacuating British forces from Dunkirk, he was chief naval planner for Operation TORCH (the invasion of North Africa) and led the British task force for the invasion of Sicily. These experiences served him well in planning the combined amphibious operations of OVERLORD. Considering the enormous scale of this endeavor, it is remarkable that Ramsay only publically tangled with two US commanders. He had to press Admiral Ernest J. King to supply additional warships for the D-Day invasion fleet and then to keep them there until the operations were completed. He also had to deal with the complaints of Rear Admiral Alan Kirk, the commander of the US D-Day Western Task Force who objected to Ramsay's detailed planning.[48]

Most notable was Ramsay's ability to work amicably with Montgomery until he called him out for the failure to clear the Scheldt Estuary and open the Port of Antwerp to remedy the Allied logistical problems. Montgomery had a very important reason for holding Ramsay in high esteem as Monty was a member of the British Expeditionary Force rescued at Dunkirk and thus was spared the fate of being interred in a German prisoner-of-war camp.

They first really got to know each other in 1941 when both held posts for the defense of Southern England. Ramsay was quick to recognize Monty's considerable ability as well as the quirky side of his personality. Ramsay wrote to his wife, "We have a new General here and his name is Bernard Montgomery but I have nicknamed him the Iron General. . . . He is without a doubt a tiger of a man, full of ideas and opinions . . . and fairly stirring everyone up."[49] Montgomery invited Ramsay to give a series of lectures to his officers on the naval aspects of combined operations.

In March 1943 Ramsay began working closely with General Miles Dempsey, Montgomery's deputy (Monty was still commanding forces in Tunisia), in planning the invasion of Sicily. Neither of them liked the look of the plan when it was presented to them—nor did Montgomery, who described it as a dog's breakfast. The original plan was scrapped and replaced by an invasion on the southeastern corner of Sicily with the American Western Task Force and the British and Canadian Eastern Task Force landing side by side.

The letters exchanged between these two men were cordial, but Ramsay also very diplomatically indicates that Montgomery must respect Ramsay's sphere of command in this operation:

> I have observed, with some disapproval and not without amusement, that in your messages to Dempsey you have been in the habit of issuing universal edicts on matters which require joint agreement. . . . As Naval Commander Eastern Task Force I have considerable responsibility for its success and intend to have my say in the framing of the plan. Incidentally my directive states that I am in executive control of the Force until the Army is firmly established ashore.
>
> I do not for one moment suggest that you would contest any of the above, but I think it is just as well that there should be a full understanding between us, my mind having been somewhat disturbed by the edicts which you have issued of late with your customary clarity.
>
> I look forward with keen anticipation to our association together.[50]

Montgomery was notorious for his lack of tact and diplomacy. Ramsay's success in working effectively and harmoniously with Montgomery through the war in Europe is a testament to his ability to get the best out of other people, even those who are particularly difficult.

Their disagreement over Antwerp was only temporary. But the clearing of the Scheldt was not the end of the problems in keeping the Port of Antwerp open, and Ramsay continued to devote his attention to these new difficulties.

As Antwerp gradually opened for business, the Germans launched a V-weapons campaign to stop the flow of supplies. This V-1 and V-2 weapon bombardment began during the operation to open the Scheldt Estuary. The first V-2 ballistic missile struck Antwerp on October 12, 1944. This was followed by the first V-1 flying bombs on October 23. By the end of March 1945, 1,214 V-weapons had bombarded sixty-five square miles of Greater Antwerp. Three thousand people were killed, and there were about twelve thousand mostly civilian casualties. But only 150 V-1s and 152 V-2s fell on the port facilities itself. Although they managed to sink two large ships and fifty-eight smaller vessels, and damage a lock, the overall V-weapons did not appreciably interdict the Allied logistics pipeline.[51]

As 1944 waned, the Germans realized that the V-weapon bombardment of Antwerp was failing to again close the port. This objective became part of

Hitler's overly ambitious Ardennes offensive launched in December. After breaking through a weakly held Allied sector, the panzers were to swing toward the northwest and drive straight toward Antwerp. If they succeeded in again closing the port, the Germans would have effectively cut the British-Canadian Twenty-First Army Group's entire logistical supply line. On New Year's Day 1945, Ramsay worked on plans for naval cooperation with the Twenty-First Army Group to counter the threat. On the following day he boarded an airplane at an airport near Versailles to fly to Montgomery's headquarters in Brussels to discuss measures for ensuring Antwerp's security. Tragically, his plane crashed shortly after takeoff, killing everyone aboard; the accident report determined that the cause was pilot error.[52]

In a eulogy delivered to the House of Commons, the first lord of the Admiralty succinctly captured the range of Ramsay's strengths: "If Dunkirk was a miracle of improvisation, the naval assault on Normandy was a masterpiece of organization, and Admiral Ramsay was the architect of both."[53]

In 1946 Alan Brooke, who witnessed all the bitter infighting and rivalries among the Allied commanders, offered this reflection: "Personally I look back on the many contacts I was privileged to have with Ramsay as some of my most cherished memories. His great charm, inspiring personality and the breadth of his outlook placed him in that category of men whom one meets only rarely in a lifetime and whose loss deprives one of an irreplaceable friend."[54]

## PATTON: THE MAVERICK COMMANDER

General George S. Patton was the only serving US general twice suspended from duty first in 1943 for slapping shell-shocked soldiers, and later in 1945 for hiring local Nazis to work in the occupation administration. Marshall would have sacked him in 1943, but Eisenhower needed this battle-tested, offensive-focused commander and kept the troublesome Patton. He had snatched Patton from obscurity for TORCH, used him as a decoy for disguising the invasion site in France, and finally called on his drive and skill to achieve the breakout from Normandy.[55]

Few generals in World War II surpassed Patton as a field commander. In Norman Davies's judgment, "Patton's drive through France following the breakout from Normandy in 1944 and his drive through central Germany in 1945 were epic feats."[56] But he also was his own worst enemy due to poor impulse management and an uncontrolled tongue. His personality was enigmatic. Known for his flamboyant appearance with pearl-handled pistols on each hip, out of sight he was a careful planner and even read poetry. General Alexander found him friendly and forthcoming but not in the least way personally aggressive, and stated in his memoirs, "In spite of all his bravura and toughness and terrific drive General George Patton was a very emotional man. He loved his men and they loved him. I have been with him at the front when he was greeted with demonstrations of affection by his soldiers; and there were—as I saw for myself—tears running down his cheeks."[57]

Several German generals thought highly of Patton. General Gunther Blumentritt, Rundstedt's chief of staff, observed, "We regarded General Patton extremely highly as the aggressive Panzer-General of the Allies, a man of incredible initiative and lightning-like action."[58]

General Heinz Guderian, one of the fathers of the German blitzkrieg, told his captors in 1945, "I hear much about General Patton. . . . From the standpoint of a tank specialist, I must congratulate him for his victory since he acted as I should have done had I been in his place."[59] General Alfred Jodl, Hitler's chief of operations, went so far as to say that Patton "was the American Guderian."[60]

Lieutenant General Fritz Bayerlein, who served with Rommel in the African Korps, said he had been amazed at the ease with which Rommel was allowed to escape after El Alamein. He commented, "I do not think General Patton would have let us get away so easily," and also repeated his own belief that Patton was Guderian's equal.[61]

As we have noted when Patton was assigned as the Third Army's commander for OVERLORD, Bradley was very concerned over whether he could control Patton's "impetuous habits." However Bradley's fears proved ill-founded. Bradley warmed to Patton as the campaign unfolded, and he later regretted his hesitation in accepting Patton as one of his army commanders. In fact Bradley concluded that the slapping incident tempered Patton's personality and helped to curb his egotism. "I shall go on believing that the private whose face he slapped in a Sicilian hospital ward did more to win the war than any other privates in the army," Bradley wrote after the war.[62]

If Bradley had overcome his apprehensions over Patton sooner, would OVERLORD have moved forward faster? Could Patton have broken out of the bocage in early July instead of weeks later? Could he then have spearheaded a breakthrough in July and even provided an incentive to his rival Montgomery for more aggressive action around Caen, so they would both encircle the Germans at Falaise and bring the war with Germany to an earlier end? We will never know. The history of a war is usually written by its winners and survivors. In their memoirs Eisenhower and Bradley criticized Patton for overconfidence and injudicious behavior. Patton did not live to refute these criticisms, as he died in an automobile accident in December 1945. But as we have seen, he complained bitterly in his diary about Eisenhower's indecisive behavior and failure to exert his authority over Montgomery.

His diary also reveals that Eisenhower held a luncheon meeting with his four American army commanders and their air officers on May 10, 1945, only two days after the German surrender in Berlin. This was not a victory banquet. Eisenhower told them, "Very confidentially on the necessity for solidarity in the event that any of us are called before a Congressional Committee." Patton then wrote, "It is my opinion that this talking cooperation is for the purpose of covering up probable criticism of strategical blunders which he unquestionably committed during the campaign. Whether or not these were his own or due to too much cooperation with the British, I don't know. I am inclined to think he over-cooperated."[63]

Military historian Martin Blumenson found Patton's judgment skewed due to his distaste for coalition warfare but states, "What Patton was trying to express was his contempt toward those who had delayed final victory because of their mediocrity. . . . Patton believed his superiors had won the war the wrong way. They had been much too slow."[64]

Blumenson's chapter on General Patton in *The War Lords* ends with this final assessment:

> Patton quickened the pace of the war, contributed *élan* to the campaigns in which he participated, and inspired his troops, as no one else, with pride, confidence and a desire to win. He was a masterful leader whose personality and exploits captivated not only his contemporaries but also subsequent generations. He was an authentic military genius.[65]

## BRADLEY—THE DEPENDABLE COMMANDER

After General Omar Bradley overcame his reluctance to have George S. Patton serve under him in Normandy, he and Patton managed to overcome their previous resentments. They worked well as a team with no political backstabbing. Bradley and Patton formed a partnership that Eisenhower could count on—Patton the maverick and the steady Bradley. He needed both.

Over the length of his career in World War II, Bradley gained the reputation as a supremely able battlefield strategist.[66] With impressive results at every turn, he successfully made the transitions from deputy corps commander under Patton in North Africa and Sicily, then to army, and finally to army group commander with Patton now under his command in Normandy.

Bradley was known as a steady, likeable officer and an excellent team player who got along very well with the other OVERLORD commanders, except for Montgomery, in the war's final months. Forrest Pogue termed him the "soldiers' general," who became renowned for "his sober dependability, dogged determination, attention to detail, and proper concern for those who served under him."[67] He was a modest man, who possessed humility, intelligence, and respect for authority.

Bradley worked carefully with Eisenhower and was a forthright go-between in handling relations among the British, French, and Patton. He made Patton's spectacular advances possible and was the essential intermediary between rival commanders.

Before Bradley left Europe at the end of the war, Eisenhower sent him a personal, sincere note recounting his deep gratitude and admiration toward him:

> Since you first joined me in North Africa in early 1942 I have consistently depended, with perfect confidence, upon your counsel and advice. . . . In my opinion you are pre-eminent among the Commanders of major battle units in this war. Your leadership, forcefulness, professional capacity, selflessness, high sense of duty and sympathetic understanding of human beings, combine to stamp you as one of America's great leaders and soldiers.[68]

Bradley's distinguished record of service continued after the war. He served as the head of the Veterans Administration from 1945 to 1947. In 1948 President Truman appointed him US Army chief of staff; in 1949 he became the first chairman of the Joint Chiefs of Staff. The following year Bradley was promoted to five-star general. He was the last person to attain this rank.[69]

## THE FINAL COMMAND

OVERLORD remains a military operation of the first magnitude in the history of war. It stands as the largest combined operation ever conducted. It also featured dazzling organization, technical ingenuity, and instances of great courage and bravery. But it also included bitter rivalries and disputes among its commanders that significantly slowed the race to victory. The differing objectives of Britain and the United States during the war and afterward added to these tensions. Churchill, in fact, very reluctantly agreed to the D-Day invasion, as he feared failure and instead pressed for an invasion through the Balkans.

While each of the Allied commanders had significant strengths, they also had deficiencies and weaknesses that hurt the overall effort. Montgomery undermined Allied operations at Falaise and elsewhere because he wanted to receive the credit for being the victorious commander. His egotism and lack of tact triggered resentment among his fellow commanders. Also in pursuing Britain's political goals, Brooke and Montgomery expended much time and effort criticizing Eisenhower's abilities and decisions rather than cooperating with him.

Eisenhower allowed his role as arbitrator to overshadow his responsibilities as supreme commander. He failed to use his authority to rein in rebellious subordinates at decisive points during OVERLORD and the subsequent European campaign.

Bradley waited too long to involve Patton in the Normandy breakout and erred in stopping Patton's drive to close the Falaise gap. Patton's grandstanding and his lapse of judgment in Sicily threatened his military career and caused him to be sidelined at a time when he was most needed.

The divisions among the Allied commanders were significant on D-Day and throughout the remaining campaign. We believe that if the strategy of speed and mobility had been further employed before and after August 1944, the futile battles of Arnhem, the Hurtgen Forest, and the Bulge would probably never have occurred. Unresolved crises in command were among the factors that prolonged the war in Europe for another nine months and produced an estimated 500,000 additional casualties.[70] The Allied leaders could and should have done better.

However OVERLORD was necessary for the Allied victory in Europe. The Russian army and Allied bombing campaign could not have guaranteed Germany's defeat. OVERLORD attained its strategic objectives by vanquishing the majority of German troops in Western Europe, liberating these nations, and advancing almost to Berlin.

When Eisenhower returned to Omaha Beach in 1964, after a time span of twenty years, he emotionally invoked the reasons for the Normandy campaign and paid a fitting tribute to those who fought there:

> These men came here—British and our allies, and Americans—to storm these beaches for one purpose only, not to gain anything for ourselves, not to fulfill any ambitions that America had for conquest, but just to preserve freedom. . . . Many thousands of men have died for such ideals as these . . . but these young boys . . . were cut off in their prime. . . . I devoutly hope that we will never again have to see such scenes as these. I think and hope, and pray, that humanity will have learned . . . we must find some way . . . to gain an eternal peace for this world.[71]

# NOTES

## INTRODUCTION: REMEMBERING D-DAY IN HISTORY AND MEMORY

1. Robert Blake and William Roger Louis, eds., *Churchill: A Major New Assessment of His Life in Peace and War* (New York: W.W. Norton, 1993), p. 294.
2. Erwin Rommel, *The Rommel Papers*, ed. B.H. Liddell Hart (London: Hamlyn Paperbacks, 1953), pp. 522–23.
3. John Keegan, *Six Armies in Normandy* (New York: Penguin Books, 1994), p. 326.
4. Michael Dolski, Sam Edwards, and John Buckley, eds., *D-Day in History and Memory: The Normandy Landings in International Remembrance and Commemoration* (Denton, TX: University of North Texas Press, 2014), pp. 52–53.
5. Al Reinert, "Lone Star," *Smithsonian*, January–February 2016, p. 110.
6. Martin Blumenson, *The Battle of the Generals* (New York: William Morrow, 1993), p. 43.
7. Niall Barr, *Eisenhower's Armies: The American-British Alliance during World War II* (New York: Pegasus, 2015), p. 1.
8. Max Hastings, *Overlord: D-Day and the Battle for Normandy* (New York: Simon and Schuster, 1984), p. 28.
9. Ibid.; Stephan A. Hart, "A Very Lofty Perch," in *D-Day*, ed. Jane Penrose (Oxford: Osprey, 2006), p. 8; Alan Axelrod, *Patton's Drive* (Guilford, CT: Lyons, 2009), p. 95.

## CHAPTER 1: SETTING THE STAGE: STRUGGLE OVER OPENING THE SECOND FRONT

1. Quoted in Carlo D'Este, *Decision in Normandy* (Old Saybrook, CT: Konecky & Konecky, 1994), p. 32.
2. Martin Gilbert, *Finest Hour: Winston S. Churchill 1939–1941* (London: Heinemann, 1983), p. 1269.
3. Winston S. Churchill, *The Grand Alliance*, vol. 3, *The Second World War* (Boston: Houghton Mifflin, 1950), pp. 605, 609.

4. Lynne Olson, *Citizens of London* (New York: Random House, 2010), p. 149; Lewis E. Lehrman, *Churchill, Roosevelt & Company* (Guilford, CT: Stackpole Books, 2017), p. 279.

5. William L. Shirer, *The Rise and Fall of the Third Reich* (New York: Simon and Schuster, 1960), pp. 892–902.

6. Winston S. Churchill, *Closing the Ring*, vol. 5, *The Second World War* (Boston: Houghton Mifflin, 1951), p. 582.

7. Max Hastings, *Overlord: D-Day and the Battle for Normandy* (New York: Simon and Schuster, 1984), pp. 19–20; Craig L. Symonds, *Neptune: The Allied Invasion of Europe and the D-Day Landings* (New York: Oxford University Press, 2014), p. 31.

8. Hastings, *Overlord*, p. 19; Lehrman, *Churchill, Roosevelt & Company*, p. 290.

9. David Fraser, *Alanbrooke* (Feltham, UK: Hamlyn Paperbacks, 1982), pp. 424, 528.

10. Ibid.

11. Alan Brooke, *War Diaries, 1939–1945*, eds. Alex Danchev and Daniel Todman (London: Phoenix Press, 2001), p. 554.

12. Hastings, *Overlord*, p. 20; Symonds, *Neptune*, pp. 13–15, 49.

13. William Weidner, *Eisenhower and Montgomery at the Falaise Gap* (New York: Xlibris, 2010), p. 261; Charles E. Kirkpatrick, *An Unknown Future and a Doubtful Present: Writing the Victory Plan of 1941* (Washington, DC: Center of Military History, United States Army, 1992), pp. 5–50, 121–139.

14. Bertram Ramsay, *The Year of D-Day*, eds. Robert W. Love, Jr. and John Mayor (Hull, UK: University of Hull Press, 1994), pp. xxx–xxxi.

15. Symonds, *Neptune*, pp. 54–55.

16. Ibid.; Maurice Matloff and Edwin M. Snell, *Strategic Planning for Coalition Warfare, 1941–1942* (Washington, DC: Office of the Chief of Military History, 1953), p. 241.

17. Amanda Mason, "The Secret British Organization of the Second World War," Imperial War Museums, http://www.iwm.org.uk/history/the-secret-organization-of-the-second-world-war (accessed May 22, 2017).

18. Hastings, *Overlord*, p. 23.

19. Ibid., p. 22–25; William F. Moore, "Overlord: The Unnecessary Invasion," *Air War College Research Report* (Maxwell Air Force Base, AL: Air University, US Air Force, March 1986), https://www.ibiblio.org/hyperwar/AAF/NoOverlord/index.html (accessed April 4, 2017).

20. Symonds, *Neptune*, pp. 32, 33.

21. Hastings, *Overlord*, p. 21.

22. John Keegan, *Six Armies in Normandy* (New York: Penguin Books, 1994), p. 53.

23. Symonds, *Neptune*, pp. 101–102; Correlli Barnett, *Engage the Enemy More Closely: The Royal Navy in the Second World War* (New York: W.W. Norton, 1991), p. 622.

24. Ramsay, *Year of D-Day*, p. xxxi.

25. Quoted in Robert Murphy, *Diplomat among Warriors* (Garden City, NY: Doubleday, 1964), p. 163.

26. Symonds, *Neptune*, pp. 98, 100; Rick Atkinson, *An Army at Dawn: The War in North Africa, 1942–1943*, vol. 1, *The Liberation Trilogy* (New York: Henry Holt, 2002), pp. 283–89.

27. Atkinson, *Army at Dawn*, pp. 283–84.

28. Keegan, *Normandy*, pp. 51–52; B. H. Liddell Hart, *History of the Second World War* (Old Saybrook, CT: Konecky & Konecky, 1970), pp. 438–39; Hastings, *Overlord*, p. 21; Symonds, *Neptune*, pp. 101–102; Winston S. Churchill, *The Hinge of Fate*, vol. 4, *The Second World War* (Boston: Houghton Mifflin, 1950), pp. 669–95.

29. Hastings, *Overlord*, p. 21; Keegan, *Six Armies*, p. 52.

30. Atkinson, *Army at Dawn*, pp. 527–28.

31. Rick Atkinson, *The Day of Battle: The War in Sicily and Italy, 1943–1944*, vol. 2, *The Liberation Trilogy* (New York: Henry Holt, 2007), pp. 75, 141–42, 168.

32. Ronald C. Rosbottom, *When Paris Went Dark: The City of Light under German Occupation, 1940–1944* (New York: Back Bay Books, 2014), p. 296.

33. Keegan, *Normandy*, p. 52; Atkinson, *Battle*, pp. 179–86, 207–29, 254–55, 297–306, 536–43.

34. Quoted in Hastings, *Overlord*, p. 22.

35. Keegan, *Normandy*, p. 54.

36. Hastings, *Overlord*, p. 22.

37. Brooke, *War Diaries*, pp. 482–488; Keegan, *Normandy*, pp. 54–55.

38. Churchill, *Closing the Ring*, p. 373.

39. Keegan, *Normandy*, p. 55.

40. John Kennedy, *The Business of War* (London: Hutchinson, 1957), pp. 301–305.

41. Samuel Eliot Morison, *The Two-Ocean War: A Short History of the United States Navy in the Second World War* (Atlantic Monthly Press, 1963), p. 385.

## CHAPTER 2: FIRST SHOTS: CONTROVERSIES OVER D-DAY PLANNING

1. Quoted in Carlo D'Este, *Decision in Normandy* (Old Saybrook, CT: Konecky & Konecky, 1994), p. 36 footnote.

2. Craig L. Symonds, *Neptune: The Allied Invasion of Europe and the D-Day Landings* (New York: Oxford University Press, 2014), p. 105.

3. Frederick Morgan, *Overture to Overlord* (London: Hodder & Stoughton, 1950), p. 105.

4. Duncan Anderson, "Remember This Is an Invasion," in *D-Day*, ed. Jane Penrose (Oxford: Osprey, 2006), pp. 35–36; Morgan, *Overture to Overlord*, pp. 29–122; Carlo D'Este, *Decision in Normandy* (Old Saybrook, CT: Konecky & Konecky, 1994), pp. 32–34.

5. Paul Kennedy, *Engineers of Victory* (New York: Random House, 2013), p. 233; Correlli Barnett, *Engage the Enemy More Closely: The Royal Navy in the Second World War* (New York: W.W. Norton, 1991), p. 547.

6. Philip Ziegler, *Mountbatten* (New York: Alfred A. Knopf, 1985), pp. 186–95; Kennedy, *Engineers of Victory*, pp. 229–35; Barnett, *Engage the Enemy More Closely*, pp. 545–48; Larry Collins, *The Secrets of D-Day* (Beverly Hills, CA: Phoenix Books, 2006), pp. 8–9; John Keegan, *Six Armies in Normandy* (New York: Penguin Books, 1994), pp. 120–25.

7. Symonds, *Neptune*, p. 117.

8. Anderson, "Invasion," p. 37.

9. Morgan, *Overlord*, pp. 123–50; Anderson, "Invasion," pp. 37–38; Symonds, *Neptune*, p. 118; Bernard Ferguson, *The Watery Maze* (London: Collins, 1961), pp. 272–81; "The Secret Files of Churchill in Largs," *Largs and Mill Port News*, February 23, 2010, http://www.largsandmillportnews.com/news/13747855.The_Secret_Files_of_Churchill_in_Largs/ (accessed April 5, 2017).

10. Symonds, *Neptune*, p. 118.

11. Collins, *D-Day*, p. 3.

12. Quoted in Ibid., p. 4.

13. Ibid.

14. Quoted in Max Hastings, *Overlord: D-Day and the Battle for Normandy* (New York: Simon and Schuster, 1984), p. 26.

15. Quoted in John S.D. Eisenhower, *Allies: Pearl Harbor to D-Day* (Garden City, NY: Doubleday, 1982), p. 437.

16. Morgan, *Overlord*, p. 72.

17. Ibid., p. 41.

18. Hastings, *Overlord*, p. 27; Philip Warner, *World War Two: The Untold Story* (London: Cassell, 1988), p. 225.

19. Quoted in Hastings, *Overlord*, p. 27.
20. Ibid.
21. Morgan, *Overlord*, pp. 146–48, 152–53; Churchill, *Chasing the Ring*, p. 582–85; Hastings, *Overlord*, p. 26–27; Eisenhower, *Allies*, p. 437–38.
22. Symonds, *Neptune*, p. 108.
23. Ibid., p. 119.
24. Martin Blumenson, *The Battle of the Generals* (New York: William Morrow, 1993), p. 71; Morgan, *Overlord*, pp. 143, 148–50, 158–59.
25. Forrest C. Pogue, *George C. Marshall: The Organizer of Victory* (New York: Viking Press, 1973), pp. 242–43; Symonds, *Neptune*, p. 119.
26. D'Este, *Normandy*, p. 38.
27. Samuel Eliot Morrison, *The Two-Ocean War: A Short History of the United States Navy in the Second World War* (Boston, MA: Atlantic Monthly Press, 1963), p. 386; Anderson, "Invasion," p. 35.

## CHAPTER 3: "WHO WILL COMMAND OVERLORD?"

1. Max Hastings, *Overlord: D-Day and the Battle for Normandy* (New York: Simon and Schuster, 1984), p. 29.
2. Winston S. Churchill, *Closing the Ring*, vol. 5, *The Second World War* (Boston: Houghton Mifflin, 1951), p. 365.
3. Quoted in David Fraser, *Alanbrooke* (London: Collins, 1982), p. 21.
4. Ibid., p. 6.
5. Carlo D'Este, *Decision in Normandy* (Old Saybrook, CT: Konecky & Konecky, 1994), p. 44; Churchill, *Closing the Ring*, p. 85; John S.D. Eisenhower, *Allies: Pearl Harbor to D-Day* (Garden City, NY: Doubleday, 1982), photo caption opposite, p. 140; Winston S. Churchill, *Their Finest Hour*, vol. 2, *The Second World War* (Boston: Houghton Mifflin, 1949), p. 96; Winston S. Churchill, *The Grand Alliance*, vol. 3, *The Second World War* (Boston: Houghton Mifflin, 1950), p. 626; T.A. Heathcote, *Dictionary of Field Marshals of the British Army* (Barnsley, South Yorkshire: Pen & Sword Military, 1999), pp. 56–59.
6. Alan Brooke, *War Diaries, 1939–1945*, eds. Alex Danchev and Daniel Todman (London: Phoenix Press, 2001), pp. 441–42.
7. Churchill, *Closing the Ring*, pp. 81–82; Forrest C. Pogue, *George C. Marshall: The Organizer of Victory* (New York: Viking Press, 1973), pp. 260–62.
8. Pogue, *Marshall*, p. xi; Antony Beevor, *The Second World War* (New York: Little, Brown, 2012), p. 180.
9. Eisenhower, *Allies*, photo caption opposite, p. 140.

10. Quoted in Craig L. Symonds, *Neptune: The Allied Invasion of Europe and the D-Day Landings* (New York: Oxford University Press, 2014), p. 167.

11. Jonathan W. Jordan, *Brothers, Rivals, Victors* (New York: Caliber, 2011), p. 222.

12. Symonds, *Neptune*, p. 168; Churchill, *Closing the Ring*, p. 301; D'Este, *Normandy*, p. 42.

13. D'Este, *Normandy*, p. 42–43.

14. Quoted in Pogue, *Marshall*, p. 321.

15. Stephen E. Ambrose, *Eisenhower: Soldier, General of the Army, President-Elect 1890–1952*, vol.1, *Eisenhower* (Simon and Schuster, 1983), p. 152; Churchill, *Closing the Ring*, p. 418.

16. Quoted in Ambrose, *Eisenhower*, p. 131.

17. Jordan, *Brothers*, pp. 7–32; Dwight Jon Zimmerman, "Eliminating the 'Dead Wood,'" Defense Media Network, September 1, 2015, http://www.denfensemedianetwork.com/stories/gen-george-c-marshall-eliminates-dead-wood/ (accessed May 29, 2017).

18. Quoted in Jordan, *Brothers*, p. 42.

19. Ibid., p. 276.

20. Jordan, *Brothers*, pp. 277–78; Symonds, *Neptune*, pp. 171–74.

21. Lewis E. Lehrman, *Churchill, Roosevelt & Company* (Guilford, CT: Stackpole Books, 2017), p. 2.

22. Martin Blumenson, *The Battle of the Generals* (New York: William Morrow, 1993), p. 27; Jordan, *Brothers*, p. 276.

23. Quoted in Fraser, *Alanbrooke*, p. 421.

24. Brooke, *War Diaries*, p. 351.

25. Hastings, *Overlord*, pp. 28–29.

26. Quoted in Jordan, *Brothers*, p. 53.

27. Ibid.

28. Quoted in Alun Chalfont, *Montgomery of Alamein* (New York: Atheneum, 1976), p. 26.

29. Ibid., p. 51.

30. Chalfont, *Montgomery*, pp. 36, 39, 41, 51, 54; Blumenson, *Generals*, p. 28.

31. Quoted in Chalfont, *Montgomery*, p. 99.

32. Ibid., pp. 102–103.

33. Nigel Hamilton, *Monty: The Making of a General* (New York: McGraw Hill, 1981), p. 275.

34. Quoted in Peter Caddick-Adams, *Monty and Rommel* (New York: Overlook, 2011), p. 194.

35. Chalfont, *Montgomery*, pp. 109–10; Brooke, *War Diaries*, p. xviii.

36. Chalfont, *Montgomery*, p. 110–12.

37. Brooke, *War Diaries*, p. 19.

38. Ibid.

39. Caddick-Adams, *Monty*, pp. 222–41; Chalfont, *Montgomery*, pp. 113–14.

40. Caddick-Adams, *Monty*, pp. 222–41.

41. Quoted in Ibid., p. 285.

42. John Harvey, ed., *The War Diaries of Oliver Harvey* (London: Collins, 1978), p. 148.

43. Brooke, *War Diaries*, p. 496.

44. Omar N. Bradley, *A Soldier's Story* (New York: Modern Library, 1999), p. 207.

45. Ibid.

46. D'Este, *Normandy*, p. 51 footnote. Eisenhower is quoted here by General Sir Miles Dempsey in a 1947 interview with historian Forrest Pogue.

47. Brooke, *War Diaries*, p. 417.

48. Ibid., p. 452.

49. Russell F. Weigley, *Eisenhower's Lieutenants* (Bloomington: Indiana University Press, 1981), p. 37.

50. Churchill, *Closing the Ring*, pp. 420, 426, 438–39.

51. Chalfont, *Montgomery*, p. 220.

52. Quoted in Ibid.

53. Churchill, *Closing the Ring*, pp. 424; Nigel Hamilton, *Montgomery: D-Day Commander* (Washington, DC: Potomac Books, 2007), p. 38.

54. Quoted in Blumenson, *Generals*, 30.

55. Barrett Tillman, *D-Day Encyclopedia* (New York: Regnery History, 2014), pp. 190–91.

56. Quoted in Martin Gilbert, *Finest Hour: Winston S. Churchill, 1939–1941* (London: Heinemann, 1983), pp. 1060–61.

57. Symonds, *Neptune*, p. 173; Michael F. Finnegan, "General Eisenhower's Battle for Control of the Strategic Bombers in Support of Operation OVERLORD: A Case Study in Unity of Command" (Carlisle Barracks, PA: US Army War College 1999), pp. 6–8.

58. Quoted in Rick Atkinson, *The Guns at Last Light*, vol. 3, *The Liberation Trilogy* (New York: Henry Holt, 2013), p. 28–29.

59. Quoted in Hastings, *Overlord*, p. 44.

60. Arthur W. Tedder, *With Prejudice: The War Memoir of Marshal of the Royal Air Force, Lord Tedder* (London: Cassell, 1966), pp. 210–45.

61. Symonds, *Neptune*, p. 172; Finnegan, "General Eisenhower's Battle," pp. 3–5; Tedder, *With Prejudice*, pp. 210–45; D'Este, *Normandy*, p. 53; Christopher

Foxley Morris, "Marshal of the Royal Air Force Lord Tedder," in *War Lords*, ed. Michael Carver (Boston: Little, Brown, 1976), p. 483–99.

62. Quoted in Finnegan, "General Eisenhower's Battle," p. 5.

63. D .K. R. Crosswell, *Beetle: The Life of General Walter Bedell Smith* (Lexington, KY: University of Kentucky Press, 2010), p. 191–257, 287–355, 551–606, 667–734; Antony Beevor, "Eisenhower's Pit Bull," review of *Beetle: The Life of General Walter Bedell Smith* by D.K.R. Crosswell, *Wall Street Journal*, October 23, 2010; Terry Shoptaugh, "Ike's Hatchet Man Emerges from the Shadows," Review of *Beetle: The Life of General Walter Bedell Smith* by D.K.R. Crosswell, H-War, H-Net Reviews, May 2012, http://www.h-net.org/reviews/showrev.php?id=35756 (accessed April 4, 2017).

64. Jim DeFelice, *Omar Bradley* (Washington, DC: Regnery, 2011), p. 19.

65. DeFelice, *Bradley*, pp. 7–38; Forrest C. Pogue, *Education of a General* (New York: Viking, 1963), p. 258.

66. Quoted in DeFelice, *Bradley*, p. 39.

67. Ibid., 48; Blumenson, *Generals*, p. 32.

68. Bradley, *A Soldier's Story* (New York: Modern Library, 1999), p. 31.

69. DeFelice, *Bradley*, p. 22.

70. Quoted in Jordan, *Brothers*, p. 250.

71. Ibid., p. 231.

72. DeFelice, *Bradley*, p. 68–69; Blumenson, *Generals*, p. 31.

73. DeFelice, *Bradley*, p. 152; Blumenson, *Generals*, pp. 33–34; Jordan, *Brothers*, p. 254; Bradley, *Soldier's Story*, p. 8.

74. Bradley, *Soldier's Story*, p. 43.

75. Rick Atkinson, *An Army at Dawn: The War in North Africa, 1942–1943*, vol. 1, *The Liberation Trilogy* (New York: Henry Holt, 2002), p. 401.

76. Alan Axelrod, *Patton's Drive: The Making of America's Greatest General* (Guilford, CT: Lyons, 2009), p. x.

77. Harry Yeide, *Fighting Patton* (Minneapolis, MN: Zenith, 2011), pp. 1–28; Ladislas Farago, *Patton: Ordeal and Triumph* (New York: Dell, 1963), pp. 1–80.

78. Quoted in Yeide, *Patton*, p. 29.

79. Ibid., 45–47.

80. Farago, *Patton*, pp. 120–22, 135.

81. Quoted in Jordan, *Brothers*, p. 33.

82. Zimmerman, "Dead Wood"; Paul G. Munch, *General George C. Marshall and the Army Staff: A Study in Effective Staff Leadership* (Washington, DC: National Defense University National War College Fort McNair, March 19, 1992), http://www.dtic.mil/get-tr-doc/pdf?AD=ADA437156 (accessed April 4, 2017); Jordan, *Brothers*, p. 32;

83. Jordan, *Brothers*, pp. 41, 46–47; Farago, *Patton*, pp. 166–68.

84. Jordan, *Brothers*, pp. 67, 70–73.

85. Yeide, *Patton*, pp. 155–75.

86. Rick Atkinson, *The Day of Battle: The War in Sicily and Italy, 1943–1944*, vol. 2, *The Liberation Trilogy* (New York: Henry Holt, 2007), pp. 123–70.

87. Quoted in Jordan, *Brothers*, p. 176.

88. Ibid.

89. Atkinson, *Day of Battle*, pp. 170–72; Jordan, *Brothers*, pp. 234–65.

90. Quoted in Jordan, *Brothers*, p. 234.

91. Ibid., p. 240.

92. DeFelice, *Bradley*, pp. 70, 152, 154–55, 162.

93. Blumenson, *Generals*, pp. 33, 37–38; Jordan, *Brothers*, pp. 247–49; DeFelice, *Bradley*, pp. 70, 152, 154–55, 162; Farago, *Patton*, pp. 349, 351, 362; Martin Blumenson, "General George S. Patton," in *War Lords*, pp. 554–61.

94. "D-Day's Forgotten Commander," University of Cambridge, March 5, 2014, http://www.cam.ac.uk/news/d-days-forgotten-commander (accessed April 4, 2017).

95. Kennedy, *Engineers of Victory*, p. 251. W.S. Chalmers, *Full Cycle: The Biography of Admiral Sir Bertram Ramsay* (London: Hodder & Stoughton, 1959); Bertram Ramsay, *Year of D-Day*, eds. Robert W. Love, Jr. and John Mayor (Hull, UK: University of Hull Press, 1994), pp. xiv–vi.

96. Ramsay, *Year of D-Day*, pp. xvi–xvii.

97. Quoted in David Stafford, *Ten Days to D-Day* (New York: Little, Brown, 2003), p. 34.

98. Correlli Barnett, *Engage the Enemy More Closely: The Royal Navy in the Second World War* (New York: W.W. Norton, 1991), p. 143.

99. *Dictionary of National Biography*, s.v. "Ramsay, Sir Bertram Home," http:www.oxforddnb.com.

100. Author interview with David Ramsay on the Backhouse relationship with his father Bertram Ramsay, July 14, 2015; Symonds, *Neptune*, pp. 174–75; Barnett, *Engage*, pp. 50, 142.

101. Paul Kennedy, *Engineers of Victory*, p. 251; Barnett, *Engage the Enemy*, pp. 141–42, 146; Hugh Sebag-Montefiore, *Dunkirk* (Cambridge: Harvard University Press, 2008), pp. 254, 447, 541; Chalmers, Full Cycle, pp. 12–54, 271.

102. "D-Day's 'Forgotten Man,'" University of Cambridge, June 6, 2014, http://www.cam.ac.uk/research/news/d-days-forgotten-man (accessed April 4, 2017).

## CHAPTER 4: THE OVERLORD GAMBLE

1. John S.D. Eisenhower, *Allies: Pearl Harbor to D-Day* (Garden City, NY, 1982), pp. 439–40; William Weidner, *Eisenhower and Montgomery at the Falaise Gap* (New York: Xlibris Corp, 2010), pp. 22–25; D.K.R. Crosswell, *Beetle: The Life of General Walter Bedell Smith* (Louisville: University Press of Kentucky), p. 554.

2. Quoted in Crosswell, *Beetle*, p. 569.

3. Quoted in Carlo D'Este, *Decision in Normandy* (Old Saybrook, CT: Konecky & Konecky, 1994), p. 55.

4. Correlli Barnett, *Engage the Enemy More Closely: The Royal Navy in the Second World War* (New York: W.W. Norton, 1991), p. 764; Alun Chalfont, *Montgomery of Alamein* (New York: Atheneum, 1976), p. 220; Martin Blumenson, *The Battle of the Generals* (New York: William Morrow, 1993), p. 74; Winston S. Churchill, *Closing the Ring*, vol. 5, *The Second World War* (Boston: Houghton Mifflin, 1951), p. 444; Bernard Montgomery, "Diary, December 31, 1943–January 2, 1944," in *Montgomery and the Battle of Normandy*, ed. Steven Brooks (Gloucestershire: History Press, 2008), p. 15.

5. D'Este, *Normandy*, pp. 56–57; Blumenson, *Generals*, pp. 73–75.

6. Paul Kennedy, *Engineers of Victory* (New York: Random House), p. 242.

7. Crosswell, *Beetle*, p. 565.

8. Barnett, *Engage the Enemy*, pp. 753–54; Andrew Gordon, "The Greatest Military Armada Ever Launched, Operation Neptune," in *D-Day*, ed. Jane Penrose (Oxford: Osprey, 2010), p. 135; Editors Robert W. Love, Jr. and John Mayor's Biography of Admiral Ramsay in Bertram Ramsay, *The Year of D-Day* (Hull, UK: University of Hull Press, 1994), p. xxxv; B.B. Schofield, *Operation Neptune* (Barnsley, South Yorkshire: Pen & Sword, 1974), pp. 28–44.

9. Barnett, *Engage the Enemy*, p. 755.

10. Quoted in Barnett, *Engage the Enemy*, p. 781.

11. Ibid., p. 763.

12. William Weidner, *Eisenhower and Montgomery* (New York: Xlibris, 2010), p. 26; Kenneth Edwards, *Operation Neptune* (London: Fonthill, 2013), p. 80.

13. Kevin M. Arnwine, *An Analysis of Operation Neptune: Lessons for Today's Naval Logistics Planners* (Newport, RI: Naval War College, 1995), p. 8.

14. Barnett, *Engage the Enemy*, pp. 796–97, 780; W.S. Chalmers, *Full Cycle: the Biography of Admiral Sir Bertram Home Ramsay* (London: Hodder & Stoughton, 1959), pp. 196–205.

15. Rick Atkinson, *The Guns at Last Light*, vol. 3, *The Liberation Trilogy*

(New York: Henry Holt, 2013), p. 28; Samuel Eliot Morison, *The Two-Ocean War* (Boston: Little, Brown, 1963), p. 391; Gordon, "Armada," p. 141.

16. Williamson Murray, "A Visitor to Hell on the Beaches," in *D-Day*, ed. Jane Penrose (Oxford: Osprey, 2010), p. 151.

17. Quoted in Craig L. Symonds, *Neptune: The Allied Invasion of Europe and the D-Day Landings* (New York: Oxford University Press, 2014), pp. 187–89.

18. Symonds, *Neptune*, p. 189–91; Thomas B. Buell, *Master of Sea Power: A Biography of Fleet Admiral Ernest J. King* (Annapolis: Naval Institute Press, 1980), p. 453; Lewis E. Lehrman, *Churchill, Roosevelt & Company* (Guilford, CT: Stackpole Books, 2017), p. 164.

19. Bernard Ferguson, *The Watery Maze* (London: Collins, 1961), pp. 321–22.

20. Quoted in Barnett, *Engage the Enemy*, p. 770.

21. Quoted in Thomas B. Buell, *Master of Sea Power* (Annapolis, MD: Naval Institute Press, 1980), p. 465.

22. Morison, *Two-Ocean War*, p. 390; Barnett, *Engage the Enemy*, pp. 771–72; Symonds, *Neptune*, p. 192–93; Ken Ford, *Operation Neptune, 1944* (Oxford: Osprey, 2014), p. 19.

23. Ferguson, *Watery Maze*, p. 312.

24. Quoted in Barnett, *Engage*, p. 785; Ferguson, *Watery Maze*, p. 312.

25. Barnett, *Engage*, p. 773.

26. Crosswell, *Beetle*, p. 567; Max Hastings, *Overlord: D-Day and the Battle for Normandy* (New York: Simon and Schuster, 1984), p. 33; D'Este, *Normandy*, p. 65.

27. D'Este, *Normandy*, p. 65; Max Hastings, *Overlord*, p. 33; Jim DeFelice, *Omar Bradley* (Washington, DC: Regnery, 2011), p. 166; Alan Moorhead, *Eclipse* (London: Soho Press, 1988), p. 91–92; Alistair Horne and David Montgomery, *Monty: The Lonely Leader 1944–1945* (New York: Harper Collins, 1994), p. 77.

28. Quoted in Hastings, *Overlord*, p. 33.

29. D'Este, *Normandy*, p. 65.

30. D'Este, *Normandy*, p. 65; Captain H.C. Butchez, "Diary, January 21, 1944," in *Voices from D-Day*, ed. Jon E. Lewis (New York: Skyhorse, 2014), pp. 4–5; Hastings, *Overlord*, p. 33; Barnett, *Engage the Enemy*, p. 765; Morison, *Two-Ocean War*, p. 385; Symonds, *Neptune*, p. 178.

31. Ramsay, *Year of D-Day*, p. 11.

32. Forrest C. Pogue, *George C. Marshall: Organizer of Victory* (New York: Viking, 1973), p. 334; Symonds, *Neptune*, pp. 182, 183, 191; Chalfont, *Montgomery*, p. 223.

33. Ramsay, *Year of D-Day*, p. 48.

34. Crosswell, *Beetle*, p. 567; Moorhead, *Eclipse*, p. 92; Collins, *D-Day*, pp. 8–11.

35. Quoted in Philip Ziegler, *Mountbatten* (New York: Alfred A. Knopf, 1985), p. 192.

36. Duncan Anderson, "Remember This Is an Invasion," in *D-Day*, ed. Jane Penrose (Oxford: Osprey, 2006), pp. 38–39.

37. Barnett, *Engage*, pp.761–63.

38. Quoted in Ladislas Farago, *Patton: Ordeal and Triumph* (New York: Dell, 1963), p. 388.

39. Ibid., p. 389.

40. Michael Arnold, *Hollow Heroes* (Oxford: Casemate, 2015), pp. 61, 131.

41. Erwin Rommel, *The Rommel Papers*, ed. B.H. Liddell Hart (London: Hamlyn Paperbacks, 1953), p. 329.

42. Quoted in Farago, *Patton*, pp. 403–404.

43. Ibid., pp.404–405.

44. D'Este, *Normandy*, pp. 73–74.

45. DeFelice, *Bradley*, pp. 166–67.

46. Hastings, *Overlord*, p. 44.

47. Arthur Tedder, *With Prejudice* (Boston: Little, Brown, 1966), pp. 512–13; Eisenhower, *Allies*, 443–47; R.J. Overy, *The Air War 1939–1945* (New York: Stein and Day, 1981), pp. 97–98.

48. Williamson Murray, "In the Air, on the Ground and in the Factories," in *D-Day*, Jane ed. Penrose (Oxford: Osprey, 2006), pp. 118–20; Glen Infield, *Big Week!* (Los Angeles: Pinnacle Books, 1974), pp. 199–209; Overy, *Air War*, pp. 98–99; Walter J. Boyne, *Clash of Wings* (New York: Simon and Schuster, 1994), p. 337.

49. Adolf Galland, *The First and the Last* (New York: Ballantine Books, 1957), p. 211.

50. Quoted in Morison, *Two-Ocean War*, p. 387.

51. Stephen A. Hart, "A Very Lofty Perch," in *D-Day*, ed. Jane Penrose (Oxford: Osprey, 2006), pp. 85–86; Hastings, *Overlord*, p. 45.

52. Nicholas Stargardt, *The German War: A Nation under Arms* (New York: Basic Books, 2015), p. 427; Nigel Cawthorne, *Fighting Them on the Beaches* (London: Capella, 2002), pp. 54–55.

53. David Stafford, *Ten Days to D-Day* (New York: Little, Brown, 2003), p. 53–54; Harry Yeide, *Fighting Patton* (Minneapolis, MN: Zenith, 2011), pp. 218–20; Christina J. M. Goulter, "The Great Shadow Boxing Match," in *D-Day*, ed. Jane Penrose (Oxford: Osprey, 2006), pp. 56–62; Farago, *Patton*, p. 400.

54. Quoted in Joshua Levine, *Operation Fortitude* (London: Collins, 2012), p. 230.

55. Cawthorne, *Fighting*, pp. 55–56; Mark A. Stoler, *Allies in War* (New York: Hodder Arnold, 2007), p. 153.

56. Philip Warner, *World War Two: The Untold Story* (London: Cassell, 1988), p. 225.

57. Cawthorne, *Fighting*, pp. 72–73.

58. Ibid.

59. Eisenhower, *Allies*, p. 46; Cawthorne, *Fighting*, pp. 72–73; Douglas Botting, *The D-Day Invasion* (Alexandria, VA: Time-Life Books, 1978), p. 54; Harry C. Butcher, *Three Years with Eisenhower* (New York: Simon and Schuster, 1946), p. 505; Matthew Hickman, "How Military Operations Get Their Code Name," Mental Floss, September 8, 2011, http://mentalfloss.com/article/28711/how-military-operations-get-their-code-names (accessed April 4, 2017).

60. Williamson Murray, "A Visitor to Hell," in *D-Day*, ed. Jane Penrose (Oxford: Osprey, 2006), pp. 151–52; Eisenhower, *Allies*, p. 455; R. Ernest Dupuy and Tremor N. Dupuy, *The Harper Encyclopedia of Military History* (New York: Harper Collins, 1993), pp. 1209–10.

61. D'Este, *Normandy*, p. 75 footnote. Bradley is quoted here in a 1946 interview with historian Forrest Pogue.

62. Ibid., pp. 76–77.

63. Blumenson, *Generals*, pp. 78–81; Hastings, *Overlord*, pp. 35–36; Nigel Hamilton, *Montgomery: D-Day Commander* (Dulles, VA: Potomac Books, 2006), pp. 46–49.

64. Symonds, *Neptune*, pp. 123–26.

65. Hastings, *Overlord*, pp. 34–35.

66. Churchill, *Closing the Ring*, p. 379; Hastings, *Overlord*, p. 34.

67. Quoted in Atkinson, *Last Light*, p. 111; Botting, *D-Day*, p. 58; DeFelice, *Bradley*, p. 214–15.

68. Quoted in Atkinson, *Last Light*, p. 111; Frederick Morgan, *Overture to Overlord* (London: Hodder & Stoughton, 1950), pp. 157–58, Blumenson, *Generals*, 72, 79; Stephen E. Ambrose, *D-Day June 6, 1944* (London: Pocket Books, 1994), p 78.

69. Barnett, *Engage*, p. 798; Symonds, *Neptune*, pp. 210–11.

70. Ramsay, *Year of D-Day*, p. 60.

71. Edwin P. Hoyt, *The Invasion before Normandy: The Secret Battle of Slapton Sands* (Lanham, MD: Scarborough House, 1999), pp. 99–138.

72. Denise Goolsby, "Vet Part of Exercise That Claimed 600 Lives," *Desert Sun*, April 24, 2010, p. B3.

73. Hoyt, *Invasion before Normandy*, p. 9.

74. Hoyt, *Invasion before Normandy*, pp. 99–138; Symonds, *Neptune*, pp.

210–17, 219, 221; Morison, *Two-Ocean War*, p. 391; Barnett, *Engage the Enemy*, p. 798.

75. Atkinson, *Last Light*, p. 3.

76. D'Este, *Normandy*, p. 82; Atkinson, *Last Light*, p. 6; Symonds, *Neptune*, p. 221.

77. Quoted in Atkinson, *Last Light*, p. 6.

78. D'Este, *Normandy*, p. 83.

79. Carlo D'Este, "A Lingering Controversy: Eisenhower's 'Broad Front' Strategy," *Armchair General*, October 7, 2009, http:www.armchairgeneral.com/a-lingering-controversy-eisenhowers-broad-front-strategy.htm (accessed April 4, 2017).

80. "Montgomery's Notes for Address on 15 May 1944: Brief Presentation of Plans before the King," in Stephen Brooks, ed., *Montgomery and the Battle of Normandy* (Stroud, UK: History Press, 2008), p. 103.

81. Quoted in Weidner, *Eisenhower and Montgomery*, p. 262.

82. Alan Brooke, *War Diaries, 1939–1945*, ed. Alex Danchev and Daniel Todman (London: Phoenix Press, 2001), p. 546.

83. D'Este, *Normandy*, pp. 82–104; Atkinson, *Last Light*, pp. 3–12; Farago, *Patton*, pp. 401–402; William B. Breuer, *Feuding Allies* (New York: John Wiley & Sons, 1996), p. 174; Anthony Kemp, *The Unknown Battle: Metz, 1944* (New York: Stein and Day, 1981), pp. 4–5.

84. Martin Hill, "The Imposter General: Bernard Montgomery's D-Day Body Double," Decoded Past, June 15, 2013, http://decodedpast.com/the-imposter-general-bernard-montgomerys-d-day-body-double/1332 (accessed April 4, 2017).

85. Levine, *Fortitude*, pp. 263–66; Hill, "Imposter General"; Ben Macintyre, "Monty's Boozy Aussie Double Fooled Nazi Spy," *Australian*, March 13, 2010, http://www.theaustralian.com.au/news/world/d-day-montgomery-spy/story-e6frg650-1225839889393 (accessed May 29, 2017).

86. Ramsay, *Year of D-Day*, p. 76 footnote notes specific new Allied intelligence on German Twenty-First Panzer Division and Ninety-First Infantry Division.

87. Quoted in Symonds, *Neptune*, p. 221; Ramsay, *Year of D-Day*, p. 77.

88. Quoted in Stafford, *Ten Days*, p. 74.

89. Ramsay, *Year of D-Day*, p. 78. Footnote explains airdrop controversy; John Keegan, *Six Armies in Normandy* (New York: Penguin Books, 1994), pp. 71, 73; Stafford, *Ten Days*, pp. 73–75; DeFelice, *Bradley*, pp. 168–69; Allan R. Millett, "Blood upon the Risers," in *D-Day*, ed. Jane Penrose (Oxford: Osprey, 2006), pp. 169–72.

90. Stafford, *Ten Days*, pp. 86–87.

91. Churchill, *Closing the Ring*, p. 619.

92. Quoted in Stafford, *Ten Days*, p. 147.

93. Ramsay, *Year of D-Day*, pp. 79–80; Barnett, *Engage*, p. 806.

94. Letter from HRH George VI to Winston S. Churchill, June 2, 1944 (Cambridge, England: Churchill Archives, Churchill College); Letter from Winston S. Churchill to HRH George VI, June 3, 1944 (Cambridge, England: Churchill Archives, Churchill College).

95. Ramsay, *Year of D-Day*, p. 80; Eisenhower, *Allies*, p. 465–66.

96. Quoted in Jonathan W. Jordan, *Brothers, Rivals, Victors* (New York: Caliber, 2011), p. 315.

97. Atkinson, *Last Light*, pp. 28–29.

98. Lewis, ed., *Voices from D-Day*, p. 1.

99. Quoted in Cawthorne, *Beaches*, p. 73; Geoffrey C. Ward, *The War: An Intimate History* (New York: Alfred A. Knopf, 2007), p. 189.

100. Stafford, *Ten Days*, pp. 232–33.

101. Ibid., pp. 50–51.

102. Symonds, *Neptune*, p. 236.

103. Quoted in Stafford, *Ten Days*, p. 234.

104. Quoted in Chalfont, *Montgomery*, p. 238.

105. Ibid., p. 233.

106. Symonds, *Neptune*, p. 237.

107. Stafford, *Ten Days*, p. 209.

108. Quoted in Stafford, *Ten Days*, p. 260.

109. Ibid.

110. Ibid., p. 263.

111. Stephen A. Hart, "A Very Lofty Perch," in *D-Day*, p. 83.

112. Samuel J. Newland, "The Great Crusade," in *D-Day*, ed. Jane Penrose (Oxford: Osprey, 2006), p. 27.

113. Deborah Cadbury, *Princes at War* (London: Bloomburg, 2015), p. 301; Gordon, "Armada," p. 141; Stafford, *D-Day*, p. 277; Richard Holmes, *The Story of D-Day* (New York: Metro Books, 2014), p. 42; Ford, *Operation Neptune*, p. 20; Kenneth Edwards, *Operation Neptune* (Sabon, UK: Foothill, 1946), p. 37. The exact number of ships that were part of NEPTUNE or the D-Day fleet has been estimated in the range of four thousand to seven thousand vessels. The figures at the high end tend to include all of the landing craft and supporting ships for supply or transport of logistical materials that supported the invasion.

114. Denise Goolsby, "Dillon Scouted Waves for Ships at Normandy," *Desert Sun*, March 7, 2010, p. B3.

## CHAPTER 5: CRACKS IN FORTRESS EUROPE

1. Nigel Cawthorne, *Fighting Them on the Beaches* (London: Capella, 2002), p. 26.

2. Dennis Showalter, *Patton and Rommel* (New York: Berkley Caliber, 2005), pp. 336–40; Cawthorne, *Beaches*, p. 26; Dennis Showalter, "Throw Them Back," in *D-Day*, ed. Jane Penrose (Oxford: Osprey, 2006), pp. 96–97; Martin Blumenson, *The Battle of the Generals* (New York: William Morrow, 1993), pp. 91–92; Douglas Botting, *The D-Day Invasion* (Alexandria: VA: Time-Life Books, 1978), p. 8; Alexander McKee, *Last Round against Rommel* (New York: Signet Books, 1966), p. 29; Henri Eberle, and Matthias Uhl, *The Hitler Book* (New York: Bristol Park Books, 2005), pp. 320, 326.

3. Blumenson, *Generals*, pp. 92–93; Showalter, *Patton and Rommel*, p. 340–41; "Disagreement in High Places: Rommel—Von Rundstedt,"The Wehrmacht in Normandy, http://www.batterie-merville.com/the-merville-battery/540-2/?lang=en (accessed April 4, 2017); Samuel W. Mitcham, Jr., *The Desert Fox in Normandy* (Westport, CT: Praeger, 1997), pp. 24–25; Günther Blumentritt, *Von Rundstedt: The Soldier and the Man* (London: Odhams Press, 1952), pp. 127, 194–95, 204; Stephen E. Ambrose, *D-Day June 6, 1944* (London: Pocket Books, 1994), p. 65.

4. Showalter, *Patton and Rommel*, pp. 339–40; Blumenson, *Generals,* pp. 93–94.

5. Erwin Rommel, *The Rommel Papers*, ed. B.H. Liddell Hart (London: Hamlyn Paperbacks, 1953), p. 455.

6. Ibid.

7. Cawthorne, *Beaches*, p. 27; Blumenson, *Generals*, pp. 93–94; David Stafford, *Ten Days to D-Day* (New York: Little, Brown, 2003), p. 43;. Hans Speidel, *We Defended Normandy* (London: Herbert Jenkins, 1951), p. 76; Ambrose, *D-Day*, p. 117.

8. Carlo D'Este, *Decision in Normandy* (Old Saybrook, CT: Konecky & Konecky, 1994), p. 115; Samuel W. Mitcham, Jr., *The Desert Fox in Normandy* (Westport, CT: Praeger, 1997), pp. 26–27; Showalter, *Patton and Rommel*, pp. 243–44; Rommel, *Papers*, p. 469.

9. Rommel, *Papers*, p. 468 footnote; D'Este, *Normandy*, p. 116.

10. Larry Collins, *The Secrets of D-Day* (Beverly Hills, CA: Phoenix Books, 2006), p. 23.

11. Collins, *D-Day*, pp. 17–23; John Keegan, *Six Armies in Normandy* (New York: Penguin Books, 1994), p. 65.

12. Showalter, *Patton and Rommel*, p. 344; Mitcham, *Desert Fox*, pp. 28–31;

D'Este, *Normandy*, p. 117; Heinz Magenheimer, *Hitler's War* (New York: Barnes & Noble Books, 1997), p. 247.

13. Quoted in Stafford, *D-Day*, p. 26; Joshua Levine, *Operation Fortitude* (London: Collins, 2012), p. 4.

14. Quoted in Beevor, *D-Day: The Battle for Normandy* (New York: Penguin Books, 2009), p. 37; Paul Carrell, *Invasion! They're Coming!* (New York: Bantam, 1964), p. 7.

15. Joseph Balkoski, *Beyond the Beachhead* (Mechanicsville, PA: Stackpole Books, 1999), p. 99.

16. Martin Blumenson, *Breakout and Pursuit* (Washington, DC: Office of the Chief of Military History, United States Army, 1961), p. 32.

17. Ibid.

18. Quoted in Beevor, *D-Day*, p. 39.

19. Ibid., p. 37.

20. Keegan, *Normandy*, p. 62; Mitcham, *Desert Fox*, p. 25; Balkoski, *Beachhead*, p. 99; Alan Moorhead, *Eclipse* (London: Soho, 1988), pp. 94, 138–41; Beevor, *D-Day*, pp. 37–39; R. Ernest Dupuy and Tremor N. Dupuy, *The Harper Encyclopedia of Military History* (New York: Harper Collins, 1993), p. 1210.

21. Beevor, *D-Day*, pp. 38–39; Moorhead, *Eclipse*, pp. 138–41; Dupuy, *Military History*, p. 1210.

22. Allan R. Millett, "Blood upon the Risers," in *D-Day*, ed. Jane Penrose (Oxford: Osprey, 2006), pp. 172–73; Blumentritt, *Rundstedt*, p. 175.

23. Balkoski, *Beachhead*, pp. 70–76; John C. McManus, *The Dead and Those about to Die* (New York: Caliber, 2014), pp. 53, 61.

24. Stafford, *D-Day*, pp. 254–55.

25. Quoted in Stafford, *D-Day*, p. 255; Barnett, *Engage*, p. 773; Mitcham, *Desert Fox*, p. 41.

26. Stafford, *D-Day*, pp. 230–32, 256; Kenneth Edwards, *Operation Neptune* (Sabon, UK: Fonthill, 1946), p. 39.

27. Rommel, *Papers*, p. 458.

28. Mitcham, *Desert Fox*, p. 18–21.

29. Ibid., p. 21.

30. Balkoski, *Beachhead*, pp. 76–77; Levine, *Fortitude*, p. 8; Stafford, *D-Day*, pp. 26–27; Mitcham, *Desert Fox*, pp. 18–21; Showalter, "Throw Them Back," pp. 100–102; Millett, "Blood upon the Risers," p. 173; Rommel, *Papers*, pp. 458–60; Ken Ford, *Operation Neptune 1944* (Oxford: Osprey, 2014), p. 34; Hans Speidel, *We Defended Normandy* (London: Herbert Jenkins, 1951), pp. 205–206; Blumentritt, *Rundstedt*, pp. 205–206.

31. Showalter, "Throw Them Back," p. 107.

32. Quoted in Levine, *Fortitude*, p. 266.
33. Showalter, "Throw Them Back," pp. 107–108.
34. Carrell, *Invasion*, pp. 1–2.
35. Balkoski, *Beachhead*, p. 78.
36. Quoted in Blumenson, *Generals*, p. 94.
37. Quoted in William Weidner, *Eisenhower and Montgomery at the Falaise Gap* (New York: Xlibris, 2010), p. 112.
38. Quoted in Blumenson, *Generals*, p. 94.
39. Weidner, *Eisenhower and Montgomery*, p. 112.
40. Rommel, *Papers*, p. 470; Stafford, *D-Day*, p. 44; Mitcham, *Desert Fox*, p. 63.
41. Collins, *D-Day*, p. 83.
42. Quoted in Ibid.
43. Ibid., p. 85.
44. Stafford, *D-Day*, p. 43; Collins, *D-Day*, p. 85.
45. Collins, *D-Day*, p. 86.
46. Stafford, *D-Day*, p. 256; Collins, *D-Day*, pp. 82–87.

## CHAPTER 6: THE "LONGEST DAY" COMES UP SHORT

1. Quoted in Deborah Cadbury, *Princes at War* (London: Bloomsbury, 2015), p. 302.
2. Correlli Barnett, *Engage the Enemy More Closely: The Royal Navy in the Second World War* (New York: W.W. Norton, 1991), p. 810.
3. W.S. Chalmers, *Full Cycle: The Biography of Admiral Sir Bertram Home Ramsay* (London: Hodder & Stoughton, 1959), p. 223.
4. Craig L. Symonds, *Neptune: The Allied Invasion of Europe and the D-Day Landings* (New York: Oxford University Press, 2014), p. 250; Antony Beevor, *D-Day: The Battle for Normandy* (New York: Penguin Books, 2009), p. 76; Larry Collins, *The Secrets of D-Day* (Beverly Hills, CA: Phoenix Books, 2006), p. 122; Douglas Botting, *The D-Day Invasion* (Alexandria: VA: Time-Life Books, 1978), p. 94; Ken Ford, *Operation Neptune 1944* (Oxford: Osprey, 2014), pp. 32–33.
5. Symonds, *Neptune*, p. 250; Beevor, *D-Day*, p. 51; Barrett Tillman, *D-Day Encyclopedia* (Washington, DC: Regnery History, 2014), pp. 3–4; Denise Goolsby, "Pilot Flew Troops over Enemy Territory," *Desert Sun*, June 6, 2010, p. G8; Carlo D'Este, "The Eyes of the World," in *D-Day*, ed. Jane Penrose (Oxford: Osprey, 2010), p. 259.
6. Quoted in Rick Atkinson, *The Guns at Last Light*, vol. 3, *The Liberation Trilogy* (New York: Henry Holt, 2013), p. 46.

7. Nigel Cawthorne, *Fighting Them on the Beaches* (London: Capella, 2002), pp. 100–101.

8. Allan R. Millett, "Blood upon the Risers," in *D-Day*, ed. Jane Penrose (Oxford: Osprey, 2010), p. 184; Cawthorne, *Beaches*, pp. 100–101; David Stafford, *Ten Days to D-Day* (New York: Little, Brown, 2003), pp. 296–301; Jim DeFelice, *Omar Bradley* (Washington, DC: Regnery, 2011), pp. 196–97; Atkinson, *Last Light*, p. 50; John Keegan, *Six Armies in Normandy* (New York: Penguin Books, 1994), pp. 112–14; Philip Warner, *World War Two: The Untold Story* (London: Cassell, 1988), p. 231; Barrett Tillman, *D-Day Encyclopedia* (Washington, DC: Regency History, 2014), p. 339.

9. Warner, *World War Two*, pp. 230–31; Cawthorne, *Beaches*, pp. 102–105; Millett, "Blood upon the Risers," in *D-Day*, pp. 177–80.

10. Collins, *D-Day*, p. 103; Joshua Levine, *Operation Fortitude* (London: Collins, 2012), pp. 271–73.

11. Hans Speidel, *We Defended Normandy* (London: Herbert Jenkins, 1951), pp. 93–95.

12. Samuel W. Mitcham Jr., *The Desert Fox in Normandy* (Westport, CT: Praeger, 1997), pp. 67–68.

13. Ibid.

14. Cawthorne, *Beaches*, pp. 101, 106–107; Collins, *D-Day*, p. 101; Samuel Eliot Morison, *The Two-Ocean War: A Short History of the United States Navy in the Second World War* (Atlantic Monthly Press, 1963), p. 394; Tillman, *D-Day Encyclopedia*, p. 200; Mitcham, *Desert Fox*, pp. 66–68; Max Hastings, *Overlord: D-Day and the Battle for Normandy* (New York: Simon and Schuster, 1984), pp. 76–78; David Stafford, *Ten Days to D-Day* (New York: Little, Brown, 2003), p. 322; Russell Hart, "With Unbelieving Eyes," in *D-Day*, ed. Jane Penrose (Oxford: Osprey, 2010), pp. 225–29; Speidel, *We Defended Normandy*, pp. 93–95; Richard Holmes, *The Story of D-Day* (New York: Metro Books, 2014), pp. 38, 44.

15. Erwin Rommel, *The Rommel Papers*, ed. B.H. Liddell Hart (London: Hamlyn Paperbacks, 1953), p. 470.

16. Quoted in Stafford, *D-Day*, ed. Jane Penrose (Oxford: Osprey, 2010), p. 322.

17. Williamson Murray, "A Visitor to Hell," in *D-Day*, ed. Jane Penrose (Oxford: Osprey, 2010), p. 147; Symonds, *Neptune*, p. 251; Barnett, *Engage*, pp. 787, 812.

18. Denise Goolsby, "Co-Pilot of B-17 Bomber Crew Recalls Normandy," *Desert Sun*, March 12, 2010, B3; Atkinson, *Last Light*, p. 55.

19. Denise Goolsby, "His Bombing Mission Paved the Way for Troops on D-Day," *Desert Sun*, June 24, 2012, B3.

20. Barnett, *Engage*, p. 814.
21. Ibid., p. 815.
22. Ibid., pp. 813–15; Symonds, *Neptune*, pp. 266–67.
23. Symonds, *Neptune*, p. 257.
24. Quoted in Cawthorne, *Beaches*, p. 195; Hart, "With Unbelieving Eyes," pp. 230–35; Mitcham, *Desert Fox*, pp. 72–73; Symonds, *Neptune*, pp. 256–57; John C. McManus, *The Dead and Those About to Die* (New York: Caliber, 2014), pp. 68–69; Millett, "Blood upon the Risers," p. 191; Cawthorne, *Beaches*, pp. 193–99; Collins, *D-Day*, pp. 127–29; Murray, "Visitor to Hell," pp. 155–59.
25. Cawthorne, *Beaches*, p. 195.
26. Quoted in Hart, "With Unbelieving Eyes," p. 224; Beevor, *D-Day*, p. 90.
27. Kenneth Edwards, *Operation Neptune* (Sabon, UK: Foothill, 1946), p. 167.
28. McManus, *Dead*, pp. 57–58; Cawthorne, *Beaches*, pp. 167–68; Mitcham, *Desert Fox*, p. 78; Symonds, *Neptune*, p. 272; Murray, "Visitor to Hell," p. 154; Hart, "With Unbelieving Eyes," p. 236; Edwards, *Operation Neptune*, p. 167.
29. Cawthorne, *Beaches*, p. 173; Warner, *World War Two*, pp. 232–33.
30. Cawthorne, *Beaches*, p. 173.
31. Warner, *World War Two*, p. 233; Symonds, *Neptune*, p. 268.
32. Quoted in Jonathan Mayo, *D-Day, Minute by Minute* (New York: Marble Arch, 2014), p. 215; Symonds, *Neptune*, pp. 263–64; Murray, "Visitor to Hell," p. 155; Edwards, *Operation Neptune*, p. 136.
33. Cawthorne, pp. 174–75.
34. Ibid., p. 176.
35. Denise Goolsby, "Navy Man Faced Challenges Prior to D-Day," *Desert Sun*, July 15, 2012, p. B3; Cawthorne, *Beaches*, pp. 174–78; Barnett, *Engage*, pp. 817–18; Symonds, *Neptune*, p. 268.
36. Quoted in Symonds, *Neptune*, p. 281.
37. Quoted in Chester Wilmot, *The Struggle for Europe* (London: Collins, 1952), p. 262; Botting, *D-Day*, p. 141.
38. Murray, "Visitor to Hell," pp. 153–58; Paul Carrell, *Invasion! They're Coming!* (New York: Bantam, 1964), pp. 90–91; Beevor, D-Day, p. 93; Joseph Balkoski, *Beyond the Beachhead* (Mechanicsville, PA: Stackpole Books, 1999), p. 149; Stephen E. Ambrose, *D-Day June 6, 1944* (London: Pocket Books, 1994), p. 342; Stewart Bryant, "D-Day: German Infantry at Omaha Beach," Jewish Virtual Library, 2002, http://jewishvirtuallibrary.org/jsource/ww2/germandef.html (accessed April 4, 2017).
39. Quoted in Hastings, *Overlord*, p. 99.
40. Ibid., p. 98.

41. Cawthorne, *Beaches*, pp. 178–80; Hastings, *Overlord*, p. 98; Symonds, *Neptune*, pp. 290–95; Tillman, *D-Day Encyclopedia*, p. 153.

42. Ambrose, *D-Day*, p. 388.

43. Quoted in Symonds, *Neptune*, p. 300.

44. Quoted in Jonathan Mayo, *D-Day: Minute by Minute* (New York: Marble Arch, 2014), p. 215; Symonds, *Neptune*, pp. 285–86; Cawthorne, *Beaches*, pp. 181–83; Adrian R. Lewis, *Omaha Beach: A Flawed Victory* (Chapel Hill: University of North Carolina Press, 2001), p. 284.

45. Quoted in Collins, *D-Day*, p. 140.

46. Quoted in Mayo, *D-Day*, p. 267; Collins, *D-Day*, pp. 140–41; Cawthorne, *Beaches*, pp. 182–84.

47. Cawthorne, *Beaches*, p. 184.

48. Botting, *D-Day*, pp. 152–53.

49. Ibid., p. 153.

50. Barnett, *Engage*, p.815; Edwards, *Operation Neptune*, pp. 139–40.

51. Botting, *D-Day*, pp. 152–53; Barnett, *Engage*, pp. 814, 818–19; Keegan, *Normandy*, p. 131; Cawthorne, *Beaches*, pp. 147–53; Ambrose, *D-Day*, p. 527; Warner, *World War Two*, p. 233; Murray, "Visitor to Hell," p. 159; Mitcham, *Desert Fox*, p. 81.

52. Mitcham, *Desert Fox*, p. 81; Keegan, *Six Armies in Normandy*, p. 131.

53. Barnett, *Engage*, p. 822; Murray, "Visitor to Hell," pp. 159–60; Keegan, *Normandy*, p. 131; Beevor, *D-Day*, pp. 133–35; Edwards, *Operation Neptune*, pp. 139–40.

54. Quoted in Ambrose, *D-Day*, p. 545.

55. Murray, "Visitor to Hell," p. 160; Barnett, *Engage*, p. 822; Cawthorne, *Beaches*, p. 139; Beevor, *D-Day*, p. 135.

56. Beevor, *D-Day*, p. 136.

57. Quoted in Symonds, *Neptune*, p. 281; Murray, "Visitor to Hell," p. 160; Beevor, *D-Day*, p. 136; Barnett, *Engage*, p. 815; Symonds, *Neptune*, p. 287; Collins, *D-Day*, p. 133.

58. Collins, *D-Day*, p. 133; Barnett, *Engage*, p. 822; Cawthorne, *Beaches*, pp. 109–19.

59. Ambrose, *D-Day*, pp. 515–17.

60. Botting, *D-Day*, p. 158.

61. Murray, "Visitor to Hell," pp. 160–61; Ambrose, *D-Day*, pp. 516–17; Peter Caddick-Adams, *Monty and Rommel: Parallel Lives* (New York: Overlook, 2011), p. 378; Botting, *D-Day*, pp. 158–60.

62. Mitcham, *Desert Fox*, p. 84; Cawthorne, *Beaches*, p. 106.

63. Quoted in Mitcham, *Desert Fox*, p. 79.

64. Quoted in Collins, *D-Day*, p. 157.

65. Mayo, *D-Day*, p. 222.

66. Günther Blumentritt, *Von Rundstedt: The Soldier and the Man* (London: Odhams Press, 1952), p. 226.

67. Liddell Hart, *The Other Side of the Hill* (London: Pan Books, 1948), p. 406.

68. Quoted in Mitcham, *Desert Fox*, p. 87.

69. Quoted in Carrell, *Invasion*, p. 106; Symonds, *Neptune*, p. 282.

70. Hastings, *Overlord*, p. 117; Botting, *D-Day*, pp. 160–61; Carrell, *Invasion*, pp. 107–108; Alexander McKee, *Last Round against Rommel: Battle of the Normandy Bridgehead* (New York: Signet, 1966), pp. 57–61; Carlo D'Este, *Decision in Normandy* (Old Saybrook, CT: Konecky & Konecky, 1994), pp. 139–40.

71. Quoted in Alexander McKee, *Caen: Anvil of Victory* (New York: Dorset, 1964), p. 63.

72. Mayo, *D-Day*, p. 264.

73. Adolf Galland, *The First and the Last* (New York: Ballantine Books, 1957), p. 213; Atkinson, *Last Light*, p. 85; Mitcham, *Desert Fox*, p. 71; Hart, "With Unbelieving Eyes," pp. 238–39.

74. Quoted in Beevor, *D-Day*, p. 150.

75. Quoted in Mitcham, *Desert Fox*, p. 87.

76. Atkinson, *Last Light*, p. 84; Stafford, *D-Day*, p. 332; William Weidner, *Eisenhower and Montgomery at the Falaise Gap* (New York: Xlibris, 2010), p. 28; Barnett, *Engage*, p. 825; Botting, *D-Day*, p. 161; Bertram Ramsay, *Year of D-Day*, eds. Robert W. Love, Jr. and John Mayor (Hull, UK: University of Hull Press, 1994), p. 84.

77. Mitcham, *Desert Fox*, pp. 83, 93–95; Weidner, *Eisenhower and Montgomery*, p. 113; Heinz Magenheimer, *Hitler's War* (New York: Barnes & Noble Books, 1997), p. 251; Murray, "Visitor to Hell," p. 153; Rommel, *Papers*, p. 474.

78. Hastings, *Overlord*, p. 121.

79. D'Este, *Normandy*, p. 149; Bernard Law Montgomery, *Normandy to the Baltic* (Boston, MA: Houghton Mifflin, 1948), pp. 116–34.

80. D'Este, *Normandy*, p. 144.

81. Quoted in DeFelice, *Bradley*, p. 203.

82. Quoted in Botting, *D-Day*, p. 155.

83. Quoted in Collins, *D-Day*, p. 161.

84. Mayo, *D-Day*, p. 162.

## CHAPTER 7: WHO WAS IN CONTROL?

1. Richard Langworth, *Churchill by Himself: The Definitive Collection of Quotations* (New York: Public Affairs, 2011), p. 577.

2. Bertram Ramsay, *Year of D-Day*, eds. Robert W. Love, Jr. and John Mayor (Hull, UK: University of Hull Press, 1994), p. 84; Ronald J. Drez, "Their Road Will Be Long and Hard," in *D-Day*, ed. Jane Penrose (Oxford: Osprey, 2010), p. 197; Douglas Botting, *The D-Day Invasion* (Alexandria, VA: Time-Life Books, 1978), p. 183; Robert A. Miller, *August 1944: The Campaign for France* (Novato, CA: Presidio Press, 1996), p. 8; Carlo D'Este, *Decision in Normandy* (Old Saybrook, CT: Konecky & Konecky, 1994), pp. 150, 161; Bernard Fergusson, *The Watery Maze* (London: Collins, 1961), p. 349; Antony Beevor, *D-Day: The Battle for Normandy* (New York: Penguin Books, 2009), p. 175; Diary notes, in Stephen Brooks, ed., *Montgomery and the Battle of Normandy* (Stroud, UK: History Press, 2008), p. 118; Jonathan W. Jordan, *Brothers, Rivals, Victors* (New York: Caliber, 2011), p. 327.

3. Keith Grint, *Leadership, Management and Command: Rethinking D-Day* (New York: Palgrave Macmillan, 2007), p. 105.

4. William Weidner, *Eisenhower and Montgomery at the Falaise Gap* (New York: Xlibris, 2010), p. 115; Botting, *D-Day*, p. 187; Martin Blumenson, *The Battle of the Generals* (New York: William Morrow, 1993), p. 95; John Keegan, *Six Armies in Normandy* (New York: Penguin Books, 1994), pp. 155–58; D'Este, *Normandy*, p. 157.

5. Quoted in "'Agent Garbo,' The Spy Who Lied about D-Day," NPR, July 7, 2012, http://www.npr.org/2012/07/07/156189716/agent-garbo-the-spy-who-lied-about-d-day.

6. Quoted in Larry Collins, *The Secrets of D-Day* (Beverly Hills, CA: Phoenix Books, 2006), p. 196; Dennis E. Showalter and Harold C. Deutsch, *If the Allies Had Fallen* (New York: MJF Books, 2010), pp. 251–52.

7. Paul Carrell, *Invasion! They're Coming!* (New York: Bantam, 1964), pp. 134–36; Keegan, *Normandy*, pp. 148–49.

8. Erwin Rommel, *The Rommel Papers*, ed. B.H. Liddell Hart (London: Hamlyn Paperbacks, 1953), p. 477; Hans Speidel, *We Defended Normandy* (London: Herbert Jenkins, 1951), p. 96; B.H. Liddell Hart, *The German Generals Talk* (New York: Quill, 1979), p. 244.

9. Weidner, *Eisenhower and Montgomery*, p. 144; Max Hastings, *Overlord: D-Day and the Battle for Normandy* (New York: Simon and Schuster, 1984), p. 125; Carrell, *Invasion*, pp. 146–50.

10. Beevor, *D-Day*, pp. 182–83; Keegan, *Normandy*, pp. 150–51; Weidner, *Eisenhower and Montgomery*, p. 264; Speidel, *We Defended Normandy*, p. 100.

11. Samuel Eliot Morison, *The Two-Ocean War: A Short History of the United States Navy in the Second World War* (Atlantic Monthly Press, 1963), pp. 407–408.

12. Adolf Galland, *The First and the Last* (New York: Ballantine Books, 1957), pp. 214–19; Alexander McKee, *Last Round against Rommel: Battle of the Normandy Bridgehead* (New York: Signet, 1966), p. 277; Morison, *Two-Ocean War*, p. 407; Craig L. Symonds, *Neptune: The Allied Invasion of Europe and the D-Day Landings* (New York: Oxford University Press, 2014), p. 312; Martin Blumenson, *Breakout and Pursuit* (Washington, DC: Office of the Chief of Military History, Department of the Army, 1961), pp. 33–34.

13. Correlli Barnett, *Engage the Enemy More Closely: The Royal Navy in the Second World War* (New York: W.W. Norton, 1991), p. 832.

14. Ken Ford, *Operation Neptune 1944* (Oxford: Osprey, 2014), pp. 86–87; Beevor, *D-Day*, p. 76; Nigel Cawthorne, *Fighting Them on the Beaches* (London: Capella, 2002), p. 185; Morison, *Two-Ocean War*, pp. 405–406; Samuel W. Mitcham, Jr., *The Desert Fox in Normandy* (Westport, CT: Praeger, 1997), p. 40; Barnett, *Engage*, pp. 830–32.

15. Beevor, *D-Day*, pp. 226–27; Carrell, *Invasion*, pp. 174–75; Horace Edward Henderson, *The Greatest Blunders of World War II* (New York: Writer's Showcase, 2001), p. 368; Kennedy Hickman, "World War II: V-1 Flying Bomb," ThoughtCo., August 12, 2015, http://militaryhistory.about.com/od/artillerysiegeweapons/p/v1.htm (accessed April 5, 2017). Later Hitler deployed the V-2, often called the "vengeance weapon." It was the world's first ballistic missile, became the prototype for the US Redstone Missile, and paved the way for the Saturn V that took America's astronauts to the moon.

16. Blumenson, *Generals*, p. 97; Beevor, *D-Day*, p. 185.

17. Quoted in D'Este, *Normandy*, pp. 151–52.

18. Quoted in Keegan, *Normandy*, p. 156.

19. Rommel, *Papers*, p. 491.

20. Diary entry, June 7, 1944, in *Montgomery and the Battle of Normandy*, p. 118.

21. Message to Field Marshal Sir Alan Brooke, June 11, 1944, in *Montgomery and the Battle of Normandy*, p. 129.

22. D.K.R. Crosswell, *Beetle: The Life of General Walter Bedell Smith* (Lexington, KY: University of Kentucky Press, 2010), p. 634.

23. Nigel Hamilton, *Montgomery: D-Day Commander* (Washington, DC: Potomac Books, 2007), pp. 58–59.

24. Stephen E. Ambrose, *The Supreme Commander: The War Years of General Dwight D. Eisenhower* (Garden City, NY: Doubleday, 1970), p. 428; Hastings, *Overlord*, pp. 37–38; David Eisenhower, *Eisenhower: At War 1943–1945* (New York: Random House, 1986), pp. 210–12; D'Este, *Normandy*, p. 202.

25. Letter to Major-General F.E. Simpson, June 8, 1944, in *Montgomery and the Battle of Normandy*, p. 122; Hastings, *Overlord*, p. 123; D'Este, *Normandy*, p. 161.

26. Beevor, *D-Day*, pp. 188–94; Drez, "Their Road," pp. 207–11; B.H. Liddell Hart, *History of the Second World War* (Old Saybrook, CT: Konecky & Konecky, 1970), p. 546.

27. Cawthorne, *Beaches*, p. 141; Hastings, *Overlord*, p. 135; D'Este, *Normandy*, p. 197.

28. Letter to Field Marshal Sir Alan Brooke, June 13, 1944, in *Montgomery and the Battle of Normandy*, pp. 141–43; Diary notes, June 15, 1944, in *Montgomery and the Battle of Normandy*, p. 145.

29. Crosswell, *Beetle*, p. 640; D'Este, *Normandy*, p. 198.

30. Keegan, *Normandy*, p. 152.

31. D'Este, *Normandy*, pp. 153–55; Beevor, *D-Day*, pp. 252–55; Keegan, *Normandy*, pp. 152–53; Joseph Balkoski, *Beyond the Beachhead* (Mechanicsville, PA: Stackpole Books, 1999), pp. 159–61; Hastings, *Overlord*, pp. 166–67; Fred Majdalany, *The Fall of Fortress Europe* (Garden City, NY: Doubleday, 1968), pp. 378–79; Dwight D. Eisenhower, *Crusade in Europe* (New York: Avon, 1968), p. 285; Antony Beevor, *Second World War* (New York: Little, Brown, 2012), pp. 597–99.

32. Quoted in Rick Atkinson, *The Guns at Last Light*, vol. 3, *The Liberation Trilogy* (New York: Henry Holt, 2013), p. 111.

33. Quoted in Jonathan Mayo, *D-Day Minute by Minute* (New York: Marble Arch, 2014), p. 275.

34. Russell F. Weigley, *Eisenhower's Lieutenants: The Campaigns of France and Germany 1944–1945* (Bloomington: Indiana University Press, 1981), p. 76.

35. Drez, "Their Road," pp. 203–205.

36. Robert Gildea, *Fighters in the Shadows* (Cambridge, MA: Belknap Press of Harvard University Press, 2015), pp. 22–29.

37. Quoted in Gildea, *Fighters*, p. 23.

38. Stafford, *D-Day*, pp. 80–81.

39. Gildea, *Fighters*, p. 162.

40. Stafford, *D-Day*, p. 81; Gildea, *Fighters*, pp. 23, 127, 162, 242, 271, 334, 342–44; Beevor, *D-Day*, pp. 16–17; Jean Edward Smith, *Eisenhower in War and Peace* (New York: Random House Trade Paperbacks, 2013), pp. 346–47.

41. Dwight D. Eisenhower, memorandum dated June 3, 1944, box 137, Crusade in Europe Documents NAID# 12005079, Dwight D. Eisenhower Presidential Library, Abilene, Kansas.

42. Quoted in Beevor, *D-Day*, p. 199; Jonathan Fenby, *The General: Charles de Gaulle and the France He Saved* (New York: Skyhorse, 2012), p. 242.

43. Gildea, *Fighters*, pp. 18, 377; Smith, *Eisenhower*, pp. 369–71; Beevor, *D-Day*, pp. 197–99.

44. Rommel, *Papers*, pp. 478–79.

45. Quoted in Blumenson, *Generals*, p. 98.

46. D'Este, *Normandy*, pp. 152–53; Beevor, *D-Day*, pp. 224–26; Keegan, *Normandy*, pp. 164–65; Speidel, *Normandy*, pp. 105–109.

47. Quoted in Liddell Hart, *The Other Side of the Hill* (London: Pan Books, 1948), p. 410.

48. Barnett, *Engage*, p. 829.

49. Morison, *Two-Ocean War*, p. 408.

50. Jim DeFelice, *Omar Bradley* (Washington, DC: Regnery, 2011), p. 198; Barnett, *Engage*, p. 828; Morison, *Two-Ocean War*, pp. 408–409; Crosswell, *Beetle*, p. 645; Symonds, *Neptune*, pp. 324–27; D-Este, *Normandy*, p. 230; Ramsay, *Year of D-Day*, pp. 86, 90–91; Barrett Tillman, *D-Day Encyclopedia* (Washington, DC: Regency History, 2014), p. 222.

51. Quoted in Keegan, *Normandy*, pp. 163–64.

52. Barnett, *Engage*, p. 835.

53. Ibid.; Ford, *Operation Neptune*, pp. 78–81, 85; Symonds, *Neptune*, pp. 323–24.

54. Denise Goolsby, "Navy's LST Ships Supplied Troops," *Desert Sun*, June 6, 2010, p. G7.

55. Andrew Gordon, "The Greatest Military Armada Ever Launched," in *D-Day*, ed. Jane Penrose (Oxford: Osprey, 2010), p. 143.

56. Directive (M504) to Lieutenant-General O.N. Bradley First US Army, June 18, 1944, in *Montgomery and the Battle of Normandy*, pp. 154–55; DeFelice, *Bradley*, p. 206.

57. Kenneth Edwards, *Operation Neptune* (Sabon, UK: Foothill, 1946), pp. 277–79; Symonds, *Neptune*, pp. 339–48.

58. D'Este, *Normandy*, pp. 230–31; Patrick Dalzel-Job, *Arctic Snow to Dust of Normandy* (Barnsley, South Yorkshire, UK: Pen and Sword Military, 1992), p. 153; Symonds, *Neptune*, pp. 336–50; Drez, "Their Road," pp. 205–207; Hastings, *Overlord*, p. 163; DeFelice, *Bradley*, p. 206; Ford, *Operation Neptune*, p. 90.

59. Quoted in William B. Brewer, *Hitler's Fortress Cherbourg* (New York: Stein and Day, 1984), p. 252.

60. Ramsay, *Year of D-Day*, pp. 100–101; Ford, *Operation Neptune*, p. 91.

61. Quoted in Hastings, *Overlord*, p. 166; DeFelice, *Bradley*, p. 206.

62. Ramsay, *Year of D-Day*, pp. 91–92, 96.

63. Ford, *Operation Neptune*, p. 91.

64. Symonds, *Neptune*, pp. 351–52.

65. Ramsay, *Year of D-Day*, p. 114.

66. Barnett, *Engage*, p. 837.

67. Beevor, *D-Day*, p. 229.

68. Quoted in Horace Edward Henderson, *The Greatest Blunders of World War II* (New York: Writer's Showcase, 2001), p. 368.

69. Directive (M502) to Lieutenant-General Omar M. Bradley, First US Army and Lieutenant-General Miles Dempsey, Second British Army, June 18, 1944, in *Montgomery and the Battle of Normandy*, p. 151.

70. Diary notes, June 19, 1944, in *Montgomery and the Battle of Normandy*, p. 156; Message (M25) to Major-General F.W. de Guingand, June 20, 1944; *Montgomery and the Battle of Normandy*, p. 158.

71. D'Este, *Normandy*, pp. 235–37.

72. Message (M30) to General Dwight D. Eisenhower, June 25, 1944, in *Montgomery and the Battle of Normandy*, p. 164.

73. D'Este, *Normandy*, pp. 240–45; Henderson, *Blunders*, pp. 368–69; Beevor, *D-Day*, p. 234; Beevor, *Second World War*, p. 595.

74. Message to (M31) to General Dwight D. Eisenhower, June 26, 1944, in *Montgomery and the Battle of Normandy*, p. 164.

75. Beevor, *Second World War*, p. 595.

76. Ramsay, *Year of D-Day*, pp. 92–93.

77. Letter to Field Marshal Sir Alan Brooke, June 27, 1944, in *Montgomery and the Battle of Normandy*, p. 166.

78. Message (M33) to the Prime Minister, June 29, 1944, in *Montgomery and the Battle of Normandy*, p. 172.

79. Directive (M505) to Lieutenant-General Omar M. Bradley, First US Army and Lieutenant-General Miles Dempsey, Second British Army, June 30, 1944, in *Montgomery and the Battle of Normandy*, p. 176.

80. Ibid., p. 174.

81. Henderson, *Blunders*, pp. 366–69; Beevor, *Second World War*, p. 596; D'Este, *Normandy*, pp. 247–48; Blumenson, *Generals*, pp. 108–109.

82. Beevor, *D-Day*, p. 243.

83. Quoted in Hart, *Other Side of the Hill*, p. 411; Blumenson, *Generals*, pp. 98–99; Beevor, *D-Day*, pp. 214–15, 243; Alun Chalfont, *Montgomery of Alamein* (New York: Athenaeum, 1976), p. 240; Rommel, *Papers*, pp. 478–83.

84. Quoted in Blumenson, *Generals*, p. 100.

## CHAPTER 8: BREAKOUT BLUES

1. Diary, July 12, 1944, in *The Patton Papers 1940–1945*, ed. Martin Blumenson (Cambridge, MA: Da Capo, 1974), p. 480.

2. Antony Beevor, *D-Day: The Battle for Normandy* (New York: Penguin Books, 2009), pp. 237–38.

3. Martin Blumenson, *The Battle of the Generals* (New York: William Morrow, 1993), p. 100; Liddell Hart, *The Other Side of the Hill* (London: Pan Books, 1948), pp. 411–13; Antony Beevor, *The Second World War* (New York: Little, Brown, 2012), p. 597; Beevor, *D-Day*, pp. 237–38; Erwin Rommel, *The Rommel Papers*, ed. B.H. Liddell Hart (London: Hamlyn Paperbacks, 1953), pp. 481–84.

4. William Weidner, *Eisenhower and Montgomery at the Falaise Gap* (New York: Xlibris, 2010), p. 30; Jonathan W. Jordan, *Brothers, Rivals, Victors* (New York: Caliber, 2011), pp. 334–35; David Fraser, *Alanbrooke* (London: Harper Collins, 1982), p. 436.

5. David I. Hall, "Much the Greatest Thing We Have Ever Attempted," in *D-Day*, ed. Jane Penrose (Oxford: Osprey, 2010), p. 246.

6. Jim DeFelice, *Omar Bradley* (Washington, DC: Regnery, 2011), pp. 212–13.

7. Jordan, *Brothers*, p. 341.

8. Ibid.

9. DeFelice, *Bradley*, p. 213; Jordan, *Brothers*, p. 341.

10. Alun Chalfont, *Montgomery of Alamein* (New York: Athenaeum, 1976), p. 238.

11. Blumenson, *Generals*, p. 116.

12. "Operation Charnwood, 8–9 July 1944," http://www/dday-overlord.com/wp-content/uploads/2016/02/operation_charnwood-1.jpg (accessed June 1, 2017).

13. Carlo D'Este, *Decision in Normandy* (Old Saybrook, CT: Konecky & Konecky, 1994), pp. 212–27, 314–20; Beevor, *D-Day*, pp. 272–73; Blumenson, *Generals*, pp. 116–17; Richard Holmes, *The Story of D-Day* (New York: Metro Books), p. 110.

14. Alistair Horne and David Montgomery, *Monty: The Lonely Leader, 1944–1945* (New York: Harper Collins, 1994), p.127.

15. Blumenson, *Generals*, p. 115.

16. D'Este, *Normandy*, pp. 259–60.

17. David Eisenhower, *Eisenhower at War 1943–1945* (New York: Vintage, 1987), p. 213; Philip Warner, *World War Two: The Untold Story* (London: Cassell,

1988), p. 221; Beevor, *D-Day*, pp. 263, 305; D'Este, *Normandy*, pp. 259–60; John Keegan, *Six Armies in Normandy* (New York: Penguin Books, 1994), p. 190.

18. Montgomery to Field Marshal Sir Alan Brooke, July 14, 1944, in Stephen Brooks, ed., *Montgomery and the Battle of Normandy* (Stroud, UK: History Press, 2008), p. 208.

19. Chester Wilmot, interview, May 18, 1946, Liddell Hart Papers, King's College, London.

20. Max Hastings, *Armageddon: The Battle for Germany, 1944–45* (New York: Alfred A. Knopf, 2006), p. 13; D'Este, *Normandy*, pp. 284–89; D.K.R. Crosswell, *Beetle: The Life of General Walter Bedell Smith.* (Lexington, KY: University of Kentucky Press, 2010), pp. 635–36; Beevor, *D-Day*, p. 264; John Buckley, *Monty's Men* (New Haven, CT: Yale University Press, 2013), p. 144; Stephen R. Taaffe, *Marshall and His Generals* (Lawrence, KS: University of Kansas, 2011), pp. 188–89; Omar N. Bradley, *A Soldier's Story* (New York: Modern Library, 1999), p. 260.

21. Quoted in Chalfont, *Montgomery*, p. 236.

22. Chalfont, *Montgomery*, pp. 236–37.

23. Beevor, *D-Day*, p. 264.

24. Max Hastings, *Overlord, D-Day and the Battle for Normandy* (New York: Simon and Schuster, 1984), p. 228.

25. Alan Brooke, *War Diaries, 1939–1945*, ed. Alex Danchev and Daniel Todman (London: Phoenix Press, 2001), p. 566.

26. Quoted in Fraser, *Alanbrooke*, pp. 530–31.

27. Quoted in D'Este, *Normandy*, pp. 302–303; Quoted in Hastings, *Overlord*, p. 228.

28. General Dwight D. Eisenhower to Montgomery, July 7, 1944, in *Montgomery and the Battle of Normandy*, pp. 186–87.

29. Montgomery to General Dwight D. Eisenhower, July 8, 1944, in *Montgomery and the Battle of Normandy*, pp. 188, 190.

30. Brooke, *War Diaries*, pp. 546, 575; Blumenson, *Generals*, pp. 110–11.

31. Blumenson, *Generals*, p. 120.

32. Quoted in Blumenson, *Generals*, p. 119.

33. Message (M49) to General Dwight D. Eisenhower, July 12, 1944, in *Montgomery and the Battle of Normandy*, p. 201.

34. Montgomery's Diary notes, July 13, 1944, in *Montgomery and the Battle of Normandy*, p. 204.

35. Message (M53) to Air Chief Marshal Sir Arthur Tedder, July 14, 1944, in *Montgomery and the Battle of Normandy*, pp. 204–205.

36. Montgomery to Field Marshal Sir Alan Brooke, July 14, 1944, in *Montgomery and the Battle of Normandy*, p. 208.

37. General Dwight D. Eisenhower to Montgomery, July 14, 1944, in *Montgomery and the Battle of Normandy*, p. 205.

38. Montgomery's Directive (M510) to Lieutenant-General O.N. Bradley, First US Army, Lieutenant-General Sir Miles Dempsey, Second British Army, Lieutenant-General G. Patton, Third US Army, and Lieutenant-General H.D. Crerar, First Canadian Army, July 10, 1944, in *Montgomery and the Battle of Normandy*, p. 195.

39. Memorandum by Montgomery headed "Notes on Second Army Operations 16 July–18 July," in *Montgomery and the Battle of Normandy*, p. 213.

40. Quoted in Buckley, *Monty's Men*, p. 96–97.

41. Peter Caddick-Adams, *Monty and Rommel* (New York: Overlook, 2011), pp. 410–11.

42. Beevor, *D-Day*, p. 314.

43. Ronald J. Drez, "Their Road Will Be Long and Hard," in *D-Day*, ed. Jane Penrose (Oxford: Osprey Publishing, 2010), p. 213; Blumenson, *Generals*, p. 122; Beevor, *D-Day*, p. 315; D'Este, *Normandy*, pp. 370–76; Beevor, *Second World War*, p. 601; Mark Urban, *Generals: Ten British Generals Who Shaped the War* (London: Faber and Faber, 2005), p. 282; Martin Blumenson, *Breakout and Pursuit* (Washington, DC: Office of the Chief of History, Department of the Army, 1961), p. 48.

44. Quoted in Drez, "Their Road," p. 214.

45. Ibid., p. 215.

46. Ibid.

47. Paul Carrell, *Invasion! They're Coming!* (New York: Bantam, 1964), p. 253; D'Este, *Normandy*, p. 379.

48. Quoted in Drez, "Their Road," p. 215.

49. D'Este, *Normandy*, p. 382.

50. Drez, "Their Road," pp. 215–16.

51. Chalfont, *Montgomery*, p. 243; Horace Edward Henderson, *The Greatest Blunders of World War II* (New York: Writer's Showcase, 2001), p. 373; D'Este, *Normandy*, pp. 385–86.

52. D'Este, *Normandy*, p. 387.

53. Alexander McKee, *Caen: Anvil of Victory* (London: St. Martin, 1987), p. 217.

54. Hastings, *Overlord*, p. 238; Weidner, *Eisenhower and Montgomery*, p. 281.

55. Quoted in Harry Yeide, *Fighting Patton*, p. 226; Blumenson, *Generals*, p. 124.

56. Quoted in Blumenson, *Generals,* p. 121.

57. Hall, "Much the Greatest Thing," p. 252.

58. Ibid.; Buckley, *Monty's Men*, p. 144.

59. Rommel, *Rommel Papers*, p. 486.

60. Ibid., pp. 486–87.

61. Ibid., p. 486.

62. Quoted in Caddick-Adams, *Monty and Rommel*, p. 421.

63. Samuel W. Mitcham, Jr., *The Desert Fox in Normandy* (Westport, CT: Praeger, 1997), p. 179; Caddick-Adams, *Monty and Rommel*, pp. 421–22.

64. Keegan, *Normandy*, pp. 221–30; Hall, "Much the Greatest Thing," pp. 253–54; Beevor, *D-Day*, pp. 330–35; William L. Shirer, *Rise and Fall of the Third Reich* (New York: Simon and Schuster, 1960), pp. 1048–76; Hans Speidel, *We Defended Normandy* (London: Herbert Jenkins, 1951), p. 87.

65. Quoted in Shirer, *Third Reich*, p. 1077.

66. Ibid.; Mitcham, *Desert Fox in Normandy*, p. 180.

67. Manfred Rommel, "The Last Days," in *Rommel Papers*, p. 500.

68. Quoted in Shirer, *Third Reich*, p. 1079.

69. Manfred Rommel, "The Last Days," in *Rommel Papers*, p. 505.

70. Quoted in Blumenson, *Generals*, pp. 124–25; Hall, "Much the Greatest Thing," p. 254.

71. Quoted in Buckley, *Monty's Men*, p. 110.

72. Blumenson, *Generals*, p. 125.

73. Message (M58) to Field Marshal Sir Alan Brooke, July 18, 1944, in *Montgomery and the Battle of Normandy,* p. 218.

74. Message (M60) to General Dwight D. Eisenhower, July 18, 1944, in *Montgomery and the Battle of Normandy*, p. 218.

75. Quoted in Hastings, *Overlord*, p. 236.

76. Chalfont, *Montgomery*, p. 243.

77. Harry C. Butcher, *Three Years with Eisenhower* (New York: Simon and Schuster, 1946), p. 531.

78. Quoted in Buckley, *Monty's Men*, p. 111.

79. Quoted in Keegan, *Normandy*, p. 217.

80. Stephen E. Ambrose, *Eisenhower Soldier, General of the Army, President-Elect, 1890–1952*) New York: Simon and Schuster, 1983), p. 320.

81. Quoted in Chalfont, *Montgomery*, p. 244.

82. Message (M49) to General Dwight D. Eisenhower, July 12, 1944, in *Montgomery and the Battle of Normandy*, p. 201; Keegan, *Normandy*, p. 215.

83. Brooke, *War Diaries*, p. 572; Montgomery to Prime Minister, July 19, 1944, in *Montgomery and the Battle of Normandy*, p. 221; Nigel Hamilton, *Montgomery: D-Day Commander* (Washington, DC: Potomac Books, Inc., 2007), p. 71.

84. General Dwight D. Eisenhower to Montgomery, July 21, 1944, in *Montgomery and the Battle of Normandy*, pp. 228–30.

85. Arthur W. Tedder, *With Prejudice: The War Memoirs of Marshal of the Royal Air Force, Lord Tedder* (London: Cassell, 1966), p. 567.

86. Message (M65) to General Dwight D. Eisenhower, July 22, 1944, in *Montgomery and the Battle of Normandy*, p. 231.

87. Chalfont, *Montgomery*, p. 245.

88. Buckley, *Monty's Men*, p. 111.

89. Brooke, *War Diaries*, p. 575.

90. Diary notes, July 21, 1944, in *Montgomery and the Battle of Normandy*, pp. 230–31; Weidner, *Eisenhower and Montgomery*, p. 289.

91. William Weidner, *Eisenhower and Montgomery at the Falaise Gap* (New York: Xlibris, 2010), p. 289; Raymond Callahan, *Churchill and His Generals* (Lawrence, KS: University of Kansas Press, 2007), p. 218.

92. Brooke, *War Diaries*, p. 575.

93. DeFelice, *Bradley*, pp. 217–18; Jordan, *Brothers*, p. 335.

94. Beevor, *D-Day*, p. 256; Blumenson, *Generals*, pp. 120–21.

95. Quoted in Hastings, *Overlord*, p. 252.

96. Martin Blumenson, *Breakout and Pursuit*, p. 206.

97. Ibid., 207.

98. Alan Axelrod, *Patton's Drive* (Guilford, CT: Lyons Press, 2009), pp. 36–37; Hastings, *Overlord*, p. 252; DeFelice, *Bradley*, pp. 227–28; Denise Goolsby, "Battalion's Aim: Keep the Enemy Distracted," *Desert Sun*, June 6, 2010, p. 69.

99. Herbert Essame, *Patton: A Study in Command* (New York: Charles Scribner's Sons, 1974), p. 138;D'Este, *Normandy*, p. 307; Axelrod, *Patton,* pp. 14–18.

100. Editor Blumenson in *Patton Papers,* p. 441.

101. Quoted in Crosswell, *Beetle*, p. 605.

102. Quoted in Bradley, *Soldier's Story*, p. 187; Ladislas Farago, *Patton: Ordeal and Triumph* (New York: Dell, 1963), pp. 416–23.

103. Diary, July 12, in *Patton Papers*, p. 480.

104. Ibid.

105. Diary, June 8, in *Patton Papers*, p. 465.

106. Diary, July 2, in *Patton Papers*, pp. 470–71.

107. Diary, July 14, in *Patton Papers*, p. 482.

108. Farago, *Patton*, p. 429.

109. Ibid., pp. 425–29.

110. Bradley, *Soldier's Story*, p. 266.

111. Farago, *Patton*, p. 440.
112. Quoted in Ibid., p. 332.
113. Diary, July 14, in *Patton Papers*, p. 481.

## CHAPTER 9: PATTON UNLEASHED

1. Diary, July 29, 1944, in *Patton Papers 1940–1945*, ed. Martin Blumenson (Cambridge, MA: Da Capo, 1974), p. 491.

2. Forrest C. Pogue, *The Supreme Command* (Washington, DC: Office of the Chief of Military History, 1954), p. 192; Robert A. Miller, *August 1944, The Campaign for France* (Novato, CA: Presidio, 1996), pp. 8–9.

3. Jonathan W. Jordan, *Brothers, Rivals, Victors* (New York: Caliber, 2011), p. 351; Alan Axelrod, *Patton's Drive* (Guilford, CT: Lyons, 2009), p. 38; Carlo D'Este, *Decision in Normandy* (Old Saybrook, CT: Konecky & Konecky, 1994), pp. 343–50.

4. D'Este, *Normandy*, pp. 339, 341; Jordan, *Brothers*, p. 357; Martin Blumenson, *The Battle of the Generals* (New York: William Morrow, 1993), pp. 134–35.

5. Blumenson, *Generals*, pp. 137–38.

6. Herbert Essame, *Patton: A Study in Command* (New York: Charles Scribner's Sons, 1974), p. 140.

7. Blumenson, *Generals*, pp. 136–38; Essame, *Patton*, pp. 140, 144; D'Este, *Normandy*, p. 401; Max Hastings, *Overlord, D-Day and the Battle for Normandy* (New York: Simon and Schuster, 1984), p. 254; Horace Edward Henderson, *The Greatest Blunders of World War II* (New York: Writer's Showcase, 2001), p. 375.

8. Quoted in D'Este, *Normandy*, p. 402.

9. Quoted in Ronald J. Drez, "Their Road Will Be Long and Hard," in *D-Day*, ed. Jane Penrose (Oxford: Osprey, 2010), pp. 220–21.

10. Quoted in Antony Beevor, *D-Day: The Battle for Normandy* (New York: Penguin Books, 2009), p. 349.

11. Quoted in Blumenson, *Generals*, p. 139; Richard Rohmer, *Patton's Gap* (Don Mills, Ontario: General Publishing, 1981), p. 151; B.H. Liddell Hart, *Strategy* (New York: Praeger, 1967), p. 316.

12. Beevor, *D-Day*, p. 349; Chester Wilmot and Daniel Christopher McDevitt, *The Struggle for Europe* (Hertfordshire, UK: Wordsworth Editions, 1997), p. 393; William Weidner, *Eisenhower and Montgomery at the Falaise Gap* (New York: Xlibris, 2010), p. 31.

13. Jordan, *Brothers*, p. 361; Hastings, *Overlord*, p. 255; D'Este, *Normandy*, p. 403.

14. Quoted in Paul Carrell, *Invasion! They're Coming!* (New York: Bantam, 1964), p. 262.

15. Ibid.

16. Beevor, *D-Day*, p. 349; D'Este, *Normandy*, p. 404; Blumenson, *Generals*, p. 144.

17. Beevor, *D-Day*, pp. 350–51; Ladislas Farago, *Patton: Ordeal and Triumph* (New York: Dell, 1963), pp. 446–52; Blumenson, *Generals*, p. 145.

18. Hastings, *Overlord*, p. 271; Beevor, *D-Day*, p. 357; Jim DeFelice, *Omar Bradley* (Washington, DC: Regnery, 2011), pp. 226–27; D'Este, *Normandy*, p. 406.

19. Quoted in Blumenson, *Generals*, p. 145; Beevor, *D-Day*, p. 357.

20. Hastings, *Overlord*, pp. 227–78; Beevor, *D-Day*, pp. 354, 359, 362.

21. Quoted in Beevor, *D-Day*, p. 353.

22. Quoted in Martin Blumenson, *Breakout and Pursuit* (Washington, DC: Office of the Chief of History, Department of the Army, 1961), p. 323; Beevor, *D-Day*, pp. 370–71.

23. Message (63324) from the Prime Minister to Montgomery, July 26, 1944, in Stephen Brooks, ed., *Montgomery and the Battle of Normandy* (Stroud, UK: History Press, 2008), p. 243.

24. Message from the Prime Minister to Montgomery, July 27, 1944, in *Montgomery and the Battle of Normandy*, p. 245.

25. Message to Prime Minister, copy to Field Marshal Sir Alan Brooke, July 27, 1944, in *Montgomery and the Battle of Normandy*, p. 245.

26. Montgomery's Directive (M515) to Lieutenant-General O.N. Bradley, First US Army, Lieutenant-General Sir Miles Dempsey, Second British Army, Lieutenant-General G. Patton, Third US Army, and Lieutenant-General H.D.G Crerar, First Canadian Army, July 27, 1944, in *Montgomery and the Battle of Normandy*, p. 248.

27. Field Marshal Sir Alan Brooke to Montgomery, July 28, 1944, in *Montgomery and the Battle of Normandy*, p. 254.

28. Message to Field Marshal Sir Alan Brooke, July 28, 1944, in *Montgomery and the Battle of Normandy*, p. 255.

29. Alun Chalfont, *Montgomery of Alamein* (New York: Athenaeum, 1976), pp. 245–46; Beevor, *D-Day*, pp. 366–71, 390; Hastings, *Overlord*, p. 265; Blumenson, *Generals*, pp. 147–48.

30. Montgomery to Sir James Grigg, August 2, 1944, in *Montgomery and the Battle of Normandy*, p. 262.

31. Omar Bradley, *A Soldier's Story* (New York: Modern Library, 1999), p. 355.

32. Quoted in Farago, *Patton*, pp. 448–49; Blumenson, *Generals*, pp. 145–46.

33. Diary, July 29, 1944, in *Patton Papers*, pp. 490–91.

34. Poem, July 1944, in *Patton Papers*, p. 492; Farago, *Patton*, p. 453.

35. Essame, Patton, pp. 141, 146, 152; Blumenson, *Generals*, pp. 146, 155; Henderson, *Blunders*, p. 376.

36. Quoted in Farago, *Patton*, p. 472.

37. Ibid., pp. 462–63.

38. Elizabeth Letts, *The Perfect Horse* (New York: Ballantine Books, 2016), pp. 136–37.

39. Essame, *Patton*, pp. 141–44; Dennis Showalter, *Patton and Rommel* (New York: Berkley Caliber, 2005), p. 367; Farago, *Patton*, p. 492–93; Axelrod, *Patton's Drive*, pp. 58–59; Blumenson, *Breakout and Pursuit*, p. 349.

40. Quoted in Essame, *Patton*, p. 143.

41. Patton to Kenyon Joyce, August 6, 1944, in *Patton Papers*, p. 502.

42. Yeide, *Fighting Patton*, p. 236.

43. Nigel Hamilton, *Master of the Battlefield Monty's War Years, 1942–1944* (New York: McGraw-Hill, 1983), p. 773.

44. Farago, *Patton*, pp. 478–82; D'Este, *Normandy*, pp. 409–10; Essame, *Patton*, p. 141.

45. Axelrod, *Patton's Drive*, pp. 70–71; Farago, *Patton*, p. 478; Showalter, *Patton and Rommel*, p. 366; Essame, *Patton*, pp. 149–50; John Keegan, *Six Armies in Normandy* (New York: Penguin Books, 1994), p. 237; Blumenson, *Generals*, p. 149; Charles R. Codman, *Drive* (Boston: Little, Brown, 1957), pp. 158–59. Colonel Codman was Patton's ADC.

46. Essame, *Patton*, p. 150.

47. Quoted in Essame, *Patton*, pp. 151–52.

48. Blumenson, *Generals*, p. 164; Essame, *Patton*, p. 153; Hastings, *Overlord*, p. 281; Farago, *Patton*, p. 498.

49. Diary, August 4, 1944, in *Patton Papers*, p. 499; Essame, *Patton*, pp. 153–54; Farago, *Patton*, p. 514.

50. Quoted in Beevor, *D-Day*, p. 379.

51. Beevor, *D-Day*, p. 401; Essame, *Patton*, pp. 157–58; Diary, August 7, 1944, in *Patton Papers*, p. 503.

52. Quoted in Carrell, *Invasion*, p. 274.

53. Quoted in D'Este, *Normandy*, p. 415.

54. Keegan, *Six Armies*, p. 245.

55. Quoted in D'Este, *Normandy*, p. 415.

56. Carrell, *Invasion*, p. 279; Hastings, *Overlord*, pp. 285–86; Essame, *Patton*, pp. 160–61; Henderson, *Blunders*, pp. 376–77.

57. Quoted in Liddell Hart, *The Other Side of the Hill* (London: Pan Books, 1948), p. 421.

58. Showalter, *Patton and Rommel*, p. 367; Peter Caddick-Adams, *Monty and Rommel* (New York: Overlook, 2011), p. 430.

## CHAPTER 10: FALAISE FOLLIES

1. George S. Patton, diary, August 16, 1944, in *The Patton Papers 1940–1945*, ed. Martin Blumenson (Cambridge, MA: Da Capo, 1974), pp. 508–509.
2. F.W. Winterbotham, *The Ultra Secret* (New York: Harper and Row, 1974), pp. 155–58.
3. Jonathan W. Jordan, *Brothers, Rivals, Victors* (New York: Caliber, 2011), p. 363.
4. Quoted in D.K.R. Crosswell, *Beetle: The Life of General Walter Bedell Smith* (Lexington, KY: University of Kentucky Press, 2010), p. 679.
5. John Keegan, *Six Armies in Normandy* (New York: Penguin Books, 1994), pp. 249–56.
6. Quoted in William Mortimer-Moore, *Paris '44: The City of Light Redeemed* (Philadelphia: Casemate, 2015), p. 142.
7. Patton, Letter to Beatrice, August 8, 1944, in *Patton Papers*, p. 504; Ladislas Farago, *Patton: Ordeal and Triumph* (New York: Dell, 1963), pp. 515, 526.
8. Herbert Essame, *Patton: A Study in Command* (New York: Charles Scribner's Sons, 1974), p. 163; Antony Beevor, *D-Day: The Battle for Normandy* (New York: Penguin Books, 2009), p. 433; Richard Rohmer, *Patton's Gap* (Don Mills, Ontario: General Publishing, 1981), p. 179.
9. Quoted in Martin Blumenson, *The Battle of the Generals* (New York: William Morrow, 1993), p. 190; Rohmer, *Patton's Gap*, p. 183; Chester Wilmot and Daniel Christopher McDevitt, *The Struggle for Europe* (Hertfordshire, UK: Wordsworth Editions, 1997), p. 415.
10. Patton, letter, August 8, 1944, in *Patton Papers*, p. 504; William Weidner, *Eisenhower and Montgomery at the Falaise Gap* (New York: Xlibris, 2010), pp. 55–56; Harry Yeide, *Fighting Patton* (New York: Zenith, 2011), p. 258; Beevor, *D-Day*, p. 434.
11. Letter to George Marshall, August 9, 1944, in Alfred D. Chandler, Jr., ed., *The Papers of Dwight David Eisenhower*, vol. 4 (Baltimore: Johns Hopkins University Press, 1970), p. 1889; Harry C. Butcher, *My Three Years with Eisenhower* (New York: Simon and Schuster, 1948), p. 636.
12. Quoted in Blumenson, *Generals*, p. 191.
13. Quoted in Farago, *Patton*, p. 540.

14. John Buckley, *Monty's Men* (New Haven, CT: Yale University Press, 2013), pp. 169–72; Weidner, *Eisenhower and Montgomery*, pp. 60–61; Beevor, *D-Day*, pp. 422–30.

15. Montgomery, Message (M85) to Field Marshal Sir Alan Brooke, in Stephen Brooks, ed., *Montgomery and the Battle of Normandy* (Stroud, UK: History Press, 2008), p. 285.

16. Wilmot, *Struggle for Europe*, p. 414.

17. Montgomery, Message (M86) to Field Marshal Sir Alan Brooke, in *Montgomery and the Battle of Normandy*, p. 287; Montgomery, diary, August 16, 1944, in *Montgomery and the Battle of Normandy*, p. 304; Beevor, *D-Day*, pp. 454–55.

18. Montgomery, Directive (M518) to 12 US Army Group, First Canadian Army and Second British Army, in *Montgomery and the Battle of Normandy*, p. 288.

19. Montgomery, diary and papers, in *Montgomery and the Battle of Normandy*, pp. 268, 273, 289, 297, 300; Blumenson, *Generals*, p. 217.

20. Letter from Field Marshal Sir Alan Brooke to Montgomery, August 13, 1944, in *Montgomery and the Battle of Normandy*, p. 294.

21. Beevor, *D-Day*, p. 43; Essame, *Patton*, p. 165; Weidner, *Eisenhower and Montgomery*, pp. 58–59; Keegan, *Normandy*, p. 253; Robert A. Miller, *August 1944, The Campaign for France* (Novato, CA: Presidio, 1996), pp. 103, 105, 109–10.

22. Patton, diary, August 13, 1944, in *Patton Papers*, p. 508.

23. Farago, *Patton*, pp. 537–38; Blumenson, *Generals*, pp. 205–206.

24. Omar N. Bradley, *A General's Life* (New York: Simon and Schuster, 1983), p. 298; Farago, *Patton*, p. 539.

25. Patton, diary, August 16, 1944, in *Patton Papers*, p. 508; Farrago, *Patton*, pp. 539–40.

26. Quoted in Farago, *Patton*, p. 534.

27. Patton, diary, August 13, 1944, in *Patton Papers*, p. 508.

28. Omar N. Bradley, *A Soldier's Story* (New York: Modern Library, 1999), p. 378.

29. Niall Barr, *Eisenhower's Armies* (New York: Pegasus Books, 2015), p. 392.

30. Weidner, *Eisenhower and Montgomery*, p. 305; Jordan, *Brothers*, p. 375.

31. Carlo D'Este, *Decision in Normandy* (Old Saybrook, CT: Konecky & Konecky, 1994), p. 451.

32. Blumenson, *Generals*, p. 207.

33. Richard Lamb, *Montgomery in Europe 1943–1945: Success or Failure?* (New York: Franklin Watts, 1984), p. 171; Weidner, *Eisenhower and Montgomery*, p. 167.

34. Quoted in Blumenson, *Generals*, p. 214.

35. Chester B. Hansen, diary, August 14, 1944, Chester B. Hansen Collection, Folder 12, US Army Military History Institute, Carlisle, Pennsylvania.

36. Field Marshal Bernard Law Montgomery, interview by Chester Wilmot, May 18, 1946, Liddell Hart Papers, Kings College, London.

37. Keegan, *Normandy*, p. 260.

38. Bradley, *Soldier's Story*, p. 376.

39. Wilmot, *Struggle for Europe*, p. 419; Nigel Hamilton, *Master of the Battlefield* (New York: McGraw-Hill, 1983), p. 785; Max Hastings, *Overlord, D-Day and the Battle for Normandy* (New York: Simon and Schuster, 1984), p. 314.

40. Essame, *Patton*, p. 167; Keegan, *Normandy*, p. 256.

41. Miller, *August 1944*, p. 112; Keegan, *Normandy*, pp. 256, 261; Weidner, *Eisenhower and Montgomery*, pp. 97, 165, 170–71, 340; Farago, *Patton*, pp. 538–39.

42. Rohmer, *Patton's Gap*, pp. 194–96.

43. Bradley, *Soldier's Story*, p. 377.

44. Essame, *Patton*, pp. 169–70; D'Este, *Normandy*, pp. 443–44.

45. Hastings, *Overlord*, p. 290; Patton, diary, August 14, 1944, in *Patton Papers*, p. 510.

46. Dwight D. Eisenhower, *Crusade in Europe* (New York: Avon, 1968), pp. 296–97.

47. Weidner, *Eisenhower and Montgomery*, pp. 327–47.

48. Ibid., p. 345; Blumenson, *Generals*, p. 217; Miller, *August 1944*, pp. 119–21.

49. Montgomery, letter to Field Marshal Sir Alan Brooke in *Montgomery and the Battle of Normandy*, p. 298.

50. Martin Blumenson, *Breakout and Pursuit* (Washington, DC: Office of the Chief of History, Department of the Army, 1961), p. 547.

51. Wilmot, *Struggle for Europe*, pp. 422, 423; Beevor, *D-Day*, pp. 467, 468, 472, 475; D'Este, *Normandy*, pp. 456, 458; Blumenson, *Breakout and Pursuit*, pp. 541, 545, 546, 553, 554; Miller, *August 1944*, p. 155.

52. Quoted in Keegan, *Normandy*, p. 257.

53. Blumenson, *Breakout and Pursuit*, p. 516.

54. Keegan, *Normandy*, p. 257; Blumenson, *Breakout and Pursuit*, pp. 517–18.

55. Wilmot, *Struggle for Europe*, p. 420; Keegan, *Normandy*, p. 257; Miller, *August 1944*, p. 131.

56. Quoted in Beevor, *D-Day*, p. 459.

57. Blumenson, *Breakout and Pursuit*, pp. 519–21; Keegan, *Normandy*, p. 257; Miller, *August 1944*, p. 131; Beevor, *D-Day*, pp. 444–45.

58. Quoted in Blumenson, *Breakout and Pursuit*, p. 522.

59. McKee, *Last Round against Rommel* (New York: Signet Books, 1966), p. 316.

60. Miller, *August 1944*, pp. 133–35; Beevor, *D-Day*, p. 464.

61. Keegan, *Normandy*, p. 259; Wilmot, *Struggle for Europe*, p. 421.

62. Quoted in Miller, *August 1944*, pp. 149–50.

63. Carrell, *Invasion*, p. 292; Liddell Hart, *The Other Side of the Hill* (London: Pan Books, 1948), p. 417.

64. Carrell, *Invasion*, p. 292; Blumenson, *Breakout*, pp. 528–31.

65. Beevor, *D-Day*, p 466.

66. Keegan, *Normandy*, p. 325.

67. Beevor, *D-Day*, pp. 476–77.

68. Rohmer, *Patton's Gap*, p. 213; Charles Perry Stacey, *The Victory Campaign: The Operations in Northwest Europe 1944–1945*, vol. 3, *Official History of the Canadian Army in the Second World War* (Ottawa: Queen's Printer, 1960), pp. 271–72.

69. Keegan, *Normandy*, p. 285; Rohmer, *Patton's Gap*, p. 214; D'Este, *Normandy*, p. 438; Beevor, *D-Day*, p. 478; Hastings, *Overlord*, p. 314; Blumenson, *Generals*, p. 259; McKee, *Rommel*, p. 328; Paul Carrell, *Invasion! They're Coming!* (New York: Bantam, 1964), p. 301.

70. Russell F. Weigley, *Eisenhower's Lieutenants: The Campaign in France and Germany, 1944–1945* (Bloomington: Indiana University Press, 1981), pp. 214–15; Miller, *August 1944*, pp. 168, 176; Weidner, *Eisenhower and Montgomery*, pp. 142–43.

71. Hastings, *Overlord*, pp. 315–17.

72. Blumenson, *Generals*, p. 263.

73. Eisenhower, *Eisenhower at War*, p. 409; Correlli Barnett, *Engage the Enemy More Closely: The Royal Navy in the Second World War* (New York: W.W. Norton, 1991), p. 843; Keegan, *Normandy*, p. 283.

74. Alistair Horne, *Monty: The Lonely Leader* (New York: Harper Collins, 1994), pp. 250–51; Stacey, *Victory Campaign*, pp. 270–71; Hastings, *Overlord*, p. 313.

75. Quoted in Beevor, *D-Day*, p. 478.

76. Montgomery, diary notes, August 18–20, 1944, in *Montgomery and the Battle of Normandy*, p. 310.

77. Nigel Hamilton, *Master of the Battlefield* (New York: McGraw-Hill, 1983), p. 786.

78. Quoted in Horace Edward Henderson, *The Greatest Blunders of World War II* (New York: Writer's Showcase, 2001), p. 379.

79. Henderson, *Greatest Blunders*, p. 378.

80. Weidner, *Eisenhower and Montgomery*, p. 143.

81. Lamb, *Montgomery in Europe*, p. 177.

82. Bradley, *General's Life*, p. 301.

83. Stacey, *Victory Campaign*, p. 276.

84. Quoted in Stacey, *Victory Campaign*, p. 276.

85. Quoted in Eddy Florentin, *The Battle of the Falaise Gap* (New York: Hawthorn Books, 1967), p. 331; Miller, *August 1944*, p. 176.

86. Patton, diary, August 13, 1944, in *Patton Papers*, p. 511.

87. Hamilton, *Montgomery*, p. 83; Crosswell, *Beetle*, p. 680; William B. Breuer, *Feuding Allies* (New York: John Wiley & Sons, 1996), p. 233.

88. Quoted in Stephen E. Ambrose, *Eisenhower Soldier, General of the Army, President-Elect, 1890–1952* (New York: Simon and Schuster, 1983), p. 328.

89. Ibid.

90. Bradley, *Soldier's Story*, p. 369.

91. Letter to Winston Spencer Churchill, August 11, 1944, #1891 in *Eisenhower Papers*, ed. Alfred D. Chandler, Jr., vol. 4 (Baltimore, MD: Johns Hopkins University Press, 1978), p. 2065.

92. Montgomery, diary notes, August 18–20, 1944, in *Montgomery and the Battle of Normandy*, pp. 308–309.

93. Francis de Guingand, *Operation Victory* (New York: Charles Scribner's Sons, 1947), p. viii.

94. Montgomery, Letter to Field Marshal Sir Alan Brooke, August 14, 1944, in *Montgomery and the Battle of Normandy*, pp. 298–99.

95. Hamilton, *Montgomery*, p. 81.

96. Lamb, *Montgomery in Europe*, p. 179; Weidner, *Eisenhower and Montgomery*, p. 331.

97. Miller, *August 1944*, p. 176; Breuer, *Feuding Allies*, p. 232.

98. Quoted in Farago, *Patton*, p. 541.

99. Quoted in Rick Atkinson, *The Guns at Last Light*, vol. 3, *The Liberation Trilogy* (New York: Henry Holt, 2013), p. 163.

100. Quoted in Essame, *Patton*, p. 172.

101. Quoted in Martin Blumenson, *The Duel for France, 1944* (Boston: Houghton Mifflin, 1963), p. 262.

## CHAPTER 11: THE LOST VICTORY

1. Patton, diary, August 21, 1944, in *The Patton Papers 1940–1945*, ed. Martin Blumenson (Cambridge, MA: Da Capo, 1974), p. 523.

2. Omar N. Bradley, *A General's Life* (New York: Simon and Schuster, 1983), p. 305.

3. Blumenson, *Breakout and Pursuit* (Washington, DC: Office of the Chief of History, Department of the Army, 1961), pp. 701–702.

4. Patton, diary, August 13, 1944, in *Patton Papers*, p. 508.

5. Ibid., August 14, 1944, p. 510; Robert A. Miller, *August 1944, The Campaign for France* (Novato, CA: Presidio, 1996), p. 122.

6. Blumenson, *Breakout and Pursuit*, pp. 564–66; Bradley, *General's Life*, p. 302; Ladislas Farago, *Patton: Ordeal and Triumph* (New York: Dell, 1963), p. 545.

7. Patton, Letter to Beatrice, August 13, 1944, in *Patton Papers*, pp. 509–10; Blumenson, *Breakout and Pursuit*, pp. 566–71; Miller, *August 1944*, pp. 141–42; Antony Beevor, *D-Day: The Battle for Normandy* (New York: Penguin Books, 2009), pp. 455–56.

8. William B. Breuer, *Feuding Allies* (New York: John Wiley & Sons, 1996), p. 234; Miller, *August 1944*, pp. 142–43.

9. Patton to Harbord and Summerall, August 18, 1944, in *Patton Papers*, p. 518.

10. Stephen R. Taaffe, *Marshall and His Generals: US Army Commanders in World War II* (Lawrence, KS: University of Kansas Press, 2011), p. 196; Blumenson, *Breakout and Pursuit*, p. 573; Jim DeFelice, *Omar Bradley* (Washington, DC: Regnery, 2011), pp. 260–61.

11. Blumenson, *Breakout and Pursuit*, pp. 575–83; Herbert Essame, *Patton: A Study in Command* (New York: Charles Scribner's Sons, 1974), pp. 180–82.

12. Essame, *Patton*, pp. 187–88.

13. Taaffe, *Marshall and His Generals*, p. 196; Blumenson, *Breakout and Pursuit*, p. 605; Essame, *Patton*, p. 179.

14. Jonathan Fenby, *The General: Charles de Gaulle and the France He Saved* (New York: Skyhorse, 2012), p. 251.

15. Ibid.; Blumenson, *Breakout and Pursuit*, p. 593.

16. Quoted in John Keegan, *Six Armies in Normandy* (New York: Penguin Books, 1994), p. 292; Robert Gildea, *Fighters in the Shadows* (Cambridge: Belknap Press, 2015), p. 391.

17. Keegan, *Normandy*, pp. 293–94; Gildea, *Fighters*, pp. 397–98.

18. Jonathan W. Jordan, *Brothers, Rivals, Victors* (New York: Caliber, 2011), p. 384; Gildea, *Fighters*, p. 18; Taaffe, *Marshal and His Generals*, p. 19.

19. Blumenson, *Breakout and Pursuit*, p. 603.

20. Martin Blumenson, *The Battle of the Generals* (New York: William Morrow, 1993), p. 270.

21. Antony Beevor, *D-Day: The Battle for Normandy* (New York: Penguin Books, 2009), pp. 488–89; Farago, *Patton*, p. 557.

22. Essame, *Patton*, p. 184.

23. Blumenson, *Breakout and Pursuit*, p. 609; Gildea, *Fighters*, p. 401.

24. Keegan, *Normandy*, pp. 304–12.

25. Gildea, *Fighters*, pp. 18, 404; Keegan, *Normandy*, p. 312.

26. Quoted in Gildea, *Fighters*, p. 3.

27. Blumenson, *Breakout and Pursuit*, p. 622; Omar N. Bradley, *A Soldier's Story* (New York: Modern Library, 1999), p. 396; Miller, *August 1944*, pp. 233–35.

28. Interview with Raymond Sola by Edward Gordon, August 10, 2016, which was Mr. Sola's one hundredth birthday. He also stated that he was disappointed because he marched that day in the middle of the column. The soldiers who were at the ends of the column received many hugs and kisses from the Parisian women who were overjoyed at finally being liberated from the Germans.

29. Jean Edward Smith, *Eisenhower in War and Peace* (New York: Random House, 2013), p. 391.

30. Beevor, *D-Day*, p. 519.

31. William B. Breuer, *Operation Dragoon: The Allied Invasion of the South of France* (Novato, CA: Presidio, 1996), p. 13.

32. Rick Atkinson, *The Guns at Last Light*, vol. 3, *The Liberation Trilogy* (New York: Henry Holt, 2013), pp. 198–99.

33. Samuel Eliot Morison, *The Two-Ocean War: A Short History of the United States Navy in the Second World War* (Atlantic Monthly Press, 1963), pp. 411–12; Atkinson, *Last Light*, p. 199; Breuer, *Operation Dragoon*, pp. 13, 246–48; John S.D. Eisenhower, *Allies: Pearl Harbor to D-Day* (Garden City, NY: Doubleday, 1982, p. 442; Paul H. Jeffers, *Command of Honor: General Lucian Truscott's Path to Victory in World War II* (New York: Nal CALIBER, 2008), p. 217; Stephen E. Ambrose, *Eisenhower Soldier, General of the Army, President-Elect, 1890–1952* (New York: Simon and Schuster, 1983), p. 330; Beevor, *D-Day*, pp. 444–45.

34. Dwight D. Eisenhower, *Crusade in Europe* (New York: Johns Hopkins University Press, 1997), p. 294.

35. Quoted in Jordan, *Brothers*, p. 389.

36. George S. Patton, Jr., *War as I Knew It* (New York: Bantam Books, 1980), pp. 129–30.

37. David P. Colley, "On the Road to Victory: The Red Ball Express,"

HistoryNet, http://www.historynet.com/red-ball-express (accessed April 5, 2017).

38. Blumenson, *Breakout and Pursuit*, p. 666; David Colley, *The Road to Victory* (Washington, DC: Brassey's, 2000), p.61.

39. D.K.R. Crosswell, *Beetle: The Life of General Walter Bedell Smith* (Lexington, KY: University of Kentucky Press, 2010), pp. 688–96, 736; Steven E. Ambrose, *The Supreme Commander: The War Years of Dwight D. Eisenhower* (New York: Anchor, 2012), p. 494; Colley, *Road to Victory*, pp. 49, 61; Blumenson, *Breakout and Pursuit*, pp. 665–66; Anthony Kemp, *The Unknown Battle: Metz, 1944* (New York: Stein and Day, 1981), pp. 22–23.

40. Farago, *Patton*, p. 559.

41. Blumenson, *Breakout and Pursuit*, pp. 662–64; B.H. Liddell Hart, *History of the Second World War* (Old Saybrook, CT: Konecky & Konecky, 1970), p. 559.

42. Quoted in Atkinson, *Last Light*, p. 220.

43. Quoted in Essame, *Patton*, p. 194.

44. Farago, *Patton*, pp. 549–51; Taaffe, *Marshall and His Generals*, p. 203; Blumenson, *Breakout and Pursuit*, p. 668.

45. Patton, diary, August 30, 1944, in *Patton Papers*, p. 531.

46. Quoted in Farago, *Patton*, p. 577; Hart, *Second World War*, p. 558.

47. Patton to Beatrice, August 30, 1944, in *Patton Papers*, p. 531.

48. Quoted in Bradley, *Soldier's Story*, p. 402.

49. Quoted in Bradley, *General's Life*, p. 314.

50. Diary notes, August 17, 1944, in Stephen Brooks, ed., *Montgomery and the Battle of Normandy* (Stroud, UK: History Press, 2008), p. 306.

51. Bradley, *General's Life*, p. 314.

52. Quoted in Fargo, pp. 576; Ambrose, *Eisenhower*, p. 341.

53. Quoted in Carlo D'Este, *Decision in Normandy* (Old Saybrook, CT: Konecky & Konecky, 1994), p. 461; Nial Barr, *Eisenhower's Armies* (New York: Pegasus Books, 2015), pp. 406–408; DeFelice, *Bradley*, p. 260.

54. Ambrose, *Eisenhower*, pp. 338, 341; D'Este, *Normandy*, p. 467; Richard Lamb, *Montgomery in Europe 1943–1945: Success or Failure?* (New York: Franklin Watts, 1984), pp. 188–89; Crosswell, *Beetle*, p. 686.

55. Niall Barr, *Eisenhower's Armies*, pp. 401–402; Carlo D'Este, "A Lingering Controversy: Eisenhower's 'Broad Front' Strategy," *Armchair General Magazine*, October 7, 2009, http://www.armchairgeneral.com/a-lingering-controversy-eisenhowers-broad-front-strategy.htm; Blumenson, *Breakout and Pursuit*, pp. 657–58.

56. Blumenson editorial comment in *Patton Papers*, p. 527.

57. Keegan, *Normandy*, pp. 313–15; "Breaching the Siegfried Line," US Army Military Center, http://www.history.army.mil/books/wwii/Siegfried/Siegfried%20 Line/siegfried-ch01.htm; Crosswell, *Beetle*, p. 737; Essame, *Patton*, p. 194.

58. Dwight D. Eisenhower, *The Papers of Dwight D. Eisenhower*, ed. Alfred D. Chandler, Jr., vol. 4, *The War Years* (Baltimore: Johns Hopkins Press, 1970), August 29, 1944, #1920, p. 2100.

59. Bradley, *Soldier's Story*, p. 401; Bradley, *General's Life*, pp. 320–21; Blumenson, *Breakout and Pursuit*, p. 659.

60. Quoted in Farago, *Patton*, p. 602; Bradley, *General's Life*, p. 322.

61. Quoted in Farago, *Patton*, p. 603.

62. Alan Brooke, *War Diaries, 1939–1945*, eds. Alex Danchev and Daniel Todman (London: Phoenix Press, 2001), p. 585.

63. Montgomery, diary notes August 17, 1944, in *Montgomery and the Battle of Normandy*, p. 57.

64. Quoted in Bradley, *General's Life*, p. 322.

65. Ibid., p. 323.

66. Patton, Letter to Beatrice, September 3, 1944, in *Patton Papers*, pp. 538–39.

67. Patton, diary, September 11, 1944, in *Patton Papers*, p. 547.

68. Hart, *Second World War*, p. 561.

69. Ibid., p. 567.

70. Ibid., p. 557.

71. Nigel Hamilton, *Montgomery: D-Day Commander* (Washington, DC: Potomac Books, 2007), p. 84.

72. Siegfried Westphal, *The German Army in the West* (London: Cassell, 1951), p. 176.

73. Essame, *Patton*, p. 198.

## CHAPTER 12: THE ANTWERP/MARKET GARDEN FIASCOS

1. Mark Urban, *Generals: The British Commanders Who Shaped the World* (London: Faber and Faber, 2005), p. 290.

2. Russell F. Weigley, *Eisenhower's Lieutenants: The Campaign in France and Germany, 1944–1945* (Bloomington: Indiana University Press, 1981), pp. 388–89; William Weidner, *Eisenhower and Montgomery at the Falaise Gap* (New York: Xlibris, 2010), p. 310; Forrest C. Pogue, *George C. Marshall: The Organizer of Victory* (New York: Viking Press, 1973), p. 426.

3. Ramsay, diary, September 1 and 5, 1944, in Bertram Ramsay, *Year of*

*D-Day*, eds. Robert W. Love, Jr. and John Mayor (Hull, UK: University of Hull Press, 1994), pp. 129, 132.

4. Love and Major, editorial notes in *Year of D-Day*, p. 130.

5. Letter from Field Marshal Sir Alan Brooke to Montgomery, September 1, 1944, in Stephen Brooks, ed., *Montgomery and the Battle of Normandy* (Stroud, UK: History Press, 2008), p. 312.

6. Omar N. Bradley, *A General's Life* (New York: Simon and Schuster, 1983), p. 319; Correlli Barnett, *Engage the Enemy More Closely: The Royal Navy in the Second World War* (New York: W.W. Norton, 1991), p. 845; Dominick Graham, *Price of Command* (Toronto: Stoddart, 1993), p. 177.

7. Kenneth Edwards, *Operation Neptune* (Sabon, UK: Fonthill, 2013), p. 311; Dwight D. Eisenhower, *Crusade in Europe* (New York: Johns Hopkins University Press, 1997), p. 309; Dennis Showalter, *Patton and Rommel* (New York: Berkley Caliber, 2005), p. 377; Rick Atkinson, *The Guns at Last Light*, vol. 3, *The Liberation Trilogy* (New York: Henry Holt, 2013), p. 242; J.L. Moulton, *Battle for Antwerp* (New York: Hippocrene Books, 1978), pp. 27–45; D.K.R. Crosswell, *Beetle: The Life of General Walter Bedell Smith* (Lexington, KY: University of Kentucky Press, 2010), p. 706.

8. Ramsay, diary, September 4, 1944, in *Year of D-Day*, p. 131.

9. Quoted in Barnett, *Engage*, p. 846; W.S. Chalmers, *Full Cycle, The Biography of Admiral Sir Bertram Home Ramsay* (London: Hodder & Stoughton, 1959), p. 244.

10. Quoted in Nial Barr, *Eisenhower's Armies* (New York: Pegasus Books, 2015), p. 414.

11. John Buckley, *Monty's Men* (New Haven, CT: Yale University Press, 2013), pp. 199–202.

12. Quoted in Richard Lamb, *Montgomery in Europe 1943–1945: Success or Failure?* (New York: Franklin Watts, 1984), p. 201.

13. Quoted in B.H. Liddell Hart, *History of the Second World War* (Old Saybrook, CT: Konecky & Konecky, 1970), p. 567.

14. Lamb, *Montgomery*, pp. 202–203.

15. Ramsay, diary, September 10, 1944, in *Year of D-Day*, p. 135.

16. Love and Major, editorial notes in *Year of D-Day*, p. 136.

17. Quoted in Jonathan W. Jordan, *Brothers, Rivals, Victors* (New York: Caliber, 2011), p. 398.

18. Ibid.

19. Eisenhower, *Crusade*, p. 327.

20. Ramsay, diary, September 11, 1944, in *Year of D-Day*, p. 137.

21. Quoted in Barnett, *Engage*, pp. 844–45.

22. Love and Major, editorial notes in *Year of D-Day*, p. 143.
23. Ramsay, diary, September 22, 1944, in *Year of D-Day*, p. 142–43.
24. Quoted in Crosswell, *Beetle*, p. 726.
25. Ibid.
26. Ibid., p. 708.
27. Quoted in Jim DeFelice, *Omar Bradley* (Washington, DC: Regnery, 2011), p. 272.
28. Patton, diary, September 15, 1944, in *Patton Papers*, p. 548.
29. Crosswell, *Beetle*, pp. 696, 727.
30. Chester Wilmot, *The Struggle for Europe* (London: Collins, 1952), p. 477; Lamb, *Montgomery*, p. 212; Milton Shulman, *Defeat in the West* (New York: E.P. Dutton, 1948), pp. 178–80.
31. Cornelius Ryan, *A Bridge Too Far* (New York: Popular Library, 1974), pp. 114–15; W.S. Chalmers, *Full Cycle: The Biography of Admiral Sir Bertram Ramsay* (London: Hodder & Stoughton, 1959), p. 248; Edwards, *Operation Neptune*, pp. 330–31.
32. Max Hastings, *Armageddon: The Battle for Germany, 1944–45* (New York: Alfred A. Knopf, 2006), pp. 20–21; Robin Neillands, *The Battle for the Rhine* (New York: Overlook, 2007), p. 160.
33. Lamb, *Montgomery*, p. 207.
34. Bradley, *Soldier's Story*, p. 416; Ryan, *Bridge*, p. 11; Graham, *Price of Command*, p. 180; Eisenhower, *Eisenhower at War*, pp. 441–42.
35. Crosswell, *Beetle*, p. 715; Ryan, *Bridge*, p. 88.
36. Crosswell, *Beetle*, pp, 717–18; Bernard Montgomery, *The Memoirs of Field Marshal the Viscount Montgomery of Alamein* (London: Collins, 1958), p. 297.
37. Crosswell, *Beetle*, p. 717; Ryan, *Bridge*, pp. 115–16; Wilmot, *Struggle*, pp. 479–80.
38. Quoted in Ryan, *Bridge*, p. 89.
39. Brian Urquhart, *A Life in War and Peace* (New York: W.W. Norton, 1987), pp. 48–76.
40. Arnold, *Hollow Heroes* (Philadelphia: Casemate, 2015), p. 162.
41. Brian Horrocks with Eversley Belfield and H. Essame, *Corps Commander* (New York: Charles Schribner's Sons, 1977), p. 83.
42. Elizabeth Anne Coble, *Operation Market Garden: Case Study for Analyzing Senior Leader Responsibilities* (Carlisle Barracks, PA: US Army War College, 2009), pp. 22–23.
43. Miles Dempsey, "The First 100 Days: Operation Overlord—From the Beaches to the Dutch Frontier" (diary written daily during course of war, 1944), p. 107.

44. Coble, *Market Garden*, p. 61.
45. DeFelice, *Bradley*, p. 271.
46. Bradley, *Soldier's Story*, p. 418.
47. Quoted in Norman Gelb, *Ike and Monty: Generals at War* (New York: William Morrow, 1994), p. 362.
48. Jordan, *Brothers*, p. 407; Crosswell, *Beetle*, p. 720; Callahan, *Churchill and His Generals* (Lawrence, KS: University of Kansas Press, 2007), pp. 220–21; Robert A. Miller, *August 1944, The Campaign for France* (Novato, CA: Presidio, 1996), p. 258.
49. Arnold, *Hollow Heroes*, p. 161.
50. Quoted in Ryan, *Bridge*, p. 217.
51. Ryan, *Bridge*, pp. 187–99; B.H. Liddell Hart, *Strategy* (New York: Praeger, 1967), p. 320; Antony Beevor, *The Second World War* (New York: Little, Brown, 2012), pp. 635–36; Alan Axelrod, *Patton's Drive* (Guilford, CT: Lyons, 2009), p. 108; Arnold, *Hollow Heroes*, pp. 164–65; Carlo D'Este, "Market Garden 65 Years On: Reflections of a Tragedy," Armchair General, September 2, 2009, http://www.armchairgeneral.com/market-garden-65-years-on-reflections-of-a-tragedy.htm (accessed June 4, 2017).
52. Bernard Montgomery, *The Memoirs of Field Marshall Montgomery* (Cleveland: World Publishing, 1958), p. 267.
53. Nigel Hamilton, *Montgomery: D-Day Commander* (Washington, DC: Potomac Books, 2007), p. 89.
54. Norman Davies, *No Simple Victory: World War II in Europe 1939–1945* (New York: Viking, 2007), p. 122.
55. Alun Chalfont, *Montgomery of Alamein* (New York: Atheneum, 1976), p. 252.
56. David Bennett, *Magnificent Disaster* (Philadelphia: Casemate, 2008), p. 196.
57. Quoted in Atkinson, *Last Light*, p. 288.
58. Quoted in Ryan, *Bridge*, p. 597.
59. Quoted in Stephen E. Ambrose, *Eisenhower: Soldier, General of the Army, President-Elect, 1890–1952* (New York: Simon and Schuster, 1983), p. 350.
60. Buckley, *Monty's Men*, p. 231; D'Este, "Market Garden."
61. Alan Moorehead, *Eclipse* (New York: Harper & Row, 1945), p. 215.
62. Ramsay, diary, September 19, 1944, in *Year of D-Day*, pp. 140–41.
63. Ibid., pp. 151–52.
64. Alan Brooke, *War Diaries, 1939–1945*, eds. Alex Danchev and Daniel Todman (London: Phoenix Press, 2001), p. 600.
65. Ramsay, diary, October 8, 1944, in *Year of D-Day*, p. 153.
66. Barnett, *Engage*, p. 848.

67. Eisenhower, *Papers*, October 10, 1944, p. 2215.
68. Quoted in Chalfont, *Montgomery*, p. 259.
69. Quoted in Jordan, *Brothers*, p. 176.
70. Chalfont, *Montgomery*, p. 259; Crosswell, *Beetle*, p. 731; Ambrose, *Eisenhower*, p. 354.
71. Quoted in Crosswell, *Beetle*, p. 732.
72. Montgomery, *Memoirs*, p. 254.
73. George C. Marshall, *The Papers of George Catlett Marshall*, ed. Larry I. Bland, vol. 4, *Aggressive and Determined Leadership* (Baltimore: Johns Hopkins University Press, 1996), p. 624.
74. Eisenhower, *Papers*, October 13, 1944, p. 2222.
75. Barnett, *Engage*, p. 849.
76. Neillands, *Rhine*, pp. 164–67.
77. Barnett, *Engage*, pp. 850–51.
78. Ibid., p. 851.
79. Ramsay, diary, November 28, 1944, in *Year of D-Day*, pp. 182.
80. Moulton, *Antwerp*, p. 230; Atkinson, *Last Light*, p. 330.
81. Barnett, *Engage*, p. 851.
82. Callahan, *Churchill and His Generals*, p. 221.
83. Montgomery, *Memoirs*, p. 297.

## CHAPTER 13: CRISIS IN COMMAND

1. Alan Brooke, *War Diaries, 1939–1945*, eds. Alex Danchev and Daniel Todman (London: Phoenix Press, 2001), p. 564.
2. Quoted in Antony Beevor, *D-Day: The Battle for Normandy* (New York: Penguin Books, 2009), p. 522.
3. Frederick Morgan, *Overture to Overlord* (Garden City, NY: Doubleday, 1950), pp. 287.
4. David Woolner, "The 'Special Relationship' between Great Britain and the United States Began with FDR," Roosevelt Institute, July 22, 2010, http://rooseveltinstitute.org/special-relationship-between-great-britain-and-united-states-began-fdr/ (accessed April 4, 2017).
5. Quoted in Maurice Matloff, *Strategic Planning for Coalition Warfare 1943–1944* (Washington, DC: Center of Military History, US Army, 1990), p. 5, http://www.history.army.mil/html/books/001/1–4/CMH_Pub_1–4.pdf (accessed June 4, 2017).
6. Brooke, *War Diaries*, pp. 465, 475.

7. Morgan, *Overture*, p. 284.

8. Don Cook, "General of the Army: Dwight D. Eisenhower," in *The War Lords, Military Commanders of the Twentieth Century*, ed. Michael Carver (Boston, MA: Little, Brown, 1976), p. 509.

9. Erwin Rommel, *Rommel Papers*, ed. B.H. Liddell Hart (London: Hamlyn Paperbacks, 1953), pp. 521–22.

10. Martin Blumenson, *Breakout and Pursuit* (Washington, DC: Office of the Chief of History, Department of the Army, 1961), p. 8.

11. Cook, "Eisenhower," pp. 509–10.

12. Ralph Ingersoll, *Top Secret* (New York: Harcourt Brace, 1946), p. 12.

13. Cook, "Eisenhower," p. 527.

14. Ladislas Farago, *Patton: Ordeal and Triumph* (New York: Dell, 1963), pp. 629–30; Carlo D'Este, "A Lingering Controversy: Eisenhower's 'Broad Front' Strategy," *Armchair General Magazine*, October 7, 2009, http://www.armchairgeneral.com/a-lingering-controversy-eisenhowers-broad-front-strategy.htm (accessed April 4, 2017).

15. William Weidner, *Eisenhower and Montgomery at the Falaise Gap* (New York: Xlibris, 2010), p. 354; Stephen E. Ambrose, *Eisenhower: Soldier, General of the Army, President-Elect, 1890–1952* (New York: Simon and Schuster, 1983), p. 344.

16. Patton, diary, July 12, 1944, in *The Patton Papers 1940–1945*, ed. Martin Blumenson (Cambridge, MA: Da Capo, 1974), p. 480.

17. Quoted in D.K.R. Crosswell, *Beetle: The Life of General Walter Bedell Smith* (Lexington, KY: University of Kentucky Press, 2010), p. 722.

18. Max Hastings, *Overlord: D-Day and the Battle for Normandy* (New York: Simon and Schuster, 1984), pp. 28–29.

19. Earl Alexander, *The Alexander Memoirs 1940–1945* (London: Cassel, 1962), pp. 40–41.

20. Correlli Barnett, *The Desert Generals* (London: Allen & Unwin, 1960), pp. 8, 310–13.

21. Correlli Barnett, *Engage the Enemy More Closely: The Royal Navy in the Second World War* (New York: W.W. Norton, 1991), p. 615.

22. Rommel, *Papers*, pp. 280, 360–61.

23. Barnett, *Desert Generals*, pp. 272, 302–303, 308–309, 312–31; Weidner, *Eisenhower and Montgomery*, p. 243.

24. Martin Blumenson, *The Battle of the Generals* (New York: William Morrow, 1993), pp. 78–79.

25. George S. Patton, Jr., *War as I Knew It* (New York: Bantam Books, 1980), pp. 112–13.

26. Rommel, *Papers*, p. 521.

27. Quoted in Henderson, *Blunders*, p. 380.

28. Stephen Hart, *Montgomery and "Colossal Cracks": The 21st Army Group in Northwest Europe, 1944–1945* (Connecticut & London: Praeger, 2000), p. 189; Horace Edward Henderson, *The Greatest Blunders of World War II* (New York: Writer's Showcase, 2001), pp. 380–81; Beevor, *D-Day*, p. 522; Hastings, *Overlord*, pp. 211, 254; Rick Atkinson, *The Guns at Last Light*, vol. 3, *The Liberation Trilogy* (New York: Henry Holt, 2013), p. 182; Jim DeFelice, *Omar Bradley* (Washington, DC: Regnery, 2011), pp. 166–67.

29. Quoted in Alun Chalfont, *Montgomery of Alamein* (New York: Atheneum, 1976), p. 329.

30. Francis de Guingand, *Operation Victory* (London: Charles Scribner's Sons, 1947), p. 182.

31. Weidner, *Eisenhower and Montgomery*, p. 210.

32. Carlo D'Este, "A Lingering Controversy: Eisenhower's 'Broad Front' Strategy," *Armchair General*, October 7, 2009, p. 5, http://www.armchairgeneral.com/a-lingering-controversy-eisenhowers-broad-front-strategy.htm (accessed April 4, 2017).

33. Mark Urban, *Generals: Ten British Commanders Who Shaped the World* (London: Faber and Faber, 2005), pp. 296–97.

34. Quoted in Atkinson, *Last Light*, p. 383.

35. Ibid.

36. Quoted in Jonathan W. Jordan, *Brothers, Rivals, Victors* (New York: Caliber, 2011), p. 458.

37. Quoted in Mark Urban, *Generals: The British Commanders Who Shaped the World* (London: Faber and Faber, 2005), p. 296.

38. Ibid.

39. Quoted in Antony Beevor, *Second World War* (New York: Little, Brown, 2012), p. 489.

40. Quoted in Tim Moreman, *Bernard Montgomery: Leadership Strategy and Conflict* (Oxford: Osprey, 2012), p. 15.

41. Quoted in Alan Moorehead, "Montgomery's Quarrel with Eisenhower," *Colliers*, October 5, 1946, p. 12.

42. Ambrose, *Eisenhower, The President*, vol. 2, *Eisenhower* (New York: Simon and Schuster, 198), pp. 329–93.

43. Glenn LaFantasie, "Monty and Ike Take Gettysburg," *Quarterly Journal of Military History*, Autumn 1995, p. 73.

44. Quoted in Ambrose, *Eisenhower: The President*, p. 392.

45. Quoted in LaFantasie, "Monty and Ike," p. 73.

46. ""Longest Day' Author Used Journalistic Accuracy for World War II History," https://www.ohio.edu/news/months/july/007.html (accessed April 4, 2017).

47. Cornelius Ryan, interview with Eisenhower, Gettysburg, 1963. Cornelius Ryan Collection of World War II Papers, Ohio University, Athens, Ohio. Though the transcripts and recording have survived, the Ohio University Archives has been unable to determine the exact date of the interview in 1963.

48. Symonds, *Neptune*, pp. 189–91; Thomas B. Buell, *Master of Sea Power: A Biography of Fleet Admiral Ernest J. King* (Annapolis: Naval Institute Press, 1980), pp. 453,465.

49. Papers of Admiral Sir Bertram Home Ramsay, Churchill Archives Centre, Cambridge University.

50. Ibid.

51. J.L. Moulton, *Battle for Antwerp* (New York: Hippocrene Books, 1978), p. 230; Kenneth Edwards, *Operation Neptune* (Sabon, UK: Fonthill, 2013), p. 332.

52. W.S. Chalmers, *Full Cycle, The Biography of Admiral Sir Bertram Home Ramsay* (London: Hodder & Stoughton, 1959), p. 266.

53. Quoted in Chalmers, *Full Cycle*, p. 268.

54. Ibid., p. 7.

55. Stephen R. Taaffe, *Marshall and His Generals* (Lawrence, KS: University of Kansas, 2011), p. 205; Norman Davies, *No Simple Victory: World War II in Europe 1939–1945* (New York: Viking, 2007), p. 241.

56. Davies, *No Simple Victory*, p. 256.

57. Earl Alexander, *The Alexander Memoirs, 1940–1945*, ed. John North (London: Cassell, 1962), p. 45.

58. Quoted in Harry Yeide, *Fighting Patton* (New York: Zenith, 2011), p. 416.

59. Ibid.

60. Ibid.

61. Quoted in Michael Arnold, *Hollow Heroes* (Philadelphia: Casemate, 2015), p. 63.

62. Omar N. Bradley, *A Soldier's Story* (New York: Modern Library, 1999), p. 357.

63. Patton, diary, May 10, 1945 in *Patton Papers*, p. 702.

64. Martin Blumenson, *The Battle of the Generals* (New York: William Morrow, 1993), p. 272.

65. Martin Blumenson, "General George S. Patton," in *The War Lords: Military Commanders of the Twentieth Century*, ed. Michael Carver (Boston: Little, Brown, 1976), p. 567.

66. Carlo D'Este, *Decision in Normandy* (Old Saybrook, CT: Konecky & Konecky, 1994), p. 506.

67. Forrest C. Pogue, "General of the Army Omar N. Bradley," in *War Lords*, p. 538.

68. Quoted in Jordan, *Brothers*, p. 526.

69. Omar N. Bradley, *A General's Life* (New York: Simon and Shuster, 1983), pp. 440–62, 463–67, 504–505, 552–53.

70. B. H. Liddell Hart, *History of the Second World War* (Old Saybrook, CT: Konecky & Konecky, 1970), p. 561.

71. Quoted in David I. Hall, "Much the Greatest Thing We Have Ever Attempted," in *D-Day*, ed. Jane Penrose (Oxford: Osprey, 2010), p. 272.

# INDEX

(Pages in **bold** indicate photographs.)